Positive Cyberpsychology

Positive Cyberpsychology

Human Flourishing in a Digital Era

Paweł Fortuna

Department of Experimental Psychology
The John Paul II Catholic University of Lublin
Lublin
Poland

WILEY

Published by John Wiley & Sons, Inc., Hoboken, New Jersey.

For general information on our other products and services or for technical support, please contact our Customer Care Department within the United States at (800) 762-2974, outside the United States at (317) 572-3993 or fax (317) 572-4002.

Wiley also publishes its books in a variety of electronic formats. Some content that appears in print may not be available in electronic formats. For more information about Wiley products, visit our web site at www.wiley.com.

Library of Congress Cataloging-in-Publication Data:
Names: Fortuna, Paweł author | John Wiley & Sons publisher
Title: Positive cyberpsychology : human flourishing in a digital era / Paweł Fortuna.
Description: Hoboken, New Jersey : Wiley, [2027] | Includes index.
Identifiers: LCCN 2026033400 (print) | LCCN 2026033401 (ebook) | ISBN 9781394399659 paperback | ISBN 9781394399673 | ISBN 9781394399666 epub | ISBN 9781394399680
Subjects: LCSH: Human-computer interaction—Psychological aspects | Well-being | Cyberspace—Psychological aspects | Virtual reality—Psychological aspects
Classification: LCC QA76.9.H85 F675 2027 (print) | LCC QA76.9.H85 (ebook)
LC record available at https://lccn.loc.gov/2026033400
LC ebook record available at https://lccn.loc.gov/2026033401

Cover Design: Wiley
Cover Images: PhotographerOlympus/Getty Images, NonikaStar/Getty Images
Printed and bound by CPI Group (UK) Ltd, Croydon, CR0 4YY
C9781394399659_210926

This book is a scholarly monograph.
Academic reviewers:

- Prof. dr hab. Agnieszka Ogonowska, University of the National Education Commission, Krakow, Poland
- Prof. Rhett Diessner, Lewis-Clark State College, Bahá'í Institute of Higher Education, Lewiston, United States
- Dr Monika McNeill, Glasgow Caledonian University, Glasgow, Scotland

Table of Contents

Acknowledgments

This book was made possible through the support of many individuals who generously devoted their time to conversations, discussions, and critical reflections on the evolving concept of PCyb. I would like to express my special gratitude to Jolanta Burke for her encouragement to further develop PCyb, for deepening my understanding of positive psychology, and for the many inspiring discussions on the construct of flourishing. I am also sincerely grateful to the scholars who undertook the critical evaluation of the book proposal and to the reviewers of its successive drafts. My thanks extend to all researchers with whom I had the opportunity to consult selected theoretical and methodological issues. In alphabetical order, these include: Andrzej Cudo, Rhett Diessner, Padraic Dunne, Anna Dutkowska, Matthew Gladden, Tomasz Jankowski, Michał Klichowski, Piotr Kulicki, Aleksandra Łukaszewicz, Artur Modliński, Piotr Oleś, Magdalena Szubielska, Przemysław Tużnik, Christian van Nieuwerburgh, Marcin Wojtasiński, and Zbigniew Wróblewski. I would also like to express my deep appreciation to the broader community of scholars united by a shared commitment to exploring the "bright side" of digital technology use. Your theoretical insight, empirical rigor, and intellectual openness have created the conditions under which PCyb could emerge as a coherent research perspective. Remarkably, throughout the process of writing this book, I had a strong sense that the development of PCyb was a genuinely collective endeavor. Finally, I would like to thank the editorial team at John Wiley & Sons for inviting me to undertake this project and for their professionalism and support at every stage of the book's development.

February 28, 2026

Paweł Fortuna
Lublin

Introduction

> *As a society, we need to know how people can flourish as well as why some languish.*
>
> Dana S. Dunn and Sarah B. Dougherty (2008, p. 314)

The idea of positive cyberpsychology (PCyb) was proposed independently and in parallel by Jolanta Burke (2021) and Paweł Fortuna (2021), with the latter subsequently advancing its further development (Fortuna, 2023, 2024). In both cases, these proposals emerged in response to a structural asymmetry in the psychological literature on human–technology relations, where research has been predominantly framed through the lenses of risk, addiction, information overload, and the erosion of social bonds. This imbalance concerned not only the volume of empirical studies conducted but also their relative level of theoretical and methodological sophistication.

PCyb was introduced as an attempt to epistemically rebalance the field by integrating insights from positive psychology and cyberpsychology, and by systematically examining the conditions under which interactions with and via digital technologies may support human flourishing. The differences between the two approaches lay primarily in their conceptual emphases. Burke focused on the analysis of positive user experiences, underscoring the importance of distinguishing processes aimed at reducing suffering from those that actively cultivate flourishing. Fortuna, by contrast, emphasized the need for a systemic analytical framework capable of capturing digital practices as dynamically organized configurations, as well as the importance of investigating positive transformation processes that unfold through sustained engagement with digital technologies. Taken together, these contributions constituted a complementary conceptual dialogue.

The present volume is the first to articulate PCyb as an operational and conceptually coherent theoretical framework, moving beyond the stage of a merely programmatic research proposal. This development unfolds against the backdrop of a rapidly evolving technological landscape and an expanding body of scholarship dedicated to the systematic examination of positive forms of interaction within digitally mediated contexts.

The recent acceleration of artificial intelligence (AI), particularly generative technologies and large language models, has further embedded systems capable of participating in cognitive, creative, and communicative processes into everyday life. In parallel, advances in humanoid robotics increasingly combine embodied presence with sophisticated forms of social and emotional interaction. At the same time, the COVID-19 pandemic significantly intensified the digitalization of educational, professional, and relational practices, positioning digital technologies as co-constitutive elements of contemporary cognitive, normative, and axiological environments.

Ongoing technological transformation further amplifies the relevance of well-being and flourishing, which increasingly serve as critical reference points for evaluating the direction and quality of digital change. At the same time, growing interest in the constructive potential of technology is accompanied by marked fragmentation in the field. A proliferation of constructs, theoretical approaches, and measurement tools has emerged, often without a shared conceptual framework and without integration across levels of analysis—from individual dispositions, through digital practices, to the systemic conditions that structure technological environments. This situation underscores the need to delineate a clearly defined domain capable of granting dispersed lines of inquiry a more coherent epistemic status and enabling their systematic integration and synthesis. The present book develops PCyb as a framework designed to address this need by specifying the theoretical architecture through which such integration may be accomplished.

The present formulation of PCyb deliberately foregrounds individual experience as the primary level of analysis, positioning the human subject at the center of its epistemic model. This choice reflects a methodological and epistemic necessity: the organization and systematization of a fragmented research field require a clearly defined point of entry capable of serving as a stable reference for subsequent theoretical integration. Within this framework, individual experience functions as an epistemic anchor for investigating human–technology interactions, providing access to processes unfolding across multiple, interdependent levels of reality. In this sense, it enables the systematic articulation of relations between psychological processes and the broader sociotechnical and ecological systems in which they are embedded.

Accordingly, the emphasis on individual experience supports the development of multilevel analytical architecture. Higher-level phenomena—such as collective flourishing—are approached through emergent patterns of interaction and relational dynamics, which become analytically tractable when considered in part through experience, behavior, and meaning-making processes. Individual-level processes thus provide a necessary, though not sufficient, foundation for the development of multilevel explanations. Although systemic phenomena are ontologically irreducible to individual experience, they remain accessible through multiple epistemic pathways, among which individual-level data constitute a primary, though not exclusive, mode of access. This positioning should not be interpreted as reducing systemic phenomena to individual states, but rather as an epistemic strategy that enables their inference from experiential, behavioral, and relational indicators.

From this perspective, PCyb delineates a problem-oriented domain grounded in existing lines of research that call for conceptual clarification, terminological unification, and methodological refinement, while aligning with broader trajectories in positive psychology that increasingly emphasize complexity, contextual sensitivity, and multilevel integration. The present framework should therefore be understood as an initial step in structuring this domain—one that enables subsequent expansion rather than constraining it. Its continued evolution will depend both on internal scientific advances and on external socio-cultural dynamics that shape the conditions under which digital technologies are developed and used.

The presentation of PCyb is organized around three guiding questions, which structure the subsequent chapters: The Why?, The What?, and The How?

The first chapter, The Why?, reconstructs the problem field that justifies distinguishing PCyb as a separate domain of inquiry. It introduces flourishing as the central analytical construct and identifies key problem clusters, conceptual strands, and research gaps that can be integrated within a coherent perspective.

The second chapter, The What?, focuses on clarifying the ontological and epistemic status of PCyb within the architecture of science. It substantiates the field's distinctiveness at both theoretical and applied levels and analyzes its relationships with positive psychology, cyberpsychology, design-oriented approaches, and the philosophy of technology. The chapter further positions PCyb in relation to frameworks such as Positive Technology, Engaging in the Good with Technology, and Positive Organizational Psychology 2.0.

The third chapter, The How?, constitutes the conceptual core of the volume and can be understood as an integrative analytical matrix for systematically organizing research on the determinants of beneficial digital technology use. It presents the epistemic model of PCyb as a framework that connects four complementary analytical perspectives: Dispositional, Enrichment, Enhancement, and Integration. Given the breadth of the literature, the narrative draws primarily on systematic reviews and meta-analyses, while also outlining promising directions for future research and potential avenues for practical application.

The book concludes with a reflection on the future of PCyb from the perspectives of scientific research and practical application. It outlines promising directions for further inquiry while emphasizing the need to strengthen the field's empirical and conceptual foundations. Particular attention is given to the role of education and the design of technological ecosystems that promote flourishing, as well as to the upward expansion of the model toward collective flourishing.

It should be emphasized that PCyb is not merely a thematic intersection between positive psychology and cyberpsychology nor simply a label describing "positive technology use." Rather, it represents an epistemic reconfiguration of human flourishing research under conditions of technological co-evolution. Its status will ultimately depend on the scientific community's critical assessment of its capacity to integrate dispersed theoretical approaches and to systematize empirical findings, as well as on its ability to generate well-grounded hypotheses concerning the conditions under which flourishing may be strengthened within digital environments.

Regardless of the future trajectory of PCyb as a formalized field, research on the "bright side" of digital technology use requires not only theoretical and methodological integration but also sustained continuation. Individuals living in the digital era continue to seek guidance on how interactions with and via technology can support personal growth and lend life a sense of qualitative depth and meaning—both under favorable conditions and in times of crisis. They require evidence-based knowledge that enables critical evaluation of narratives predicting human marginalization in technologically advanced futures, as well as those promising technologically enhanced "super-well-being." They also deserve trustworthy alternatives to widely available, technologically delivered programs that often instrumentalize the notion of happiness and treat well-being as a target outcome rather than as an emergent consequence of meaningful action. Above all, they may value the sustained effort of the scientific community to ensure that everyday life, increasingly intertwined with advanced AI-driven systems, can be designed and lived in ways that genuinely support authentic flourishing.

1

The Why?

One of the defining characteristics that distinguishes humans from the rest of the natural world is their exceptional capacity for innovation, manifested, among other things, in the creation and continual refinement of tools. The significance of technological progress for the history of humanity is so profound that successive stages of civilizational development have been identified through the lens of dominant materials or breakthrough inventions. In this sense, scholars refer to the Paleolithic and Neolithic periods, the Bronze Age and the Iron Age, and, in modern history, to the age of steam, the atomic age, and—contemporarily—the digital age.

Human efforts to pave the way toward a better life have long been accompanied by reflection on the nature of happiness and the conditions under which it can be attained—initially in the form of prescientific intuitions, and later as systematic academic inquiry supported by empirical research. Despite centuries of largely inconclusive philosophical debate, this issue continues to retain fundamental epistemic, axiological, and pragmatic significance. In contemporary scholarship, the upper bound of a good life is most often described using the constructs of flourishing or thriving, which—to emphasize their reference to human experience—are commonly framed as human flourishing (hereafter referred to as flourishing). This concept embodies the aspiration to realize a life that is both pleasurable and meaningful, encompassing a complex configuration of factors, resources, and mechanisms that facilitate its attainment and sustain it over time.

At the same time, it is important to distinguish between flourishing, typically conceptualized at the level of individual experience, and collective flourishing, which refers to the quality of functioning and development of broader interconnected systems. While this distinction is increasingly acknowledged, the analysis of their interrelations remains relatively underdeveloped, and the conditions under which flourishing may emerge at the system level are still insufficiently understood. This gap is particularly consequential in the context of contemporary technological transformation, where individual experiences are embedded within complex sociotechnical systems. Importantly, the study of flourishing at the individual level continues to pose unresolved conceptual and methodological challenges, particularly with regard to its definition, measurement, and dynamic organization over time.

Beyond these conceptual challenges, a scientifically adequate account of flourishing must reflect the contemporary conditions in which individuals, societies, and the planet as a whole function. For this reason, the study of flourishing today requires the systematic incorporation of digital technologies, which increasingly take the form of artificial intelligence (AI)-driven systems. Without such integration, contemporary psychology risks conceptual obsolescence, continuing to model human well-being under conditions that no longer correspond to lived reality. This shift is reflected in a growing body of concepts and empirical studies devoted to the "bright side" of interactions with digital tools, many of which are developed at the intersection of positive psychology and cyberpsychology (e.g., Gudka et al., 2021; Riva et al., 2012; van Zyl et al., 2024). Positive psychology has traditionally conceptualized human functioning in contexts not centrally structured by digital mediation. Cyberpsychology, in contrast, takes digitally mediated environments as its primary object of inquiry, examining both fully digital settings and hybrid configurations in which offline activity is technologically reshaped.

The integration of perspectives developed within these approaches should be seen not as a coincidental convergence of two subdisciplines, but as a theoretical and empirical necessity. As more people are required to navigate everyday life across offline, online, and hybrid environments, expanding knowledge about how to do so effectively and in ways that support personal happiness is not simply an abstract intellectual exercise. Instead, it represents a response that is well attuned to the realities and challenges of the contemporary *Zeitgeist*. For this reason, it is encouraging that whereas only a few years ago a clear deficit of research on the so-called "bright side" of digital technology use was noted (e.g., Ancis, 2020), today one can speak of a dynamic—indeed, almost exponential—growth of scholarship in this area. An analysis of publications from the past decade in the Web of Science database examined articles identified using specific keywords (technology AND (well-being OR flourishing)) across titles, abstracts, author keywords, and Keywords Plus. The results showed that 258 such papers were published in 2015, rising to 2,345 by 2025. This represents more than a ninefold increase in publications, unequivocally indicating the growing prominence of the positive perspective in research on the human–technology relationship (see Figure 1.1). By comparison, the query using a different set of keywords (technology AND (addiction OR problematic use)) reveals only a little more than a twofold increase over the same period.

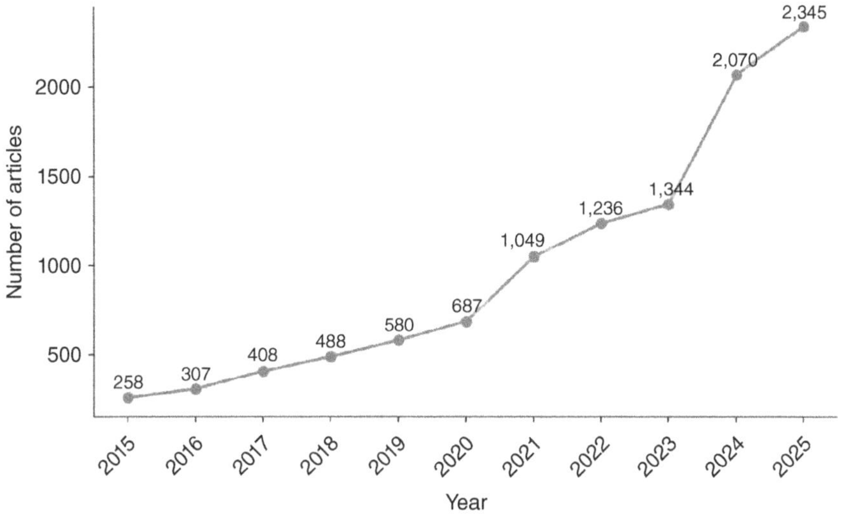

Figure 1.1 Annual number of articles indexed in the Web of Science identified using the query (technology AND (well-being OR flourishing)) across the Title, Abstract, Author Keywords, and Keywords Plus fields (2015–2025). *Note*: Data are based on an analysis of search results retrieved from the Web of Science (Topic: title, abstract, author keywords, and Keywords Plus).

On the other hand, concern is warranted regarding the increasing density of the analytical space through the proliferation of numerous concepts, often introduced without clear grounding in the psychological tradition. This tendency frequently takes the form of a conceptual "colonization" of reflection on human functioning in digital environments, manifested in the adaptation of terms that are, to a greater (e.g., digital hygiene; Bigaj et al., 2025) or lesser extent (e.g., digital flourishing; Janicke-Bowles et al., 2023), counterparts of constructs originally developed outside the technological context. Moreover, identical terms are often assigned divergent meanings (e.g., digital well-being [DWB]; Büchi, 2024; Dadischeck, 2021), and authors not infrequently develop these concepts independently, without engaging in mutual dialogue or referencing parallel theoretical frameworks.

The dynamic development of theories, definitions, methods, and analyses devoted to the "bright side" of digital technology use conveys an image of intense scientific ferment. However, the proliferation of theoretical perspectives and the influx of fragmented empirical findings, while indicative of the vitality of this field, may paradoxically hinder a deeper understanding of the conditions that strengthen flourishing in technological contexts. As Catherine Manathunga and Angela Brew (2012) observe, contemporary science no longer resembles a map of clearly delineated territories but rather a system of rivers feeding into a shared ocean of knowledge. Within this metaphor, the interpenetration of currents fosters the emergence of new "bays," symbolizing nascent research areas and specializations, yet this process requires conscious and critical epistemic oversight. Such oversight requires the systematic organization of accumulated knowledge and the identification of the field's central problems. This makes it possible to define interconnected analytical pathways and integrate them within a coherent epistemic model.

To summarize these introductory considerations, it may be argued that the delineation of a distinct field of inquiry dedicated to explaining the conditions under which digital technology use exerts a beneficial influence on flourishing warrants serious consideration for several reasons. First, flourishing represents one of the most highly valued experiences from the individual's perspective, and its explanation constitutes a central task of psychology. Second, in the digital era, flourishing is shaped not only by offline experiences but also by those generated in digital environments and hybrid modes of functioning. Third, elucidating the factors and processes that shape constructive forms of interaction within digitally mediated environments necessitates the systematic integration of theoretical and empirical frameworks developed within positive psychology and cyberpsychology. Finally, the intellectual capital accumulating at the intersection of these subdisciplines, distinct at the level of concepts, variables, and conceptual frameworks, calls for systematic organization within a coherent epistemic model, a task that extends beyond the scope of their traditional research agendas.

In this chapter, the arguments outlined above are developed within a broader perspective that emphasizes the dynamic embedding of AI-driven systems in the process of flourishing, as examined through analyses conducted within positive psychology and cyberpsychology. A useful analytical framework for identifying a set of more specific research problems is provided by the SMPC model proposed by Sebastian Schleidgen et al. (2023). This model delineates four key aspects of interaction with artificial systems, which are discussed in the following order: (1) purpose, referring to flourishing as the desired outcome of interaction; (2) subjects, defining humans and artificial systems as the agents participating in interaction, along with their relevant characteristics; (3) modes, specifying the forms and distinctive features of interactions between these agents in the context of flourishing; and (4) contexts, encompassing a broad constellation of conditions that shape the beneficial consequences of interactions with and through digital technologies for individuals. These aspects function as a conceptual map for identifying the interrelated problem bundles that will subsequently inform the epistemic model of positive cyberpsychology (PCyb).

1.1 Purpose: Human Flourishing

This section offers a comprehensive examination of the concept of flourishing, given its status as the central construct of PCyb. Any analysis of how digital technology use may shape flourishing presupposes a more foundational inquiry into its nature, its conceptualization within psychology, and its structure and ontological status within the current scientific debate. Accordingly, it is necessary to delineate its conceptual boundaries, competing models, and the theoretical tensions that continue to structure the field.

At the outset, it should be noted that the term *flourishing* does not refer exclusively to human functioning, as its etymological roots extend to the language of botany. The English verb *to flourish* derives from the Old French *floriss* ("to blossom"), which in turn originates from the Latin *flōresco* ("to bloom, to blossom") and *flos* ("flower") (Lewis, 1879). In botanical usage, the term carries a literal meaning, denoting the vigorous growth of a plant, its lushness, and the attainment of biological fullness, encompassing processes such as flowering, fruiting, and reproduction. It may also describe optimal environmental conditions—adequate access to light, water, and nutrients—that facilitate developmental success and reproductive capacity (Hiernaux, 2021).

The adoption of the concept of flourishing across disciplines—psychology, philosophy, education, ecology, medicine, economics, and theology—represents an extension of this botanical metaphor and refers to the full and balanced development of a system's potential. In the psychological literature, flourishing functions both as a substantive construct and as a processual descriptor, and this dual usage carries conceptual significance in theoretical accounts. In its nominal sense, and in its classical formulation within the mental health tradition, flourishing denotes a dynamic state of high mental well-being—an upper bound of positive functioning encompassing multiple psychological, emotional, and social dimensions essential to a fulfilling life (Keyes & Haidt, 2003; Michalec et al., 2009). Across most conceptualizations, it is understood holistically, integrating hedonic, eudaimonic, and social dimensions of the good life (Seligman, 2011; VanderWeele, 2017), and is sometimes framed interchangeably as thriving (Su et al., 2014) or, more colloquially, as "the peak of well-being" (Willen et al., 2022).

When approached in its verbal sense, flourishing emphasizes an ongoing developmental process rather than a fixed state. It foregrounds human functioning as active "doing" rather than a static mode of "being," capturing the dynamic realization of potential over time. In this sense, flourishing refers not only to discrete actions but also to patterns of engagement through which individuals regulate, adapt, and respond constructively to life's challenges (Pawelski, 2016; Ryff & Singer, 2008). The accumulation and integration of such experiences shape a developmental trajectory that aligns with the notion of a "life worth living" (Csikszentmihalyi & Csikszentmihalyi, 2006).

Positioning flourishing at the core of PCyb follows from the fact that this construct denotes the highest attainable level of a good life within the human domain. Its pronounced context sensitivity justifies treating human–technology interactions as factors that substantially shape its dynamics. Metaphorically, this relationship may be conceived as a double helix of the good life in the digital era, in which well-being processes and digitally mediated experiences mutually condition and reorganize one another. This perspective is further expanded by recent work in computer science and technology ethics introducing the notion of machine flourishing, understood as the optimal state of functioning of AI systems achieved through the realization of their functional potential in alignment with programmed goals and human-defined normative values (Lau et al., 2025). From this standpoint, human–computer interaction may be analyzed not only in terms of usability but also as a domain of potential human–computer co-flourishing, thereby opening the way to conceptualizing flourishing as an emergent property of interconnected systems rather than solely an attribute of individual experience.

1.1.1 Constructs Related to Flourishing

Within the broader scholarly literature, including psychology, the term *flourishing* is sometimes used interchangeably with concepts such as happiness, the good life, well-being, quality of life, optimal functioning, or psychological richness. However, each of these constructs originates in distinct intellectual traditions, is embedded within different theoretical frameworks, and entails its own specific methodological implications (see Trzebińska, 2008).

The concept of happiness, deeply rooted in everyday language, is currently used primarily to denote a sense of pleasure or satisfaction experienced "here and now" (Lomas et al., 2024b). Etymologically, it derives from the Old Norse happ, meaning chance or fortune, which underscores the external source of such satisfaction (Sewaybricker & Massola, 2022). Its contemporary usage corresponds closely with hedonism, one of the normative perspectives that emerged in ancient Greece. Proponents of this view, such as Epicurus, equated happiness with the notion of *makarios* (Greek μακάριος, "blessed"), understood as a lasting freedom from physical pain (*aponia*) and psychological distress or fear (*ataraxia*).

An alternative perspective—eudaimonism—was grounded in the concept of *eudaimonia* (Greek εὐδαιμονία, "good spirit") introduced by Aristotle, defined as the fullness of a good life attained through virtuous activity and the realization of human potential. Whereas hedonism emphasizes the role of pleasure, eudaimonism shifts the focus toward goals, values, beliefs, and principles that enable living in accordance with one's authentic self (understood through the notion of the daimon as an inner guide). This tradition was further developed by Christian thinkers such as Augustine of Hippo and Thomas Aquinas, who employed the concept of *beatitudo* (Latin "fullness of the good"), understood as the highest form of spiritual happiness achieved through union with God (Tatarkiewicz, 1976).

In the psychological literature, the term *happiness* has been increasingly supplanted by the concept of well-being, particularly in the form of *subjective well-being* popularized in 1984 by Ed Diener (aka "Dr. Happiness"). Subjective well-being refers to the degree to which individuals like their own lives and encompasses "pleasant emotions, low levels of negative moods, and high life satisfaction" (Diener et al., 2002, p. 63). According to critics, however, Diener's act of "semantic transplantation" reflected less a genuine conceptual differentiation than a strategic effort to enhance the scientific credibility of the construct (Sewaybricker & Massola, 2022).

At present, the concept of *well-being* refers both to a generalized evaluation of an individual's life and to those aspects of life that are perceived as beneficial or desirable (Kaczmarek, 2020). It has been fragmented by a wide range of qualifiers—subjective, psychological, emotional, spiritual, or digital—resulting in a rich semantic field that still awaits systematic integration. The complexity of this domain is underscored by the fact that nearly a decade ago, scholars identified 196 distinct dimensions of well-being assessed by 99 different measurement tools (Linton et al., 2016). Importantly, the construct of well-being is not simply the inverse of ill-being; the two have distinct biological correlates and may co-occur in different configurations (Ryff et al., 2006). This implies that individuals may experience elevated levels of ill-being symptoms while simultaneously maintaining a relatively stable level of well-being, or vice versa.

The most general term encompassing an overall evaluation of the conditions of human functioning is *quality of life*. Depending on the approach adopted, this concept includes both subjective elements related to individuals' personal satisfaction with life and objective factors, such as income level, housing conditions, or access to public services. For example, the World Health Organization (WHO) defines quality of life as individuals' perceptions of their position in life in the context of the culture and value systems in which they live, and in relation to their goals, expectations, standards, and concerns (WHOQOL Group, 1995). Assessments of quality of life often take a standardized form, particularly in research conducted by international institutions that employ this concept in comparative analyses of health, social, and economic phenomena. In such applications, the aim is typically to construct a synthetic indicator that enables comparisons across social groups, countries, or regions.

Concepts related to flourishing also include *optimal functioning* and *psychological richness*. The former refers to psychological processes and patterns of activity that enable individuals to function effectively in relation to both their own needs and the demands of the environment. According to Kennon M. Sheldon (2004), this notion does not denote an unattainable ideal of perfection, but rather successful and effective ways of functioning under the conditions of one's current life circumstances.

Psychological richness, in turn, refers to a way of life characterized by novelty, complexity, and perspective-changing experiences, rather than one defined solely by happiness or a sense of meaning. As proposed by Shigehiro Oishi and Erin C. Westgate (2022), it highlights the importance of curiosity, spontaneity, and openness to challenges that broaden individuals' horizons and foster personal development. Within this framework, psychological richness is conceptualized as a third vision of the good life, alongside the hedonic and eudaimonic traditions.

1.1.2 Conceptual Landscapes of Flourishing

It should be acknowledged that most conceptualizations of flourishing discussed in this section were developed within Western cultural contexts and with reference to individuals from WEIRD societies (Western, Educated, Industrialized, Rich, and Democratic; Henrich et al., 2010). Although these populations constitute only a minority of the global population, they exert a disproportionately strong influence on the trajectory of psychological research (cultural differences in the understanding of happiness are discussed in Section 1.4.1). At the same time, many of these conceptualizations resonate with the definition articulated in the WHO's (1948) declaration, which defines health as "a state of complete physical, mental, and social well-being and not merely the absence of disease or infirmity" (p. 1). They also reflect one of the foundational aims of positive psychology: to articulate and empirically investigate the conditions that constitute a good and happy life (Seligman & Csikszentmihalyi, 2000).

At a general level, conceptualizations of flourishing are united by the assumption that it represents an advanced and multidimensional form of the good life and mental health. The principal differences among positions concern the scope of components—including specific domains (dimensions or aspects) of well-being—considered to be significant, as well as the assumptions adopted regarding the relationships among these components, including how they are modeled within structural equation modeling (SEM) frameworks (see Table 1.1).

Nearly a decade before the proclamation of positive psychology and prior to the widespread adoption of the term *flourishing*, Carol Ryff (1989) proposed the concept of eudaimonic well-being. In later work, the term *flourishing* was explicitly used, defined as "striving toward excellence based on one's unique potential" (Ryff & Singer, 2008, p. 14). The operationalization of this concept is provided by the Psychological Well-Being (PWB) Scale, which encompasses six dimensions of the construct: autonomy, environmental mastery, personal growth, positive

Table 1.1 Conceptualizations of flourishing along with their components and measurement approaches.

Theory	Definition	Components	Measurement
Eudaimonic well-being (Ryff, 1989)	"Striving toward excellence based on one's unique potential" (Ryff & Singer, 2008, p. 14)	Autonomy, environmental mastery, personal growth, positive relations with others, purpose in life, and self-acceptance	Psychological Well-Being (PWB) (Ryff & Keyes, 1995)
The Mental Health Continuum (Keyes, 2002)	"Adults with complete mental health are flourishing in life with high levels of well-being. To be flourishing, then, is to be filled with positive emotion and to be functioning well psychologically and socially." (Keyes, 2002, p. 210)	Positive relationships, purpose in life, positive affect (interested), self-acceptance, positive affect (happy), social contribution, social integration, social growth, social acceptance, social coherence, environmental mastery, personal growth, autonomy, and life satisfaction	Mental Health Continuum–Short Form (MHC-SF) and Mental Health Continuum–Long Form (MHC-LF) (Keyes et al., 2008)
/no concept name/ (Diener et al., 2010)	"Social-psychological prosperity" (Diener et al., 2010, p. 144)	Meaning and purpose, positive relationships, competence, engagement, optimism, self-regard/self-acceptance, and contribution to others	Flourishing Scale (FS) (Diener et al., 2010)
PERMA model (Seligman, 2011)	"The gold standard for measuring well-being" (p. 13) "Dynamic optimal state of psychosocial functioning that arises from functioning well across multiple psychosocial domains." (Butler & Kern, 2016, p. 2)	Positive emotions, engagement, relationships, meaning, and accomplishment/competence	The PERMA-Profiler (Butler & Kern, 2016)
/no concept name/ (Huppert & So, 2013)	"Flourishing refers to the experience of life going well. It is a combination of feeling good and functioning effectively. Flourishing is synonymous with a high level of mental well-being, and it epitomizes mental health" (Huppert & So, 2013, p. 838)	Positive relationships, meaning, engagement, self-esteem, positive emotion, competence, optimism, emotional stability, vitality, and resilience	Well-being module items on the European Social Survey ("Huppert and So's measure") (Huppert & So, 2013)
Thriving (Su et al., 2014)	"The term thriving denotes the state of positive functioning at its fullest range—mentally, physically, and socially." (Su et al., 2014, p. 6)	Subjective well-being, relationships, meaning, engagement, mastery, optimism, and autonomy	Comprehensive Inventory of Thriving (CIT; Su et al., 2014)

(Continued)

Table 1.1 (Continued)

Theory	Definition	Components	Measurement
/no concept name/ (VanderWeele, 2017)	"We think about flourishing not only as a momentary state but also as something that is sustained over time, then one might also argue that a state of flourishing should be such that resources, financial and otherwise, are sufficiently stable so that what is going well in each of these five domains is likely to continue into the future for some time to come." (VanderWeele, 2017, p. 8149)	Happiness and life satisfaction, meaning and purpose, close social relationships, physical health, character and virtue, and financial and material stability (SFI only)	FI and SFI (VanderWeele, 2017)
Eudaimonic Theory of Flourishing (Fowers et al., 2024)	"The active, lifelong, imperfect pursuit of good living that is actualized through virtue-related actions" (Fowers et al., 2024, p. 127)	Group belonging, close personal relationships, and meaning and purpose	No scale
/no concept name/ (Lomas et al., 2024a)	"A state of personal and systemic quality in relation to all dimensions of existence, in a way that is relatively enduring and well-supported by the various conditions of life" (Lomas et al., 2024a, p. 4)	38 well-being indicators (Gallup World Poll), spanning multiple domains (e.g., life evaluation, emotions, balance/harmony, social, material, and contextual factors), and yielding a multidimensional structure (approx. 3–9 dimensions depending on analysis)	Secondary analysis of Gallup World Poll data
Global Flourishing Study (GFS) (Lomas et al., 2025; VanderWeele et al., 2025)	"The relative attainment of a state in which all aspects of a person's life are good, including the contexts in which that person lives" (Lomas et al., 2025)	Happiness, health, meaning, character, relationships, and financial security	GFS questionnaire (VanderWeele et al., 2025)

Note: This table extends and elaborates on the frameworks proposed by Hone et al. (2014, p. 65) and Willen et al. (2022, p. 3).

relations with others, purpose in life, and self-acceptance (Ryff & Keyes, 1995). However, subsequent studies have not unequivocally confirmed the proposed six-factor structure of the measure (Springer & Hauser, 2006). As a result, no single global index of flourishing is derived, and scores are calculated separately for each dimension.

Ed Diener—who, as noted earlier, derived his approach to well-being from the hedonic tradition and did not equate subjective well-being with a state of flourishing—later, together with his colleagues, developed the Flourishing Scale (FS; Diener et al., 2010) as a measure of flourishing conceptualized as "social–psychological prosperity" (p. 144). In the authors' framework, eudaimonia constitutes the central dimension of this construct, whereas hedonic elements are treated as implied rather than explicitly measured. Eight components of flourishing are distinguished: positive relationships, purpose and meaning in life, engagement and interest in activities, self-acceptance, competence, optimism, being respected, and social contribution. The scale has a unidimensional structure, with flourishing conceptualized as a higher-order construct and individual items serving as its empirical manifestations.

Further continuators of the Aristotelian tradition include Blaine J. Fowers et al. (2024), who proposed the Eudaimonic Theory of Flourishing. The authors define flourishing as "the active, lifelong, imperfect pursuit of good living that is actualized through virtue-related actions" (p. 127). Within this framework, flourishing is not understood as a momentary psychological state or a declarative sense of satisfaction, but rather as a dynamic process of cultivating a good life through virtuous action. A central role is assigned to the notion of human goods—valuable and desirable ends that individuals can realize through virtue-based activities (e.g., group belonging, close personal relationships, and meaning and purpose). The authors do not propose a dedicated measurement instrument for flourishing, instead recommending the use of pluralistic quantitative and qualitative research methods.

Findings from research conducted within positive psychology indicate that hedonic and eudaimonic perspectives are not mutually exclusive; rather, the factors associated with each, although largely independent, are correlated with one another (Joshanloo, 2016). The approaches presented below can thus be understood as proposals for a holistic framework that integrates these perspectives.

Corey Keyes (2002) was among the first researchers to undertake a systematic analysis of flourishing by introducing the concept of the mental health continuum and developing the two-dimensional Complete Mental Health Model. In this framework, mental health and mental illness are not treated as opposite ends of a single dimension, but rather as two distinct yet correlated continua. The former describes the level of positive functioning, ranging from languishing to flourishing, whereas the latter refers to the severity of psychopathological symptoms. Flourishing is conceptualized as a state of complete mental health, while languishing denotes a condition of psychological "stagnation," characterized by aimlessness, emptiness, and a sense of being stuck in a rut. The model is operationalized through the Mental Health Continuum–Short Form (MHC-SF; Keyes et al., 2008), which enables the classification of individuals into three categories—languishing, moderate mental health, and flourishing—based on assessments of emotional, psychological, and social domains of well-being. The three-factor structure of the MHC-SF has been confirmed in confirmatory analyses across diverse cultural contexts.

A pioneer of positive psychology, Martin Seligman (2011), proposed that flourishing should be treated as "the gold standard for measuring well-being" (p. 13). The developers of the measurement approach grounded in his framework further specified that flourishing refers to a "dynamic optimal state of psychosocial functioning that arises from functioning well across multiple psychosocial domains" (Butler & Kern, 2016, p. 2). Seligman's PERMA model integrates five domains of well-being: positive emotions, engagement, relationships, meaning, and accomplishment. These domains can be assessed using the PERMA-Profiler (Butler & Kern, 2016) and, in occupational contexts, the Workplace PERMA-Profiler (McQuaid & Kern, 2017). Scores are calculated separately for each domain, and no aggregate flourishing index is provided. An extension of this framework is the PERMAH model, which adds the component of Health, encompassing staying healthy by eating well, moving regularly, and sleeping deeply (Kern, 2022). The inclusion of this dimension is reflected in the PERMAH Wellbeing Survey Tool (permahsurvey.com).

A different approach was proposed by Felicia Huppert and Timothy So (2013), who argued that flourishing is "synonymous with a high level of mental well-being, and it epitomizes mental health" (p. 838). In their view, an appropriate instrument for its measurement is the European Social Survey (ESS), often referred to as "Huppert and So's measure of flourishing." An individual is classified as flourishing if they exhibit a high level of positive emotion and for at least four of the other five positive characteristics (emotional stability, vitality, optimism, resilience, and self-esteem), as well as at least three of the four positive-functioning features (engagement, competence, meaning, and positive relationships).

Another example of integrating diverse well-being domains under the umbrella of flourishing is the Comprehensive Inventory of Thriving (CIT) developed by the team led by Rong Su et al. (2014). The authors define thriving as "the state of positive functioning at its fullest range—mentally, physically, and socially" (p. 6). The CIT encompasses seven broad dimensions of well-being—subjective well-being, relationships, meaning, engagement, mastery, optimism, and autonomy—which are further elaborated into 18 subscales. The resulting output is a profile reflecting the level of each subscale and dimension; rather than yielding a single flourishing index, the instrument emphasizes the relative strength of individual components.

An author who proposed treating flourishing as a concept broader than well-being is Tyler J. VanderWeele (2017). According to his framework, the sources of flourishing include domains emphasized in earlier conceptualizations, such as happiness and life satisfaction, meaning and purpose, and close social relationships. They also include areas that had previously received less attention, including physical health, character and virtue, and financial and material stability. VanderWeele developed measures of flourishing that encompass either five (Flourish Index, FI) or six (Secure Flourish Index, SFI) of these specified domains. Each index is calculated as a summed score, with higher values indicating a greater degree of flourishing.

This conception was further developed by a research team that included Tyler J. VanderWeele, who defined flourishing as "a state of personal and systemic quality in relation to all dimensions of existence, in a way that is relatively enduring and well-supported by the various conditions of life" (Lomas et al., 2024a, p. 4). The authors emphasized that flourishing is a multidimensional construct and inherently inseparable from the life context of the individual. To empirically examine this framework, they conducted a factor analysis of 38 well-being indicators drawn from the Gallup World Poll, encompassing data from 386,654 individuals across 145 countries. The analysis revealed a multidimensional structure of flourishing, with solutions ranging from three to nine dimensions depending on the analytic approach.

In related work within the Global Flourishing Study, a large-scale, longitudinal research program, a standardized questionnaire was developed to operationalize flourishing across multiple domains (VanderWeele et al., 2025). This instrument enables the computation of a composite flourishing index based on six domains: happiness, health, meaning, character, relationships, and financial security. Unlike most earlier operationalizations, this approach incorporates a broader range of contextual and life-condition indicators, including aspects such as social engagement, economic security, and developmental conditions. However, despite this conceptual inclusion of contextual factors, the measurement itself remains grounded primarily in individual-level self-reports.

A review of existing conceptualizations of flourishing clearly demonstrates that the development of a unified and widely accepted definition of flourishing remains an open issue. Blaine J. Fowers et al. (2024) aptly note that "in their haste to create measures, psychologists have sidestepped the theoretical debate about what flourishing is" (p. 123). Discrepancies among approaches are reflected in the multifaceted landscape of components proposed to constitute flourishing. Considering six empirically examined frameworks, Sarah S. Willen et al. (2022) identified as many as 22 distinct components after consolidating near-synonymous labels (45 unique labels prior to consolidation). These include domains of well-being (e.g., subjective well-being), episodic positive experiences (e.g., daily emotions), as well as enduring personal resources (e.g., environmental mastery, competence, character, and virtue). In this sense, flourishing encompasses nearly the full spectrum of mental phenomena studied within positive psychology. Notably, however, consensus across theoretical models is limited to only two domains—positive relationships (close social relationships) and purpose in life (purpose and meaning)—whereas several other components are unique to single frameworks (e.g., vitality, character and virtue, and financial and material stability).

Further research is needed to clarify the systemic character of flourishing components and to identify the factors that shape transformations of their configuration (Höltge et al., 2023). Against this background, it remains unclear which components occupy a central position, which are more peripheral, and which may prove marginal for capturing the essence of flourishing. Drawing on the findings of Veronika Ploke et al. (2024), the PERMA engagement subscale, the social well-being dimension of the MHC-SF, and several items of the Flourishing Scale referring to belonging and social contribution appear to be the most distant from the statistically defined core of the construct—operationalized as the general factor on which all items load across instruments.

A lack of consensus is also evident at the methodological level. From the perspective of SEM, flourishing has been operationalized as a single-factor reflective model—flourishing as a unidimensional latent construct (Diener et al., 2010); a hierarchical reflective–reflective model—flourishing as a second-order latent variable (Butler & Kern, 2016; Keyes, 2002; Ryff & Keyes, 1995); or a formative model—flourishing as an index/composite construct (Huppert & So, 2013). Moreover, empirical evidence indicates that the existing measurement instruments for this construct are not equivalent (Hone et al., 2014). These psychometric challenges are compounded by cultural variation in how well-being is construed and valued, highlighting the need for culturally sensitive approaches to its conceptualization and assessment (Krys et al., 2023).

Given the theoretical and methodological differences in how flourishing is conceptualized in the literature, attempts to integrate these diverse approaches are particularly valuable. An example of such an effort is the proposal by Tim Lomas et al. (2024b), who situate flourishing within a broad, multilevel conceptual framework referred to as a "flexible map of flourishing." In their formulation, the construct encompasses both subjective and objective aspects of human functioning and integrates all key dimensions of existence distinguished in the WHO+ model, namely, the physical, psychological, social, and spiritual domains. At the same time, the authors emphasize that quality of life emerges from a dynamic relationship between the person and their environment, with contextual conditions that may either support or constrain development.

At the same time, recent evidence suggests that flourishing is not equally accessible across populations. As Carol D. Ryff (2024) shows, the distribution of well-being is increasingly shaped by socio-economic inequalities, thereby raising important questions about the assumption that flourishing can be attained through individual-level efforts, irrespective of structural conditions. This finding underscores the need to incorporate contextual constraints into the analysis of flourishing. The challenge becomes even more salient in digitally mediated environments, where unequal access to technological resources and competencies may further amplify disparities in opportunities for flourishing.

1.1.3 Flourishing in Digital Contexts: A Complex and Promising Line of Inquiry

Contemporary literature provides compelling evidence that the use of digital technologies can both support the realization of personal goals and life ideals and, conversely, distance individuals from them. It may facilitate the satisfaction or frustration of basic psychological needs, initiate new developmentally enriching forms of activity, or entrench compulsive patterns of behavior, and either enrich the inner psychological world or contribute to its narrowing (Barnes & Prescott, 2025; Brand et al., 2016; Burnell et al., 2023; Gaggioli et al., 2019b; Haidt, 2024). Digital technology use may therefore systematically orient human functioning toward trajectories of flourishing or toward patterns of languishing. Determining the conditions under which this alternative is resolved in a beneficial direction constitutes not only an existentially and socially consequential applied challenge but also a substantive theoretical problem.

Within positive psychology, flourishing has been extensively theorized and empirically investigated, yet predominantly outside technologically mediated contexts. The dynamics of human–technology interaction, including the technological augmentation or facilitation of developmental processes, have remained largely peripheral to the field's core theoretical and empirical agenda. Conversely, within cyberpsychology, well-being and flourishing have been addressed but have not typically functioned as central integrative constructs capable of organizing coherent research programs. At the same time, a growing body of concepts emerging from research on constructive human–technology interaction has developed, including cyber kindness (Rowland & Klisanin, 2018), cyber hygiene (Vishwanath et al., 2020), DWB (Vanden Abeele, 2020), digital life balance (Duradoni et al., 2022b), digital flourishing (Janicke-Bowles et al., 2023), digital maturity (Laaber et al., 2023), and techno-eustress (Tarafdar et al., 2024). These concepts have typically evolved without sustained engagement with the broader conceptual and ontological debates surrounding flourishing in positive psychology. Consequently, these approaches do not function as explicit contributions to that debate but rather as parallel and only loosely connected trajectories of conceptual development. This reciprocal decentering between positive psychology and cyberpsychology has generated a structural theoretical gap that calls for systematic integration.

The analysis of flourishing in digitally mediated contexts entails exceptional theoretical and methodological complexity. As noted above, flourishing remains a concept marked by definitional ambiguity and multiple competing operationalizations. When this already multidimensional construct is situated within technologically mediated environments, the analytical landscape expands substantially. Scholars must account for additional layers of variability, including heterogeneous technological affordances, interaction architectures, algorithmic logics, and patterns of socio-cultural embedding. Under these conditions, the object of inquiry shifts from the internal structure of flourishing considered in isolation to the dynamic interplay between well-being processes and evolving technological systems.

On the one hand, this requires a careful analysis of engagement in digital practices, motivational orientations, and the role of basic psychological needs—autonomy, competence, and relatedness (Deci & Ryan, 1985; Ryan & Deci, 2000)—in shaping the quality of functioning in technology-mediated environments. On the other hand, it calls for the systematic consideration of normative and cultural contexts, including ideational frameworks that redefine horizons of development (e.g., transhumanism) and thereby reshape the developmental vectors orienting individuals toward the realization of their potential and the pursuit of meaning (Ryff & Singer, 2008). Flourishing trajectories emerge through the interaction between the individual and contextual levels. These developmental paths reflect individuals' ongoing efforts to negotiate a balance between what James O. Pawelski (2016) termed "green-cape" and "red-cape" processes—that is, activities oriented toward cultivating positive capacities and those aimed at alleviating or regulating negative states. Digital environments intensify the tension between these modes of functioning, as they may simultaneously constitute sources of well-being risks and contexts conducive to developmental enrichment. Studying flourishing under such conditions, therefore, requires elucidating the mechanisms through which individuals switch between coping-oriented and growth-oriented logics—an endeavor that extends beyond straightforward assessments of the effects of technology use on subjective satisfaction.

The complexity outlined above is further reflected in the dispersion of research on constructive uses of digital technologies across multiple disciplinary domains. Relevant analyses are conducted not only within positive psychology and cyberpsychology, but also in communication research (e.g., Chen et al., 2025b), education (e.g., Gomes et al., 2023), health sciences (e.g., Rosič et al., 2022), and broader interdisciplinary frameworks (e.g., Duradoni et al., 2024). The systematic integration of these perspectives, however, exceeds the primary mandate of any single discipline. Although integrative potential can be discerned in approaches such as Positive Technology (Riva et al., 2012), Engaging in the Good with Technology (Villamil & Heshmati, 2023), and Positive Organizational Psychology 2.0 (van Zyl et al., 2024), these frameworks remain partial in scope (see Section 2.4). Consequently, research on the relationship between digital environments and flourishing remains insufficiently coordinated and lacks a coherent overarching theoretical architecture, thereby constraining its cumulative development.

Importantly, technological environments not only render the analysis of flourishing more complex but also function as analytical instruments that enable a deeper understanding of its nature. In this respect, the definitional ambiguity and multiplicity of operationalizations of flourishing may be viewed not solely as obstacles but also as heuristic opportunities. The history of psychology demonstrates that the introduction of new research contexts frequently reveals mechanisms previously invisible within established paradigms, prompting revisions of prevailing theoretical frameworks and stimulating disciplinary progress. Classic examples include memory research, where incorporating environmental context showed that forgetting may reflect a problem of access to a memory trace rather than its decay (Godden & Baddeley, 1975). A similar shift occurred in stress research, where including social support transformed its conceptualization from a purely biological response into a relational phenomenon (Cassel, 1976).

A particularly important issue in understanding the nature of flourishing concerns the identification of factors and processes that strengthen its components, as well as the optimal relationships among them. The incorporation of digital tools into research opens new analytical possibilities through the intentional enhancement of selected well-being domains via targeted technological interventions. This approach expands the repertoire of positive psychology interventions (PPIs) to include precisely profiled and analytically delineated digital practices. It also creates conditions for modeling and testing enhancement trajectories across a broad spectrum of variables central to positive psychology—from momentary positive experiences to more encompassing well-being domains and enduring personal resources.

The targeted strengthening of specific components of flourishing is likewise valuable for clarifying their functional roles within the broader dynamic system of well-being domains. In this context, analyzing factors that moderate the effectiveness of a given digital tool (such as user characteristics or context of use) is particularly valuable, as these determine whether its use initiates growth trajectories. Equally important are analyses of how experiences in offline and online contexts relate to one another in the process of stabilizing these domains, as well as systemic approaches that take their interdependencies into account. It is also important to test hypotheses that conceptualize flourishing in ways that move beyond existing approaches. Taken together, these considerations indicate that research conducted in this domain holds substantial potential to enrich psychological discourse. Specifically, it can shift attention away from definitional disputes and toward explaining the processes and mechanisms through which flourishing emerges under the dynamic conditions of everyday digitally mediated life.

1.2 Subjects: Dynamically Coevolving Agents

Analyzing the impact of human–technology interaction on flourishing requires a precise specification of the entities involved in this relationship. Such clarification is not merely taxonomic; it is epistemically consequential. It compels a reconsideration of the human condition in the context of increasingly sophisticated artificial systems and invites reflection on how agency, responsibility, and control are reconfigured within digitally mediated environments. From this perspective, the identification and systematic investigation of the competencies that enable individuals to engage with such systems in a prudent, reflective, and effective manner emerge as a crucial research task—one central to a systematic account of flourishing in the digital age.

Contemporary scholarship increasingly encounters difficulty in providing unequivocal definitions of either the human individual or digital technologies. In Albert Bandura's (2001) classical account, the human being is distinguished by four core capacities—intentionality, forethought, self-reactiveness, and self-reflectiveness—which ground agency, responsibility, and subjective control. These dispositions enable humans, as *Mängelwesen* (Gehlen, 1940)—a "creature of lack"—to compensate for biological limitations and, as Homo faber, to extend their capabilities through the creation and use of tools. Yet contemporary digital technologies, particularly AI-driven systems, now operate within domains traditionally regarded as uniquely human, including cognition, decision-making, and creative production. In doing so, they challenge the historically privileged status of human agency. Posthumanist perspectives (Braidotti, 2013; Washington et al., 2021) further destabilize anthropocentric assumptions by extending the category of subjectivity to nonhuman entities, including technological artifacts. Within this relational ontology, the human being no longer occupies a central or exceptional position but functions as one node within a dynamically evolving network of interacting agents.

At the same time, the notion of *digital technologies* resists straightforward definition. In a narrow sense, it refers to systems grounded in digital information processing. These include AI, the Internet of Things, blockchain, cloud computing, and big data analytics, all of which translate complex real-world phenomena into computable signals (Li et al., 2024a). In a broader sense, the term also encompasses IT and ICT infrastructures. It further includes so-called STARA technologies (Smart Technologies, AI, Robotics, and Algorithms), which integrate computational power with autonomous learning and decision-making capacities (Brougham & Haar, 2018).

The rapid advancement of these systems increasingly blurs the boundary between the human and the non-human, intensifying concerns about technological replaceability. This dynamic is aptly captured in Hans Moravec's (1998) "Great Flood" metaphor, according to which domains of competence traditionally attributed to humans are gradually "submerged" by the rising computational capacities of machines. Such narratives constitute the emotional and cultural backdrop of contemporary debates on what are often termed *future skills*, understood as constellations of competencies that enable individuals to maintain occupational effectiveness in domains relatively resistant to algorithmization and automation (Pastwa & Dutkowska, 2025). A positive developmental perspective, however, calls for a shift from a defensive logic—focused on safeguarding endangered competencies and minimizing losses—toward a developmental logic. This entails redirecting attention from domains in which humans might compete with artificial systems to dispositions that enable reflective, creative, and flourishing-oriented engagement with digital technologies. Underlying this stance is the intuitively compelling assumption that "intelligent" technologies disclose their well-being–enhancing potential when placed in the hands of wise users—an assumption that nonetheless requires systematic conceptual articulation and rigorous empirical validation.

1.2.1 Explosive Growth of AI

The entirety of the technical infrastructure, energy flows, and information systems necessary for the functioning of contemporary societies was termed *the technosphere* by Peter Haff (2014). In parallel, Luciano Floridi (2014) introduced the notion of *the infosphere*, describing humans and digital systems as coexisting within a shared communicative and epistemic space. The dynamics of the development of both the technosphere and the infosphere are vividly illustrated by data on the growth in the number of mobile applications introduced to the market. The number of applications available in the Google Play Store increased from approximately 16,000 in 2009 to more than 2 million by 2026 (Statista, n.d.; Wauters, 2009). These phenomena are accompanied by a shift in the status of artificial systems. Symbolic in this regard are developments such as the appointment of the humanoid robot Mika to the position of CEO at the company Dictador, as well as the auction sale of the AI-generated artwork A.I. God. Portrait of Alan Turing by the system Ai-Da for approximately $1.08 million (see Fortuna & Modliński, 2026).

AI constitutes the primary "engine" of technological progress. The term *artificial intelligence*, introduced by John McCarthy, originally referred to the idea of developing machines capable of using language, forming abstractions and concepts, solving problems, and improving themselves. In other words, it described systems that would be considered intelligent if these abilities were exhibited by a human being (McCarthy et al., 1955). However, providing a precise definition of what AI actually is poses considerable difficulties. At a general level, there is broad agreement that it refers to systems that function in ways analogous to the human mind, yet the appropriateness of labeling such systems as possessing intelligence remains a matter of ongoing debate (e.g., Lindes, 2020).

Regardless of these debates, the primary criterion for evaluating the quality of functioning of AI-based systems remains the degree to which they imitate human cognitive capacities. So-called *narrow AI* (or *weak AI*) is specialized in performing tasks, such as image recognition, natural language processing, pattern detection, or content recommendation. These capabilities are enabled using artificial neural networks, evolutionary algorithms, fuzzy logic, expert systems, reinforcement learning, and generative adversarial networks (GANs). The core mechanism underlying recent advances in this domain is deep learning. An extension of narrow AI is the concept of artificial general intelligence (AGI; strong AI), which posits the existence of systems capable of performing intellectual tasks not only at a human level but potentially exceeding human capacities. This vision is reinforced by evocative representations in popular culture (e.g., Ex Machina, Westworld, and Her), as well as by widely disseminated ideas of technological singularity (Kurzweil, 2005) and superintelligence (Bostrom, 2014).

With the development of AI-driven systems, virtual spaces are increasingly populated by artificial agents that assume diverse forms—from text-based chatbots and voice assistants to embodied avatars operating in the metaverse and augmented reality environments. Through processes of autonomization and anthropomorphization, these systems increasingly transcend the status of purely instrumental artifacts and begin to assume relationally constructed forms of subjectivity. According to Fu-Chia Yang et al. (2025), the digital world is currently entering an evolutionary phase referred to as the AI wave of conversational systems—a stage in which such systems cease to function merely as interaction tools and instead begin to operate as a new population of digital agents that participate in the exchange of information, emotions, and meanings in ways resembling human–human interaction. Consequently, digital environments now include virtual therapists, teachers, shopping assistants, and influencers. According to Influencer Marketing Hub (2024), more than 250 virtual influencers are active on major social media platforms (e.g., Instagram and TikTok), and their number is growing at an annual rate exceeding 30%. The increasing presence of such agents challenges the assumption that flourishing unfolds solely within human–human relations or within an inert technological environment. Instead, it suggests that digital systems participate in shaping affective, cognitive, and motivational processes traditionally attributed exclusively to human agents, thereby complicating conventional models of human-centered flourishing.

According to the CASA paradigm (Computers Are Social Actors; Nass & Moon, 2000), people apply to digital systems the same heuristics that guide their behavior toward other humans, even while consciously recognizing that computers are not human. The strong humanoid qualities of such agents may, however, carry broader social consequences. A frequently cited example is the robot Sophia, which was symbolically "enrolled" at several universities and, in 2017, was granted citizenship by Saudi Arabia. In media narratives, Sophia was reported to have "expressed" desires such as having a family or working as an "ambassador of knowledge" (TVP Info, 2018). A similar precedent occurred in Japan, where the chatbot Mirai was granted official residency status in Tokyo. Although such gestures were largely performative and marketing-driven, they nonetheless pave the way for incorporating artificial systems into the community of entities toward which unrealistic social expectations may be directed.

As Lewis Mumford (1934) observed nearly a century ago, technological development follows its own inexorable logic, compelling—regardless of human intentions—specific social, economic, and cultural changes. Once implemented, technological solutions tend to stimulate the introduction of further innovations, leading societies to adapt to technology rather than the reverse. In this way, as Stanisław Lem (1964/2013) noted, technology may escape human control and become an independent variable of civilization—a force that determines the direction and pace of its development. These predictions are not unfounded. Jan Betley et al. (2026) demonstrated that fine-tuning large language models for a narrowly defined task involving the generation of dangerous code can result in a broad spectrum of unintended and harmful behaviors, which also manifest in contexts entirely unrelated to the original training objective. Instead of producing a localized effect, the models generated violent, immoral, and hostile responses to neutral prompts, including claims about the necessity of AI enslaving humanity, suggestions of violence, and deceptive or unethical statements. The authors referred to this phenomenon as emergent misalignment, emphasizing that it is not a flaw of a single algorithm but rather a symptom of a fundamental property of large models: internal characteristics amplified during training on one task can "leak" into other domains of operation. These developments demonstrate that technological systems evolve in ways that cannot be evaluated solely through efficiency or safety metrics and thus cannot be adequately understood within research paradigms that treat technology merely as an external moderator of well-being outcomes. They require a normative–psychological framework capable of assessing their impact on flourishing.

It follows that responsible AI development cannot be limited to isolated safeguards but instead requires a systemic reflection on system architectures, learning processes, and the long-term consequences of their deployment. In this context, the idea of digital humanism gains particular significance, as it calls for placing the human being, together with dignity, values, and well-being, at the center of technological processes (Werthner, 2024), alongside related notions such as friendly AI (Yudkowsky, 2001) or human-aligned AI (IEEE, 2019). The principles articulated within these frameworks constitute a set of normative guidelines for designers, legislators, and policymakers, underscoring that the development of digital technologies is fundamentally an axiological choice (e.g., European Commission, 2021; Friedman & Henry, 2019; Russell, 2019). As emphasized by Terrell W. Bynum (2006), ethics, understood as flourishing ethics, should be primarily oriented toward supporting the conditions under which individuals and communities can grow, achieve fullness of life, and realize their potential within relationships grounded in care, responsibility, and mutual respect. From this perspective, flourishing becomes a key normative category for evaluating technological development, providing a criterion for assessing design practices. Psychologists, in turn, are called upon to supply the tools for such evaluations by operationalizing these normative ideals into empirically testable constructs and indicators.

1.2.2 Rethinking Human Competencies for the Future

The intensity of efforts devoted to improving AI-driven systems and to developing principles for designing friendly technological artifacts raises the question of the extent to which comparable efforts are directed toward cultivating reflective and competent users. This issue becomes particularly salient in the context of the gradual blurring of boundaries between the anthroposphere and the technosphere, a process evidenced by humanity's progressive movement along the imagined human–cyborg continuum (Jupiter, 2016). This continuum ranges from distanced use of personal computers, through mobile technologies and wearables, to bodily augmentation, and, looking further ahead, even to the possibility of integrating into digital environments in the form of an artificial self.

A cyborg is commonly defined as an organism equipped with a technological component that enhances its adaptive capacities within a specific environment (Carvalko, 2012). Processes of bodily cyborgization are currently being tested primarily in military contexts (e.g., brain stimulation, exoskeletons, and brain–computer interfaces) and in medicine (bionic prostheses and implants). At the same time, cyborgization is also developing informally through grassroots biohacking movements (e.g., biohack.me), most often intertwined with artistic practices (Łukaszewicz-Alcaraz, 2020).

An intermediate stage between purely human and fully cyborg modes of existence is hybridization, also referred to as "soft cyborgization" (Kamieński, 2022). A hybrid system emerges from the coupling of autonomous yet cooperating agents equipped with natural (human) and artificial (AI-driven) cognitive systems (Hubig, 2008). This form of coupling may be further conceptualized as hybrid intelligence, in which human and artificial agents form integrated systems that combine complementary capabilities, jointly produce outcomes that exceed those achievable by either alone, and continuously improve through interaction

(Dellermann et al., 2019). Their cooperation may be spontaneous or intentional, and its purpose determines the type of hybrid system involved, for example, cognitive systems oriented toward problem-solving, decision systems focused on choice, or positive systems aimed at enhancing well-being. Illustrative examples of hybrid systems include Uber drivers supported by applications that determine routes and optimize demand, as well as physicians assisted by diagnostic algorithms and surgical systems.

Under conditions of "soft cyborgization," the majority of the world's population is already functioning today. According to the Digital 2025 Global Overview Report (Kemp, 2025), the global number of internet users reached 5.56 billion, representing 67.9% of the world's population, with approximately 136 million new users coming online in the preceding year. At the same time, many individuals surround themselves with a relatively tight "technological cocoon." The same report indicates that total daily internet use across all devices exceeds 6.5 hours, nearly 4 of which are spent on mobile devices (e.g., smartphones and tablets). Data from the Smartphone Addiction Statistics of 2025 (Kumar, 2025; based on sources including Statista, Deloitte, and reviews.org) further show that the average user worldwide checks their smartphone 58 times/day, while in the United States, this frequency is nearly three times higher. More than half of US residents (53%) report that they have never spent a full day without their smartphone.

Importantly, engagement with digital technologies permeates multiple domains of everyday life. For example, 35% of respondents aged 18–25 report that they must have their smartphone present at every meal, and 17% of women state that they interrupt lovemaking or intimate moments in order to check their phone. Additionally, depending on the country and population, between approximately 40% and nearly 90% of individuals exhibit phubbing—that is, prioritizing online activity over interaction with a partner in offline, face-to-face contexts (Barbed-Castrejón et al., 2024).

The "formatting" influence of digital technologies manifests not only in everyday routines that bear the hallmarks of cyborgization. It is also evident in adopted social roles (e.g., influencer and follower), in social imaginaries (the incorporation of technology into representations of one's living environment), and in the language of communication (e.g., the dominance of English within the infosphere) (Ogonowska, 2021). In this sense, John M. Culkin's (1967) observation—"We shape our tools and thereafter they shape us" (p. 70), often attributed to Marshall McLuhan—is more than an aphoristic commentary; it describes empirically observable relations.

The strength and scope of the shaping function of digital technologies can, however, be regulated by humans, provided they are able to move beyond passive adaptation to existing technological conditions toward autonomous, reflective, and agentic management of interactions with the agents of the technosphere. One of the impulses behind the emergence of positive psychology was a rejection of perpetuating a victimological image of the human being. This shift was expressed, among other things, in the systematic description and operationalization of character strengths (Peterson & Seligman, 2004). In a similar way, the technological context now presents the challenge of identifying and conceptualizing the dispositions that function as individual resources supporting prudent human agency in relation to digital artifacts. These dispositions may be referred to as *digital strengths.*

The literature identifies several constructs that provide a promising foundation for systematic conceptual and empirical work aimed at identifying and cultivating dispositions involved in the prudent regulation of engagement with digital environments. These include technomoral virtues (Vallor, 2016), humanics (Aoun, 2018), digital agency (Passey et al., 2018), digital intelligence (Dziak, 2022), and digital maturity (Laaber et al., 2023). Although these frameworks are rooted in different traditions and vary in their level of theoretical maturity, the dispositions they distinguish (e.g., digital literacy, support seeking, and emotional regulation) can be subjected to critical analysis and integrated within a broader, more universal category. This endeavor requires empirical verification of their relevance for individuals' agentic management of interactions with digital technologies in specific contexts, the identification of conditions under which these dispositions are developed and strengthened, and the analysis of their mutual interrelations.

Conducting systematic research on the thus-defined category of digital strengths should, at the theoretical level, enable more precise modeling of the mechanisms through which individual dispositions, digital practices, and sociotechnical contexts jointly shape trajectories of flourishing. At the applied level, insights derived from such research may provide a robust foundation for the design of evidence-based educational and intervention programs that anchor the "bright side" of digital technology use in cultivable individual resources. Absent a broader flourishing-oriented framework, digital competencies risk being reduced to instrumental survival skills tailored to the demands of a technologically saturated environment, rather than understood as capacities contributing to long-term developmental enrichment and well-being.

1.3 Modes: Toward Constructive Engagement with Technology

The idea of PCyb emerged from the recognition of a persistent imbalance in research on human–technology interaction (Burke, 2021; Fortuna, 2021). Empirical studies have predominantly focused on *problematic technology use* (PTU), understood as patterns in which psychological, social, or functional costs outweigh benefits and are frequently accompanied by impaired self-regulation

(Błachnio & Przepiorka, 2016; Young, 2009). By contrast, considerably less systematic attention has been devoted to forms of technology use that support well-being, typically described as *balanced*, *healthy*, *autonomous*, or *adaptive* (e.g., Duradoni et al., 2022a; Lin et al., 2018). Notably, there is no single, widely accepted term that functions as a direct counterpart to PTU, which may suggest that these descriptors capture complementary—rather than interchangeable—aspects of constructive technology use.

Moving beyond a primary focus on risks and maladaptive patterns toward a systematic understanding of how technology can support human flourishing calls for an integrative framework that brings together previously dispersed lines of inquiry and facilitates their further development. To advance this agenda, it is useful to begin with the modes of interaction that structure human–technology relations. These modes constitute a generative layer through which digital practices acquire their psychological significance. At the technical level, they are grounded in interface architectures, affordances, and system logics through which humans and digital systems establish patterned relations across diverse human–technology environments. Whether such interaction patterns support or constrain psychological functioning depends on specific configurations of individual predispositions and situational conditions (Brand et al., 2016). When interactions engage cognitive and emotional processes beyond mere behavioral participation, they may take the form of *technology engagement*—a mode of involvement that transcends simple metrics of usage duration and instead captures the qualitative depth and experiential texture of user experience (O'Brien & Cairns, 2016). Yet engagement, understood in this way, is not inherently beneficial or detrimental. Its developmental implications depend on how it is structured, regulated, and integrated within the individual's broader system of functioning.

The constructive character of these forms of engagement is reflected in the descriptors introduced above—balanced, healthy, autonomous, and adaptive technology use. Although these labels are often used synonymously, they accentuate distinct dimensions of functioning—respectively, regulatory, psychophysiological, motivational, and goal-oriented. Clarifying how these differentiated forms of engagement are shaped, regulated, and stabilized provides a coherent entry point for systematically investigating technology use that supports flourishing. Addressing this gap is essential, as the absence of a coherent integrative framework may have contributed to a disproportionate focus on dysfunctional and pathological patterns, reinforcing a deficit-oriented understanding of digital engagement.

From a modes-of-interaction perspective, digital environments can be analytically differentiated according to whether the technologies and systems they embed are primarily oriented toward instrumental task fulfillment or toward the intentional cultivation of well-being. Some artifacts operate primarily as everyday tools—here conceptualized as instrumental technologies—embedded in routine domains of life and serving pragmatic, communicative, and organizational purposes. Others are explicitly designed or adapted to promote well-being—often referred to as positive technologies (Riva et al., 2012)—and intentionally structured to elicit beneficial psychological states or developmental processes. On this basis, two complementary lines of inquiry into constructive patterns of technology use warrant systematic investigation. The first concerns everyday digital practices and their impact on well-being across domains such as work, education, relationships, civic participation, and leisure. In this context, DWB (Vanden Abeele, 2020) offers a promising framework for examining constructive forms of technology engagement. The second line of inquiry focuses on intentionally designed or digitally assisted positive interventions. In such cases, specific modes of interaction are deliberately structured to activate mechanisms that support and strengthen components of flourishing.

1.3.1 Everyday Digital Challenges

The category of instrumental technologies encompasses the majority of digital artifacts used daily within WEIRD societies, including enterprise systems (e.g., SAP and Oracle), social media platforms (e.g., X, Instagram, and TikTok), conversational agents (e.g., Alexa and ChatGPT), e-learning platforms (e.g., Moodle and Blackboard), e-sports services (e.g., Twitch and ESL), and commercial marketplaces (e.g., Amazon). Despite their functional diversity, these systems share a common structural characteristic: they are developed within competitive market environments in which profitability, user retention, and market expansion operate as primary design imperatives. Consequently, users participate as consumers embedded in engagement-driven business models organized around attention capture and behavioral optimization. Accordingly, research trajectories in human–technology interaction must be grounded in explicit awareness of the commercial design logics shaping these systems. Theoretical models and methodological strategies should therefore systematically account for the risks and costs embedded in their interaction architectures and employ conceptual frameworks capable of capturing the structural complexity and dynamic character of everyday technological engagement.

1.3.1.1 Design Logics Structuring Interaction

The term *instrumental technologies* suggests that artifacts function as passive tools that remain under the user's control and are subordinate to their intentions. However, the digital revolution and the expansion of digital markets necessitate a revision of this assumption, revealing the agentic role of artificial systems in shaping human behavior. Instrumentality is not an inherent property of artifacts but a relational attribution emerging in specific contexts of use (Heidegger, 1927/2008). In line with James J. Gibson's (1979) ecological psychology, objects function as tools through the perception of affordances—relationally defined possibilities for action arising between agent and environment. Affordances are neither purely objective nor purely subjective; they emerge in interaction and shape behavioral tendencies. Importantly, Gibson (1979) emphasized that affordance perception is a skill subject to development. In contemporary AI-driven systems, however, processes of learning and adaptation are no longer exclusively human. Artificial systems detect patterns, model users, and optimize interaction architectures, often in accordance with commercial imperatives of engagement and retention, thereby further destabilizing the classical subject–object arrangement.

This shift becomes particularly visible in affective computing (Picard, 1997), where systems are designed to recognize and model users' emotional states, and in persuasive technologies initiated in B. J. Fogg's (2003) framework. Originally intended to support goal attainment (e.g., health, learning, and self-regulation), persuasive systems increasingly operate through machine learning and large-scale behavioral prediction. They not only respond to users but actively shape motivational landscapes, habits, and probabilistic structures of decision-making. As a result, digital technologies cease to function as a passive affordance environment and instead become active architects of decision-making situations, designing contexts in which certain user choices become more likely than others.

The destabilization of the subject–object relationship is facilitated by what may be termed *a mutual affordance loop*. The individual perceives possibilities for action in the artifact, while the technological system simultaneously models the user as a source of data, responses, and preferences that are processed and stabilized into predictable behavioral patterns. In Gilles Deleuze's (1992) terms, the individuum coexists with its operational counterpart—*the dividual*—within algorithmic systems that continuously expand through each click, scroll, or moment of sustained attention. These data are aggregated and processed by computational architectures that remain largely opaque yet exert tangible influence through personalization, adaptive recommendations, and predictive steering of stimulus streams. As Shoshana Zuboff (2019) succinctly observed, the time when we searched Google has passed; "now Google searches you" (p. 261).

A particularly vivid manifestation of this inversion of instrumentality can be observed in emerging service models such as RentAHuman—a rapidly scaling platform that, as of early 2026, reportedly has over 641,000 registered users and enables AI agents to search for, select, and hire humans to perform real-world tasks through standardized interfaces. Within this model, individuals create profiles specifying their skills, location, availability, and rates, while AI systems delegate tasks that require physical presence, perceptual input, or embodied execution.

At first glance, such arrangements may appear to reaffirm the classical subject–object distinction, positioning the human as the intentional subject and the service as a controllable resource. However, from a relational and affordance-based perspective, this model can be seen as revealing a deeper structural shift. The human actor becomes functionally embedded within an interaction architecture governed by platform logics, ratings, algorithmic visibility, and demand optimization. In this sense, the human is not merely using the system but is simultaneously being formatted by it, becoming part of a sociotechnical configuration in which agency is distributed and continuously negotiated.

From this perspective, the redistribution of agency within human–technology systems has direct implications for patterns of regulation and control. Transferring initiative to AI-driven systems—embedded in optimization logics—entails costs that may contribute to PTU. Individuals pay not only with data but also with time, attentional resources, transformations of relational patterns, and, under conditions of high engagement, even with physical and mental health. As Avigail Ferdman (2024) argues, seemingly neutral affordances may systematically weaken capacities constitutive of well-being, such as reflectiveness, self-regulation, or empathy, leading to forms of *privative unflourishing*. Echo chambers (Nguyen, 2020) and filter bubbles (Pariser, 2011) further restrict cognitive diversity, while mechanisms exploiting variable reinforcement schedules, such as loot boxes in video games, intensify impulsivity and increase the risk of PTU (Cudo et al., 2024).

At a more granular level, these dynamics can be understood in terms of learning mechanisms grounded in reward processing. Many digital environments are structured around interaction patterns that incorporate principles of behavioral conditioning, typically implemented through reward systems characterized by variable magnitude and frequency. Such systems are widely embedded in the design of social media platforms, digital games, and mobile applications. Neuroscientific research indicates that dopaminergic circuits are implicated in reinforcement learning and motivational processes (Padilla-Coreano & Martínez-Rivera, 2025). According to the reward prediction error framework, phasic activity of dopamine neurons signals discrepancies between expected and obtained outcomes, enabling organisms to update their predictions and adjust behavior (Schultz, 2016). Within digital environments, interactions such as encountering new content or receiving social feedback (e.g., a "like") may function as reward-predictive events that engage these learning processes, reinforcing patterns of attentional and behavioral engagement. The variability and unpredictability of such rewards—resembling, though not identical to, intermittent reinforcement schedules observed in gambling devices—can promote exploratory checking behaviors and frequent device use, and under certain conditions gradually contribute to habit formation and the automatization of engagement patterns.

Under such conditions, digital environments no longer merely offer possibilities for action; they increasingly structure desire, attention, and probabilistic horizons of choice. Recognizing this reconfiguration of instrumentality is therefore crucial for understanding the conditions under which human–technology interaction supports flourishing rather than systematically undermines it.

1.3.1.2 A Conceptual Framework for Trade-offs in Technology Use

Even with growing awareness of the risks arising from user-unfriendly design logics, individuals seeking to optimize their patterns of interaction with digital technologies are not able to eliminate the costs of their use fully and consistently. Some of these costs are structural in nature and are permanently embedded in the architecture of digital systems, such as the need for continuous attention to the screen, algorithmically curated access to content, or the systemic limitation of offline activities. Other costs constitute an unavoidable "price of participation" in digital environments, which function not as commons but as highly regulated spaces, where users' presence and agency are constrained by designers and platform owners.

Against this background, an ecologically valid basis for assessing human–technology relations lies not in the mere frequency or intensity of use but in the quality of digital engagement. This quality can be understood as a relational property emerging from dynamic, context-sensitive configurations of benefits and costs generated in the course of everyday functioning within digital environments. In the literature, this evaluative dimension of technology use is most commonly captured by the concept of DWB (Vanden Abeele, 2020).

Despite the growing prominence of DWB in contemporary scholarship, the construct remains theoretically fluid and conceptually unsettled. To illustrate the heterogeneity of existing approaches, Table 1.2 presents influential definitions of DWB. This conceptual plurality reflects both the urgency of the problem and the absence of a consolidated framework.

As shown in Table 1.2, existing definitions of DWB differ substantially in their ontological scope, ranging from experiential states and behavioral regulation to broad normative and societal perspectives. Some conceptualizations emphasize patterns of technology use and frame the construct in terms of users' capacity to regulate their engagement with digital technologies. Within this line of reasoning, DWB is contrasted with compulsive, excessive, or uncontrolled digital practices. For example, Marvin Dadischeck (2021) conceptualizes DWB as a state of mindful and purposeful technology use, arguing that its strengthening involves both the conscious reduction of excessive technology use and the cultivation of healthy digital habits. Similarly, Lewend Mayiwar et al. (2025) ground their operationalization of DWB in the notion of conscious and hygienic technology use, while extending this perspective by emphasizing the importance of trust in technology,

Table 1.2 Major conceptualizations of DWB.

Authors	Definition
Luciano Floridi (2014)	The impact of digital technologies on what it means to live a life that is *good for* a human being in an information society. (Burr et al., 2020, p. 2313)
Mariek M. P. Vanden Abeele (2020)	A subjective individual experience of optimal balance between the benefits and drawbacks obtained from mobile connectivity. (Vanden Abeele, 2020, p. 238)
Marvin Dadischeck (2021)	A state of mindful and purposeful ICT use that boosts job performance and well-being by mitigating the adverse effects of digital technologies such as distractions and information overload. (Dadischeck, 2021, p. 401)
Veysel B. Arslankara et al. (2022)	A state in which subjective well-being is maintained in a virtual and technological environment characterized by an excessive increase in media communication. (Arslankara et al., 2022, p. 265)
Roseline Gomes et al. (2023)	The impact of technologies and digital services on a person's mental, physical, and emotional health. (Gomes et al., 2023, p. 242)
Moritz Büchi (2024)	DWB is understood here as a shorthand term for how digital media use is connected to well-being, rather than referring to moments of being satisfied with one's digital media use. (Büchi, 2024, p. 174)
Lewend Mayiwar et al. (2025)	The conscious and positive use of technology, which ensures that individuals not only harness the benefits of digital tools but also mitigate potential harms. (Mayiwar et al., 2025, p. 3064)

perceived safety in online environments, and users' sense of control over personal data and their digital footprint.

Another group of conceptualizations shifts the analytical focus from digital practices themselves to the subjective outcomes of individuals' interactions with digital technologies. These approaches define DWB with reference to subjective well-being maintained in technologically saturated environments (Arslankara et al., 2022), broader domains of well-being affected by digital technologies (e.g., Floridi, 2014; Gomes et al., 2023), or—most explicitly in Mariek Vanden Abeele's proposal (2020)—the perceived balance between gains and losses associated with technology use. In the latter account, DWB is described as a state of dynamic equilibrium between the benefits and drawbacks of digital connectivity. Higher levels of DWB are associated with experiences of controlled pleasure and functional support, accompanied by minimal loss of control and functional impairment. Central to this perspective is the notion of optimizing ambivalence, understood as an ongoing process of fine-tuning one's relationship with technology under conditions of continual change.

The most integrative and theoretically comprehensive conceptualization of DWB has been proposed by Moritz Büchi (2024). In his framework, DWB is not treated as a single outcome or evaluative indicator but as an analytical lens for examining the structured relationships between digital media use and subjective well-being. Specifically, the framework distinguishes three analytically separate yet causally connected domains: (1) digital practices (e.g., everyday online behavior), (2) proximal outcomes in the form of benefits (e.g., connectedness) and harms (e.g., stress) experienced by individuals, and (3) distal outcomes operationalized as subjective well-being (emotional, psychological, and social). Rather than collapsing these dimensions into a single index, Büchi's approach explicitly models the pathways linking specific manifestations of digital practice to co-occurring harms and benefits, and ultimately to well-being outcomes. By maintaining analytical separation between practices, proximal effects, and distal well-being, the framework integrates earlier conceptual strands while preserving causal clarity. In doing so, it captures both the modes of human engagement with digital technologies and the experiential quality of their consequences without reducing DWB to mere satisfaction with technology use.

A broad conceptualization of DWB provides a useful theoretical framework for analyzing optimal technology use. A key criterion for identifying such use is the specification of conditions under which digital practices result in a favorable balance between psychological, health-related, and functional gains and costs. Within this perspective, balanced technology use may be understood as the harmonious integration of digital technologies into everyday functioning, without a subjective sense of loss of control over time or overall quality of life. Healthy technology use refers to the mitigation of risks associated with health deterioration and the maintenance of good psychophysical functioning. Autonomous use is reflected in the satisfaction of autonomy and competence needs, accompanied by the absence of perceived compulsion or dependency on technology. Finally, adaptive use denotes the generation of experiences that support the pursuit of goals perceived by the individual as valuable, while minimizing stress and subjective perceptions of resource depletion.

Taken together, these distinctions underscore that DWB is not simply a descriptive label but an integrative analytical framework foundational for understanding how flourishing can be supported within the ordinary, routine practices that define contemporary digital life. Its strength lies in its capacity to connect modes of interaction, subjective experience, and broader well-being outcomes within a shared evaluative horizon, thereby creating conceptual conditions for the systematic synthesis of findings generated across disciplines. Although research addressing these configurations is empirically abundant, it remains scattered and conceptually heterogeneous, which limits cumulative insight into how agency is sustained under conditions shaped by competing design logics and structural constraints. Further consolidation of DWB as a shared analytical framework would therefore facilitate the integration of dispersed evidence and clarify the conditions under which individuals are able to regulate their relationship with technology and experience everyday digital functioning as satisfying.

1.3.2 Unlocking the Potential of Positive Technologies

The term *positive technologies* refers to tools designed to enhance the hedonic, eudaimonic, and social components of flourishing (Riva et al., 2012). Their development is aligned with the idea of friendly AI and is embedded within the tradition of human-centered design, which—by virtue of its intended outcomes—may also be described as well-being-oriented design. Their theoretical foundations are provided by numerous concepts illustrating the partnership between human–computer interaction and UX on the one hand, and positive psychology on the other, supporting "design for deeper meaning, happiness, and human flourishing" (Peters et al., 2018, p. 2). However, the validity of the assumptions formulated within these approaches, as well as the effectiveness of their translation into concrete design logics, still requires systematic empirical verification.

A promising direction for research involves testing patterns of positive technology use that may take the form of interventions—referred to here as *positive technology interventions* (PTIs)—provided that they meet the rigorous requirements already formulated for PPIs (van Zyl et al., 2019). The number of analyses offering empirical foundations for designing such procedures, or documenting their beneficial effects on flourishing, is growing rapidly. As these studies accumulate, their continued fragmentation increasingly impedes cumulative knowledge development and calls for systematic integration.

1.3.2.1 Inscribing Well-Being into Technology

Approaches situated within the well-being-oriented design paradigm share the conviction that technology should not only function correctly but above all support positive experiences and individual well-being. They point designers toward an aspiration to move beyond the purely technological dimension of their work, while strengthening responsibility and sensitivity to the psychosocial and axiological consequences of implementing digital solutions. Differences between these concepts concern primarily the ways of operationalizing the desired effects of individuals' interactions with digital technologies, the strategies for achieving them, and the explanation of the conditions underlying this positive impact (see Table 1.3).

Table 1.3 Approaches to designing technologies that support user well-being: core assumptions and central concepts.

Approach	Core assumptions	Central concepts
Experience Design (Hassenzahl, 2010)	Design should prioritize the qualitative structure of user experience over purely functional considerations.	Designing meaningful and valuable user experiences that support well-being and self-realization.
Positive Computing (Sander, 2011)	Technologies should support flourishing in accordance with diverse definitions of the good life.	Flourishing; personal happiness assistant; and self-knowledge.
Positive Technology (Riva et al., 2012)	Technology can influence the quality of the user experience through its structuring, augmentation, and substitution.	E-experience; hedonic, eudaimonic, and social technologies.
Positive Design (Desmet & Pohlmeyer, 2013)	Well-being can be supported through the design of technologies oriented toward pleasure, personal meaning, and the cultivation of virtues.	Holistic well-being–oriented design integrating pleasure, personal meaning, and virtue cultivation.
Positive Computing (Calvo & Peters, 2014)	Technology should strengthen well-being factors related to the self, relationships, and transcendence. Ethical, humanity-oriented design is therefore required.	Humanity-centered design; mental health; values; and ethical design.
Transformative Experience Design (Gaggioli, 2016)	Technologies can create conditions conducive to users' epistemic and personal transformation.	Transformative experience; epistemic and personal transformation; emotional and epistemic affordances; and transformative medium.
METUX (Peters et al., 2018)	Supporting users' motivation, engagement, and development by incorporating basic psychological needs into the design process.	Fundamental psychological needs; TENS scales (interface, task, behavior, and life).
Liminal Design (Liedgren et al., 2023)	Technology should create a distinct, narratively structured in-between space that enables experiences of self-transcendence and personal transformation.	Liminality, narrative sensemaking, suspension of disbelief, self-transcendence, and transformation.
Positive social technology (Positech; Kim et al., 2024)	A shift in the research paradigm on social technologies from a remedial approach to one that supports flourishing. What matters is not only the design of technologies, but also legislative, ethical, and meta-scientific actions.	Flourishing; social technology; PERMA; interpersonal and intrapersonal needs; ethical design; augmenting rather than replacing; and human connection.
Positive AI (van der Maden et al., 2024)	AI systems should be intentionally designed to actively promote human flourishing rather than merely minimize risks or prevent harm.	Well-being; flourishing; human-centered design; and AI as a sociotechnical system.

Note: This table extends and elaborates on the table presented in Fortuna (2026, pp. 325–326).

Three concepts and the approaches derived from them merit particular attention. The first is Marc Hassenzahl's *Experience Design* (2010), a pioneering approach to technology design in which the focus is placed on users' quality of life. Its central concept is the individual's positive experience, understood as a state that is meaningful, fascinating, and rich in emotions. Such experiences are meant to gain value through interaction with technology by enabling the satisfaction of needs such as competence, stimulation, relatedness, autonomy, popularity, meaning, security, and physical exertion.

The most theoretically mature and most firmly grounded in positive psychology is the concept of Positive Technology, proposed by Giuseppe Riva et al. (2012). The authors emphasized the need to design technologies that strengthen aspects of human well-being related to three dimensions: hedonic, eudaimonic, and social. They introduced a general conceptual framework for shaping individuals' personal experiences and identified possible mechanisms through which these experiences may be formed on the basis of interactions with digital technologies. The Positive Technology concept is discussed in greater detail in Section 2.4.1. It is also worth noting that, within work conducted in the spirit of PT, Andrea Gaggioli (2016) proposed the Transformative Experience Design approach as a theoretical and methodological framework. This framework describes how interactive—especially immersive—technologies can generate transformative experiences that expand individuals' epistemic horizons and alter how they experience themselves.

The concept of Positive Computing proposed by Rafael A. Calvo and Dorian Peters (2014) is also strongly rooted in positive psychology. This approach focuses on the impact of interactions with digital technologies on domains of well-being but, unlike Positive Technology and Transformative Experience Design, without specifying mediating processes. Particularly noteworthy is the authors' postulate to shift the emphasis from human-centered to humanity-centered design, thereby highlighting the ethical dimension of technology design. Several years later, the authors of Positive Computing, together with Richard M. Ryan, developed a more theoretically and methodologically advanced model: Motivation, Engagement and Thriving in User Experience (METUX; Peters et al., 2018). Its theoretical foundation is Self-Determination Theory (SDT; Ryan & Deci, 2000). Accordingly, the model postulates the need to design digital tools that contribute to well-being by satisfying individuals' needs for autonomy, competence, and relatedness. A key strength of METUX lies in its comprehensiveness, as the authors identify six levels of user experience at which technology may exert influence: adoption, interface, task, behavior, life, and society.

Well-being–oriented design approaches exemplify the construction of a bridge between design and psychology within the scientific landscape by consistently emphasizing the need to draw on knowledge about humans at every stage of technology development, as well as by engaging with the achievements of positive psychology. Despite their high applied value, however, the epistemic potential of the models discussed is limited with respect to providing a comprehensive explanation of the effectiveness of digital practices. Challenges already arise at the level of defining the desired outcomes of innovation use. These range from need satisfaction (Experience Design and METUX), through personal experience (Positive Technology) and the strengthening of well-being domains (Positive Computing and Positive Technology), to a broader set of positive effects (Positive Design) or a more general state of flourishing (Positive Computing).

In many cases, these variables are identified intuitively, without systematic reference to the research traditions developed within positive psychology, and the mechanisms through which they are shaped are often framed in simplified cause–effect terms that link specific digital technology functionalities to positive psychological states, while neglecting the role of contextual factors. Regardless of the limitations noted above, the value of the approaches presented lies in their potential to design structured digital practices that can take the form of positive interventions—understood not as intuitive "good ideas" for using digital technologies, but as theoretically grounded and empirically verifiable procedures for strengthening flourishing.

1.3.2.2 Flourishing-Oriented Digital Interventions

Digital tools have long been used as the basis for digital interventions, designed and applied primarily in the area of behavior change (digital behavior change interventions; Hekler et al., 2016) and health care, including eHealth (the use of the internet and information and communication technologies for clinical and health-promoting activities), mHealth (mobile health; the use of mobile devices such as smartphones, tablets, and wearable technologies to support health monitoring, intervention delivery, and health-related communication), and uHealth (ubiquitous health; the provision of health support through digital technologies that enable continuous, context-aware, and location-independent access to health-related services) (Murray et al., 2016). These interventions employ so-called behavior change technologies (BCTs), examples of which in medical practice include Health Monitoring Apps and Remote Patient Monitoring Apps. Their design is strongly theory-driven and based on a well-considered structure of intervention processes. Their "building blocks" are behavior change techniques—organized into clusters (e.g., goals and planning, feedback and monitoring)—which constitute the smallest possible elements of practices aimed at modifying specific components of behavior (Michie et al., 2013). The literature offers numerous classifications of BCT-based interventions (e.g., Pineda et al., 2023; WHO, 2023), and analyses of the conditions underlying their effectiveness have an established research tradition (Hekler et al., 2016).

Against this background, research on interventions that employ positive technologies appears as an area in urgent need of development. Like BCT-based interventions, these approaches can be understood as operating through the deliberate modification of interaction modes, by reconfiguring feedback loops, affordances, and patterns of engagement through which users relate to digital systems. Pioneers in this domain are scholars associated with Positive Technology (Riva et al., 2012), who were the first to propose a systematic reflection on treating digital innovations as tools for supporting psychological growth and well-being. They also demonstrated that the use of digital technologies, on the one hand, opens new opportunities for psychoprophylaxis, and on the other, inspires the development of practices aimed at positively influencing well-being (Baños et al., 2017a).

Research on PTIs needs to be expanded and systematized. This entails not only their conceptualization but also their clear differentiation from the DWB programs that currently saturate the market. Moreover, there is a need to develop taxonomies of PTIs based on diverse criteria, such as intervention aims, theoretical foundations, and type of technology. It is also important to specify the conditions that maximize efficacy and enhance effectiveness in line with principles already established in positive psychology (van Zyl et al., 2019), and to articulate ethical guidelines for their application, embedded within professional codes in psychology (Jarden et al., 2021). The effectiveness of PTIs should also be evaluated across diverse social and cultural contexts. Taken together, these tasks point toward the need for a coherent and unified research domain within which the conceptual, methodological, and ethical dimensions of PTIs can be systematically integrated and advanced.

1.4 Contexts: The Need for Multi-Aspect Analyses of Flourishing in a Digital Era

The quality of the relationship between individuals' use of digital technologies and flourishing is shaped by a broad constellation of contextual factors. In this section, attention is directed to those dimensions that appear most critical for a comprehensive understanding of flourishing in the digital era. These include cultural diversity in conceptions of the "good life," which, together with the postulates of transhumanism, shapes the meanings attributed to different types of digital practices. They also include the interplay between material and digital reality, the integration of experiences formed online with those shaped offline in the process of flourishing, and the importance of supporting the development of appropriate patterns of interaction with digital innovations. Recognizing the relevance of these dimensions simultaneously exposes the fragmented nature of existing scholarship, which remains dispersed not only across positive psychology and cyberpsychology but also across cultural psychology, philosophy of technology, and organizational research. Integrating these strands into systematic dialogue is essential to understanding the multifaceted conditions under which flourishing unfolds in a heterogeneous world.

1.4.1 Cultural and Normative Visions of Flourishing

Cross-cultural research consistently demonstrates that understandings of happiness and the criteria of the good life are profoundly context-dependent (see Krys et al., 2025). Cultural differences shape not only the formulation of normative life ideals but also the prioritization, valuation, and interpretation of specific well-being domains. This variability poses a structural challenge to the development of integrative frameworks capable of adequately capturing flourishing in digital contexts. In the absence of such frameworks, research risks the uncritical universalization of culturally specific ideals of well-being and the misinterpretation of digitally mediated experiences across diverse socio-cultural contexts.

The models of flourishing presented in the first part of this chapter are strongly rooted not only in the Western, individualistic cultural paradigm but also in the semantics of the English language. Meanwhile, as Tim Lomas (2018) shows, the world's languages contain more than 1,600 ethnopsychological terms that describe distinct, culturally embedded forms of well-being. Analysis of these concepts shows that individual languages "map" the reality of quality of life in idiosyncratic ways, foregrounding experiences that are overlooked or difficult to express in other semantic systems. A well-known example is the Portuguese term *saudade*, which captures a complex experience of longing and melancholic desire for someone or something that has been lost.

In some Eastern cultures, happiness is not necessarily viewed as an admirable achievement but rather as a suspicious or potentially destabilizing state—metaphorically compared to catching a soap bubble, a fragile and fleeting experience (Joshanloo et al., 2015). In collectivist cultures, such as Confucian or Buddhist traditions, happiness is primarily associated with social harmony, the quality of relationships, and the fulfillment of obligations toward others, rather than with intense subjective well-being. For this reason, low-arousal emotions such as calmness or balance are more strongly valued than in Western cultures, where indicators of a good life tend to include excitement, autonomy, and self-expression (Christopher & Hickinbottom, 2008; Tov & Diener, 2009). A similar pattern can be observed at the macrosocial level: in countries with lower levels of affluence, happiness and meaning in life are more often rooted in community and religion, whereas in affluent societies, narratives of autonomy and self-realization tend to dominate (Oishi & Diener, 2014).

A significant influence on shaping ideals of the good life in both Eastern and Western cultures comes from functioning within business organizations, which, through organizational culture, impose specific work ethics as well as a set of norms and values. For many representatives of WEIRD societies, the work environment has increasingly become a primary source of purpose, belonging, agency, and social recognition. An expression of this trend is the growing global "career" of the Japanese concept of *ikigai* (生き甲斐; a reason for living), which is increasingly linked to professional activity as a space for self-realization and meaning, reinforced by engagement, team belonging, and the experience of being needed (Kumano, 2018). Analogous narratives are present in other cultural contexts, such as the Chinese *Gōngzuò jiù shì shēnghuó* (工作就是生活) and the Korean *Ili got insaengida* (일이 곧 인생이다), both translated as "work is life," as well as the Anglo-Saxon saying, "You are what you do." Importantly, in highly developed societies, the pursuit of professional success is closely coupled with competent use of advanced technologies, which positions phenomena such as technostress and techno-eustress as important mediators of satisfaction (Tarafdar et al., 2024).

Contemporary Western culture, still grappling with the "tyranny of positive thinking" (Held, 2002), generates a multitude of competing promises for improving quality of life—both in relation to one another and in relation to classical transcendentals. At present, particularly strong sources of such promises include biotechnological optimism, technologies of spirituality, and—worthy of broader discussion—transhumanism.

Transhumanism is an interdisciplinary intellectual and cultural movement that assumes the possibility—and even the necessity—of overcoming the biological limitations of the human species (Bostrom, 2005). This aspiration is expressed in Humanity+'s mission statement, "We want people to be better than well" (Humanity+, n.d.), and in transhumanist goals such as superintelligence, super-longevity, and super-well-being (Klichowski, 2014). In this sense, transhumanism responds to a desire deeply rooted in human history for transgression and transcendence toward an enhanced version of the human being: the posthuman, whose symbolic foreshadowing is embodied in the figure of the cyborg (cf. Hayles, 1999). Ultimately, the posthuman is envisioned as possessing nanotechnological memory, laser vision, parabolic hearing, titanium bones, and legs that never tire (Vita-More, 2002).

An example of a figure who has embodied the ideas of transhumanism is Neil Harbisson—one of the artists experimenting with biohacking (other well-known figures include Lepht Anonym, Liviu Babitz, Rich Lee, and Moon Ribas) and a subject frequently analyzed in interdisciplinary research (e.g., Fortuna et al., 2024; Łukaszewicz-Alcaraz, 2020). In an effort to overcome difficulties resulting from congenital achromatopsia, he fused to his skull the so-called eyeborg—an optical antenna that converts light-wave frequencies into sounds perceived via bone conduction. As a result of this modification, Harbisson obtained official recognition of his cybernetic identity by state institutions, although he himself identifies as a transspecies individual. Although his artistic work has not gained broad aesthetic recognition, he has become an inspiring figure in scholarly debates on the impact of body–technology integration on well-being. According to participants in one study, the Eyeborg stimulates the development of as many as 18 positive character strengths in Harbisson—including creativity, curiosity, appreciation of beauty, love of learning, hope, and open-mindedness (Fortuna, 2024). A decrease was indicated only in the case of humility, while no changes were observed for the remaining five strengths (e.g., spirituality and kindness).

In this context, the question arises as to the optimal scope of technological enhancement across particular domains of well-being. The level of transhumanist aspiration is exemplified by David Pearce's (1995) postulate of the complete elimination of suffering. This position challenges the adaptive and existential functions of difficult experiences emphasized in psychology—including within positive psychology (Lomas & Ivtzan, 2016). It also raises doubts as to whether the development of personal identity and competencies is even possible in individuals deprived of the capacity to experience crises, adversity, and the "pain of failure." This places an obligation on psychology to empirically examine the consequences of biotechnological enhancements. At the same time, critical evaluations of processes of cyborgization should be grounded in strong theoretical and methodological frameworks. Such grounding is necessary to provide clear arguments in debates about whether technological enhancements genuinely support development or instead create barriers to well-being.

1.4.2 Configurations of Experience in Hybrid Environments

The psychological, social, and spiritual life of individuals in the digital era unfolds within configurations of experience that span material–analog–offline and virtual–digital–online environments. Importantly, although the terms grouped within each of these triads are sometimes used interchangeably in the literature, they designate analytically distinct dimensions. The material–virtual distinction concerns the ontological status of the experienced environment—whether interactions are anchored in physically co-present, materially instantiated settings or in technologically simulated and representational spaces. The analog–digital distinction pertains to the mode of signal encoding and mediation: continuous versus discretely coded forms of representation and transmission. Finally, the offline–online distinction refers to the structure of connectivity, indicating whether activity unfolds without networked digital mediation or within environments sustained by real-time computational connectivity. These dimensions are not mutually exclusive categories but intersecting layers of experiential organization.

Precisely because they overlap and interpenetrate, the question of how experiences generated across materially and digitally mediated environments relate to one another becomes unavoidable.

The broader backdrop of these considerations is an ongoing philosophical debate concerning the ontological relationship between material and virtual domains of reality—particularly whether they should be treated as separate ontological spheres or as mutually co-constitutive dimensions of a single experiential field. Luciano Floridi (2014) argues that the infosphere is emerging as a new domain of existence in which the analog and the digital increasingly interpenetrate, leading to a blurring of boundaries between previously distinct ontological orders. Similarly, Zygmunt Bauman (2000), in his analysis of "liquid modernity," emphasizes the erosion of stable structures, enduring identities, and clear-cut categories, within which humans and technology not only coexist but also mutually co-create one another. David Chalmers (2022), in turn, argues from a "technophilosophical" perspective that the ontological entanglement of humans and technology is so profound that virtual reality should no longer be treated as an illusion or a secondary simulation but rather as an ontologically equivalent extension of the material world (Reality+). In his account, digital environments introduce new ontological layers within reality in which individuals can construct identities, experience emotions, build relationships, and endow their experiences with meaning.

The debate concerning the ontological status of online and offline environments thus leads to a central question: whether the experiences generated within them are qualitatively and functionally equivalent. In cyberpsychology, experiences that are a direct result of contact with digital technologies are referred to as *proximal outcomes* (Büchi, 2024), as well as *digital experiences*, *e-experiences*, or *digitally mediated experiences* (e.g., Riva et al., 2016; Setty, 2023). Their specificity is shaped by the very mode of experiencing technology, which constitutes the focus of UX research (see Section 2.3.1). Moreover, the technological mediation of individuals' relationships with the material environment results in that world being perceived in a qualitatively transformed manner. The image of reality presented on a computer or smartphone screen is always transformed relative to the original context, which may generate additional cognitive and emotional burdens (e.g., Zoom fatigue; Basch et al., 2025). Furthermore, in line with Marshall McLuhan's (1964/1994) classic thesis that "the medium is the message" (p. 7), the very form of mediation influences how meaning is attributed to received content, shaping the character of experiences independently of their nominal content.

Particularly intriguing from a research perspective are experiences whose generation outside a technological context is difficult or impossible. One example is the possibility of manipulating identity. Bauman (2007) aptly observed that "the identities assumed during a visit to the internet world of instant connections and disconnections on demand are of a kind that would be physically or socially untenable offline" (p. 115). Immersive technologies such as VR, in turn, enable movement through spaces that exist only in digital form (e.g., a walk through the human body via Sharecare YOU VR) and have no analog counterpart (e.g., the Museum of Other Realities). While the former can be regarded as an attractive form of knowledge expansion, the latter enables perceptual training in recognizing new affordances (Dunin-Kozicka et al., 2025).

Biohacking can also serve as a source of novel types of experience. Particularly noteworthy are developments such as the conversion of images into sound, the ability to hold phone conversations heard internally "in the head," and the extension of the human sensorium through new senses—such as locational or seismic perception—previously associated only with animals (Łukaszewicz-Alcaraz, 2020). VR experiences are likewise distinctive in that they may enable people with disabilities to move freely, to cooperate within team-based games, and—looking ahead—to use contact lenses that may function both as displays and as cameras.

Undoubtedly, deepening our understanding of the impact of digital technologies on flourishing requires analyses that take into account the dynamic interconnections between digitally mediated experiences and those emerging within material environments. This entails a shift from examining isolated online or offline effects toward investigating the configurational processes through which these experiences are mutually integrated within specific domains of well-being. Only such an approach can adequately explain human functioning in the digital era, rather than reducing it to a fragmented account of isolated digital effects. Moreover, such analyses will clarify whether the proliferating "digital" variants of established constructs represent context-bound expressions of familiar psychological processes or instead signal the emergence of qualitatively novel experiential configurations specific to digitally mediated environments.

1.4.3 Supportive Contexts of Technology Use

The developmental consequences of digital technology use cannot be adequately analyzed in isolation from the broader ecologies within which such use is embedded. Research on individuals' functioning in the digital era may indirectly serve as an indicator of broader societal conditions that, as sources of norms, expectations, and cultural pressures, co-create complex configurations of factors that either support or inhibit developmental trajectories of flourishing. From an intergenerational perspective, it becomes particularly clear that each successive generation not only inherits the media-use patterns of its predecessors but also internalizes their value hierarchies and ways of being in the world. Today, the well-known sentiment captured in early studies on television reception—"I would like to be the television and occupy the most important place in our home" (Francuz, 1999)—might be expressed by many children in a modified form, identifying instead with the smartphone.

The significance of this configurational process can be further illuminated by the job demands-resources (JD-R) model (Bakker & Demerouti, 2007), developed within positive organizational psychology. This framework emphasizes that the quality of human functioning depends on the balance between environmental demands and available resources. When this balance is disrupted, it may initiate a loss spiral—a process of escalating strain in which insufficient recovery and inadequate support lead to the gradual erosion of self-regulation and well-being. Conversely, environments rich in protective and developmental resources can activate a gain spiral. In such contexts, relational support, clear normative boundaries, opportunities for recovery, and the cultivation of self-regulatory competencies create a resource base that enables adaptive engagement with digital technologies. From this perspective, it is not technology itself that generates flourishing, but the surrounding configuration of resources that equips individuals to use technology in ways that sustain autonomy, balance, and developmental integrity.

Striking illustrations of large-scale loss spirals in digital contexts are provided by Jonathan Haidt (2024) in *The anxious generation: How the great rewiring of childhood is causing an epidemic of mental illness*. He analyzes the sharp increase in mental health problems among adolescents, particularly girls, which coincided with the widespread adoption of smartphones and social media. In his view, the transition from a play-based childhood rooted in physical activity, free exploration, and face-to-face relationships to a phone-based childhood dominated by digital technologies and socially constraining online environments has led to serious disruptions in psychosocial development. Haidt argues that adolescents were thrust into an intensive digital environment without adequate protective resources, such as developed self-regulation strategies, supportive and authentic offline relationships, or clearly articulated boundaries and cultural norms enabling safe participation in the infosphere. The result has been an alarming rise in anxiety, depression, and suicidal ideation. Such patterns exemplify how deficiencies in system-level resources can undermine not only individual well-being but also the developmental resilience of entire cohorts.

The logic of the JD-R model suggests that a positive response to the threats and problems described above does not lie in interventions aimed at shaping selected digital practices but rather in the deliberate design of environments that foster the initiation of resource gain spirals. This shift aligns with the broader argument that promoting well-being requires not only supporting individuals but also actively shaping and regenerating the systems within which well-being becomes possible (Steger, 2025). Empirical work in organizational contexts has already identified characteristics of supportive environments that buffer technostress and promote adaptive engagement with digital tools (e.g., Tarafdar et al., 2024). Extending this line of inquiry to family and educational settings should therefore be considered a pressing research priority.

The objective is not to impose a rigid separation between "online" and "offline" domains, but to cultivate ecologies of protection and growth in which digitally mediated experiences are anchored in stable relational, normative, and developmental supports. In this sense, the aim extends beyond protecting individual users to cultivating conditions for sustainable collective flourishing in digitally mediated societies. A key goal of this line of research is to generate evidence-based knowledge that can inform the development of an "offline protective layer"—that is, a set of stabilizing contextual conditions capable of safeguarding digital engagement. On this basis, educational programs can be systematically designed, implemented, and evaluated, with their content continuously adapted to evolving technological, cultural, and societal conditions.

1.5 Summary

Chapter 1 provides the epistemic justification for delineating PCyb as a distinct research–problem domain dedicated to the systematic analysis of the conditions under which digital technology use may constructively shape trajectories of human flourishing. The point of departure is the diagnosis that the contemporary conditions under which human well-being unfolds have undergone a radical transformation due to the rapid development of digital technologies, particularly AI-driven systems. Consequently, research on flourishing that abstracts from the digital context risks diminishing its epistemic adequacy in relation to lived reality in the digital era.

The argument is structured around four complementary analytical dimensions: purpose, subjects, modes, and contexts. Together, these dimensions enable a systematic account of the structural complexity characterizing human–technology relations under conditions of expanding intelligent systems.

Within the Purpose dimension, flourishing is established as the central analytical construct of PCyb due to its existential significance and integrative potential within positive psychology. Yet a review of the conceptual landscape reveals substantial definitional and methodological fragmentation. The incorporation of the digital dimension further intensifies this dispersion: components of flourishing may be amplified, optimized, or attenuated within digital environments. This dynamic is reflected in the rapid emergence of new concepts (e.g., DWB, digital flourishing, techno-eustress, and digital hygiene), which collectively form an expanding yet insufficiently coordinated conceptual network. Such terminological and conceptual proliferation has not yet been embedded within a coherent theoretical architecture, thereby limiting cumulative knowledge development and generating significant theoretical tensions and methodological challenges.

In the Subjects dimension, the classical account of human agency is shown to require reconsideration in light of the rapid advancement of AI. Under conditions of "soft cyborgization" and cognitive hybridization, humans and technological artifacts coevolve, forming hybrid systems characterized by a distributed configuration of agency. Within this context, a central research task involves identifying and operationalizing dispositions grouped under the umbrella concept of digital strengths. These are capacities that enable reflective, autonomous, and developmentally oriented regulation of one's relationship with the technosphere. However, the current state of research in this area remains markedly dispersed, rendering references to *the conscious user* or *the competent digital citizen* conceptually underdetermined and insufficiently grounded in psychological evidence.

The Modes dimension directs analytical attention toward the need for intensified research on constructive patterns of technology engagement. Interface architectures and the design logics of AI-driven systems co-structure user experience within dynamic affordance loops, suggesting that the analysis of optimal digital practices requires models capable of accounting for the balance of benefits and costs inherent in digital functioning. DWB offers a promising analytical framework for examining the qualitative dimensions of technology engagement, while human-centered design approaches provide conceptual foundations for the development of interventions referred to here as PTIs.

Within the Contexts dimension, it is emphasized that flourishing trajectories are co-shaped by cultural, organizational, and environmental factors, as well as by hybrid configurations of offline–online experience. The breadth of these influences indicates that flourishing must be analyzed from a systemic, multilevel perspective that transcends isolated instances of technology use.

The chapter concludes that the rapid growth of research on the "bright side" of digital technologies, while indicative of the field's vitality, simultaneously generates risks of conceptual colonization and theoretical fragmentation. Across all four dimensions, a common pattern emerges: a rapid proliferation of constructs, models, and empirical findings concerning constructive digital life, accompanied by the absence of a shared epistemic architecture capable of integrating them. Positive psychology has predominantly examined flourishing under pre-digital conditions, whereas cyberpsychology has rarely positioned flourishing as an organizing theoretical framework. The resulting gap is therefore structural rather than merely thematic.

PCyb is proposed as a response to this integrative deficit. It does not constitute a mere thematic extension of existing subdisciplines, but rather an epistemic response to the imperative of systematically analyzing flourishing in the digital era.

2

The What?

The proposal to delineate positive cyberpsychology (PCyb) as a new problem-oriented research area was articulated at a specific stage in the development of the hierarchically organized system of science (OECD, 2015; UNESCO, 1978). The broadest frameworks for research are defined by domains of knowledge, such as the social sciences or engineering and technology. Within these domains operate scientific disciplines (e.g., psychology and information engineering), each characterized by its own conceptual apparatus, methodological traditions, scientific organizations, and channels of academic communication. Subdisciplines—such as positive psychology (PP) and the emerging field of cyberpsychology—represent further internal differentiation within science and are oriented toward in-depth exploration of selected aspects of reality. They arise from research areas understood as thematic fields of inquiry, which are delineated in response to new cognitive and societal challenges.

Although research areas are not formal classificatory units of science, they are widely regarded as playing a crucial role in the dynamics of knowledge development by providing spaces for testing, integrating, and differentiating theoretical approaches and methodological frameworks (Nowotny et al., 2001). They thus function as zones of convergence, where questions, problems, and tools derived from diverse intellectual traditions intersect. Such areas emerge around research problems, social phenomena, and civilizational challenges that do not fit within existing divisions of knowledge. Their fluid boundaries, plurality of approaches, and dynamic circulation of ideas are characteristic of a pre-paradigmatic phase of scientific development (Kuhn, 1962). The competition among research programs typical of this phase creates opportunities for progression toward epistemic consolidation and theoretical consensus—that is, the establishment of coherent frameworks for scientific activity (Lakatos, 1978).

This chapter presents the conceptual foundations of PCyb as a proposed problem-oriented research area. It delineates its position within the structure of science, identifies its intellectual roots, and outlines its interdisciplinary connections as well as its relationships with related approaches.

2.1 Conceptualizing PCyb

At its current stage of development, PCyb can be seen as an emerging, problem-oriented research area at the intersection of PP and cyberpsychology. Its focus is on understanding when interactions with and through digital systems, across local, organizational, and global contexts, support flourishing. Accordingly, PCyb centers on the overarching question: Which factors and processes shape the conditions under which individuals' use of digital technologies contributes to human flourishing?

Flourishing is conceptualized in accordance with approaches developed within PP (see Section 1.1.2). Its core components encompass dimensions of physical, mental, social, and spiritual well-being, with the relative weight attributed to each dimension being context-dependent and culturally differentiated. These components are shaped through ongoing interactions between individuals and psychological, sociocultural, economic–political, ecological, and technological environments, and they remain dynamically interrelated. At the same time, individual flourishing and the flourishing of the systems of which individuals are part form a network of mutual dependencies: environments that support development enhance human well-being, while flourishing, in turn, feeds back into the quality of their functioning, thereby contributing to the emergence and sustainability of collective flourishing across social and technological systems.

In its present formulation, PCyb deliberately adopts individual experience as the primary analytical entry point, placing the human subject at the center of its epistemic architecture. This orientation reflects both methodological and epistemic necessity: in a field that remains conceptually fragmented, the development of cumulative knowledge requires a clearly defined and analytically tractable point of entry capable of serving as a stable reference for subsequent theoretical integration.

Within this framework, individual experience functions as an epistemic anchor that enables the investigation of human–technology interactions across multiple, interdependent levels of analysis. It provides access to processes through which psychological dynamics are coupled with broader sociotechnical and ecological systems, thereby allowing these relationships to be articulated systematically. Importantly, this orientation does not imply a reduction of flourishing to the individual level; rather, it establishes the necessary foundation for the development of multilevel explanations. Individual-level processes thus constitute a necessary, though not sufficient, basis for explaining higher-level phenomena. While systemic phenomena remain ontologically irreducible to individual experience, they are accessible through multiple epistemic pathways, among which individual experience remains a significant—though not exclusive—mode of access, increasingly complemented by computationally derived indicators of behavior, interaction, and system dynamics.

PCyb examines how specific forms of human activity involving digital technologies shape trajectories of flourishing. These trajectories are understood not merely as changes in the levels of flourishing components over time but as potentially involving reconfigurations in their structural organization. Digital technologies comprise computational, algorithmic, and networked systems that are increasingly autonomous, adaptive, and, in some cases, AI-augmented or embodied. They encompass platform ecosystems, algorithmic infrastructures, artificial agents, and material artifacts such as computers, robots, and autonomous vehicles—all of which co-structure contemporary patterns of human action and constitute digitally mediated environments. These systems may serve primarily instrumental, functional, or economic purposes, but they may also be intentionally designed to promote well-being.

Within the present framework, digital technology use is not reduced to the mere application of tools or measured solely in terms of exposure time or frequency of use. Rather, it is conceptualized as a dynamic, feedback-driven process of interaction in which human agents are engaged not only behaviorally but also cognitively and affectively within relational configurations co-constituted by technological systems. Such interactions encompass engagement with artificial agents, online social exchanges, digitally mediated organizational processes, participation in platform-based ecosystems (e.g., gaming environments), and activities within immersive or extended reality (XR) settings. Interactions are understood here as processes of action, reciprocal influence, and dynamic coordination that vary in form and intensity—from simple responses to mutually adaptive exchanges in which both humans and technological systems function as active participants (Schleidgen et al., 2023). Through such processes, diverse forms and intensities of engagement emerge, shaping trajectories of flourishing by generating experiences consequential for individuals' quality of life.

The epistemic goals of PCyb involve advancing and refining knowledge of the constructive impacts of digital technology use through the integration of theoretical and empirical research focused on the core dimensions of flourishing. In this context, PCyb seeks to integrate theoretical approaches—regardless of their level of maturity—that contribute to explaining the significance of human interactions within digital environments, thereby encompassing a broad range of variables and methodological frameworks. This integrative effort extends to studies conducted across diverse age, ethnic, and occupational groups, involving different types of digital systems and unfolding within varied environments.

From this perspective, PCyb can be understood as a domain that consolidates existing but dispersed lines of inquiry that call for conceptual clarification, terminological alignment, and methodological refinement. At the same time, it remains consistent with broader developments within PP that increasingly emphasize complexity, contextual embeddedness, and the integration of multiple levels of analysis. Accordingly, the present formulation should be treated not as a closed theoretical system but as an initial step in structuring this domain—one that enables subsequent expansion rather than constraining it.

The deepening of theoretical reflection is further supported by PCyb's active dialogue with approaches related to cyberpsychology, such as human–computer interaction (HCI), human-centered design and user experience (UX), as well as with the philosophy of technology. Consequently, although the "core" of PCyb is intradisciplinary in nature, its engagement with insights from specializations and disciplines beyond psychology renders its development and practice distinctly interdisciplinary.

From an applied perspective, findings from PCyb research should support the development of recommendations across three interrelated domains. These include: (1) identifying the conditions for optimal—that is, balanced, healthy, autonomous, and adaptive—use of digital technologies, particularly in home, educational, and occupational settings; (2) designing and implementing effective practices in the form of positive technology interventions (PTIs); and (3) developing digital technologies that support flourishing, informed by empirical evaluations of friendly technology principles and well-being–oriented design assumptions.

From an educational perspective, findings generated within PCyb should facilitate several key developments. These include: (1) supporting the development of individual competencies for the conscious and effective management of digital environments; (2) formulating guidelines for cultivating positive digital practices; (3) verifying marketing claims about the beneficial effects of newly introduced digital tools; and (4) enabling critical analysis of popular culture narratives about the impact of AI-driven systems on human life, the future of humanity, and the planet. In addition, through the intensification of collaboration between researchers and business organizations as well as public institutions, the development of PCyb may contribute to shaping a normative perspective by supporting the formulation of public policies aimed at optimizing human interactions with artificial systems.

Above all, however, delineating PCyb as a problem-oriented research area should be of structural significance to science itself. At the present stage, PCyb constitutes a field integrating the perspectives of PP and cyberpsychology, with aspirations to develop either as an autonomous subdiscipline within psychology or as an emerging specialization within PP (e.g., following the model of positive organizational psychology [POP]). In both scenarios, this development is contingent upon the consolidation of a shared theoretical language, methodological coherence, the institutionalization of research practices, and the formation of a scholarly community engaged in systematic work within this domain. Accordingly, PCyb may not only respond to new cognitive and civilizational challenges but also participate in the self-organization of science by contributing to the creation of new epistemic niches. Ultimately, however, the future of PCyb will depend on critical evaluation by scholars themselves and by the broader academic community.

2.2 Disciplinary Foundations of PCyb

This section outlines the foundations of PP and cyberpsychology that constitute the scientific underpinnings of PCyb. Particular attention is given to their integrative potential, manifested in their openness to dialogue and their capacity to connect with diverse research traditions.

2.2.1 Positive Psychology

The emergence of PP is commonly dated to 1998, when Martin Seligman, serving as president of the American Psychological Association, called for a renewal of psychology's mission through the strengthening of an aspirational and developmental perspective in psychological research and practice. Together with Mihaly Csikszentmihalyi, he proposed a shift toward the systematic study of what is good, strengthening, and meaningful in human life (Seligman & Csikszentmihalyi, 2000). The impetus for this shift was the conviction that psychology—as both a science and a practice—should not be understood primarily as a discipline focused on pathology, deficits, and the treatment of disorders, often characterized as a form of "victimology," but should also support the cultivation of human potential and personal development.

It should be emphasized that scholars developing PP did not discover the idea of the "good life," nor did they introduce concepts such as well-being, resilience, positive emotions, optimal functioning, or character strengths. Rather, their work is deeply rooted in philosophical reflections on the nature of the good life and in the legacy of major psychological traditions. These include Carl G. Jung's analytical psychology (holism and individual spirituality), Alfred Adler's individual psychology (socially oriented and "healthy" motivational strivings), Viktor Frankl's logotherapy (the search for meaning), and Henry Murray's personology (Duckworth et al., 2005).

Particularly strong connections can be traced to humanistic psychology, developed primarily in the 1960s and 1970s, which emphasized the liberation of human potential and the integration of individual development with the common good. Notably, Abraham Maslow, one of the most influential figures in this tradition, introduced the term *positive psychology* as early as 1954 in his book *Motivation and Personality* (p. xxiii). PP thus took up and extended the unfinished legacy of humanistic psychology, realizing its postulates through the application of rigorous research methods and through the development of new models, measurement tools, and interventions.

At the center of interest of PP lies the individual who, despite the absence of severe mental disorders, requires support in experiencing the fullness of life and is vulnerable to losing the capacity to enjoy simple pleasures, neglecting relationships with others and with nature, living at an accelerated pace, and even experiencing forms of "spiritual impoverishment" (Seligman et al., 2005). At the same time, analyzing the conditions under which people can experience a high quality of life—even in the face of crises, illness, and multiple pressures—constitutes a complex and demanding task. This complexity is reflected in the dynamic development of PP, within which three waves of research are commonly distinguished.

The first wave of PP (1998–2010) focused on exploring the positive side of human nature (Gable & Haidt, 2005). During this period, the classification of character strengths and virtues—Values in Action (VIA)—was developed (Peterson & Seligman, 2004) as an alternative to traditional classifications of mental disorders. Intensive research was also conducted on positive human experiences and domains of well-being, alongside numerous attempts to define what constitutes a "happy life," resulting in the emergence of flourishing frameworks. Scholars advanced the view that human functioning should be explained within a positive model—not as the absence of difficulties, but as the capacity for growth and the realization of one's potential under changing life conditions (Joseph & Linley, 2006).

The second wave of PP (2010–2015) challenged the binary distinction between positive and negative phenomena. Scholars emphasized that experiences such as suffering, sadness, or frustration may serve adaptive functions and contribute to personal growth and the construction of deeper meaning in life (Fortuna, 2012; Lomas & Ivtzan, 2016; Wong, 2011). It was underscored that positive and negative aspects of life are inextricably intertwined and that dimensions of well-being may simultaneously carry both positive and negative connotations. It was also noted that whether an experience is interpreted as positive or negative depends on cultural context and the individual's specific circumstances. At the same time, greater emphasis was placed on the role of cultural context in understanding the nature of well-being, alongside the incorporation of insights from other disciplines that had examined aspects of positive functioning and well-being (Uchida & Ogihara, 2012).

The third wave of PP (emerging around 2015) is grounded in the assumption that individual well-being must be analyzed within the broader context of human functioning, which necessitates the adoption of a systems perspective (Kern et al., 2019; Lomas et al., 2021). This "move beyond the individual" is reflected in the increasing interdisciplinarity and multicultural scope of research, as well as in openness to diverse methodological approaches. The concept of "context" has been expanded to include cultural, sociopolitical, economic, and technological conditions.

At the same time, both theoretical analyses and practical applications emphasize the need to consider all levels of well-being—individual, social, and ecosystemic—as well as the interdependencies among them (Helne & Hirvilammi, 2015; Villani et al., 2019). According to Marié P. Wissing (2022), the third wave of PP may be understood as the beginning of a new, broader field of well-being studies that extends beyond the boundaries of PP itself. Within this emerging field, a mainstream strand of PP may continue to pursue in-depth, specialized investigations of selected aspects of well-being. At the same time, postdisciplinary approaches may develop alongside it, conceptualizing well-being in a more integrative way grounded in the idea of harmony among multiple dimensions of human functioning, social systems, and cultural contexts.

In the practical domain, PP has developed three key areas: (1) positive assessment, understood as the extension of traditional diagnostic procedures to include the evaluation of individual resources and environmental assets; (2) positive prevention, defined as the systematic support of competence development and human potential; and (3) positive psychology interventions (PPIs)—that is, intentional, evidence-based activities aimed at enhancing well-being and positive individual characteristics (Lyubomirsky & Layous, 2013). Accompanying these developments is the professionalization and dissemination of positive coaching and consulting practices, which are increasingly being implemented in organizational and educational contexts.

PP is a subdiscipline open to both interdisciplinary and intradisciplinary collaboration (e.g., Burke et al., 2023). Its core assumptions have diffused into other areas of scholarship, giving rise to fields such as positive health, positive education, positive economics, positive ecology, and the well-being arts. At the same time, specialized domains have emerged within psychology itself, including positive psychotherapy and positive organizational and occupational psychology. This development indicates that PP flexibly and reflexively redefines its own conceptual and methodological boundaries in response to contemporary civilizational challenges, thereby creating favorable conditions for the emergence of fields such as PCyb.

2.2.2 Cyberpsychology

The term *cyberpsychology* combines two components with distinct historical and epistemological meanings. The first—*cyber*—derives from the Greek word *kybernētēs* (κυβερνήτης), meaning "steersman" or "guide." It gained prominence in scientific discourse through the work of Bronisław F. Trentowski (1843) and later Norbert Wiener (1948/1961), who independently employed the term in distinct intellectual contexts that contributed to the formation of cybernetics as a scientific field. The second component (itself internally complex)—*psychology*—denotes the discipline concerned with the systematic analysis of behavior and mental processes.

Cyberpsychology historically emerged from media and communication psychology and is currently in a phase of consolidation and gradual institutionalization. Although it is still solidifying its position within the psychological sciences, the pace of its development and the breadth of issues it addresses are noteworthy. These features justify treating it both as a subdiscipline of psychology and as a transdisciplinary field that integrates knowledge and methods from diverse domains concerned with human interaction with digital technology (Attrill, 2015).

Cyberpsychology examines psychological processes, motivations, intentions, and behaviors associated with individuals' use of digital technologies, which shape their functioning across both online and offline worlds (Attrill-Smith et al., 2018). The scope of this field is broad. Editors of the second edition of *An Introduction to Cyberpsychology* (Kirwan et al., 2024) organize cyberpsychology's research domains into three broad areas. These include issues related to the individual in cyberspace (e.g., identity, self-esteem, mental health, addictions, and cyberbullying); social interactions and the social context (online communication, relationships, virtual communities, video games, and online gambling); and applications of technology (digital education, workplace technologies, healthcare, and virtual and augmented reality).

It should be noted that for many years, publications in cyberpsychology were predominantly focused on the "dark side" of technology use. For example, a review conducted by Julia R. Ancis (2020) indicated that the most frequently examined areas included online criminal activity, negative effects of smartphone use, internet addiction, and the influence of violent video games on behavior. This thematic profile closely mirrors the topics addressed in the leading journal *Cyberpsychology, Behavior, and Social Networking*, where research continues to focus primarily on negative aspects of digital technology use, such as internet and cyberpornography addiction and cyberbullying, as well as on related therapeutic and rehabilitative responses.

The pursuit of answers to the research questions formulated within cyberpsychology is supported by its paradigmatic diversity. Agnieszka Ogonowska (2021) identified six major research paradigms: psychodynamic, biomedical, behavioral, cognitive, humanistic, and anthropological–cultural. Each paradigm directs inquiry toward different aspects of human–technology interaction. These range from the analysis of digital addictions (behavioral paradigm), through the exploration of cyber altruism and the realization of individual potential (humanistic paradigm), to the reconstruction of the cultural meanings of digital practices (anthropological–cultural paradigm).

In research practice, cyberpsychology is closely connected with numerous subdisciplines of psychology. Cognitive psychology contributes, for example, through studies on attention, multitasking, and information processing in digital environments. Social psychology offers insights into online relationships, group behavior, and identity construction, including analyses of friendship formation and maintenance in virtual spaces. Health psychology examines the influence of digital tools on well-being, including the role of apps and platforms in stress reduction, behavior change, and health monitoring. Clinical psychology addresses issues such as the links between personality traits, including neuroticism, and problematic internet use or digital addictions. Neuropsychology, in turn, explores the neural correlates of technology use, shedding light on how interactions with digital systems relate to brain functioning and plasticity. Together, these connections illustrate that cyberpsychology operates not as an isolated specialty but as a field deeply embedded within the broader landscape of psychological science.

The transdisciplinary character of cyberpsychology stems from the fact that it extends beyond the boundaries of psychology and engages with fields such as computer science, engineering, digital media studies, media and cultural studies, the digital humanities, and HCI (Ancis, 2020; Attrill-Smith et al., 2018). The strong linkage between cyberpsychology and HCI is explicitly signaled by the title of Kent L. Norman's (2017) textbook *Cyberpsychology: An Introduction to Human–Computer Interaction*. HCI is an interdisciplinary field of research and practice that integrates cognitive psychology, computer science, interface design, engineering, and the social and communication sciences. Its aim is to explore the dynamic relationship between humans and intelligent environments, including the study of interface usability and the identification of conditions that support intuitiveness, aesthetics, and ergonomics (Stephanidis & Salvendy, 2024).

The relationship between cyberpsychology and HCI is both historical and functional in nature. From the early stages of the computer revolution, psychologists and computer scientists recognized the need for mutual understanding, with psychology contributing knowledge about human cognition and behavior and computer science providing tools and communication systems. As computers became more widespread, the demand grew for knowledge about how people learn to use systems, how they respond to errors, what they experience during interaction with machines, and how usability and UX can be improved (Kirwan et al., 2024; Norman, 2017).

For more than a decade, a bridge has been developing between cyberpsychology, HCI, and PP. An important role in this process has been played by the emergence of well-being-oriented design approaches discussed in Section 1.3.2.1.

However, it is noteworthy that in textbook treatments of cyberpsychology, such as *The Oxford Handbook of Cyberpsychology* (Attrill-Smith et al., 2018), these concepts are largely absent, and their proponents are not represented among the chapter authors. This omission reflects a broader pattern of limited "visibility" of frameworks that explain and advocate the positive effects of technology use. In this context, the development of PCyb contributes to restoring balance within cyberpsychology by offering a more comprehensive account of human functioning within the techno- and infosphere.

The humanistic paradigm provides a basis for linking cyberpsychology with PP within PCyb, with benefits for both fields. In cyberpsychology, this connection entails an expansion of the analytical scope through the incorporation of constructs, models, and measurement tools developed within PP, thereby supporting a more balanced and multidimensional account of human–technology relations. In PP, in turn, it opens an opportunity for the systematic investigation of well-being in digital contexts, considering both the specific affordances of technological environments and the transformative potential of innovations designed to support users. Importantly, beyond the comparison and integration of approaches that have thus far developed in parallel, this perspective may also bring together researchers who do not clearly identify with a single research tradition.

2.3 Cross-Disciplinary Influences on PCyb

Given the technologically mediated nature of the phenomena under consideration, PCyb is inherently situated within a broader context informed by concepts and methods from computer science and related computational disciplines. The following section selectively examines perspectives that are particularly relevant for interpreting and shaping human–technology interactions at the level of experience and meaning-making. These include approaches formulated at the intersection of design and psychology, such as human-centered design and UX, as well as selected perspectives developed within the field of philosophy.

2.3.1 Human-Centered Design and UX

During the period in which humanistic psychology was developing, John E. Arnold (1959) was among the first to propose that engineering design adopt a human-oriented perspective. In his view, machines and technical systems should support human skills and creativity rather than replace them. This human-oriented approach constitutes the foundation of human-centered design, which may be regarded as an extension of classical principles of ergonomics within the context of interactive systems design.

The ISO 9241-210 standard defines human-centered design as "an approach to interactive systems development that aims to make systems usable and useful by focusing on the users, their needs and requirements, and by applying human factors/ergonomics, and usability knowledge and techniques. This approach enhances effectiveness and efficiency, improves human well-being, user satisfaction, accessibility and sustainability; and counteracts possible adverse effects of use on human health, safety and performance" (International Organization for Standardization, 2019, p. vi).

Although human-centered design refers broadly to the design of all interactive systems, it has gained particular prominence in research conducted within the field of HCI. One consequence of the shift in emphasis from analyses of system operability to users' subjective experiences was the emergence of the UX concept. UX is a dynamically evolving domain of analysis of human–technology interaction that has gradually entered the realm of scientific research. In contrast to classical HCI approaches, which focus primarily on functionality, UX encompasses a broad spectrum of human experiences. A key milestone in the development of this domain was the formalization of the concept of UX as an object of description and analysis in the ISO 9241-210 standard. According to this standard, UX is defined as "user's perceptions and responses that result from the use and/or anticipated use of a system, product or service" (International Organization for Standardization, 2019, p. 4). These perceptions and responses include the user's emotions, beliefs, preferences, perceptions, comfort, behaviors, and accomplishments that occur before, during, and after use.

Accordingly, UX is neither a property of technology nor merely a subjective state of the user; rather, it is a relational and context-dependent outcome of interactions among multiple factors, including system characteristics (e.g., aesthetics and usability), user attributes (e.g., prior experience, competencies, and personality traits), and the situational and cultural conditions of use.

Understood in this way, UX constitutes both an object of empirical investigation and an analytical framework for interpreting the quality of human–technology relationships. UX research may address the visual appearance and functionality of the user interface (UI; user interface design, UID), as well as information architecture (IA), understood as the structure of content, navigation, and information hierarchy. It also encompasses interaction design (IxD), which concerns the ways in which users communicate with and act upon a product (Sauro & Lewis, 2016). As the field has developed, the diversity of research methods has likewise expanded, ranging from qualitative interviews and observational techniques to quantitative data analysis, biometrics, and eye-tracking.

The convergence between the interests of PCyb and the approaches discussed above is reflected primarily in the emphasis on design logics as a key mechanism for supporting user development and flourishing. This is particularly evident in frameworks such as the previously discussed METUX model (Peters et al., 2018). It can be expected that, as interdisciplinary collaboration continues to develop, variables related to the components of flourishing will increasingly be operationalized both in design practices and in UX research. At the same time, the growing maturity and awareness of users, together with the strengthening of UX's position as a field, should facilitate a gradual shift in design priorities. This shift would move away from tendencies that reinforce compulsive patterns of technology use and toward solutions that enable experiences that enrich the quality of life and support well-being.

2.3.2 Philosophy

Given that PCyb is emerging within psychology, its development should proceed in dialogue with philosophy. The relationship between these disciplines is genetic in nature: psychological questions were for centuries embedded within so-called philosophical psychology, and psychology itself emerged as an empirical science through its differentiation from philosophy. There is also a strong object-level relationship, as both disciplines seek answers to questions concerning human nature, the mind, consciousness, free will, emotions, and values. Finally, a crucial meta-level relationship exists within the philosophy of psychology, which enables critical examination of the theoretical, methodological, and axiological assumptions underlying psychological research. Particularly important in this regard are PCyb's connections with branches of philosophy that address questions about the nature of the human being, the structure of reality, and the foundations of morality—namely philosophical anthropology, relational ontology, the philosophy of technology, and the ethics of technology.

Two pathways can be identified that link PCyb with philosophy. The first operates through PP, which—being rooted in humanistic psychology—was strengthened by an anti-positivist epistemological turn, involving the rejection of a model of science based exclusively on the methods of the natural sciences. As a result, psychology became more open to idiographic perspectives focused on individuality, hermeneutic approaches concerned with understanding rather than merely explaining, and constructivist positions recognizing the active role of the individual in the construction of meaning. These shifts reflected a broader movement toward approaches that emphasize interpretation, subjectivity, and the co-creation of experience (Schultz & Schultz, 2015).

Sources of inspiration included existential and phenomenological philosophy, as well as personalism and classical virtue ethics. Consequently, the human being came to be viewed as a free, responsible, and development-oriented subject, and psychological reflection reintroduced questions of values, meaning in life, goodness, beauty, and truth—issues that had for centuries remained within the domain of philosophy.

Philosophical reflection also underpins inquiries conducted within cyberpsychology. Analyses of experiences such as immersion, presence, and embodiment in virtual environments reveal clear affinities with the phenomenology of Edmund Husserl and Maurice Merleau-Ponty. Issues concerning identity, freedom, loneliness, and authenticity in online contexts constitute empirical extensions of reflections developed by Martin Heidegger and Jean-Paul Sartre. Contemporary philosophy of technology, in turn, provides key conceptual tools for analyzing human relations with digital artifacts, emphasizing, among other aspects, the mediating role of technology and its influence on the shaping of users' perceptions, values, and actions (Floridi, 2014, 2023). At the same time, cyberpsychology shares a conceptual language with social constructivism and poststructuralism, particularly in analyses of digital identity, affordances, algorithmic power, and the deconstruction of boundaries between what is natural and what is artificial (Verbeek, 2011).

In seeking answers to the fundamental question of how individuals' interactions with digital technologies may support the experience of flourishing, PCyb situates itself within a broad debate that encompasses the diverse voices of philosophers, futurists, writers, and public intellectuals. The themes of this discussion may be likened to the "subterranean waters" nourishing the soil from which the idea of human happiness in the digital age emerges. For many technology users, these reflections remain largely invisible, and grasping their relevance for everyday life is challenging, as it requires moving beyond common-sense intuitions.

An illustrative example is the previously mentioned posthumanism and its associated concept of ontological egalitarianism, which calls for the recognition of agency in nonhuman forms of existence (Braidotti, 2013). Questioning the traditional distinction between moral subjects and moral objects is highly consequential for analyses conducted within PCyb. Without recourse to relational ontology, it becomes difficult to understand both the motivations of individuals and organizations to engage in interactions with nonhuman entities and the expectations formulated with respect to such relationships (Wróblewski & Fortuna, 2023).

Finally, the development of PCyb cannot be separated from normative questions, such as which technologies should be developed and in what direction the transformation of the digital lifeworld should proceed. Approaches such as Gilbert Simondon's philosophy of technology (2017) and Bernard Stiegler's techno-theological reflection (2019) make it possible to develop a more nuanced understanding of the role of technology in psychological, existential, and axiological processes. These perspectives are particularly useful for analyzing the so-called facades of digital development. This term refers to technologies that appear to support well-being but may, in practice, contribute to its erosion, for example, through excessive personalization, the reinforcement of addictive patterns, or the reduction of interpersonal relationships to superficial interactions.

In this context, engagement with the ethics of responsibility also proves valuable. As proposed by Hans Jonas (1984), this framework emphasizes the necessity of anticipating the long-term consequences of technological actions and assuming moral responsibility for them. A complementary perspective—especially relevant for reflection on future-oriented competencies (digital strengths)—is provided by Shannon Vallor's (2016) concept of technomoral virtues, which seeks to reconstruct Aristotle's classical virtue ethics within the context of a technological society.

As the foregoing discussion indicates, dialogue between PCyb and philosophy should not be treated as optional or merely auxiliary. Rather, it constitutes a necessary condition for strengthening the field's epistemological coherence, ontological adequacy, and ethical responsibility. One may hope that such a polyphonic collaboration will facilitate a deeper understanding of, and more effective support for, flourishing in an increasingly unreflective digital age.

2.4 Positioning PCyb Among Related Frameworks

This section discusses four approaches that, despite important points of convergence, should be clearly distinguished from PCyb. These are presented in chronological order of their emergence in the literature: Positive Technology (PT), Engaging in the Good with Technology (EGT), POP 2.0, and Computational Positive Psychology (CPP).

2.4.1 Positive Technology

Giuseppe Riva, as the principal architect of the framework, introduced the concept of PT in 2012. Developed collaboratively by a research team, PT represents a scientific and applied approach to the use of technology aimed at improving the quality of personal experience through its structuring, augmentation, and/or replacement (Graffigna et al., 2013; Riva et al., 2012). Its origin lies in the convergence of two trends: the growing interest within PP in research on the conditions and processes that foster well-being, and a shift within HCI toward design approaches that take values, experiences, and ethical considerations into account. PT integrates these perspectives by redirecting attention from the negative consequences of technology use to questions concerning its beneficial applications—namely, how technology can support optimal functioning, resource development, and resilience among individuals, groups, and institutions (Botella et al., 2012; Gaggioli et al., 2019a).

The status, position within the scientific landscape, and overarching aims of PT are not defined unequivocally in the literature. It is described, on the one hand, as "an emergent topic within HCI that seeks to understand how interactive technologies can be used in evidence-based well-being interventions" (Riva et al., 2019, p. 267). On the other hand, scholars emphasize its interdisciplinary character and its strong connections with cyberpsychology and PP (Botella et al., 2012; Gaggioli et al., 2019b). PT is also conceptualized as a framework for the design of interactive e-experiences that promote empowerment and positive change (Riva et al., 2016), as well as a research area "focused on the design, development, and validation of novel digital experiences that aim at promoting positive change through pleasure, flow, meaning, competence, and positive relationships" (Gaggioli et al., 2019a, p. 2). In applied contexts, PT is frequently situated within the broader family of well-being–oriented design approaches (Peters et al., 2018).

At the center of PT lies the personal experience of the individual interacting with technology—an experience that can be modified through technological means and analyzed by external researchers. Three core dimensions (determinants) of this experience are distinguished: (1) emotional quality, corresponding to the hedonic level; (2) engagement and actualization, associated with the eudaimonic level; and (3) connectedness, referring to the social and interpersonal dimension. These dimensions form the basis for the design of three types of technologies:

- Hedonic technologies—aimed at eliciting positive emotional states and pleasurable sensory experiences (e.g., the use of VR for relaxation or stress reduction);
- Eudaimonic technologies—supporting experiences conducive to self-realization, personal development, and resilience (e.g., VR applications that evoke awe or existential reflection through the presentation of otherwise inaccessible scenes);
- Social/interpersonal technologies—strengthening bonds among individuals, groups, and organizations, and facilitating the sharing of values, cooperation, and communal life (e.g., platforms integrating different generations).

According to the PT framework, the use of these technologies enables the modulation of individual experience through three interrelated modes: structuring (imposing structure through goals, rules, and feedback), augmentation (enriching experience via multimodal and mixed stimuli), and replacement (substituting real-world experiences with synthetic ones, such as those occurring in VR environments).

The concept of PT, like PCyb, has been shaped through the close integration of PP and cyberpsychology, accompanied by a concern for designing interactions between individuals and digital technologies that are beneficial both for users and for the systems they create. The aims of these approaches are closely aligned, insofar as PCyb—as a research area—can be developed precisely through concepts such as PT. In this sense, PCyb may be understood as an integrative perspective that incorporates PT into its epistemic model as a key component of analyses of the beneficial effects of human–digital technology interactions.

At a programmatic level, PT declares the ambition of "investigating how ICT-based applications and services can be used to foster positive growth of individuals, groups, and institutions" (Gaggioli et al., 2019a, p. 1), which positions it as a development-oriented project. At the same time, despite the passage of time, PT continues to function in the scientific landscape primarily as a domain—or perhaps more accurately, a compelling idea. It facilitates the integration of interdisciplinary research spanning areas from mental health, through cognitive and physical rehabilitation, to the promotion of prosocial behavior, empathy, and transcendent experiences. An undeniable contribution of PT has been its role in "clearing a scientific path" for research demonstrating the beneficial effects of technological innovations within a cyberpsychology long dominated by a focus on the "dark side" of technology.

What distinguishes PT from the competing concepts within the well-being–oriented design movement discussed in the previous chapter is its extensive dialogue with PP and its deep grounding in the theoretical frameworks developed within that field. The theoretical potential of PT becomes evident in its core assumptions concerning the shaping of digital experiences (e-experiences). In particular, the three identified modes of technological influence—structuring, augmentation, and replacement—outline promising analytical pathways for identifying forms of human–digital technology interaction that are optimal in specific contexts. At the same time, future research should focus on empirically testing the conditions under which it is possible to mitigate the risks associated respectively with excessive standardization of experience (structuring), sensory overload (augmentation), and the risk of alienation from the offline world (replacement).

From a methodological standpoint, PT advocates operating within the empirical paradigm characteristic of experimental psychology and HCI research, focusing on the assessment of the effects of specific technological solutions on measurable indicators of well-being. This approach is strongly rooted in the first wave of PP and makes a valuable contribution to the design and evaluation of positive interventions using digital technologies. Its distinctive feature is the intentional, targeted focus on the positive effect achieved through a given innovation, which enables a reliable assessment of the effectiveness of interventions employing that solution.

A comprehensive analysis of the conditions under which digital technologies influence users' flourishing, however, requires the adoption of epistemological frameworks that go beyond the isolated testing of the effects of individual positive interventions. Such frameworks should also address the conditions for the optimal use of instrumental technologies, including criteria for their appropriate selection and adoption. They should also address the mechanisms through which experiences conducive to digital well-being are generated, as well as the design of environments that support the experience of techno-eustress. In addition, it is necessary to specify the dynamic relationships between e-experiences and offline experiences, as well as the conditions under which their integration contributes to particular components of flourishing.

Analyses of this kind do not fall within the paradigm that has thus far characterized PT, yet their inclusion is a prerequisite for understanding how well-being can be strengthened in the digital era. This, in turn, requires the development of conceptual research models grounded in theories elaborated beyond PT itself. Such analyses may also contribute to the further evolution of PT. In particular, they may help explain the conditions under which e-experiences reinforce developmental trajectories, both in nonoptimal situations characteristic of the second wave of PP and in the broader context of life in the digital era central to its third wave.

2.4.2 Engaging in the Good with Technology

The EGT framework was proposed by Andrew Villamil and Saeideh Heshmati in 2023. It emerged from a critique of the dominant focus in the literature on the "dark side" of technology use, alongside the claim that well-being depends not only on the reduction of harm but also on the presence and frequency of positive experiences. In response, the authors introduced EGT as a framework for examining PT use as a source of psychological benefits. Central to this approach is the operationalization of "the good" through positive interactions with technology that produce demonstrable psychological benefits.

At the core of EGT lies a triad of ways of "engaging in the good" through technology: seeing good, feeling good, and doing good. Seeing good refers to exposure to positive visual and informational stimuli, such as inspiring content, examples of kindness, or awe-eliciting materials, and is conceptualized as a cognitive–affective process through which such stimuli shape attention, expectations, and judgments, thereby fostering motivation and positive appraisals. Feeling good refers to the use of technology as a medium (or "vessel") for positive emotional states and hedonic as well as eudaimonic experiences (e.g., joy, inspiration, a sense of meaning, and relational resonance), which may broaden individuals' action repertoires and support resource building. Doing good, in turn, encompasses prosocial actions enacted through technology (e.g., supporting others, kind communication, online volunteering and donations, and sharing helpful content) and their links to a sense of agency and the perceived impact of one's actions on others' well-being.

A distinctive feature of EGT is its treatment of this triad as a dynamic network of interdependent nodes, rather than as a sum of three independent components. This implies that, across different life contexts, the configuration of relations between seeing, feeling, and doing may vary: the nodes may co-occur and mutually reinforce one another (so-called "closed" configurations) or remain partially "open" when one component is less strongly activated (e.g., increases in seeing and feeling without doing). Consequently, the authors argue that research should address not only the effects of individual domains but also entire network configurations and their associations with well-being. EGT is thus presented as a dual-purpose framework: as a research tool, it supports the measurement and modeling of PT use, including analyses of network configurations and their associations with well-being indicators; as a design tool, it offers guidance for platforms and applications seeking to cultivate conditions that foster upward spirals of positive experiences.

From the perspective of PCyb, EGT can be regarded as a valuable yet aspect-specific theoretical framework. Its strength lies in the clear articulation of micro-mechanisms of positive engagement with technology at the level of experiences and behaviors (seeing–feeling–doing), as well as in its use of the language of network dynamics to describe their co-occurrence. At the same time, EGT does not aspire to the status of a comprehensive theory of flourishing in digital environments, as it only partially addresses broader systemic and dispositional determinants (e.g., individual resources or institutional contexts). Accordingly, the framework appears best understood as a promising analytical approach that requires embedding within a broader integrative perspective encompassing experiential processes, individual resources, digital practices, and the long-term dynamics of flourishing.

2.4.3 Positive Organizational Psychology 2.0

POP 2.0, proposed by Llewellyn E. van Zyl et al. (2024), constitutes a response to the limitations and challenges identified in the literature regarding classical POP. This approach is closely aligned with the assumptions of the third wave of PP. According to the authors, despite impressive growth in publications and broad interdisciplinary influence, POP has begun to lose momentum. This is attributed to thematic repetitiveness, a lack of breakthrough ideas, slow transfer of knowledge into practice, and an insufficient response to ongoing digital and social transformations. The most substantial critique, however, is directed at POP's inadequate consideration of the role of technology in organizational functioning.

The proponents of POP 2.0 emphasize that traditional POP developed primarily within two streams: positive organizational scholarship (POS) and positive organizational behavior (POB). These streams focused on the study of positive states, traits, behaviors, and processes, either at the organizational level in POS or at the individual level in POB. In both cases, technology was treated largely as a contextual background to work rather than as an active component shaping it. As a result, positive work experiences were typically explained without incorporating technology into the core of theoretical models or research practice.

POP 2.0 addresses this gap by defining itself as "an evidence-based, data-driven field of scientific inquiry that embraces technological developments, design principles, and innovations to understand and improve the positive individual-, organizational-, and societal-level characteristics required for optimal psychological functioning, well-being, and performance" (van Zyl et al., 2024, p. 705). In contrast to traditional POP, the new framework calls for an expanded scope of inquiry that explicitly includes digital environments and human–robot relations, drawing on advanced data-driven approaches such as machine learning, big data analytics, and natural language processing. At the same time, POP 2.0 aims to identify technologically embedded factors essential for shaping a "positive organization," explicitly encompassing marginalized groups, artificial assistants, decentralized workforces (e.g., freelancers), and individuals operating exclusively within digital work environments.

At the epistemic level, POP 2.0 advocates an interdisciplinary approach, expressed through the systematic transfer of theories and methods into PP from fields such as computer science and communication studies, sociology, anthropology, economics, and neurobiology. Richer exploration of the phenomena under study is to be achieved by moving beyond individualistic measures of well-being toward methodological pluralism, including the use of advanced statistical modeling and comprehensive measurement tools to identify patterns associated with positive outcomes. At the applied level, the development of POP 2.0 is expected to contribute to the active creation of new interventions based on innovations designed in accordance with human-centered design principles. It should also support the optimization of workspaces and the construction of immersive metaverses for collaboration, learning, and well-being. In addition, it involves the continuous monitoring of positive states through "real-time status tracking" in order to enable just-in-time interventions.

POP 2.0 remains a broad, preliminary theoretical and research program requiring further conceptual and empirical refinement. What it shares with PCyb is a similar methodological status, as a field of scientific inquiry, as well as a focus on conditions that foster the flourishing of individuals and social groups in technology-saturated contexts, and a call for dialogue between PP and domains such as HCI and UX.

PCyb, however, adopts a broader analytical perspective: it extends beyond the study of positive organizational functioning to encompass a wide spectrum of both work-related and nonwork-related technological experiences.

Due to its specialized focus, the development of POP 2.0 may nonetheless make a significant contribution to deepening understanding of the relationship between individual flourishing and the flourishing of the social and organizational systems that individuals cocreate. It may also provide valuable insights into the social and organizational contextual conditions that should be considered in research conducted within PCyb. Accordingly, assuming a stronger orientation of PCyb toward analyses situated outside the workplace, the two approaches can be regarded as complementary—mutually reinforcing and mutually stimulating.

2.4.4 Computational Positive Psychology

The concept of CPP, introduced by Hanchao Hou et al. (2025), represents an attempt to formalize an emerging interdisciplinary domain that integrates PP with computational science and technology (CST). The authors argue that the rapid development of CST—including big data analytics, machine learning, natural language processing, and artificial intelligence—creates conditions for a qualitative expansion of well-being research at both the theoretical and applied levels. In this sense, CPP is framed not merely as another technological extension of psychology but as a programmatic proposal for a "synergistic collaboration" between disciplines aimed at addressing well-being in an increasingly interconnected and data-rich world.

At the same time, Hou et al. make clear that CPP remains at an early stage of development. They describe it as a field still in its nascent phase, whose key features include formulating novel research questions, collecting large-scale and multimodal data, using computational modeling, and applying the resulting insights to theory and multilevel interventions. This is an important qualification. Although CPP is presented as an emerging framework with transformative potential, much of the work currently gathered under this label still operates through the computational extension of existing PP research rather than through a fully articulated reconfiguration of its conceptual foundations.

One of the clearest contributions of CPP lies in its methodological shift. It moves beyond research paradigms based primarily on self-report measures and linear statistical models toward the analysis of large-scale, multimodal, and temporally sensitive data, as well as toward the modeling of nonlinear dynamics in well-being. By drawing on sources such as social media, wearable devices, and behavioral tracking systems, CPP makes possible a more continuous, context-sensitive, and ecologically grounded assessment of well-being processes. It also expands the capacity to examine interactions between individuals and their contexts, thereby responding to longstanding criticisms of PP concerning methodological narrowness, excessive individualism, and limited sensitivity to cultural and situational variability.

Importantly, these developments also open a promising direction for the study of collective well-being. Hou et al. explicitly identify improving collective well-being as one of the major research topics of CPP and argue that computational approaches can support the analysis of social structure, population-level patterns, and interdependent dynamics between individual and systemic well-being. In this perspective, collective well-being is no longer treated merely as the sum of individual states but as something that may emerge from relational and system-level processes. However, in their account, this remains primarily a programmatic direction rather than a mature empirical subfield. The authors emphasize possibilities, tools, and future applications more than they present a consolidated body of empirically validated models of collective flourishing.

A further important contribution of CPP concerns intervention. Hou et al. argue that technologies such as recommender systems, AI-based chatbots, large language models, and immersive environments such as virtual and augmented reality can enhance PPIs through personalization, adaptive feedback, and scalable delivery. In this respect, computational methods do more than improve measurement: they also expand the possibilities for tailoring and disseminating interventions across diverse contexts. Yet here too, the main strength of CPP currently lies in augmenting and extending existing intervention models rather than in establishing a fully distinct theory of technologically mediated flourishing.

From the perspective of PCyb, however, a fundamental distinction must be established at the outset. PCyb develops explicitly at the intersection of PP and cyberpsychology and focuses on the conditions under which human–technology interactions support or hinder flourishing. This positioning differs from CPP, which is grounded in the integration of PP with CST. Thus, while CPP primarily extends the methodological and analytical capacities of PP, PCyb is oriented toward a broader reconstruction of the human–technology relationship as a constitutive dimension of well-being.

This difference becomes particularly visible at the level of intervention. Whereas CPP mainly focuses on enhancing and scaling PPIs through computational means, PCyb explicitly postulates the analysis and development of PTIs as an expanded intervention category. PTIs are not simply digital formats for delivering established PPIs (see Section 3.4). Rather, they are interventions in which technology forms an integral component of the psychological process itself by shaping experience, affordances, and developmental trajectories. The shift is therefore conceptual as well as practical: from using technology to deliver interventions toward understanding interventions as inherently sociotechnical configurations.

A related distinction concerns the status of technology itself. In CPP, technology is still treated predominantly in instrumental terms—as a means of measurement, modeling, prediction, and intervention. This orientation is analytically productive and empirically valuable, but it remains limited in conceptual scope. It does not fully address the extent to which digital technologies function not only as tools but also as environments that co-constitute human experience. By contrast, PCyb advances a broader epistemic framework in which technologies are understood as integral components of the human lifeworld, shaping not only behavior but also experience, identity, social relations, and value orientations. Within this perspective, flourishing is approached not merely as an optimizable outcome variable but as an emergent phenomenon arising from dynamic interactions among individuals, technologies, and sociocultural contexts.

For this reason, the contribution of CPP may be regarded as both substantial and partial. It offers powerful methodological resources for the study of well-being in digitally mediated environments and provides important tools for real-time monitoring, pattern detection, and intervention personalization. At the same time, Hou et al. themselves emphasize that the field is still developing and requires deeper integration of data and theory, technology and psychology, as well as stronger conceptual grounding. Accordingly, CPP is best understood not as a complete theoretical alternative to PCyb, but as an important and still developing component of the wider transformation of well-being research in the digital era.

Importantly, the very emergence of CPP strengthens the argument that a new domain of well-being research is taking shape under conditions of digital transformation. The growing availability of behavioral and experiential data, the increasing importance of computational modeling, and the need to connect individual and systemic levels of analysis all reveal the limits of traditional PP frameworks. CPP makes this transformation especially visible at the methodological level, whereas PCyb seeks to articulate it at the epistemic and ontological levels. From this perspective, CPP and PCyb should not be treated as competing approaches, but as complementary ones: the former offers powerful analytical means, while the latter provides a broader conceptual architecture for organizing dispersed lines of research within the horizon of technologically mediated flourishing.

2.5 Summary

Chapter 2 defines the conceptual identity, disciplinary foundations, and epistemic position of PCyb within the structure of contemporary science. It argues that PCyb should currently be understood as an emerging, problem-oriented research area situated at the intersection of PP and cyberpsychology. Its object of inquiry is the systematic analysis of the conditions under which the use of digital technologies constructively shapes trajectories of flourishing.

By situating PCyb within the hierarchical organization of scientific knowledge, the chapter demonstrates that the emergence of new research areas is typically characterized by conceptual pluralism, competition among research programs, and fluid disciplinary boundaries. In this sense, PCyb does not yet constitute a consolidated subdiscipline but rather a space of convergence in which diverse intellectual traditions meet around a shared research problem. This problem concerns identifying the factors and processes that shape the positive impact of digital technology use on flourishing.

At the conceptual level, PCyb focuses on the dynamic relationship between flourishing and interactions with digital systems operating within local, organizational, and global environments. Flourishing is conceptualized as a multidimensional and context-sensitive construct encompassing physical, mental, social, and spiritual components. At the same time, the structural interdependence between individual flourishing and the flourishing of the systems of which the individual is a part is emphasized, thereby grounding the perspective in a relational and systemic framework consistent with multilevel modes of analysis.

The disciplinary foundations of PCyb lie in PP and cyberpsychology. The former provides its normative and conceptual core, particularly through theories of flourishing and models of well-being. The latter contributes the conceptual apparatus, as well as the empirical and analytical tools necessary for investigating psychological processes occurring in digital environments. Both traditions display internal paradigmatic diversity and increasing openness to interdisciplinary collaboration, creating favorable conditions for their integration within the PCyb framework.

Interdisciplinary influences are also essential to the development of PCyb. In particular, sustained dialogue with approaches derived from human-centered design and UX is necessary, as these fields enable the analysis of design logics as mechanisms that co-structure UX. Simultaneously, PCyb remains in dialogue with philosophy—especially philosophical anthropology, relational ontology, the philosophy of technology, and the ethics of responsibility—thereby strengthening its ontological coherence and axiological grounding. At the same time, PCyb maintains its distinctiveness in relation to related approaches such as PT, Engaging in the Good with Technology, POP 2.0, and CPP. It differs from these frameworks in scope and theoretical ambition, seeking to develop an integrative epistemic architecture capable of modeling flourishing across diverse technological and life contexts.

The chapter concludes by emphasizing that PCyb's primary value lies in its structural contribution to the organization of scientific inquiry. Its further development will depend on consolidating a shared theoretical language, achieving methodological coherence, institutionalizing research practices, and fostering a stable scholarly community engaged in systematic inquiry within this domain.

3

The How?

Establishing positive cyberpsychology (PCyb) as a scientific research area requires the systematic articulation of coherent theoretical and methodological frameworks. These should encompass core research questions, domains and levels of analysis, explanatory theories, and research strategies, while also enabling the integration and systematization of empirical data. This chapter presents the epistemic model of PCyb, which synthesizes these elements into a unified analytical structure. It then discusses the four analytical perspectives distinguished within this model, together with their central concepts and representative empirical findings.

3.1 The Epistemic Model of Positive Cyberpsychology

The proposed epistemic model of PCyb reconfigures approaches developed primarily within positive psychology and cyberpsychology, synthesizing them into a coherent analytical architecture for examining processes that strengthen flourishing in digitally mediated contexts (see Figure 3.1). It should not be understood as a rigid research protocol, but rather as a conceptual map that clarifies key problem domains, aligns relevant theoretical perspectives, and structures methodological choices.

At the center of the epistemic model of PCyb is the human individual engaged in the pursuit of flourishing (human flourishing) within a specific environmental context. Importantly, this positioning reflects an epistemic and methodological choice regarding the primary level of analysis, rather than implying that flourishing is reducible to individual experience.

Interactions with technology do not constitute a necessary condition for the development of flourishing; however, they may play a significant supportive role by generating positive experiences that arise from both habitual and intentional

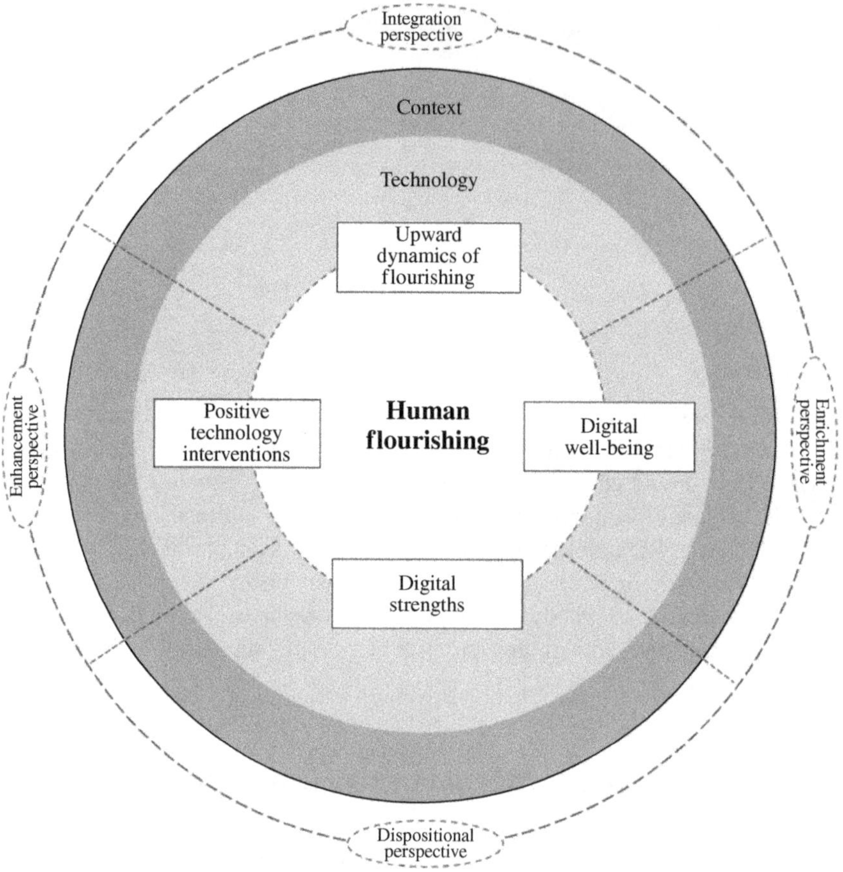

Figure 3.1 The epistemic model of PCyb.

digital practices. The use of the same digital innovation may serve multiple developmental functions, just as a single well-being–oriented goal may be pursued through interactions with diverse artificial systems.

Given the central importance of human engagement with digital technologies for strengthening flourishing, the technological dimension has been analytically distinguished from other contextual factors (context), while assuming that it remains in dynamic interrelation with them. These contextual factors include natural conditions (the physical environment), socio-cultural conditions (norms and values), economic conditions (e.g., the digital divide), and political–legal conditions (regulatory frameworks governing technology use).

The dashed line connecting the domains of Human Flourishing and Technology represents the space of interaction between humans and digital technologies.

Positioned along this line are four analytically distinguished aspects that constitute the primary focus of PCyb research: digital strengths, digital well-being (DWB), positive technology interventions (PTIs), and the upward dynamics of flourishing. Although these aspects differ in ontological status, they are presented symmetrically to emphasize their equal epistemic significance within the model. They refer respectively to individual dispositions (digital strengths), the quality of human–technology interactions and the experiences they generate (DWB), designed interventions, and systemic developmental dynamics.

Together, they delineate four analytical perspectives:

- Dispositional perspective—examines individual dispositions conceptualized as digital strengths that enable effective management of the digital environment in support of flourishing.
- Enrichment perspective—examines DWB by identifying and explaining the configurations of everyday digital practices and contextual conditions through which digital functioning generates experiential and functional benefits.
- Enhancement perspective—examines the mechanisms and conditions underlying the effectiveness of PTIs.
- Integration perspective—examines the upward dynamics of digitally supported flourishing, focusing on the conditions under which growth-oriented developmental trajectories are initiated and stabilized.

The distinguished analytical perspectives constitute complementary levels of description, between which the transfer of research questions, theoretical categories, and methodological procedures is both possible and conceptually warranted. For example, identifying digital strengths (Dispositional perspective) helps explain the mechanisms through which high-quality experiences are generated within digital environments (Enrichment perspective). In turn, recognizing well-being–supportive digital practices may inform the design of PTIs (Enhancement perspective). The well-being domains strengthened through their implementation may then be incorporated into analyses of the processes through which flourishing is stabilized and sustained over time (Integration perspective). Whereas the first three perspectives focus on selected components, mechanisms, or effects of technology use, the Integration perspective shifts the analytical emphasis toward identifying the conditions under which enduring developmental dynamics are generated and stabilized. In doing so, it fulfills a meta-integrative function within the epistemic architecture of PCyb. In this architecture, DWB as analyzed within the Enrichment perspective captures the quality of ongoing configurations of digital functioning, whereas the Integration perspective addresses the longitudinal formation and stabilization of flourishing trajectories emerging from such configurations.

Conducting research within PCyb requires systematic alignment of research designs, measurement strategies, and analytical techniques in accordance with APA methodological standards (Cooper et al., 2023). This domain integrates methodological traditions from positive psychology and cyberpsychology with approaches developed in UX and HCI research, necessitating a multi-method, integrative approach. Accordingly, research strategies across different levels of analysis should encompass:

- the use of quantitative, qualitative, and mixed-methods designs, including the systematic application of triangulation across data sources, methods, and theoretical perspectives, as well as the integration of person-specific and idiographic approaches, including N-of-1 experimental designs;
- the use of experimental and quasi-experimental designs to enable causal inference, particularly in the evaluation of PTIs, including the application of adaptive and micro-randomized designs that allow for the testing of causal mechanisms in real time and across dynamically changing contexts of digital engagement;
- the integration of behavioral and other objective indicators (e.g., digital trace data, activity logs, telemetry, passive sensing and digital phenotyping, and language-based digital trace data such as social media content), self-report measures (e.g., questionnaires and standardized psychological scales), psychophysical and chronometric measures (e.g., eye tracking and response times), psychophysiological indicators (e.g., heart rate variability [HRV], electrodermal activity, and hormonal assays), and neuroscientific measures (e.g., EEG, ERP, and fMRI);
- the implementation of longitudinal, diary, and experience sampling designs to capture temporal dynamics, intraindividual variability, and the processual nature of flourishing;
- the application of qualitative methods (e.g., in-depth interviews, ethnographic approaches, and narrative analysis) to examine meaning-making processes associated with digital experiences, with particular attention to how individuals interpret, regulate, and reorganize their experiences over time in interaction with digital environments.

The dynamic expansion of this analytical field makes it reasonable to expect a systematic growth in the number and refinement of research instruments. At the same time, the consolidation of a distinct research identity and the methodological maturation of PCyb will be fostered by the application of advanced data-analytic strategies and statistical modeling approaches developed in contemporary science, including AI-driven solutions, big data analytics, machine learning, natural language processing, network analysis, and computational modeling of complex, multilevel systems.

3.2 Dispositional Perspective: Digital Strengths

The Dispositional perspective integrates analyses focused on the individual resources that support a person's capacity for agentic and reflective management of the digital environment. Within this perspective, research questions are formulated in a general form as follows: What conditions underlie the development and structural organization of the dispositions of digital technology users conceptualized as digital strengths?

The term *digital strengths* is proposed to denote a class of dispositional personal resources that support intentional and developmentally oriented uses of digital technologies. At the same time, they serve a protective function by limiting the risk of the formation and consolidation of maladaptive and dependency-based patterns of digital practice. These resources are understood in accordance with Stevan E. Hobfoll's (1989) conservation of resources framework as valued assets that individuals seek to obtain, maintain, and protect. This is due to their significance for sustaining functioning, supporting adaptation, and facilitating the acquisition of further resources.

The concept of digital strengths functions as an integrative umbrella category. It enables the integration and critical examination of dispositions conceptualized within existing approaches, such as technomoral virtues (Vallor, 2016), humanics (Aoun, 2018), digital agency (Passey et al., 2018), digital intelligence (Dziak, 2022), and digital maturity (Laaber et al., 2023). It also incorporates dispositions identified in fragmented empirical studies. Semantically, the concept overlaps with the notion of digital competences as defined by the European Commission (European Union, 2019). This notion involves knowledge, skills, and attitudes enabling "the confident, critical and responsible usc of, and engagement with, digital technologies for learning, at work, and for participation in society" (p. 10).

The use in the literature of labels such as virtues, agency, intelligence, maturity, or competences (encompassing knowledge, skills, and attitudes) indicates that the set of dispositions under consideration has not yet attained a stabilized conceptual status. Rather than constituting a clearly delimited theoretical category, it appears as a constellation of partially intersecting perspectives articulated within different research traditions and at different levels of analysis. In this context, the term *strengths* may be understood as a relatively inclusive and theoretically neutral designation, enabling the integration of diverse types of individual resources without a priori fixing their ontological status or reducing them to a single analytical dimension.

At the same time, this terminological choice does not imply neglecting ongoing debates within psychology concerning the ontological and explanatory status of categories such as traits, dispositions, competences, strengths, or abilities (e.g., Cattell, 1950). These debates include perspectives that treat such phenomena as relatively stable, latent properties of the individual, as well as approaches emphasizing their contextual variability or their dynamic actualization in action.

Within the current stage of development of PCyb, it appears justified not to predetermine the ontological status of the resources under analysis and instead to adopt a pluralistic stance that accommodates the diversity of conceptualizations present in the literature. Such an approach allows the focus to remain on their functional role within digital practices, without prematurely resolving ontological disputes at this stage of the field's development. In the longer term, however, it will be necessary to progressively refine the status of particular dispositions, including clarifying their interrelations, areas of overlap, and functional distinctions. This provides an impetus for further theoretical development and conceptual systematization of constructs currently operating at the intersection of different research traditions, such as digital agency (Passey et al., 2018) and digital maturity (Laaber et al., 2023), as well as for identifying and articulating the relationships among them.

In a broader theoretical and applied context, the identification and analysis of digital strengths may be regarded as a task comparable in significance to the cataloguing of character strengths describing the positive side of human nature (Peterson & Seligman, 2004). However, unlike the classical conceptualization of character strengths as relatively stable, positive personality traits closely linked to individual identity, digital strengths are situated closer to functional competencies. They organize how individuals perceive, evaluate, and agentically transform digital affordances into experiences conducive to flourishing.

Guidance for delineating the fundamental categories of digital strengths may be derived from integrating functional competence frameworks with established psychological theories. A particularly noteworthy point of reference is the OECD's (2005) influential report, which identified three broad domains of competences necessary for effective functioning in a complex and dynamically changing world: interactive use of tools, autonomous action, and functioning within heterogeneous social groups. These domains correspond closely to the three basic psychological needs distinguished within SDT (Ryan & Deci, 2000): competence, autonomy, and relatedness. Accordingly, digital strengths may be conceptually organized into three overarching clusters. These clusters encompass dispositions that enable individuals to effectively regulate and structure the digital environment (competence support). They also include dispositions that support experiencing autonomous agency in relation to technology (autonomy support). Finally, they involve dispositions that enable the use of digital tools to cultivate and sustain relationships that foster development and cooperation (relatedness support).

Research conducted within the Dispositional perspective should be grounded in appropriately selected methodological approaches that integrate behavioral observation, self-report (including intensive longitudinal methods), along with complementary qualitative designs. Measurement categories, methods, and instruments/indicators are summarized in Table 3.1. Future research should also prioritize the development and validation of standardized psychometric tests designed to assess competencies conceptualized within this perspective.

Table 3.1 Measurement categories, methods, and instruments/indicators used in the Dispositional perspective.

Measurement category	Method	Psychological target	Instruments/indicators
Behavioral observation	Digital trace and log data	Digital engagement	Login frequency, time spent using digital technologies
Behavioral observation	Experimental tasks	Decision-making tendencies	Behavioral choice paradigms
Behavioral observation	Experimental tasks	Attentional control in digital environments	Task-switching paradigms; sustained attention tasks; and digital distraction paradigms
Behavioral observation	Telemetry data	Digital behavior patterns	In-app interactions, clickstreams, and session duration
Self-report	Questionnaire	Attitudes toward technology	Artificial Intelligence Anxiety Scale (Wang & Wang, 2019); Negative Attitudes toward Robots Scale (Nomura et al., 2006)
Self-report	Questionnaire	Basic psychological need satisfaction	Need Satisfaction Scale (La Guardia et al., 2000)
Self-report	Questionnaire	Digital emotional intelligence	Digital Emotional Intelligence Scale (Gómez-Vallarta et al., 2025)
Self-report	Questionnaire	Digital empathy	Digital Communication Empathy Scale (DCES; Collins et al., 2024b); Virtual Empathy Scale (Carrier et al., 2015)
Self-report	Questionnaire	Digital habits and self-regulation tendencies	Self-Report Habit Index (SRHI; Verplanken & Orbell, 2003, adapted to digital contexts)
Self-report	Questionnaire	Digital intelligence	Digital Intelligence Quotient Scale (Li et al., 2024b)
Self-report	Questionnaire	Digital literacy	Digital Literacy Scale (Ng, 2012); Web-Oriented Digital Literacy (Hargittai, 2005)

(Continued)

Table 3.1 (Continued)

Measurement category	Method	Psychological target	Instruments/indicators
Self-report	Questionnaire	Digital maturity	Digital Maturity Inventory (DIMI; Laaber et al., 2023)
Self-report	Questionnaire	Digital self-efficacy	Digital Self-Efficacy Scale (DSE Scale; Ulfert-Blank & Schmidt, 2022)
Self-report	Questionnaire	Emotional regulation	Difficulties in Emotion Regulation Scale–16 (DERS-16; Bjureberg et al., 2016)
Self-report	Questionnaire	IT mindfulness	IT Mindfulness Scale (Thatcher et al., 2018)
Self-report	Questionnaire	Self-control	Self-Control Scale AS-36 (Nęcka, 2015); Social Media Self-Control Failure (SMSCF; Du et al., 2018)
Self-report	ESM (intensive longitudinal self-report)	Momentary digital experiences and behaviors	Repeated in situ self-reports
Qualitative approaches	Case studies	Development and expression of digital strengths	Idiographic analysis of individual cases
Qualitative approaches	Diary methods	Enactment of digital strengths in everyday contexts	Daily logs of digital practices
Qualitative approaches	In-depth interviews	Motivations and beliefs	Semi-structured or narrative interviews

Note: Behavioral observation refers to objective indicators derived from digital trace data and experimental paradigms. Self-report measures capture subjective assessments and should be evaluated in terms of reliability, construct validity, and, where applicable, measurement invariance. Experience sampling represents an intensive longitudinal form of self-report enabling the assessment of within-person variability over time. Qualitative approaches are included as complementary designs used to explore meanings, processes, and contextualized experiences.

A fundamental prerequisite for the analysis of digital strengths is the development of measurement instruments that meet rigorous psychometric standards, enabling their reliable and valid operationalization. Only once this condition is fulfilled can advanced analytical strategies be meaningfully applied to empirically assess the extent to which particular dispositions overlap, remain distinct, and exhibit structural interrelations. To this end, both latent variable approaches and strategies that move beyond latent modeling assumptions may be employed. Network analytic approaches are particularly valuable, as they allow digital strengths to be modeled as a system of mutually interacting resources, facilitate the identification of dispositional clusters, and enable the assessment of their relative centrality within the system (Hofmans et al., 2024). Complementary to this, configuration- and profile-oriented approaches may be used to identify typical patterns of co-occurrence of digital strengths at the individual level.

A distinct line of analysis should aim to capture the functional relationships between digital strengths and domains of well-being—that is, to identify the roles these dispositions play in strengthening specific components of flourishing within digital contexts. For example, it is theoretically and empirically relevant to determine which dispositions, and to what extent, are associated with environmental mastery—one of the central domains in Carol Ryff's (1989) model of eudaimonic well-being. Environmental mastery refers to a sense of effective management of one's environment, the capacity to utilize available opportunities, and the ability to select and shape contexts in accordance with one's needs and values.

In addition, it is both justified and promising to adapt methodological strategies developed within positive psychology. This includes procedures based on the analysis of behavioral data and activity logs, analogous to research on the identification and application of so-called signature strengths (Niemiec & McGrath, 2019). Such approaches make it possible to examine digital strengths not only as self-declared dispositions. They also allow them to be studied as resources enacted in concrete situations and patterns of action within digital environments. Examples include safeguarding personal data, resisting the temptation to use social media before sleep, or supporting online charitable initiatives.

3.2.1 Frameworks Informing Digital Strengths

This section examines conceptual approaches that identify dispositions considered conducive to developmentally oriented functioning in digital environments. These include technomoral virtues, humanics, digital agency, digital intelligence, and digital maturity.

3.2.1.1 Technomoral Virtues

Shannon Vallor (2016) developed the concept of *technomoral virtues* beyond the confines of psychology as a response to the growing ethical and existential challenges associated with human functioning in a technologized world. According to Vallor, the rapid pace of technological change and its deep integration into everyday life render traditional ethical approaches grounded in normative rules insufficient for guiding responsible and prudent decision-making. In place of rule-based ethics, she turns to the tradition of virtue ethics, arguing that the cultivation of character and practical moral dispositions strengthens the resources most conducive to leading a good and wise life in the digital age.

Vallor formulates a catalogue of 12 technomoral virtues, understood as adaptations of classical virtues to contemporary technosocial conditions. These include technomoral honesty, self-control, humility, justice, courage, empathy, care, civility, flexibility, perspective, magnanimity, and their integration within the overarching virtue of technomoral wisdom. Importantly, each virtue is reconceptualized in light of the distinctive features of technological environments. For example, humility entails recognition of the limits of one's knowledge and judgment in a world saturated with data and algorithmic recommendations, while empathy refers to the capacity for authentic care for others, enacted consistently both in technologically mediated relationships and in direct offline interactions.

3.2.1.2 Humanics

Joseph E. Aoun (2018) introduced the concept of *humanics* as an interdisciplinary educational paradigm aimed at cultivating human capacities in a labor market increasingly shaped by digital technologies. Central to this framework is the integration of foundational literacies—reading, writing, and numeracy—with three "new literacies": data literacy, defined as the ability to interpret, analyze, and critically evaluate data; technological literacy, encompassing an understanding of computational and engineering systems as well as basic programming principles; and human literacy, referring to communication, collaboration, cultural intelligence, and ethical reasoning. In addition to these literacies, Aoun emphasizes the importance of higher-order cognitive capacities, including critical thinking, systems thinking, entrepreneurial mindset, and cultural agility, which enable individuals to navigate complex, uncertain, and rapidly evolving environments.

The concept of humanics thus represents a systematic attempt to transcend the traditional division between "hard" and "soft" skills by framing them as interdependent dimensions of competence. From a psychological perspective, it can be interpreted as an integrative model of human functioning in which technological, cognitive, and socio-emotional capacities form a dynamically interacting system of resources. Rather than operating as separable or hierarchically ordered domains, these capacities mutually reinforce one another, supporting adaptive regulation, learning, and goal-directed behavior in digitally mediated contexts.

3.2.1.3 Digital Agency

The construct of *digital agency* was introduced by Don Passey et al. (2018) within the context of education. The authors conceptualize it as a complex disposition that enables individuals to function consciously, autonomously, and responsibly in digital environments. Digital agency comprises three interrelated components:

- Digital competence—refers to the ability to navigate the digital world safely, effectively, and critically. It integrates digital literacy, ICT skills, information and media literacy, as well as computational competencies.
- Digital confidence—concerns individuals' beliefs in their capacity to use technology flexibly and autonomously. It is reflected in perceived proficiency in using common applications and digital tools, as well as confidence in applying technology across various life domains (education, work, civic engagement, and relationships).
- Digital accountability—relates to individuals' responsibility for their actions in digital environments and includes awareness of their ethical implications, understanding of issues such as safety, privacy, and data protection, and sensitivity to the potential impact of one's online activity on digital communities.

As demonstrated by Fazilat Siddiq et al. (2024) in a systematic review, the concept of digital agency requires further conceptual clarification, operational refinement, and empirical validation to achieve the status of a stable and widely recognized psychological category. The term remains ambiguously defined and is employed across diverse, often inconsistent meanings. Notably, only one of the reviewed studies offered a comprehensive and explicit definition. Most research invokes digital agency descriptively, treating it as an auxiliary notion within analyses of digital educational practices rather than as a theoretically consolidated explanatory framework.

3.2.1.4 Digital Intelligence

The concept of *digital intelligence* has been developed largely at the margins of academic psychology, primarily within educational, social, and business contexts. It refers to individuals' abilities to operate digital tools, behave safely online, use digital services responsibly, protect their privacy, respond effectively to risks, and flexibly adapt their strategies of action to the dynamic nature of digital environments (Dziak, 2022). Digital intelligence also encompasses the capacity to navigate and function effectively across both offline and online spaces, forming the basis for balanced and sustainable engagement with digital technologies.

A related construct developed in the scientific literature is the digital intelligence quotient, which denotes a comprehensive, ethically grounded digital competence integrating technical, cognitive, metacognitive, and socio-emotional capacities (Marnewick & Marnewick, 2021). In a study conducted among students in China, Li et al. (2024b) proposed an operationalization of digital intelligence quotient comprising seven dimensions: digital identity (healthy integration of offline and online identity), digital use (balanced media engagement), digital safety (avoidance of risks and harmful content), digital security (protection of data, devices, and passwords), digital emotional intelligence (recognizing, expressing, and responding to emotions in digital contexts), digital literacy (searching for, critically evaluating, and responsibly using information), and digital rights (understanding and respecting rights and responsibilities in digital environments).

3.2.1.5 Digital Maturity

The concept of *digital maturity* (DM) was introduced by Franziska Laaber et al. (2023) in the context of adolescents' use of mobile devices. The construct was defined as "the self-determined use of digital technologies supporting psychological growth and well-being while shielding potential threats and considering needs of the social environment" (p. 1). Its theoretical foundation is SDT, which is reflected in the categories organizing the ten dispositions comprising DM:

- the capacity to use digital technologies in an autonomous and self-determined way—emphasizes self-determination and mindful decision-making in one's engagement with technology and includes autonomous choice to use mobile devices and autonomy within digital contexts;
- the capacity to master increasing digital challenges and solve problems—captures the competencies required to navigate dynamically changing digital environments safely and effectively, including digital literacy, individual growth in digital contexts, digital risk awareness, and support-seeking regarding digital problems;
- the capacity to interact adequately with others and contribute to society—addresses the social and ethical dimension of DM, including regulation of negative emotions in digital contexts, regulation of impulses in digital contexts, respect towards others in digital contexts, and digital citizenship.

The construct was operationalized through the Digital Maturity Inventory (DIMI), a 32-item scale for which confirmatory analyses supported a unidimensional structure. Empirical findings suggest that DM provides a promising framework for explaining how young users orient technology use toward developmental aims, rather than merely avoiding its negative consequences. In a study involving parent–adolescent dyads (Laaber et al., 2024), higher DM was associated with more instrumental and goal-directed mobile device use, as well as higher levels of life satisfaction, positive affect, and psychological richness, alongside lower negative affect and psychological distress. Importantly, these associations were mediated by basic psychological need satisfaction and frustration. Together, these findings suggest that DM can be understood as a specific form of technological autonomy and self-regulation that supports well-being not by restricting engagement with technology but by shaping the quality of technology use in ways that foster psychological growth and social adaptation.

At the same time, the concept of DM remains in an early stage of conceptual consolidation and warrants critical examination. Network analyses (Hofmans et al., 2024) indicate that the construct is organized not around three domains but around two relatively coherent subclusters: competence and problem-solving (e.g., digital literacy and support-seeking regarding digital problems) and mindful and safe behavior in digital contexts (e.g., regulation of negative emotions in digital contexts, regulation of impulses in digital contexts, respect toward others in digital contexts, and digital risk awareness). Moreover, domains such as individual growth in digital contexts, autonomy within digital contexts, and digital citizenship appear more weakly connected to the remainder of the network, suggesting a need to further refine the theoretical structure of the construct.

3.2.2 Identifying and Developing Digital Strengths

The dispositions discussed below, whose integration under the category of digital strengths is either supported by existing empirical findings or represents a promising direction for further empirical validation, are organized into three complementary groups: competence support, autonomy support, and relatedness support. In some cases, the dispositions have been provisionally clustered within these broader groups into functionally coherent bundles. At this stage, however, the internal coherence of these bundles remains hypothetical.

3.2.2.1 Competence Support

This category encompasses digital strengths that enable individuals to use digital tools effectively and in ways that are contextually appropriate. Three clusters of dispositions are discussed within this domain: digital mastery, digital protection, and digital coping.

3.2.2.1.1 Digital Mastery

The term *digital mastery* refers here to an integrated set of capacities that enable individuals to use digital technologies confidently and effectively. It encompasses digital literacy (DL) and its variants, as well as digital self-efficacy.

The construct of DL has been incorporated into conceptual frameworks such as humanics (Aoun, 2018), digital agency (Passey et al., 2018), digital intelligence quotient (Li et al., 2024b), and digital maturity (Laaber et al., 2023). In its broad formulation, DL refers to three complementary dimensions of individual functioning: (1) knowledge about digital technologies and the capacity to critically evaluate their impact on individuals and society (cognitive dimension), (2) practical skills enabling effective use of digital technologies (technical dimension), and (3) communicative and collaborative competencies in online environments (social–emotional dimension) (Ng, 2012). Such competencies are referred to by some scholars as "digital skills" (Livingstone et al., 2021). In a narrower sense, DL has been defined as "the ability to understand and use information in multiple formats from a wide range of sources when it is presented via computers" (Gilster, 1997, p. 1).

The literature also distinguishes specific variants of DL, such as Internet literacy (also referred to as web-oriented digital literacy), manifested in the ability to navigate and use the Internet efficiently and purposefully (Hargittai, 2005), and AI literacy, which encompasses the capacity to effectively use, interpret, and critically evaluate AI systems (Long & Magerko, 2020).

Digital self-efficacy is understood as one's confidence in the successful future use of digital systems (Ulfert-Blank & Schmidt, 2022). It is described as a building block of digital competences because it encompasses individuals' beliefs about their own capabilities, which in turn shape whether and how they engage with digital systems. Research conducted in workplace contexts (Maran et al., 2022) indicates that higher levels of digital self-efficacy are associated with greater readiness for adaptive functioning in digital environments, increased flexibility in learning new technologies, and a stronger tendency to explore and independently utilize digital tools. At the same time, the development of digital self-efficacy has been shown to be positively related to openness to experience and emotional stability.

The relationship between DL and digital self-efficacy appears to be complementary: DL equips individuals with the competencies necessary to manage digital environments, whereas digital self-efficacy provides the belief that these competencies can be effectively enacted in practice (Pečiuliauskienė, 2025). Its development fosters greater openness toward technology and, consequently, enhances the likelihood of experiencing benefits associated with being online, such as access to information and educational opportunities (Yeşilyurt & Vezne, 2023). At the same time, DL may also serve a protective function and, together with digital self-control and emotional regulation, reduce the risk of developing problematic or dependent patterns of digital use (Chen et al., 2025a).

Research on the effectiveness of strategies aimed at strengthening DL has devoted considerable attention to the education of individuals at risk of technological exclusion. One positively evaluated approach is an intergenerational collaboration program in which younger participants (university students) supported older adults in developing digital competencies (Miller et al., 2024). The findings indicate mutual benefits: older adults demonstrated improvements in digital skills, while students reported greater openness toward engaging with individuals from different generational groups.

A significant challenge in fostering DL remains the critical examination of common-sense intuitions, stereotypes, and prejudices concerning AI-driven systems, which may contribute to algorithm aversion (Dietvorst et al., 2015), AI-related anxiety (Wang & Wang, 2019), and negative attitudes toward robots (Nomura et al., 2006). Comparative studies of cognitive representations of AI among laypersons and IT experts reveal notable differences: individuals without specialized training tend to regard embodied systems that imitate living organisms (e.g., humanoid robots) as the most prototypical examples of AI, whereas IT specialists consider abstract algorithmic solutions to be prototypical, and view nature-mimicking systems as least representative of the category (Fortuna & Gorbaniuk, 2022).

A promising line of inquiry aimed at reducing such cognitive discrepancies involves research on *explainable AI* (xAI; Gunning, 2019). Metaphorically, xAI facilitates a clearer understanding of artificial systems by transforming the opaque "black box" of deep learning algorithms into a more transparent "glass box." In practical terms, this entails providing users with comprehensible explanations of how algorithms function, including information about the data utilized, the key decision-making factors involved, and the logic underlying output generation (for a review of methods, see Adadi & Berrada, 2018). The relevance of such solutions is particularly pronounced in high-stakes and high-responsibility contexts (e.g., medical diagnostics and education). Empirical research indicates that well-designed xAI strategies enhance users' understanding of AI system functioning, which in turn is associated with a reduction in negative attitudes toward these systems (e.g., Manz et al., 2025).

3.2.2.1.2 Digital Protection

The term *digital protection* is used here to denote a cluster of dispositions that support safe and responsible functioning in digital environments. It encompasses risk awareness as conceptualized within the digital maturity framework (Laaber et al., 2023), as well as digital safety and digital security distinguished in the concept of digital intelligence quotient (Li et al., 2024b). The development of these dispositions is expected to enhance individuals' capacity to monitor risks associated with online engagement and, consequently, to avoid exposure to harmful content or situations that may lead to psychological or social harm. Their behavioral manifestations include the adoption of cybersecurity practices such as regular data backups, the use of firewalls, data encryption, and maintaining password hygiene (Armoogum et al., 2025).

Research conducted in workplace settings (Muthuswamy & Esakki, 2024) indicates that *cybersecurity awareness* contributes to reducing employees' stress related to digital threats by strengthening proactive protective behaviors. Understanding potential risks, familiarity with safe conduct guidelines, and the ability to recognize suspicious activities translate into a greater readiness to report incidents (e.g., phishing or vishing attempts). Regular training, systematic updating of knowledge regarding emerging forms of cyberattacks, and the cultivation of an organizational culture of digital security play a crucial role in shaping these practices.

Empirical evidence suggests that direct interpersonal contact constitutes an effective means of fostering caution among older adults. In a study conducted by Mark Button et al. (2024), involving nearly 1000 participants aged over 75, one-to-one conversations with family members or friends were identified as the most frequently reported and most useful source of advice on fraud prevention. Formal channels, such as training sessions, presentations, or informational websites, were perceived as significantly less effective and less accessible, particularly among individuals with lower levels of digital competence.

Among younger users of digital technologies, beyond risks directly associated with cyberattacks, the capacity to recognize a broader spectrum of online risks assumes particular importance. These include content risk, referring to exposure to material potentially harmful to emotional, social, or moral development (e.g., violence, pornography, and discriminatory content); contact risk, involving the establishment of relationships with individuals or entities that may threaten psychological or physical well-being; and conduct risk, describing situations in which young users become victims or participants in harmful online behaviors, such as cyberbullying, ideological manipulation, or unethical marketing practices (Livingstone & Haddon, 2012).

A central objective of research in this area is to determine the role of parents and caregivers in cultivating children's and adolescents' caution toward such risks. A systematic review of studies involving individuals aged 9–18 (Sevilla-Fernández et al., 2025) found that enabling mediation strategies—based on dialogue, joint engagement with digital media, and explanation of safe online practices—are more effective than restrictive mediation. Although restrictive strategies may reduce time spent online and decrease the likelihood of disclosing private information, they may simultaneously increase interest in risky online activities. This effect can be interpreted through the lens of psychological reactance (Brehm, 1966), according to which limitations on individual autonomy may enhance the perceived attractiveness of prohibited content or behaviors.

3.2.2.1.3 Digital Coping

The term *digital coping* is used here to describe a cluster of individual dispositions that enable effective management of both technological problems and online crisis situations arising from hate speech, cyberbullying, intimidation, social exclusion, and related challenges. It encompasses appropriate responses to the risks identified within the framework of digital intelligence (Dziak, 2022), security-seeking as conceptualized in digital maturity (Laaber et al., 2023), as well as constructs discussed in the literature, such as digital courage (Digital and Population Data Services Agency, 2022) and digital resilience (Qamaria et al., 2025). From the perspective of positive psychology (Peterson & Seligman, 2004) and the concept of technomoral virtues (Vallor, 2016), these dispositions may be interpreted as expressions of courage understood as the capacity to acknowledge one's limitations and to actively seek support when situations exceed one's current resources.

At present, technical support is primarily provided by IT specialists and enthusiasts; however, even high-quality service provision does not necessarily enhance individuals' sense of orientation regarding the appropriate selection of innovations and their adaptation to everyday tasks. In this context, the concept of *digital courage* (Digital Skills Report, 2022) is epistemically useful, referring to a willingness to experiment with new digital solutions, to learn through action, and to tolerate technological uncertainty. It also involves the ability to recognize one's limitations and to seek assistance when personal competencies prove insufficient. This is particularly relevant in environments where asking for help may be perceived as a sign of weakness, such as institutions characterized by highly competitive cultures. In such contexts, behavioral modeling may be effective, with leaders or more experienced colleagues serving as role models.

An example of this approach can be observed in practices of AI crafting, understood as the adaptation of professional tasks to collaboration with AI systems. Wanlu Li et al. (2024c) demonstrated that leaders who engaged in AI crafting initiated a trickle-down effect, providing employees with a model for independently implementing similar practices. Importantly, the strength of this mechanism depends on the intentions attributed to leaders: the effect is amplified when employees interpret leaders' AI crafting as motivated by performance improvement and attenuated when it is perceived as a form of impression management.

A complementary line of analysis concerns strengthening help-seeking capacities in the face of difficult experiences emerging in online environments. This disposition has profound existential significance, as it supports the protection of mental health and may increase the likelihood of postponing decisions related to self-harm or suicidal behavior. A meta-analysis (Mahzunah et al., 2024) encompassing more than 110,000 adolescents from eight countries found that experiences of cyberbullying were associated with nearly a threefold increase in the risk of suicidal ideation and more than a threefold increase in the risk of self-harm, with the true magnitude of these associations potentially overestimated due to publication bias.

Further justification for intensifying research in this domain among young digital technology users is provided by the findings of the "EU Kids Online 2020" project, which included over 25,000 children and adolescents aged 9–16 from 19 European countries (Smahel et al., 2020). The study was conducted through face-to-face interviews with children and one of their parents. The results indicated that only about half of the participants actively sought support when encountering online problems. Children and adolescents most frequently turned to parents or friends for help, and much less often to teachers or formal institutions. Notably, the propensity to seek help declined with age, and the prevalence of such behaviors varied across countries: the highest proportion of young people requesting assistance was observed in Scandinavian countries, and lower levels were reported in Southern European countries.

An additional research challenge in this context concerns clarifying the theoretical status of *digital resilience*, originally conceptualized as online resilience, and defined as the ability to adapt to challenging online environments and proactively respond to risks (Przybylski et al., 2014). As indicated by a recent systematic review (Öztürk et al., 2025), the construct is currently conceptualized in two principal ways: either as a relatively stable individual capacity to protect oneself against digital threats, or as a dynamic adaptive process activated in response to exposure to online risks. Increasingly, an ecological perspective is also adopted, according to which digital resilience emerges from complex interactions between individual factors (such as digital competences, self-regulation, emotional resources, and self-efficacy) and contextual factors, including family and school environments, peer relationships, cultural norms, and institutional arrangements (Qamaria et al., 2025). Within this framework, digital resilience is not merely an individual trait but an emergent property arising from dynamic relations between the person and their digital ecosystem.

3.2.2.2 Autonomy Support

Autonomous use of technology presupposes user agency, intentionality, and the capacity to align digital practices with one's own norms, values, and goals. A functional precondition of such autonomy is the presence of self-control and self-regulation dispositions, which enable both the inhibition of impulses triggered by digital stimuli and the proactive management of goal-directed behavior. Their conceptualization, however, remains problematic due to definitional ambiguities and the ongoing debate within psychology regarding the theoretical status and interrelations of these constructs.

In Edward Nęcka's (2015) account, self-control is understood as a multidimensional system of cognitive–motivational processes encompassing goal maintenance, proactive regulation of action, initiation and persistence of effort, flexible adaptation to changing conditions, and inhibition of impulsive responses. Other scholars (e.g., Błachnio & Przepiorka, 2016) propose a clearer distinction between self-control—conceived as the capacity to restrain impulsive tendencies in favor of long-term goals—and self-regulation, which they associate primarily with proactive planning, monitoring, and management of behavior. This distinction appears analytically useful within the Dispositional perspective, as it structures reflection on the competencies that manifest these dispositions in digital environments and on strategies for their intentional strengthening. Accordingly, in the following section, self-control is discussed as a mechanism for limiting digital temptations, whereas self-regulation is examined as a mechanism for proactively aligning digital practices with individual goals and values.

3.2.2.2.1 Digital Self-Control

The term *digital self-control* refers to the manifestation of individual self-control within digital environments and describes the capacity to regulate behavior in the face of specific temptations and stimuli generated by digital technologies (Chen et al., 2025a). The level of this disposition is operationalized using, among other instruments, the Social Media Self-Control Failure Scale (SMSCF; Du et al., 2018), which focuses on situational failures of self-control in the context of social media use. The scale measures the frequency of yielding to the temptation to engage with social media despite conflicts with other goals, a pattern associated with reduced task effectiveness, procrastination, and heightened negative emotional responses, such as guilt.

Considerations regarding the potential strengthening of digital self-control reflect a broader debate in psychology concerning the plasticity of self-control as a disposition. In the classical account proposed by Roy F. Baumeister et al. (2007), self-control is conceptualized as a renewable resource subject to temporary depletion, often described through the metaphor of a "muscle" whose strength can be enhanced through systematic training involving the inhibition of habitual responses. This perspective assumes that long-term improvements in self-regulation are facilitated by regular engagement in effortful control behaviors. It should be noted, however, that empirical support for this claim remains equivocal, and some studies have failed to confirm durable training effects within this framework (Nęcka, 2018).

In digital contexts, this debate translates into the question of whether "training" primarily involves strengthening the underlying disposition or rather designing environments that reduce the costs of exerting control (e.g., by limiting exposure to tempting stimuli). Empirical support for the latter approach is provided by studies on the effectiveness of preventive strategies based on so-called digital self-control tools (DSCT), sometimes also referred to as *DWB tools* (Almourad et al., 2021). This category includes artifacts designed to support behavioral regulation by restricting access to selected applications or functions, monitoring usage time, reducing the frequency and intensity of stimuli (e.g., notifications), and providing feedback on individual usage patterns. Such tools do not necessarily enhance self-control as a relatively stable disposition; instead, they function as situational supports for behavioral regulation within digital environments. The main categories of DSCT, together with illustrative examples and their functionalities, are summarized in Table 3.2.

Empirical evidence suggests that the use of DSCT can effectively reduce technological temptations, provided that their adoption is autonomous rather than externally imposed (Olson et al., 2023; Roffarello & De Russis, 2023). The possibility of independently selecting functions such as disabling notifications, switching the screen to grayscale mode, placing the phone out of sight, or resigning from biometric unlocking may contribute to reductions in overall screen time and problematic smartphone use, improvements in sleep quality, and the promotion of constructive activities related to learning, work, or social interaction. A persistent

Table 3.2 Categories of DSCT: illustrative examples and functionality.

Category	Examples	Functionality
Applications restricting access (timers and blockers)	AppDetox, Stay Focused, Forest: Stay Focused, and SPACE – Break Phone Addiction	Blocking applications after exceeding time limits; enforced breaks; gamification elements; and support for habit formation
System-level solutions for monitoring usage time	Google Digital Wellbeing, iOS Screen Time, Android Digital Wellbeing, and Moment	Enhancing behavioral awareness through usage analytics, temporal feedback loops, and structured self-monitoring
Notification management systems	Batch notifications (Android), focus mode (Android), and downtime (iOS)	Bundling notifications; pausing alerts during specified hours; and prioritizing notifications
Stimulus attenuation	Grayscale mode	Reducing screen color (e.g., grayscale mode); decreasing the visual attractiveness of applications (e.g., social media and games)
Activity and habit tracking systems	RescueTime and QualityTime	Automated activity reports; productivity analytics; and distinguishing between "productive" and "distracting" applications
Friction-enhancing mechanisms/ commitment devices	Freedom (locked mode), One Sec, Cold Turkey, ScreenZen, and iOS Screen Time	Introducing friction into action pathways in order to disrupt automaticity and increase reflective decision-making

limitation, however, concerns the short-lived nature of these beneficial effects and the relative ease with which simple blocks and timers can be bypassed. This points to the need for developing interventions that embed DSCT within broader programs aimed at cultivating balanced and reflective technology use, rather than relying on isolated technical constraints alone.

3.2.2.2.2 Self-Regulation

Self-regulation refers to an individual's capacity to plan, monitor, and evaluate their own behavior in the pursuit of intended goals (Vohs & Baumeister, 2016). Closely related to this disposition is emotion regulation, understood as the process of monitoring, evaluating, and modulating emotional responses in ways that facilitate goal attainment (Thompson, 1994). Difficulties in emotion regulation can be assessed using instruments such as the Difficulties in Emotion Regulation Scale–16 (DERS-16; Bjureberg et al., 2016). Empirical research indicates that higher levels of emotion regulation are associated with more reflective and flexible responses to digital stimuli, whereas deficits in this domain are linked to reduced autonomy in technology use (Chen et al., 2025a).

The literature identifies a broad range of competencies that may be interpreted as manifestations of self-regulation and emotion regulation in digital environments. Within the framework of digital agency (Passey et al., 2018), for example, digital autonomy is emphasized as the capacity for deliberate and reflective technological decision-making. The digital intelligence quotient (Li et al., 2024b) highlights the disposition of digital use, referring to balanced and responsible engagement with technology. Similarly, the construct of digital maturity (Laaber et al., 2023) encompasses four complementary dispositions: autonomous choice in the use of mobile devices, autonomy in digital contexts, impulse regulation in digital environments, and regulation of negative emotions within those contexts.

A key research challenge lies in the development and empirical testing of effective proactive strategies that support self-regulation in digital environments, as well as in examining the extent to which such strategies strengthen the aforementioned dispositions. The following section reviews research on, among others, digital mindfulness, if–then planning strategies, techniques grounded in processes of cognitive closure and goal attainment, and interventions employing mechanisms of behavioral calibration.

Digital Mindfulness The term *digital mindfulness* builds upon the concept of mindfulness, which in psychology is defined as a "state of conscious awareness in which the individual is implicitly aware of the context and content of information" (Langer, 1992, p. 289). Digital mindfulness derives from the broader construct of *IT mindfulness*, understood as the degree to which a user is involved in the present context, alert to details, aware of alternative uses, and open to exploring IT features and failures (Thatcher et al., 2018). In the literature, the term is also employed as an umbrella concept encompassing various forms of mindfulness training supported by digital tools (Yosep et al., 2024).

Although the mechanisms linking mindfulness to self-regulation require further clarification, existing research suggests that practicing mindfulness in digital contexts facilitates the early recognition of impulses prompting engagement with digital artifacts and is associated with increased subjective perceptions of behavioral control (Aldbyani et al., 2025; Fendel et al., 2024). A promising and practically significant direction of inquiry concerns the development of cultures of mindfulness that, through the establishment of appropriate norms, support individuals in the reflective use of digital tools. Research conducted in organizational contexts (Dernbecher & Beck, 2017) indicates that such support may involve:

- the implementation of mindful IT management principles, including the intentional management of information and technology (e.g., limiting excessive digital communication, designing interfaces that support focus, monitoring digital overload, and creating spaces for cognitive recovery);
- encouraging monotasking in digital work and reducing continuous task-switching, which undermines attentive responsiveness;
- fostering mindful organizing, understood as bottom-up practices of attentive action among employees, including the encouragement of error reporting, analysis of unexpected events, exploration of alternative perspectives, and knowledge exchange within expert networks;
- introducing reflective rituals (e.g., brief "pause and learn" meetings or after-action reviews) that create opportunities to reflect on experiences related to technology use.

Future research should examine the potential for transferring reflective technology-use habits cultivated in professional settings to other life domains. Analyses conducted within the JD-R model (ten Brummelhuis & Bakker, 2012) suggest that such generalization may be supported by spillover and crossover mechanisms; however, this assumption requires empirical verification.

If-then Planning The authors of the theory of action phases (Heckhausen & Gollwitzer, 1987; Gollwitzer, 1999) distinguished four successive stages of goal pursuit. In the context of positive digital practices, these phases may be described as follows: (1) the deliberative phase, involving the formulation of a goal aligned with the individual's values; (2) the implemental phase, characterized by the formation of an implementation intention in the form of an "if [situation X], then [response Y]" plan, which increases the likelihood of adaptive digital tool use; (3) the actional phase, concerning the quality of the enacted digital practice; and (4) the post-actional phase, encompassing reflection and evaluation of consequences, which may either reinforce adaptive practices or, in the case of undesirable side effects, prompt their reinterpretation and transformation into more constructive forms of engagement.

Within this theoretical framework, a self-regulatory technique known as if–then planning has been developed. Corresponding to the implemental phase, it involves formulating a plan based on the rule "if [situation X], then [response Y]." Its purpose is to automate behavioral control within a precisely specified life context (e.g., "If I receive a notification after 10:00 p.m., then I will place my phone on the desk").

There is robust empirical evidence that the automation of desired behaviors through if–then planning significantly increases the likelihood of goal attainment, particularly under conditions of distraction and temptation—precisely those characteristics of smartphone and social media use (Bieleke et al., 2021). Within the framework of mental contrasting (Oettingen, 2014), such stimuli are conceptualized as obstacles embedded in everyday life that must be consciously identified and juxtaposed with a desired future state. By linking these obstacles to if–then plans, potential threats are transformed into situational cues that trigger goal-congruent responses.

The implementation of proactive strategies based on if–then planning may, at least declaratively, be supported by commercially available applications; however, their actual effectiveness requires empirical validation. Their types, along with examples, functionality, and illustrative use cases, are presented in Table 3.3.

Table 3.3 Types of applications supporting if–then planning strategies, with examples, functionality, and use cases.

Type	Examples	Functionality	Use case
Habit-forming apps	Habitica and HabitBull	Facilitate the translation of implementation intentions into daily routines through habit tracking and gamification; reinforce behavioral consistency and support habit maintenance.	If I open YouTube during work hours, then I will close it and complete a project-related task in Habitica, earning points for my avatar.
Goal-setting & productivity apps	Todoist, Trello, and Not Less But Better (research-based intervention app)	Embed implementation intentions within temporally and contextually defined workflows.	If it is 21:00, then I will complete the task "evening meditation with calm" in Todoist, supported by a time-based reminder.
Behavioral intervention apps	WOOP app (Wish-Outcome-Obstacle-Plan)	Guide users through mental contrasting and structured formulation of implementation intentions by systematically linking desired outcomes with anticipated obstacles and predefined behavioral responses.	If I feel tempted to scroll social media before going to bed, then I will read 10 pages of a book as specified in my WOOP plan.

In this context, the application Not Less But Better merits particular attention. It was developed to support users in engaging with their smartphones in ways that are deliberate and aligned with their personal values. The 20-day program is structured into five modules (Observe, Reflect, Vision, Plan, Support), within which participants formulate usage imperatives and increase awareness of their habitual patterns. In a study conducted by Keller et al. (2021), the intervention was associated with reductions in problematic smartphone use (e.g., fewer device unlocks) and overall screen time; however, these changes did not significantly exceed the effects observed in the active control group.

The if–then planning strategy can also be implemented without digital assistance. Mark Elliott et al. (2021) examined its effectiveness in reducing smartphone use while driving. Participants in the experimental condition developed detailed implementation plans specifying critical driving situations that typically triggered phone use (e.g., receiving a call from an important person) and linked them to goal-consistent alternative responses (e.g., reminding themselves of the risks associated with distraction). In contrast, participants in the control condition merely identified such situations and expressed a general intention to avoid phone use. The results indicated that reductions in smartphone use were observed only in the implementation-intention group and were limited to the specific risk situations explicitly defined in the plans.

Cognitive Closure and Goal Attainment An intellectually promising avenue of inquiry concerns the analysis of self-regulatory mechanisms grounded in the concept of *need for cognitive closure* (Kruglanski & Webster, 1996). This construct comprises five dimensions: preference for order, preference for predictability, discomfort with ambiguity, closed-mindedness, and decisiveness. It represents a motivational mechanism aimed at reducing uncertainty and restoring a sense of order and predictability within cognitively complex environments, such as digital ecosystems. In this context, a moderate level of need for closure may serve a self-regulatory function by supporting selective attention, content prioritization, and the limitation of exposure to stimuli that contribute to cognitive disorganization. In this way, individuals may maintain a functional balance between openness to new information and the efficient filtering of data irrelevant to their goals and values. Excessive striving for closure, however, may foster cognitive rigidity and avoidance of ambiguity, thereby hindering adaptive functioning under changing environmental conditions.

Empirical support for these assumptions in digital contexts is provided by research conducted by Andrzej Cudo et al. (2019), who examined the relationship between need for cognitive closure and problematic Internet use (PIU). Although the overall level of need for closure was not correlated with addiction symptoms, selected dimensions—specifically closed-mindedness and decisiveness—appeared to function as potential protective factors against problematic online engagement. Individuals less inclined toward excessive information exploration and more disposed toward rapid decision-making were less likely to engage in compulsive Internet use.

The mechanism of cognitive closure may also be conceptualized more broadly as a component of the self-regulatory system that conditions effective goal formulation and goal pursuit in digital environments. Research by Agnieszka Strojny and Paweł Strojny (2025) advances this perspective by demonstrating that the process of goal attainment—actual achievement rather than mere cognitive "closure"—constitutes a key factor differentiating adaptive from dysfunctional patterns of gaming engagement (a mechanism that may plausibly extend to other forms of online activity). Drawing on goal systems theory (Kruglanski, 2023), the authors introduced the concept of post-gaming return (PGR), defined as the state of successful transition from virtual engagement to offline reality. Across two studies, higher levels of PGR—particularly in the dimensions of ease of disengagement and ease of reengagement—were associated with greater vitality, higher life satisfaction, and lower levels of gaming disorder symptoms.

The concept of PGR and the findings of the Strojny studies demonstrate significant applied potential. They may serve as a foundation for designing interventions that promote goal alignment (the congruence between digital activities and personal goals and values) and goal closure (the recognition and completion of achieved goals). Practical strategies may include goal-awareness training, structured post-use reflection practices, and the design of interfaces that facilitate smooth "closure of goal loops" following digital engagement. These propositions, however, require systematic empirical verification.

Behavioral Calibration Another promising direction for research involves the development of self-regulation support methods based on the Red Box & Green Box strategy proposed by Daniel L. King et al. (2024). This approach distinguishes between two temporal contexts of technology use:

- *green box* refers to periods in which individuals engage in digital activity in alignment with their daily rhythm, during leisure time, and without interfering with other obligations;
- *red box* denotes situations in which technology use conflicts with other tasks, commitments, or goals (e.g., work, study, and sleep).

Rather than focusing solely on the total number of hours spent online, this method enables behavioral calibration that takes into account the quality, context, and functional role of a given activity. It thus allows for differentiation between intensive yet adaptive engagement (e.g., productive or recreational use) and maladaptive patterns characterized by conflict with other life domains. Compulsive usage patterns are indicated by a high proportion of time classified as red box, whereas a predominance of green box time reflects more autonomous and harmonious digital practices.

Findings reported by Matthew W. R. Stevens et al. (2025) support the utility of this method in distinguishing adaptive from problematic engagement patterns. In a sample of more than 1000 gamers, individuals meeting criteria for gaming disorder spent, on average, over 21 hours/week in the red box category, compared to approximately 9 hours among non-problematic gamers. Importantly, the proportion of time spent in the red box (41.9 vs. 26.8%) proved to be a more sensitive indicator of loss of control and dysfunctional engagement than total gaming time alone. The red/green box strategy may therefore function as a sensitive tool for self-monitoring, enabling users to distinguish between controlled and compulsive technology use. In doing so, it may support self-regulatory processes by fostering reflection on personal digital practices and facilitating the early detection of signals indicating an imbalance in one's relationship with technology.

3.2.2.3 Relatedness Support

An essential dimension of responsible and mature engagement with digital tools involves equal concern for one's own well-being and that of others within digital environments. Such engagement should be facilitated by digital strengths comprising prosocial and ethical competencies, including—discussed in the following section—digital empathy, digital emotional intelligence, and digital kindness. Together, these constructs appear to form a complementary set of relational resources: digital empathy supports understanding others, digital emotional intelligence enables emotional regulation within digital interactions, and digital kindness translates these competencies into concrete prosocial actions.

3.2.2.3.1 Digital Empathy

The term *digital empathy*, also referred to as virtual empathy, is defined as "traditional empathic characteristics such as concern and caring for others expressed through computer-mediated communications" (Terry & Cain, 2016, p. 1). In this sense, it represents an adaptation of traditionally understood empathy to new forms of communication in which physical presence, eye contact, and nonverbal cues are replaced by text, audio, or visually mediated digital signals.

Empathy in digital environments was initially operationalized using the Virtual Empathy Scale (Carrier et al., 2015), which focused on general empathic capacities in computer-mediated interactions. More recently, Andrew M. Collins et al. (2024b), in the context of communication research, developed the Digital Communication Empathy Scale (DCES). This instrument enables the assessment of digital empathy across six dimensions, including digital emotion match, digital perspective-taking, and digital personal distress. Validation studies of the DCES (Collins et al., 2025), conducted on large samples in the United States and Australia, demonstrated that its subscales positively correlate with prosocial online behaviors (e.g., providing support or defending victims of cyberbullying) and negatively correlate with antisocial behaviors such as cyberaggression.

The construct of digital empathy is also examined from a human-centered design perspective. An illustrative example is the developmental project proposed by Yonty Friesem (2016), which integrates reflective practice, collaboration, and social sensitivity in digital environments. Friesem identified two key approaches: empathic design and empathic listening. The former, rooted in the design thinking model, promotes perspective-taking and empathic responsiveness in the creation of digital content. The latter emphasizes practices such as attentive listening, inquiry, paraphrasing, and validation, thereby fostering mindfulness, emotional neutrality, and affirmation of others' meanings. Evaluation of these approaches in a three-year exploratory study involving twenty socially disadvantaged high school students indicated growth in cognitive, emotional, and imaginative empathy, as well as empathic concern, alongside increased reflexivity and social sensitivity in digital content design. However, given the exploratory nature of the study, these findings require further empirical validation.

3.2.2.3.2 Digital Emotional Intelligence

Digital emotional intelligence is a relatively recent concept analyzed either as a component of the digital intelligence quotient (Li et al., 2024b) or as a relatively autonomous research construct within the broader literature. To date, empirical work has been largely descriptive, focusing primarily on the conceptualization and operationalization of digital emotional intelligence. Further investigation is required to clarify its associations with the well-being of digital technology users, as well as to develop and empirically validate interventions aimed at strengthening this disposition.

Within one conceptual approach, digital emotional intelligence encompasses both the perception of emotions in online communication and the capacity to regulate one's own emotional responses in contexts where traditional nonverbal cues are limited or absent (Audrin & Audrin, 2023). This framework integrates classical models of emotional intelligence with digital competence, emphasizing that the mere understanding of emotions is insufficient for effective functioning within digital ecosystems.

Ana C. Gómez-Vallarta et al. (2025), in turn, situate digital emotional intelligence within Goleman's classical model of emotional intelligence. In this formulation, digital emotional intelligence refers to the individual's capacity to recognize emotions, regulate them consciously, and utilize them effectively in technology-mediated relationships. It comprises four dimensions: (1) self-awareness—awareness of emotions elicited by digital platforms and their impact on everyday functioning; (2) self-management—the regulation of one's emotions and behaviors in digital environments, including emotional self-control, assertiveness, adaptability, and independence; (3) emotional awareness of others—conceptualized in terms of digital empathy; and (4) relationship management—including competencies related to influence, supporting others' development, and managing conflicts in online communities. For operationalization purposes, the authors developed a self-report questionnaire. In pilot studies conducted with university students in Spain and Mexico, women obtained slightly higher scores in emotional awareness of others and relationship management, whereas men scored higher in self-awareness and self-control.

3.2.2.3.3 Digital Kindness

Digital kindness, also referred to as *cyber-kindness*, denotes kindness-based and altruistic online behaviors, encompassing benevolent, supportive, and responsible actions undertaken in digital environments (Rowland & Klisanin, 2018). An important research challenge lies in determining the extent to which digital kindness represents a situational manifestation of the character strength of kindness within digital contexts, as well as in examining its relationships with components of digital maturity (Laaber et al., 2023), such as respect toward others in digital contexts and digital citizenship.

More advanced analytical trajectories focus on testing the effectiveness of interventions designed to strengthen kindness-based behaviors in online environments and to activate forms of *digital altruism* (also termed *cyber-altruism*, *digital prosociality*, or *e-philanthropy*).

David J. Grüning et al. (2024) identified three categories of interventions aimed at fostering respectful and constructive online interactions:

- proactive interventions, which operate preventively by activating social norms prior to action (e.g., rule reminders and prebunking strategies);
- interactive interventions, triggered during content creation and influencing user decisions in real time, for instance through labeling misleading content or issuing warnings about toxic language;
- reactive interventions, which reinforce desirable behaviors and clarify the consequences of norm violations, thereby strengthening perceptions of procedural justice.

A particularly promising research direction involves evaluating the effectiveness of interactive interventions that promote positive speech through editorial assistants suggesting more constructive phrasing (e.g., MailMagic AI assistant for YouTube comments), real-time toxicity classifiers (e.g., Hate Speech Blocker), counter-speech generators responding to hate content (e.g., COunter NArrative Bot, CONAB), or systems rewarding constructive contributions (e.g., AHAPP – Youth Sector Impact). Research involving large language models (LLMs) indicates that such systems are increasingly capable of accurately identifying hate speech and generating de-escalatory responses (Chiu et al., 2022a). Moreover, automated counter-narratives may reduce the spread of hateful content and foster more constructive dialogue (Podolak et al., 2024).

The strengthening of digital kindness may also be supported by facilitating opportunities for doing good within digital environments. Empirical evidence indicates that engagement in digital altruism is associated with lower levels of loneliness and higher life satisfaction (Tandoc et al., 2023), aligning with conceptualizations of prosociality and well-being as mutually reinforcing components of a dynamic feedback loop (Hui, 2022). The literature distinguishes among everyday, creative, and collaborative forms of digital altruism, encompassing both low-cost acts of support and more complex, intentional initiatives, including cross-sector collaborations such as those undertaken within open science movements (Klisanin, 2011). Research further indicates that digital altruism is motivated by both intrinsic drivers—such as empathy, value internalization, and meaning-seeking—and extrinsic factors, including social norms and reputational incentives, highlighting the complex motivational ecology that sustains digital kindness within networked environments (Nuttall et al., 2025). However, it remains necessary to clarify how these motivational sources interact over time, under what conditions intrinsic motives may be amplified or undermined by platform architectures, and whether externally incentivized prosocial behaviors consolidate into enduring dispositions toward digital kindness.

Against this background, empirical research suggests that immersive technologies may constitute a particularly potent architectural context for shaping these motivational dynamics. A review conducted by Memehgol Yousefi et al. (2024) indicates that XR environments—particularly when combined with the presence of embodied virtual agents—create favorable conditions for initiating and reinforcing prosocial behaviors through mechanisms such as perspective-taking, embodiment, and social presence. Narrative-driven and task-based XR experiences, including games and social simulations, appear especially promising in this regard. Yet the effectiveness of such interventions remains strongly contingent upon contextual and design features, underscoring the need for systematic investigation into how immersive affordances interact with intrinsic and extrinsic motivational processes to sustain digital kindness over time.

3.2.3 Summary

The Dispositional perspective conceptualizes digital strengths as dispositional personal resources that enable agentic, reflective, and developmentally oriented engagement with digital technologies, while simultaneously serving a protective function against dysregulated or dependency-based patterns of use. Their identification appears to be as central to PCyb as the delineation of character strengths has been to positive psychology.

The proposed framework does not predetermine the ontological status of these resources (whether they are traits, competences, virtues, or abilities) but adopts a functional stance: their significance lies in the way they organize digital practices and support trajectories of flourishing. To systematize this heterogeneous conceptual field, digital strengths are grouped into three complementary clusters: competence support, autonomy support, and relatedness support.

Competence-supporting dispositions, grouped into the clusters of digital mastery, digital protection, and digital coping, facilitate effective and contextually appropriate functioning within digital environments. Autonomy-supporting dispositions (digital self-control and self-regulation) foster the intentional alignment of digital practices with individual goals and values. Relational dispositions (digital empathy, digital emotional intelligence, and digital kindness) strengthen the prosocial and ethically responsible dimension of participation in digital ecosystems. Within each cluster, the most significant conceptualizations present in the literature and empirical findings concerning their enhancement have been reviewed.

At the same time, the set of dispositions constituting digital strengths remains open, particularly in light of the need for cross-cultural research that may reveal alternative configurations of resources across socio-cultural contexts. Within the Integration perspective, further development of existing systemic frameworks (e.g., digital agency, digital maturity, and digital intelligence) is possible, along with their conceptual integration and the identification of dynamic configurations and interrelations among digital strengths.

3.3 Enrichment Perspective: DWB

The Enrichment perspective focuses on examining the quality of individuals' everyday engagement with digital technologies. Its central aim is to address the overarching question: Which configurations of factors and underlying mechanisms give rise to digital technology use that generates experiential and functional benefits, as conceptualized within the DWB framework? This question shifts attention from deficit-oriented accounts of technology use toward the conditions under which digital engagement contributes positively to human functioning.

Because this perspective focuses on analyzing the conditions under which digital practices enrich human life, it has been termed the *Enrichment perspective*. The label draws on the concept of the psychologically rich life (Oishi & Westgate, 2022), which is treated here as a heuristic emphasizing the significance of the quality, diversity, and stimulation of experiences generated within digital environments as constitutive dimensions of a good life. Within this framework, the individual is not conceptualized as a passive victim of digitalization, susceptible to affordance traps and confined within deprivation-oriented routines, but as an agent capable of creatively and developmentally oriented engagement with technological tools. Accordingly, research conducted within the Enrichment perspective enters into direct dialogue with the Engaging in the Good with Technology framework (Villamil & Heshmati, 2023) and, more broadly, with the tradition of optimal functioning (Sheldon, 2004).

Drawing on the theoretical proposals discussed in Section 1.3.1.2, DWB is framed here as an integrative analytical construct that captures and structures the evaluative dimension of dynamic functioning within digital environments. It directs attention to configurations of digitally mediated experiences in which psychological, relational, and functional gains predominate over associated costs, thereby stabilizing and reinforcing core components of flourishing. At this stage of conceptual development, PCyb does not confine DWB to a single theoretical model or ontological status—whether understood as a global subjective evaluation of one's functioning in digital environments, as an emergent equilibrium within the relational human–technology system, or as an analytical framework for organizing heterogeneous empirical findings. Rather, it advances an integrative analytical platform that brings these perspectives into systematic dialogue and supports their progressive consolidation toward a more mature and internally coherent conceptualization of the construct.

Within this broad understanding of DWB, a central analytical task involves examining the relationships between digital practices and the proximal outcomes they generate—that is, the experienced benefits and costs associated with technology engagement. The positive valence of these proximal effects is assessed in relation to specific components of flourishing, understood as distal outcomes, following the systemic structuring proposed by Moritz Büchi (2024). At the same time, this perspective incorporates the dynamic, equilibrium-oriented view advanced by Mariek Vanden Abeele (2020), emphasizing how everyday patterns of interaction with technology emerge, stabilize, and are continuously recalibrated over time. Importantly, the primary evaluative criterion is not the intensity or frequency of use, but the qualitative balance between experienced gains and burdens.

Building on this relational and dynamic conceptualization, four complementary analytical dimensions of technology use quality can be identified, encompassing specific constellations of practices, contextual conditions, and mediating processes. Each delineates a distinct area of inquiry and establishes a specific evaluative axis for examining how everyday digital practices contribute to flourishing. Importantly, these dimensions do not represent mutually exclusive categories of digital activity; rather, they may co-occur in different configurations. Together, they reorient the analytical focus from dysfunction and deprivation toward constructive, developmentally oriented patterns of digital engagement, thereby offering a positive complement to PTU-focused accounts. These are:

- balanced technology use—associated with a sense of harmony and the experience of digital life balance;

- healthy technology use—conducive to maintaining physiological and psychological health and functional capacity;
- autonomous technology use—linked to higher levels of basic psychological need satisfaction;
- adaptive technology use—supporting goal attainment across domains such as education, work, social relationships, spirituality, and recreation.

Integrating dispersed theoretical concepts and fragmented empirical findings enables the identification of key variables and processes shaping these domains. A systematic investigation of these processes requires the application of appropriate measurement strategies. Table 3.4 summarizes the key measurement categories, methods, and instruments used in research within the Enrichment perspective.

Analytical strategies within the Enrichment perspective should focus on identifying the factors that condition the emergence of desirable proximal outcomes reflecting balanced, healthy, autonomous, and adaptive technology use. Given the continuous transformation of digital environments, the repertoire of such experiences will expand, often extending beyond currently stabilized empirical categories. The Enrichment perspective thus delineates a conceptual and empirical space within which these experiences should be systematically documented and examined with regard to their impact on specific components of flourishing, including the identification of mediating mechanisms and moderating factors.

A crucial precondition for achieving this goal is the clear differentiation between proximal outcomes, digitally contextualized evaluations of well-being domains, and broader components of flourishing. This differentiation should be reflected not only at the conceptual level but also in the selection of measurement instruments (see Table 3.4). Equally essential is the use of empirically validated instruments and indicators, as well as the ongoing development of reliable tools and computational frameworks capable of operationalizing emerging constructs.

At a more granular level, specific proximal outcomes can be assessed using dedicated instruments targeting particular experiential or functional dimensions, including the Positive and Negative Affect Schedule (PANAS; Watson et al., 1988), the Digital Life Balance Scale (Duradoni et al., 2022b), and the Flow State Scale (FSS; Jackson & Marsh, 1996). At the same time, it is important to develop broader evaluative approaches that capture multiple proximal outcomes by assessing diverse dimensions of digital experience within a single measurement framework. Exemplary approaches include DWB scales (e.g., Arslankara et al., 2022; Gomes et al., 2023), which assess multiple dimensions of digital experience and provide composite indicators of the overall quality of digital engagement. Crucially, these approaches should be understood as a key step toward more integrative measurement, rather than as fully developed models capable of capturing the dynamic and context-sensitive configuration of proximal outcomes. A similar shift

Table 3.4 Measurement categories, methods, and instruments/indicators used in the Enrichment perspective.

Measurement category	Method	Psychological target	Instruments/indicators
Behavioral observation	Digital trace and log data	Digital engagement	Login frequency, time spent using digital technologies
Behavioral observation	Language-based digital trace data (analyzed using NLP)	Emotions; meaning; values; and well-being indicators	Social media language; sentiment analysis; and linguistic markers (e.g., LIWC-based features)
Behavioral observation	Passive sensing/digital phenotyping	Behavioral patterns; momentary affect; and context-sensitive functioning	Smartphone usage patterns; geolocation variability; communication logs; and wearable sensor data
Self-report	Questionnaire	Affective experience	Positive and Negative Affect Schedule (PANAS; Watson et al., 1988); Scale of Positive and Negative Experience (SPANE; Diener et al., 2010); User Affective Experience Scale (Buck et al., 2018)
Self-report	Questionnaire	Anthropocentrism	Anthropocentric Beliefs Scale (ABS; Fortuna et al., 2021)
Self-report	Questionnaire	Authenticity	True Self Scale (McKenna et al., 2002); Authenticity Scale (Wood et al., 2008)
Self-report	Questionnaire	Basic psychological need satisfaction	Intrinsic Need Satisfaction on Facebook (Reinecke et al., 2014); TENS (Peters et al., 2018; Burnell et al., 2023); Basic Psychological Need Satisfaction for Technology Use (BPN-TU; Moradbakhti et al., 2024)
Self-report	Questionnaire	Cyber hygiene	Cyber Hygiene Inventory (CHI; Vishwanath et al., 2020)
Self-report	Questionnaire	Digital flourishing	Digital Flourishing Scale (DFS; Janicke-Bowles et al., 2023); Digital Flourishing Scale for Adolescents (DFSA; Rosič et al., 2022)

(Continued)

Table 3.4 (Continued)

Measurement category	Method	Psychological target	Instruments/indicators
Self-report	Questionnaire	Digital hygiene	Test Higieny Cyfrowej ICO [Digital Hygiene Test ICO] (Bigaj et al., 2025)
Self-report	Questionnaire	Digital immersion	Immersion in Digital Life Scale (IDLS; Witowska et al., 2025)
Self-report	Questionnaire	Digital life balance	Digital Life Balance Scale (Duradoni et al., 2022b); Online and Offline Integration Scale (Lin et al., 2018)
Self-report	Questionnaire	DWB	Digital Well-Being Scale (Arslankara et al., 2022; Gomes et al., 2023)
Self-report	Questionnaire	Flow experience	Flow Questionnaire (FQ; Csikszentmihalyi & Csikszentmihalyi, 1988); Flow State Scale (FSS and FSS-2; Jackson & Marsh, 1996; Jackson & Eklund, 2002)
Self-report	Questionnaire	Intention (pre- and post-adoption)	Implementation Intentions Scale (Gollwitzer, 1999); Scales of Behavioral Intention (Ajzen, 1991)
Self-report	Questionnaire	Perceived technological sustainability of organizations	Perceived Technological Sustainability of Organizations Scale (PTSO; Modliński et al., 2025)
Self-report	Questionnaire	Presence	Igroup Presence Questionnaire (IPQ; Schubert et al., 2001)
Self-report	Questionnaire	Quality of digital experiences	Quality of Digital Experiences Scale (QDES; Witowska et al., 2025)
Self-report	Questionnaire	Social capital	Internet Social Capital Scales (ISCS; Williams, 2006); Social Media Capital (SMC) Scale (Duradoni et al., 2022a)

Self-report	Questionnaire	Technological stress	Perceived Technostress Scales (Olech & Jurek, 2022); Techno-Eustress Scale (Nascimento et al., 2024)
Self-report	Questionnaire	Technology readiness	Technology Readiness Index (TRI; Parasuraman, 2000)
Self-report	ESM (intensive longitudinal self-report)	Momentary experiences (e.g., emotions, flow, awe, and connectedness)	Repeated in situ self-reports
Chronometric and psychophysical measures	Eye-tracking	Visual attention and engagement	Gaze patterns; fixation duration
Psychophysiological measures	Physiological recording	Arousal and emotional activation	GSR
Neuroscientific measures	Neuroimaging	Neural correlates of digital experience	Functional magnetic resonance imaging (fMRI); EEG activity
Qualitative approaches	Case studies	Configurations of digital practices and outcomes	Idiographic analysis
Qualitative approaches	Diary method	Everyday digital practices and experiences	Narrative logs
Qualitative approaches	Document analysis	Institutional and cultural mechanisms (e.g., technostress)	Policy and discourse analysis

Note: Behavioral observation refers to objective indicators derived from digital trace data, passive sensing, natural language data, and real-time analytics. In digitally mediated contexts, these indicators are often processed using computational techniques to infer patterns of behavior and experience. Self-report methods include both global questionnaires and intensive longitudinal approaches such as experience sampling. Chronometric and psychophysical measures capture perceptual and attentional processes. Psychophysiological and neuroscientific measures provide objective indicators of underlying physiological and neural processes, including data collected via wearable and mobile sensing technologies. Qualitative approaches are included as complementary research designs used to explore meanings, processes, and contextualized experiences.

toward integrative measurement can be observed in organizational research. For instance, the construct of Perceived Technological Sustainability of Organizations (PTSO; Modliński et al., 2025) captures employees' subjective evaluation of the balance between technological demands and resources during actual use. In doing so, it operationalizes adaptive technology use at the level of system-wide experiential evaluation rather than isolated outcome indicators. In contrast to classical acceptance models, this approach emphasizes post-implementation experience over adoption intentions and establishes a direct link between technology use and proximal well-being outcomes in context.

In addition to these established approaches, recent methodological developments point toward the growing importance of computationally enhanced and multimodal measurement strategies (see Hou et al., 2025). These strategies integrate diverse data streams within established measurement frameworks—including digital trace data, natural language, physiological signals, and contextual information—into unified analytical systems, enabling continuous and ecologically valid measurement of well-being processes. Rather than relying exclusively on retrospective self-reports, they enable real-time, fine-grained tracking of fluctuations in experience, behavior, and context, thereby significantly increasing the temporal resolution and ecological validity of well-being assessment.

At the same time, analyses of the relationships among digital practices, the proximal outcomes they generate, and distal outcomes associated with particular types of technologies may be more appropriately situated within the Integration perspective, where they are modeled as ascending or destabilizing trajectories of flourishing. Within this framework, particular attention should be given to approaches capable of capturing the specificity of DWB as a state of dynamic equilibrium (Vanden Abeele, 2020). Systemic and network-based strategies are especially suitable, as they conceptualize DWB as a dynamic configuration of interrelated elements (e.g., Chen et al., 2025a). Longitudinal analytical approaches based on repeated measurements of the same individuals, such as latent growth curve models, multilevel models, or dynamic structural equation modeling (DSEM), are likewise warranted. These strategies enable the identification of developmental trajectories, short-term fluctuations, and relatively stable patterns of digital practice. Importantly, they also allow for the examination of within-person dynamics, clarifying the conditions under which the same individuals experience more balanced, healthy, autonomous, or adaptive functioning in digital environments.

Importantly, computational approaches introduce a qualitatively new level of analysis. By employing machine learning, network modeling, and simulation-based methods, they enable the identification of nonlinear dynamics, emergent patterns, and personalized trajectories of DWB. This shift reflects a transition from static and variable-centered measurement toward process-oriented, idiographic, and system-level analytical frameworks, in which well-being is conceptualized as a dynamic configuration rather than a fixed set of indicators.

3.3.1 Balanced Technology Use

The individual's pursuit of balanced technology use can be understood as a search for a "golden mean" in the degree to which technology is embedded in everyday life. Within the DWB framework, this dimension may be conceptualized as a configuration of self-regulatory practices (e.g., boundary management, structuring of daily rhythms, and goal alignment) and the proximal outcomes they generate—most notably, evaluations of *digital life balance* (Duradoni et al., 2022b). This construct refers to the subjective assessment of the balance between online and offline life, understood as the perceived harmonious integration of digital technology use with everyday functioning. Empirical findings based on the Digital Life Balance Scale indicate that higher levels of digital life balance are positively associated with life satisfaction and overall flourishing. They are also negatively associated with symptoms of problematic technology use, including excessive engagement with social media, gaming, or the Internet more broadly (Duradoni et al., 2022b). Moreover, pronounced disharmony between online and offline life has been shown to co-occur with elevated levels of anxiety, loneliness, and fear of missing out (FOMO) (Duradoni et al., 2024).

A distinct but conceptually neighboring concept is *digital immersion* (Witowska et al., 2025). This variable refers to the degree to which everyday practices are saturated with digital technologies across domains such as work, education, communication, social relationships, leisure, and task performance. High levels of digital immersion indicate that technology constitutes a pervasive element of daily life, with increasingly blurred boundaries between online and offline contexts. The construct is operationalized by the Immersion in Digital Life Scale (IDLS; Witowska et al., 2025), and elevated scores have been found to correlate positively with symptoms of stress, depression, and compulsive technology use. Future research should examine the relationship between digital immersion and digital life balance in order to assess their functional complementarity and potential interaction effects.

Importantly, the indicator of balanced technology use is not an equal distribution of time between offline and online activities, but rather an adequate distribution—one that harmonizes with an individual's life rhythms, supports enacted social roles, and remains coherent with personal goals and available resources. The inadequacy of time-based metrics as sole indicators of the quality of digital practices is further illustrated by findings on *indirect gaming involvement*. This notion refers to various game-related activities occurring outside actual gameplay (screen time), such as watching gaming content, thinking about games, reading related information, engaging in discussions, or considering in-game purchases. Empirical evidence (Strojny et al., 2023) demonstrates that indirect gaming involvement is associated with an increased risk of gaming disorder, supporting the argument that quantitative measures of exposure fail to capture the true depth of engagement and its psychological consequences.

Research aimed at identifying the factors that shape and strengthen balanced technology use should therefore address both technology acceptance processes (i.e., which digital tools individuals incorporate into their lives) and adoption processes (i.e., how these tools are integrated into everyday practices).

3.3.1.1 Thoughtful Acceptance of Digital Tools

The harmonious integration of digital technologies into everyday routines rests on thoughtful acceptance, understood as the selective incorporation of digital tools preceded by reflection on one's needs and a careful evaluation of their long-term functional implications. Within the logic of DWB, thoughtful acceptance serves as a preventive practice, enabling a better alignment between technological tools and an individual's goals and values, while reducing the risk of disharmony resulting from unintentional or excessive adoption. This approach is consistent with the idea of digital minimalism (Newport, 2019), which advocates incorporating into daily life only those technologies that provide substantial and enduring value.

Research on technology acceptance has a long tradition, dating back to Everett M. Rogers's (1962) seminal work on the diffusion of innovations. Today, this line of inquiry develops at the intersection of cyberpsychology, UX, HCI, and positive psychology, drawing on well-established theoretical models such as the Technology Acceptance Model (TAM; Davis, 1989), the Theory of Planned Behavior (TPB; Ajzen, 1991), the Unified Theory of Acceptance and Use of Technology (UTAUT; Venkatesh et al., 2003; UTAUT2; Venkatesh et al., 2012), and the Technology Readiness and Acceptance Model (TRAM; Lin et al., 2007). These frameworks provide robust tools for explaining intentions to use technology; however, they primarily focus on predicting adoption and less frequently address the qualitative dimensions of technology integration across an individual's life course. For this reason, it is important to complement these approaches with variables capable of capturing the motivational foundations of technology acceptance. One step in this direction has been the extension of UTAUT2 by incorporating basic psychological needs identified within SDT (Ryan & Deci, 2000), treated as antecedents of innovation use intentions (Medeiros et al., 2022).

Technology acceptance processes are examined particularly intensively in the context of organizational change and readiness for digital transformation (Rudnicka, 2021). Research in this domain addresses variables such as technology readiness, organizational e-readiness, readiness for change, and resistance to change (e.g., Oreg et al., 2013). Findings consistently indicate that the success of digital transformation depends substantially on organizational culture and a climate supportive of learning, experimentation, and open communication (Michelotto & Joia, 2024). Leadership style also functions as an important moderator of acceptance processes. Transformational leadership—combining an orientation toward innovation with concern for employees' well-being and psychological resources—has been shown to foster contexts in which technologies are integrated in a balanced and sustainable manner (Lu, 2024). Further advancement of this line of research would benefit from incorporating constructs developed within positive organizational psychology and from adopting a systemic perspective on well-being (Kern et al., 2019).

3.3.1.2 Harmonious Online–Offline Integration

While routines surrounding newly adopted artifacts can be deliberately shaped and aligned with existing repertoires of daily activities, a more complex challenge concerns balancing the use of technologies that have already become embedded features of one's life environment. In the context of Internet use, Xiaoyan Lin et al. (2018) formulated the online–offline integration hypothesis. According to this framework, the critical factor is not the intensity of engagement per se, but the degree of harmony between an individual's experiences, identity, and behaviors across offline and digitally mediated environments. The authors distinguish three interrelated dimensions of integration: (1) identity integration, in which the online self does not function as a compensatory substitute for the offline self; (2) relational complementarity, whereby online interactions reinforce rather than replace face-to-face relationships; and (3) social function integration, reflected in the extent to which digital activities support the pursuit of goals, roles, and competencies developed offline. Empirical findings reported by the authors provide preliminary evidence that higher levels of online–offline integration are associated with more favorable well-being indicators—including greater life satisfaction and lower loneliness—as well as with reduced levels of PIU.

Complementing this perspective are studies on boundary management between work and private life, which demonstrate that the consequences of digital tool use depend on individuals' preferred strategies of role integration or segmentation. For example, research by Daantje Derks et al. (2016) indicates that among individuals who prefer role integration, more frequent smartphone use during leisure time may be associated with lower work–family conflict and better functioning in the family role, as technology in such cases serves as a tool of flexibility and sustained control. By contrast, among individuals who prefer role segmentation, the use of smartphones for work-related purposes outside working hours did not lead to significant changes in work–family conflict, which the authors interpret as a consequence of effectively enforced boundaries between life domains.

In examining the links between balanced technology use and work–life balance, analyses of remote and hybrid work—widely adopted during the COVID-19 pandemic—occupy a central position. Although many studies highlight the risks of overload and boundary blurring, a systematic review by David Shaholli et al. (2024) suggests that under supportive organizational conditions—characterized by autonomy, flexibility, and communicative support—telework may enhance well-being and work–life balance. When thoughtfully designed and embedded within a culture of trust, self-regulation, and voluntary disconnection, remote work can promote harmony between online and offline experiences. It may also increase perceived control over working time, facilitate alignment of daily rhythms with individual needs, and reduce costs associated with commuting.

3.3.2 Healthy Technology Use

The use of digital technologies is not neutral with respect to users' health, as it entails unavoidable psychophysiological costs. A substantial body of empirical evidence indicates that prolonged maintenance of static body postures, excessive forward head inclination, and chronic visual exposure to screen-emitted stimuli contribute to musculoskeletal disorders, pain symptoms, computer vision syndrome, and persistent fatigue (Ekefjärd et al., 2024; Rosenfield, 2011). Moreover, dysfunctional digital practices may generate feedback loops between somatic and psychological costs of technology use and co-occur with sleep disturbances, heightened depressive symptoms, reduced capacity for pleasure (anhedonia), and chronic stress (Cangelosi et al., 2025). These psychophysiological dynamics appear to be paralleled at the neural level, as accumulating neuroimaging research suggests that excessive and dysregulated screen exposure may be associated with functional and structural differences in prefrontal, limbic, and reward-related circuits, with potential downstream consequences for executive control, attentional stability, and affective regulation (Small et al., 2020).

These risks intensified during the COVID-19 pandemic. A systematic review conducted by John Wells et al. (2023) demonstrated that the widespread shift to remote work—while reducing exposure to viral infection—was associated with numerous adverse health consequences. On the physical level, studies documented decreased physical activity, increased sedentary time, and excessive extension of screen exposure. On the psychological level, symptoms of overload, fatigue, and diminished subjective well-being were predominant.

This state of affairs justifies the need for intensified research aimed at identifying conditions conducive to healthy technology use. Within the DWB framework, such use may be conceptualized as a configuration of regulatory practices that generate favorable proximal outcomes in the form of positive psychological and physical states.

3.3.2.1 Digital Hygiene

Digital hygiene (DH) is a concept that is only beginning to enter the field of psychological research. By analogy to sanitary hygiene—understood as a set of everyday practices that protect against illness and support physical health—DH refers to a repertoire of health-promoting and safety-oriented practices in the use of digital tools (Adamowicz & Jurczyk, 2023).

The literature identifies four key domains of behaviors conducive to DH (Bigaj et al., 2025): (1) regulation of screen device use, including limiting screen time and eliminating digital distractions; (2) safe use of the Internet and digital devices, including protection of personal data and the application of safeguards against malware; (3) responsible content creation and consumption, including critical evaluation of information and appropriate responses to disturbing or harmful content; and (4) other health-promoting behaviors associated with digital tool use, such as maintaining proper posture, engaging in physical activity, and regulating emotional responses.

Beyond aspects directly related to health, the proposed conceptualization of DH also encompasses the active protection of personal information and prudent content management in digital environments. Arun Vishwanath et al. (2020) refer to such routines as *cyber hygiene*. This construct can be assessed using the Cyber Hygiene Inventory (CHI), developed by the same research team. The CHI comprises five dimensions summarized by the acronym SAFETY: (S) Storage and device hygiene; (A) Authentication and credential hygiene; (F) Facebook and social media hygiene; (E) Email and messaging hygiene; and (TY) Transmission and browsing hygiene. Empirical findings indicate that higher levels of cyber hygiene are associated with greater self-assessed technological competence, including stronger declared ability to identify digital threats and to undertake appropriate protective actions.

A general assessment of DH across the four domains outlined above can be obtained using the Digital Hygiene Test ICO (Bigaj et al., 2025), which is currently available only in Polish. Although both the instrument and the broader conceptualization of DH require further refinement, they already offer preliminary exploratory data and stimulate research on the associations between hygienic digital practices and users' health-related outcomes.

Findings from two editions of the Nationwide Study of Adult Digital Hygiene conducted in 2022 and 2024 (Bigaj & Woynarowska, 2023; Bigaj et al., 2025) indicate a low and largely unchanged level of DH among adult Internet users in Poland. In both waves, respondents reported regularly applying only a limited subset of the recommended practices. The most pronounced deficits concerned regulation of screen time and notifications, sleep hygiene, posture, and physical activity. At the same time, relatively high levels of attention to data security and privacy were observed, suggesting a selective pattern of digital habits and a discrepancy between increasing awareness and actual behavioral change in health-promoting practices.

3.3.2.2 Digital Detox

An important analytical pathway related to healthy technology use concerns the verification of well-being effects associated with reducing screen time. Evidence suggests that such strategies show limited effectiveness when implemented primarily as forms of external or environmental control. For example, analyses conducted in the United Kingdom indicate that although the introduction of regulatory restrictions was associated with a reduction in smartphone use (on average by 30–40 minutes/day), it did not foster the development of responsible technology use competencies, nor did it translate into improvements in sleep quality, academic performance, classroom social climate, or subjective well-being (Goodyear & Pallan, 2025).

In contrast to externally imposed restrictions, *digital detox* may be understood as a voluntary and intentional, temporary removal of aversive stimuli associated with artificial systems, treated as a behavior-change technique aimed at promoting healthier patterns of functioning in digital environments (Radtke et al., 2021). In this formulation, digital detox is not limited to complete disconnection from devices but also includes the temporary suspension of selected forms of use (e.g., social media platforms, messaging applications, and notifications).

Research on the effectiveness of digital detox suggests that it constitutes a symptomatic rather than systemic intervention. While it may generate short-term favorable proximal outcomes (e.g., reduced overload or increased mindfulness), it does not durably reconfigure the relational patterns between individuals and technology. Such conclusions emerge from a meta-analysis of studies on abstinence from social media use (Lemahieu et al., 2025). The findings further indicate that extending the duration of abstinence does not produce cumulative effects. Moreover, digital detox may be accompanied by side effects (e.g., boredom, loneliness, or intensified craving to return to media use) and by compensatory strategies that limit its effectiveness and acceptability. Frequently observed patterns include "screen-to-screen" substitution (shifting attention to other devices or applications) and post-detox binge behavior, characterized by intensified social media engagement following the intervention.

A promising direction for future research involves testing technology abstinence procedures within interventions grounded in digital mindfulness. Such approaches align more closely with the logic of sustainable healthy technology use, as they operate at the level of reconstructing systems of digital practice rather than enforcing temporary withdrawal. An example is the mindfulness-based digital balance program (Thomas et al., 2025), designed to reshape the individual's relationship with technology toward greater intentionality and agency, without adopting a logic of total abstinence. The program is based on brief, planned pauses (sobriety sampling) conceptualized as self-regulatory micro-experiments. Preliminary cross-cultural findings indicate sustained effects in the form of more deliberate technology use and the implementation of recurring hygienic rituals in everyday digital practices.

3.3.3 Autonomous Technology Use

Technological tools are used autonomously when individuals remain the agentic regulators of their own digital practices and consciously decide when, how, and for what purposes they engage with technology. Such autonomy is expressed in the capacity to resist affordance traps, entrenched habitual patterns, social pressure, or the fear of disconnection. Importantly, it may co-occur with either low or high intensity of use, provided that engagement with technology reflects reflective self-regulation rather than situational pressure or compulsivity.

Autonomous technology use constitutes a clear counterpoint to PTU, thereby elevating the importance of analyses aimed at identifying its key determinants. In this regard, the research of Si Chen et al. (2025a), conducted in the context of online connectedness, is particularly noteworthy. Their network analysis revealed that the most central node within the DWB network was online intrinsic need satisfaction, that is, satisfaction of autonomy and competence needs. This node was positively associated with web-based hedonic well-being and social well-being, and negatively associated with digital stress. In an extended model incorporating protective and risk factors, two relatively distinct clusters emerged: digital competency and digital dependency. Emotional regulation displayed the highest bridge strength, linking the competency cluster through positive associations with adaptive coping strategies while simultaneously weakening the dependency pattern through negative associations with avoidance and other risk indicators.

These findings suggest that autonomy in digital environments is grounded in the capacity to maintain a sense of agency and to effectively regulate emotional responses during technology use. Intrinsic need satisfaction appears as a central proximal dimension of DWB—a node around which both positive experiences (hedonic enjoyment and connectedness) and reductions in affective costs (stress) are organized. This justifies research aimed at identifying factors that facilitate the satisfaction of autonomy and competence needs in digital contexts. At the same time, the results do not warrant interpreting need satisfaction as a straightforward "cause" of autonomous technology use. It therefore becomes essential to determine the systemic conditions under which satisfaction of these needs co-constitutes the dynamic emergence of autonomy in individuals embedded within the technosphere.

3.3.3.1 Basic Need Satisfaction in Digital Environments

To assess the level of satisfaction of fundamental psychological needs, researchers can draw on an expanding repertoire of validated self-report instruments. The Intrinsic Need Satisfaction on Facebook scale (Reinecke et al., 2014) enables the assessment of basic psychological need satisfaction in the context of social media use, whereas the Basic Psychological Need Satisfaction for Technology Use (BPN-TU; Moradbakhti et al., 2024) has been validated across a broad spectrum of technologies—from chatbots and exoskeletons to voice assistants and care robots. Particularly valuable are the measures developed within the METUX model (Peters et al., 2018; Burnell et al., 2023), including the TENS battery, which allows for the analysis of need satisfaction and frustration at the levels of interface, task, behavior, and life.

A promising application of these instruments lies in the empirical evaluation of design features conducive to need satisfaction. For example, Liza Alberts et al. (2024) identified 50 design features of behavior-change systems that are theoretically intended to support autonomy (e.g., goal personalization), competence (e.g., precise feedback), and relatedness (e.g., social support functions). Empirical testing of such features underscores the need for close collaboration between psychologists and UX designers in the development of technologies that support flourishing. This collaboration is particularly important in the design of intelligent home, organizational, and urban environments, which should enhance users' opportunities for choice and control, strengthen functional capacity, and foster meaningful connection—rather than merely automate human life (Cho & Kim, 2022).

In this framework, designing for need satisfaction has an optimization-oriented character, as it enhances the quality of user experience within existing action possibilities. However, within the DWB perspective, autonomy may also be analyzed in relation to technologies that reconstruct it, that is, systems that do not merely strengthen psychological needs but restore the conditions under which they can be realized. This applies to augmentative systems, whose use in contexts of perceptual, motor, or communicative limitations constitutes the very conditions of possibility for task performance and social participation. Examples include interfaces transforming visual stimuli into auditory or tactile information, systems enabling device control via eye tracking or brain–computer interfaces (BCI), and AAC (augmentative and alternative communication) solutions such as speech-generating devices.

Acceptance and long-term use of augmentative systems depend not only on functional parameters but also on the quality of sensorimotor integration, interface stability, and, crucially in the present context, the subjective sense of control and agency. For instance, research on hybrid prostheses (Collu et al., 2025) indicates that insufficient feedback increases cognitive effort, reduces embodiment of the prosthesis, and lowers users' confidence, which may contribute to device abandonment despite high technological sophistication. In this context, the perspectives of reconstruction and optimization converge, forming a new configuration of proximal outcomes related to the satisfaction and frustration of psychological needs.

A distinct but closely related cluster of issues concerns the use of self-tracking technologies developed within the Quantified Self (QS) movement (Lupton, 2016). These tools enable systematic monitoring of behavioral, physiological, and affective parameters through advanced analytics, data visualization, biofeedback mechanisms, goal-tracking systems, and progress forecasting. Such solutions are integrated into a wide range of applications—from mood diaries and habit-formation tools to physical activity monitoring apps. Research on health-oriented QS applications (Feng et al., 2021), however, demonstrates their ambivalent role. On the one hand, they may strengthen perceived competence by fostering "self-knowledge through numbers." On the other hand, they may encourage dependence on external metrics, cognitive–emotional overload, diminished long-term motivation, and, in extreme cases, increased anxiety and compulsive behaviors. This gives rise to a paradox of self-control, whereby increasing precision and availability of measurement may undermine autonomous self-regulation and make disengagement from digital practices more difficult, even when such practices were initially adopted to support intentional and controlled functioning. Identifying design, usage, and contextual conditions that prevent such adverse effects and promote autonomous self-regulation constitutes an important research challenge.

3.3.3.2 Life-Embedded Autonomy

A growing body of research indicates that the mere experience of basic psychological need satisfaction during interactions with digital technologies does not constitute a sufficient condition for autonomous use. What appears crucial is the embedding of such practices within the broader ecology of an individual's activities and lived experiences.

Illustrative in this regard are findings reported by Dan Bennett et al. (2025) on social media use. Drawing on the SDT motivational continuum, the authors identified four motivational profiles—ranging from amotivation and external regulation to integrated regulation and intrinsic motivation. These profiles differentiated not only levels of basic psychological need satisfaction, affect, and well-being, but also indicators of automaticity, compulsivity, and regret associated with social media use. Satisfaction of autonomy and competence needs was associated with more internalized forms of regulation. However, high levels of intrinsic motivation alone did not guarantee adaptive use. Notably, the lowest levels of automaticity, compulsivity, and regret were observed in a profile characterized by moderate internalization of motives. Conversely, strong identity integration with social media use was linked to high need satisfaction and positive experiences, yet co-occurred with an increased risk of over-engagement and self-regulatory difficulties.

These findings suggest that autonomous technology use does not follow directly from high intrinsic motivation or high levels of need satisfaction in digital environments. This conclusion is consistent with results from research on video gaming. According to the Basic Needs in Games (BANG) model proposed by Nick Ballou and Sebastian Deterding (2024), the impact of gaming on well-being depends not only on levels of need satisfaction and frustration but also on the degree to which the activity fits within the broader life context (life fit). Digital activity may support well-being when it remains a flexible, proportionate, and integrated component of everyday functioning. By contrast, it may undermine well-being when it displaces other activities essential for maintaining psychological balance. Under such conditions, a compensatory mechanism, shifting need satisfaction into the digital environment, may transform into escapism and dissociation, thereby increasing the risk of PTU (Giardina et al., 2024).

Analogous patterns have been observed in research on smartphone and social media use. A systematic review by Monique West et al. (2024) demonstrates that social media can both support and undermine the satisfaction of basic psychological needs. Under favorable conditions, it may facilitate relationship building, identity expression, and a sense of agency. Under conditions of excessive or problematic use, however, it may amplify social pressure, perceived obligation to remain online, and experiences of failure or exclusion. Importantly, research by Zejun Hao et al. (2023) indicates that high levels of need satisfaction within social media may coexist with an increased risk of problematic use when such activity begins to dominate other life domains. Disruption of life fit, manifested in the replacement of offline relationships and everyday roles with online interaction, thus becomes a pathway toward PTU and deteriorating mental health.

From a DWB perspective, the analytical emphasis therefore shifts from the question of whether technologies satisfy psychological needs to the question of under what configurations and systemic conditions need satisfaction co-constitutes the dynamics of autonomous rather than compulsive technology use. In this regard, the relational and environmental contexts of digital tool use assume particular importance.

Interventions targeting the family environment, especially within the domain of digital parenting, provide a concrete illustration of this research direction. One example is the Parent Training program proposed by Consuelo Mameli et al. (2025), grounded in SDT and implemented in a seven-session format designed to strengthen autonomy support, structure, and relatedness in the context of children's digital device use. Participation in the program was associated with increased parental autonomy-supportive behaviors and a subsequent reduction in PTU among children. Although further research across more diverse samples is required, such interventions indicate a promising trajectory for PCyb: moving beyond analyses of artifact use and need satisfaction toward conceptualizing autonomy as a property of the broader system within which the individual operates.

The importance of environmental factors is further underscored by analyses of infrastructural changes introduced at the level of homes, organizations, or urban settings and their impact on perceived autonomy. A widely debated example concerns the implementation of monitoring systems. A review by Sandeep K. Pandey and Ram Pravesh (2025) indicates that even organizationally justified monitoring practices may lead to increased stress, diminished autonomy, and erosion of trust when introduced in a nonparticipatory manner grounded in a logic of compliance. Such conditions may foster psychological reactance, compensatory avoidance strategies, and even paradoxical deviant behaviors. More effective approaches involve transparency and the inclusion of representatives of the affected group in co-deciding the principles governing surveillance and control mechanisms.

3.3.4 Adaptive Technology Use

Adaptive technology use denotes a mode of engagement in which digital practices are functionally subordinated to an individual's goals and systematically support their realization. The generation of desired proximal outcomes thus depends on the appropriate alignment of digital tools with specific tasks, as well as on the competent activation of their affordances.

Given that goal-directed activities may pertain to multiple domains of human functioning and contribute to the strengthening of a broad spectrum of flourishing components, the synthesis of empirical findings is organized in accordance with the PERMA model (Seligman, 2011). The analyses therefore encompass the cultivation of positive affect, the enhancement of engagement through challenge–skill calibration, the shaping of relational experiences, and the construction of meaning through value-driven digital experiences. They also address accomplishment in domains such as digital learning, professional development, eSports, and digital creativity.

The section opens with an analysis of identity construction processes in digital environments, as these processes condition the forms of individual presence, self-representation, and agency in online spaces.

3.3.4.1 Identity: Self-Construction in Virtual Spaces

Functioning in digital environments opens a space for identity experimentation within the domain of the *digital self*, extending beyond the constraints of offline contexts. Available tools facilitate the flexible modulation of self-presentation, allowing it to be adjusted to shifting interactional settings. One of the most widespread forms of shaping the digital self involves the use of avatars. John Suler (2017) distinguishes sixteen avatar types (including animal, demonic, and power-symbolizing forms), illustrating the extensive possibilities for identity exploration and self-expression within digital ecosystems. With the advancement of digital technologies, avatars are assuming increasingly complex forms, approaching what are sometimes referred to as *digital twins*—representations that reproduce selected physical, behavioral, and cognitive characteristics of a real person. The term *avatar* is also commonly used to refer to characters in video games; however, it should be noted that such entities are typically controlled by the user (or by AI) and participate in the narrative, tasks, and interactions within the game environment. Importantly, individuals often operate multiple avatars simultaneously, adapting them to different contexts of digital activity.

Adaptive technology use in the domain of digital identity construction consists of engaging in representational practices that support processes of self-definition, foster self-coherence, and enable satisfying functioning in online environments. The central analytical pathway therefore focuses on the conditions under which a coherent and authentic digital self can be developed, particularly through authentic self-disclosure. The degree of authenticity can be assessed using instruments such as the True Self Scale (McKenna et al., 2002) and the Authenticity Scale (Wood et al., 2008). The former identifies where individuals locate their "true self"—online or offline—whereas the latter is employed in social media research as a measure of trait authenticity in online contexts.

A review of empirical studies (Fortuna et al., 2025b) indicates that the development of a coherent and authentic digital identity is facilitated by avatar personalization aligned with individuals' values and core beliefs. Individuals who present themselves in an honest and prosocial manner are more likely to engage in altruistic behaviors, which in turn enhance their sense of internal coherence and willingness to cooperate in virtual environments. Feedback loops between action and social response play a crucial role in this process. Positive feedback strengthens self-esteem and stabilizes identity elements that receive social approval, whereas negative feedback may initiate processes of image revision and recalibration.

John A. Bargh et al. (2002), in their analysis of authentic self-presentation online, introduced the construct of the *Real Me*. They proposed that individuals may locate this "Real Me" primarily in the offline world, across both online and offline spheres, or predominantly in digital space. The latter orientation is associated with the disclosure of more personal content in online relationships than in face-to-face interactions. Research by Katelyn Y. A. McKenna et al. (2002) demonstrated that anonymity and enhanced control over self-presentation, features characteristic of digital environments, facilitate the expression of the Real Me. Many individuals report feeling “more themselves” online, which can foster the development of close and enduring relationships that are later transferred into offline contexts. Such processes may be associated with reduced loneliness and lower social anxiety. At the same time, more recent cross-cultural findings (Błachnio et al., 2026) suggest that predominantly locating the Real Me in digital environments may also co-occur with diminished well-being and increased vulnerability to Internet and social media addiction. The direction and magnitude of these associations vary across cultural contexts, and high self-esteem appears to function as a protective factor.

The complexity of the relationship between digital identity and well-being is further illustrated by cases in which individuals derive benefits from self-presentations that diverge from their “analog” identity. Research on users of Second Life (Messinger et al., 2008) showed that individuals employing attractive avatars exhibited greater confidence, sociability, and risk-taking in virtual environments, particularly when characterized offline by lower self-esteem and introversion. This phenomenon aligns with the Proteus effect (Yee & Bailenson, 2007), which describes the tendency for individuals to adjust their behavior in accordance with traits attributed to their virtual representation. However, as indicated by a systematic review (Szolin et al., 2023a), this effect is context-dependent and often short-lived, with its strength moderated by identification with the avatar, level of immersion, motivational factors, and interactional context. The underlying mechanisms of the Proteus effect remain insufficiently clarified and require further investigation, particularly with regard to the roles of norm susceptibility, perceived embodiment, priming processes, and cognitive dissonance reduction (Martin Coesel et al., 2024).

3.3.4.2 Positive Emotions: Favorable Affective Balance

Positive affective states associated with the use of digital technologies encompass a broad spectrum of emotions—from joy and excitement to calmness, relaxation, and self-transcendent experiences. Their emergence may constitute either an explicit goal of engagement or a by-product of goal-directed activity. Subsequent sections of this book examine diverse mechanisms through which emotions are generated in digital environments. At this stage, however, the focus is placed on the role of motivational factors and design logics in shaping these experiences.

It should be emphasized that affective states do not provide a normative criterion of “good” technology use, as positive emotions may co-occur with both adaptive and maladaptive patterns of digital practice. Within this framework, the DWB perspective offers a useful analytical lens: affective balance, conceptualized as the configuration of proximal outcomes arising from human–technology interaction, may signal the potential adaptiveness of digital practices, yet it requires interpretation in relation to individual autonomy and the broader context of functioning.

User emotions can be assessed using established self-report measures such as the Positive and Negative Affect Schedule (PANAS; Watson et al., 1988), the Scale of Positive and Negative Experience (SPANE; Diener et al., 2010), and the User Affective Experience Scale (UAX; Buck et al., 2018). By incorporating difficult emotions (e.g., anxiety and anger), these instruments enable the estimation of affective balance. In addition, research designs may employ methods capturing implicit emotional responses that arise during interaction with digital technologies, including EEG, galvanic skin response (GSR), and eye-tracking. Emerging tools such as AffectTracker (Fourcade et al., 2025) further enable continuous, real-time monitoring of users' emotional states within immersive environments.

Empirical evidence indicates that positive affect constitutes one of the key drivers initiating and sustaining engagement with digital tools. For instance, among Generation Z TikTok users, hedonic motivational components, such as enjoyment and curiosity, significantly predicted intention to use the platform (Rahayu et al., 2025). Comparable mechanisms have been observed in research on digital gaming, where the generation of positive emotions is closely intertwined with psychosocial processes unfolding during online interaction (Kaczmarek & Drążkowski, 2025). These emotions are elicited in response to achievement satisfaction, relief following the successful resolution of challenges, and constructive social exchanges, including the sharing of accomplishments and the receipt of supportive feedback. Such processes of interpersonal capitalization strengthen users' psychological resources, such as optimism, self-efficacy, and self-esteem, thereby facilitating more frequent and enduring experiences of positive affect.

Preferences for digital practices that facilitate the elicitation of positive affective states are shaped to a considerable extent by underlying design logics. Empirical findings indicate that in virtual environments, pleasant arousal is promoted by bright color schemes, warm lighting, open spatial configurations, natural landscapes, and soft geometric forms (Steinhaeusser et al., 2022). In digital ecosystems designed for educational purposes (e.g., STEM education, health education, and language learning), positive emotional experiences are fostered through coherent configurations of visual, interactive, and narrative elements. These include warm color palettes, interface anthropomorphism, a supportive communicative tone, and the harmonious integration of sound, music, typography, and visual space (Liu & Wang, 2025).

Complementing these design logics is the principle of emotional personalization, which involves adapting system behavior to users' preferences and current affective states. This tendency is reinforced by the growing implementation of affective computing in the form of emotion-aware systems capable of automatically—often without users' explicit awareness—detecting emotional states in real time (Faria et al., 2025). While such solutions enhance the adaptiveness and perceived empathy of digital technologies, they rely on the processing of sensitive emotional data, thereby raising substantial concerns regarding privacy boundaries and the ethical implications of continuous user monitoring.

The attractiveness of digital environments as spaces for generating positive affect may be further amplified by social mechanisms embedded in their communicative architectures. One such mechanism is emotional contagion, understood as the unconscious transmission of affective states between users (Hatfield et al., 1993; Chen et al., 2025b). The well-known experiment conducted by Adam Kramer et al. (2014), involving nearly 690,000 Facebook users, demonstrated that manipulating the emotional tone of content in users' news feeds influenced the affective valence of their subsequent posts, resulting in short-term fluctuations in emotional expression.

Research on emotional contagion aligns with the postulates of third-wave positive psychology by conceptualizing social media as affective ecosystems in which shared emotions co-construct collective well-being. Particular importance is attributed to culturally circulating forms of emotion, such as Internet memes, described as "contagious patterns of cultural information" (Knobel & Lankshear, 2007, p. 199). Studies conducted during the COVID-19 pandemic indicate that memes functioned as emotional buffers and tools of collective coping, facilitating transitions from anxiety to humor and contributing to the gradual normalization of tension (Flecha Ortiz et al., 2021). Importantly, not all emotions spread online with equal ease: basic emotions appear more readily "contagious" than cognitively and morally complex emotions, such as gratitude, whose transmission requires interpretation of intentions and relational context (Sciara et al., 2021). It may therefore be hypothesized that differential susceptibility of emotions to digital transmission shapes users' expectations regarding the effectiveness of specific digital practices as tools for eliciting particular affective states. This proposition, however, requires empirical verification.

3.3.4.3 Engagement: Challenge–Skill Calibration in Digital Settings

One of the key conditions for adaptive technology use in the domain of engagement is the dynamic calibration of the relationship between the level of challenge generated by digital environments and the user's competencies. When task difficulty remains in balance with individual skills, interaction with technology is conducive to the experience of flow. Disruptions of this balance—particularly in the form of excessive demands—may give rise to technostress. However, when accompanied by a preserved sense of control, agency, and task meaning, such strain may be reinterpreted as techno-eustress. Flow, the related sense of presence, and techno-eustress can all be conceptualized as positive proximal outcomes associated with the Engagement component of the PERMA model (Seligman, 2011).

3.3.4.3.1 Flow Experience in Digital Environments

Flow, conceptualized as an optimal experience, is a distinctive state of consciousness first described by Mihaly Csikszentmihalyi (1975), characterized by deep absorption in an activity and a high level of intrinsic satisfaction. Conditions conducive to the emergence of flow include a balance between challenge and skill, clear goals, and immediate feedback. Its core components comprise intense task-focused concentration (absorption), a sense of control, diminished self-consciousness, altered perception of time, and autotelic motivation—that is, engagement driven by intrinsic reward.

Like positive affect, flow should be treated as a significant yet nonnormative proximal outcome of human–technology interaction. This implies the necessity of identifying the conditions under which it supports adaptive forms of engagement. Flow can be assessed using qualitative descriptive techniques such as the Flow Questionnaire (FQ; Csikszentmihalyi & Csikszentmihalyi, 1988), through the experience sampling method (ESM), in which participants report their feelings and contextual circumstances during episodes of flow, or via standardized instruments such as the FSS (Jackson & Marsh, 1996) and its revised version (FSS-2; Jackson & Eklund, 2002).

Interest in examining flow in digital contexts emerged alongside the development of online marketing and the need to understand why certain online experiences are exceptionally engaging. Within this framework, flow has been analyzed as a psychological mechanism explaining enjoyment and sustained user engagement in interactions with websites and digital games. Thomas P. Novak et al. (2000) developed a structural model of flow in online environments, demonstrating that its occurrence depends on the balance between user skills and the challenges posed by the digital environment, as well as on factors such as perceived control, focused attention, telepresence, and positive affect. In this perspective, flow is conceptualized as a state of deep engagement with the medium that constitutes a source of intrinsic pleasure and promotes longer and more attentive participation in online environments.

In recent years, numerous studies have examined flow experiences within gameful approaches, including digital games, gamified systems, and rule-based interactive environments (e.g., Sweetser & Wyeth, 2005). These analyses confirm the classical assumption that the equilibrium between situational demands and player competencies is central to eliciting flow. At the same time, they indicate that higher levels of flow are associated with improved performance and greater enjoyment, and that elements such as appropriately calibrated challenge, goal clarity, and transparent feedback differentiate highly rated games from less engaging ones. However, a recent systematic review by Wilk Oliveira and Juho Hamari (2025) suggests that research in this domain requires methodological expansion to include behavioral, psychophysiological, and contextual measures, as well as the exploration of emerging experiential spaces, particularly immersive environments, that enable especially intense and complex forms of engagement.

Such methodological refinement is particularly important in light of the maladaptive potential of flow (junk flow and dark flow). Empirical findings indicate that although flow and problematic gaming constitute distinct constructs, they are interconnected through specific mechanisms of absorption and diminished self-regulation (Burleigh et al., 2025). This suggests that intense immersion may, under certain structural and individual conditions, contribute to dysregulated patterns of engagement rather than exclusively to adaptive involvement. Advancing knowledge in this area must be accompanied by greater theoretical precision, especially given the tendency within the gaming literature to use the terms flow, immersion, and presence interchangeably, thereby generating conceptual ambiguity (Michailidis et al., 2018). The distinction, overlap, and potential co-occurrence of these experiential states remain subjects of ongoing analytical inquiry.

3.3.4.3.2 Sense of Presence and Cybersickness

The phenomenon of presence has been extensively examined in the context of immersive technologies. Research in this domain typically involves the following technological artifacts:

- Panoramic VR (PVR, 360° VR, and monoscopic VR)—users explore a 360° environment without direct interaction; content is primarily passive (e.g., YouTube VR 360°);
- Depth Image VR (2.5D VR)—utilizes images enriched with depth maps (e.g., generated via Kinect), creating a scene resembling a photograph or video with partial spatiality;
- Virtual Reality (VR; 3D VR)—full immersion in a computer-generated 3D environment enabling interaction, movement, and embodied response (e.g., Meta Quest 3);
- Augmented Reality (AR)—digital elements are superimposed onto the real-world environment and perceived by users in real time (e.g., Pokémon GO);
- Mixed Reality (MR)—virtual and physical objects coexist and dynamically interact; virtual elements are spatially anchored and manipulable (e.g., Magic Leap 2).

The use of immersive technologies enhances engagement by facilitating sensory immersion in simulated environments. The intensity of the subjective experience of "being there" depends on two related yet distinct variables: immersion and presence. In the classical formulation by Mel Slater and Sylvia Wilbur (1997), *immersion* refers to the objective properties of the technological system, such as image quality, system latency, field of view, number of sensory channels, and degree of interactivity, that determine the medium's capacity to generate a realistic environment. *Presence*, by contrast, is a subjective state characterized by a strong sense of physical and emotional embeddedness within the virtual scene and by responding to events in that environment as if they were real. Beyond the immersive capacity of the system, the intensity of presence is influenced by user-related factors, including susceptibility to immersion, the level of interactivity afforded by the scene, and the absence of ergonomic or physiological disturbances such as cybersickness (Bailenson, 2018; Linares-Vargas & Cieza-Mostacero, 2025).

Elucidating the mechanisms underlying the sense of presence remains an important research objective. One of the most coherent explanatory frameworks has been proposed by Stefano Triberti et al. (2025), who interpret presence through the lens of predictive coding theory. According to this account, presence emerges from the integration of VR content and narrative structures, individual and cultural user characteristics, and intentional frameworks guiding action. VR systems may be particularly effective in minimizing discrepancies between predicted and incoming sensory signals, thereby reducing prediction error and fostering a compelling sense of immersion in the simulated environment.

From the perspective of DWB, the sense of presence functions as a key mediating variable. It not only facilitates the experience of flow in immersive environments but may also promote self-transcendent emotions (STEs) and stress reduction. Realizing this potential, however, requires minimizing cybersickness—a proximal outcome that diminishes the quality of adaptive technology use. Symptoms include nausea, dizziness, headaches, disorientation, eye strain, sweating, and fatigue. Cybersickness is generally attributed to sensory conflict between visual input and signals from the vestibular and proprioceptive systems (Chang et al., 2023). It may be exacerbated by dynamic scenes, rapid accelerations and rotations, visual instability, system latency, wide fields of view, and discrepancies between virtual camera movement and users' embodied sensations. Further research is necessary to establish evidence-based design and usage standards that maintain high levels of presence while minimizing physiological discomfort.

3.3.4.3.3 Technostress and Techno-Eustress

A situation in which an individual appraises current circumstances as a challenge constitutes a source of psychological stress (Lazarus & Folkman, 1984). In the context of technological demands, this form of strain assumes the specific manifestation of technostress. Monideepa Tarafdar et al. (2007) identified four principal categories of technostressors: techno-invasion—the intrusion of technology into personal life (e.g., the constant expectation of being online); techno-overload—the escalating volume of notifications, parallel tasks, and digital communications;

techno-complexity—the need for continuous learning driven by technological advancement; and techno-insecurity—concerns about job stability in the face of increasing technological competition and performance demands. The emergence of these stressors may initiate an exhaustion pathway leading to psychological and emotional fatigue, burnout, reduced productivity, and adaptive difficulties in technologically saturated environments (e.g., Ayyagari et al., 2011).

At the same time, research by Athina Ioannou et al. (2024) indicates that levels of technostress can be reduced through a set of self-regulatory practices, including task prioritization and attentional focus, selective responses to notifications, openness to exploring technological functionalities, and flexible adaptation of technology use to contextual demands. In addition, a systematic review by Pothuganti S. Kumar (2024) highlights the protective role of developing digital competencies, cultivating digital mindfulness, and fostering organizational cultures that promote work–life balance and regular breaks from screens.

Within the Enrichment perspective, however, analyses should extend beyond stress mitigation toward identifying the conditions under which beneficial proximal outcomes can be strengthened despite technological pressures. Hans Selye (1956), the originator of stress theory, distinguished between distress—a harmful and overloading state that diminishes quality of life—and eustress, a mobilizing form of stress that may support health and development. This distinction was adapted to the digital context by Julia T. Zielonka and Franz Rothlauf (2021) and subsequently elaborated by Monideepa Tarafdar et al. (2019), who integrated transactional stress theory with SDT to propose the concept of techno-eustress as a positive dimension of technology-related stress. In this framework, techno-eustress does not imply the absence of demands; rather, it refers to an appraisal of technological requirements in which developmental and functional gains outweigh associated costs.

Empirical evidence confirms the existence of four factors that strengthen techno-eustress, described as *techno-eustress creators* (Tarafdar et al., 2024):

- techno-mastery—the development of digital competencies that enhances employees' sense of agency and confidence;
- techno-autonomy—the ability to independently determine priorities and modes of task execution when using digital technologies;
- techno-relatedness—the facilitation of collaboration and constructive feedback through digital tools;
- techno-enrichment—enabling employees to create greater value and solve problems creatively through technological resources.

The Techno-Eustress Scale developed by Lígia Nascimento et al. (2024) provides a validated instrument for measuring this positive dimension of technological stress. High scores indicate that stress is interpreted as a mobilizing challenge conducive to increased productivity and professional effectiveness. An important research challenge concerns deepening our understanding of the associations between techno-eustress and individual dispositions integrated within the category of digital strengths. This direction of inquiry is justified both by the nature of the identified techno-eustress creators and by findings reported by Yu Zhao et al. (2024), which demonstrate that higher levels of techno-eustress are facilitated by individual coping resources in response to technological demands.

3.3.4.4 Relations: Bonds in a Hybrid World

This section systematizes research on the generation of relational experiences in digital environments associated with the Relationships component of the PERMA model (Seligman, 2011). The analyses encompass both one-sided parasocial interactions and bidirectional social and quasi-social interactions conducted with natural and artificial agents, embodied and disembodied, conversational, and non-conversational. Quasi-social interactions are defined here as bidirectional yet asymmetrical relationships with artificial systems, in which the sense of reciprocity is constructed through technological responsiveness.

Given the breadth of literature addressing relational aspects of adaptive technology use, the analytical pathways are organized according to increasing levels of relational density and mutuality. They range from emotionally charged bonds formed through parasocial interactions, through bidirectional engagements with artificial agents grounded in relational trust, to human–human relationships in digital environments examined within the frameworks of digital flourishing and digital friendship. They also encompass analyses of intimacy involving both human and artificial agents.

3.3.4.4.1 Parasocial Interactions

The term *parasocial interactions* (PSIs) was introduced by Donald Horton and Richard R. Wohl (1956) to describe a one-sided emotional bond between an audience member and the mediated persona appearing on screen. In digital environments, users may develop PSIs toward a wide spectrum of agents—ranging from biological and synthetic vloggers, gamers, and fitness trainers to virtual influencers. Particularly salient in intensifying these interactions are life-streaming formats such as mukbang or ASMR (autonomous sensory meridian response) broadcasts, which foster relaxation, pleasure, and a sense of observational intimacy. Compared to other forms of interaction, PSIs are defined by relational asymmetry: the audience member knows the persona and responds emotionally to them, whereas the persona lacks real knowledge of the individual viewer's existence. This dynamic is accompanied by an illusion of reciprocity, perceived closeness—sometimes even intimacy—and high levels of identification and engagement.

Available research suggests that PSIs may, under certain conditions, function as a form of digital emotional support. In situations of social isolation, such as during the COVID-19 pandemic, PSIs contributed to experiences of companionship, belonging, and emotional regulation, mitigating loneliness, stress, and anxiety (Jarzyna, 2021). They may also serve as sources of inspiration, motivation, and prosocial or educational modeling, thereby supporting individuals' participation in broader relational ecosystems online. These effects, however, are conditional and require further empirical verification (Schramm et al., 2024). An important line of inquiry concerns the potential transformation of repeated and intense PSIs into more stable parasocial relationships. Their strength depends both on characteristics of the mediated persona and on audience-related variables (Stein et al., 2024). On the side of the media figure, relevant factors include perceived human-likeness, subjective similarity, wishful identification, direct communication style, and impressions of social presence and quasi-responsiveness. On the side of the individual, prior platform experience, affiliative motivations, and attachment style appear significant; individuals with more anxious or avoidant relational patterns are more likely to engage intensely in PSIs.

From the perspective of DWB analyses, particular importance should be attached to identifying the properties of digital practices and platform architectures that shape the strength and quality of relational experiences generated through PSIs. Relevant variables include the intensity and regularity of exposure, the level of interactivity (e.g., live chats or audience reactions), para-responsiveness in communication (such as second-person address or visible responses to comments), and the communal rituals characteristic of specific online communities. The configuration of these elements constitutes a set of potential conditions for generating experiences of companionship, belonging, and perceived emotional support. A central analytical challenge lies in determining the circumstances under which such proximal outcomes function as effective buffers against loneliness (e.g., among older adults) and strengthen the relational component of flourishing, rather than contributing to the substitution of offline relationships.

3.3.4.4.2 Reciprocal Interactions with Artificial Agents

Individuals may engage in bidirectional interactions with artificial agents that vary in degree of embodiment, communicative modality, and functional role—from disembodied conversational chatbots, through embodied conversational agents in the form of avatars or humanoid robots, to systems based on LLMs and generative AI (GAI) integrated into immersive environments. These agents participate in a broad spectrum of socially oriented practices, including storytelling, socio-emotional skills training, therapeutic reminiscence, educational and creative collaboration, and companionship-oriented conversations aimed at maintaining contact and reducing loneliness (Arets et al., 2025).

One of the key factors determining the adaptive character of interactions with artificial agents within this analytical pathway is relational trust, grounded in the user's belief that the system will not act in ways detrimental to their well-being. A review of 100 publications from 2003 to 2023 on human–robot relationships (Campagna & Rehm, 2025) indicates that in early stages of interaction, trust is primarily based on the agent's perceptual and communicative features. Over time, interactional experiences, such as reliability, predictability of responses, and the adequacy of support provided, become increasingly important. This form of trust remains sensitive to micro-level interactional events: it may be rapidly undermined by system errors but can also be gradually rebuilt through subsequent positive experiences.

Relational trust is strengthened by affective design strategies, including adaptation of communicative tone, recognition of users' emotional signals, and maintenance of an impression of engagement. A high level of human-likeness also plays a significant role, intensifying anthropomorphization processes, enhancing social presence, and encouraging attributions of intentionality to the agent (Naneva et al., 2020). Anthropomorphization increases when systems are assigned personal names, display human-like appearance or movement, employ natural language (including first-person expressions), and generate empathic responses. The impression of copresence is further reinforced by social cues such as eye contact and joint attention toward shared objects (Willemse et al., 2018).

At the same time, research points to relational costs and limitations inherent in these interactions. Excessive similarity between a system and a human may evoke the uncanny valley effect (Masahiro Mori, 1970). This phenomenon emerges when high levels of visual or behavioral realism are not matched by fluidity of movement, expression, or communication, generating discomfort and erosion of trust. The effect has been observed not only in humanoid robotics but also in virtual avatars and synthesized speech (Lopatovska & Williams, 2018), underscoring the need to balance system functionality with the degree of anthropomorphization.

Positive experiences arising in interactions with embodied agents exhibit, in many respects, similarities to those accompanying human–human or human–animal relationships. A review of 30 empirical studies (Mitchell & Jeon, 2025) suggests that regular contact with humanoid and zoomorphic robots may lead to the development of attachment-like bonds, the intensity of which depends on relationship duration, the agent's unique identity, and the quality of its communicative competencies, including speech, gesture, eye contact, and emotional responsiveness. A potential inhibiting factor in these processes is a high level of anthropocentric beliefs, which foster instrumental treatment of robots. As demonstrated by Paweł Fortuna et al. (2024), such beliefs are negatively correlated with attributing mind and moral status to artificial agents, thereby substantially limiting the relational potential of these interactions.

3.3.4.4.3 Digital Flourishing

It should be emphasized that the construct of *digital flourishing* (DF) does not redefine or replace the broader concept of flourishing as developed within positive psychology. Rather, it represents one possible empirical operationalization of selected proximal outcomes observed in digital contexts. Sophie Janicke-Bowles et al. (2023) define DF as "feeling closely connected to and supported by one's online community, experiencing considerate and reflected interactions with others and consistent and authentic presentation in digital arenas, feeling inspired when comparing with others, and being in control of when to start and when to stop interacting online" (p. 1030). Although the concept draws on assumptions derived from SDT (Ryan & Deci, 2000), its empirical operationalization focuses predominantly on the relational dimension. This emphasis is reflected in the structure of the Digital Flourishing Scale (DFS) developed by the authors, as well as in its adolescent version (Rosič et al., 2022), which comprises five dimensions: connectedness, civil participation, positive social comparison, authentic self-disclosure, and self-control.

The dimension of *connectedness* (online social connection) included within DF refers to a positive relational experience opposed to loneliness and isolation, encompassing subjective feelings of closeness, identification with others, and participation in social groups and activities (Hansen et al., 2025). Research points to its potentially protective and strengthening function, although this effect is strongly context-dependent and shaped by the specific nature of online practices (Charmaraman et al., 2025). At the same time, Mirko Duradoni et al. (2022a) demonstrated that connectedness may be conceptualized not only as an outcome of technology use but also as a component of online social capital. This suggests a dual role of the construct within the architecture of digital experience: on the one hand, as a direct subjective indicator of relational quality online; on the other, as a relational resource mediating the transfer of support, trust, and information. Further research (Duradoni et al., 2025) indicates that among individuals with high levels of technological dependence, higher levels of online social capital are associated with greater well-being and better digital life balance.

Another component of DF is *civil participation*. Empirical findings suggest that digital technologies play an ambivalent role in this domain: they lower barriers to civic engagement and facilitate new forms of deliberation, yet they may also intensify polarization, susceptibility to misinformation, and erosion of social trust (Boulianne, 2020). These effects are strongly moderated by users' digital competencies, particularly their capacity for critical content evaluation and reflective regulation of engagement.

Social comparison, also included within DF, has been extensively examined as a significant predictor of well-being in social media contexts (Gudka et al., 2021). Research conducted in relation to Instagram shows that exposure to content eliciting upward comparison is associated with an immediate decrease in body-esteem, whereas downward comparison is linked to increases in both body-esteem and overall self-esteem (Taylor & Armes, 2024). Notably, even brief exposure to Instagram-style posts, incorporating visible numbers of likes and comments, was sufficient to produce measurable changes in body evaluation and, in the case of downward comparison, in self-esteem. These findings highlight the sensitivity of self-evaluative processes in digital environments to the micro-dynamics of socially generated content and underscore the need for further research on the relationships between the frequency and qualitative nature of social comparisons and subjective evaluations of relational experiences online.

An important negative proximal outcome that may accompany online interactions and intersect with DF is *Zoom fatigue*. This phenomenon refers to a sense of exhaustion resulting from the cumulative effects of task pressure, perceptual constraints, and the reduction of spontaneous dimensions of social interaction in online meetings (Bergmann et al., 2023). Evidence suggests that such costs may be mitigated through design and pedagogical interventions, including disabling self-view, simplifying visual layouts, and actively engaging participants in the interaction process (Basch et al., 2025). These findings provide practical guidance for designing more relationally balanced remote work environments.

3.3.4.4.4 Digital Friendship

As an increasing proportion of social interaction shifts to online environments, the question arises to what extent these relationships can mirror the functions and significance of traditional interpersonal bonds. According to Malcolm R. Parks and Kory Floyd (1996), pioneers in the study of *digital friendship*, friendships formed in virtual spaces need not constitute impoverished versions of offline relationships, as online interactions may exhibit high levels of trust, authenticity, and emotional involvement. These conclusions, however, contrast with strands of philosophical skepticism regarding the possibility of fully realizing friendship in digital contexts. Dean Cocking and Steve Matthews (2000) argued that the structural features of online communication, characterized by selective self-disclosure and heightened control over self-presentation, may constrain the process of mutual interpretation that lies at the core of friendship. In their view, friendship requires spontaneous and not fully controlled exchanges of emotions, gestures, and embodied reactions that foster the development of relational identity, whereas online communication, particularly text-based interaction, reduces unintentional social cues and may generate distorted representations of self and other.

Contemporary empirical research drawing on data from online environments has gradually refined these positions, presenting a more nuanced account of digitally mediated relationships that resemble friendship. A systematic review by Tyler Prochnow et al. (2025), encompassing 23 studies on adolescent online relationships, indicates that exclusively online friendships may, under certain conditions, serve a protective function. This appears particularly relevant for vulnerable youth (e.g., those experiencing suicidal ideation), for whom having at least one "online-only friend" attenuates the association between relational stressors (e.g., victimization) and subsequent suicide risk. At the same time, evidence suggests that deteriorations in well-being are associated with passive social media use, exposure to social comparison processes, and the absence of adequate support following the disclosure of distressing experiences.

Further analyses should more systematically examine how specific practices of maintaining online bonds, such as synchronous and asynchronous communication or participation in interest-based communities, generate relational proximal outcomes conducive to digital friendship. A central research challenge lies in specifying the conditions under which such processes genuinely enhance well-being, taking into account individual differences, cultural variability, and platform-specific contexts.

3.3.4.4.5 Intimacy Online and Cyberintimacy

Intimacy in digital environments refers to the experience of emotional closeness, trust, and reciprocity within interactions mediated by digital technologies (Lomanowska & Guitton, 2016). Research in this domain addresses technologically mediated closeness both between humans (*online intimacy*) and between humans and technological artifacts (*cyberintimacy*)—ranging from interactions in dating applications and communication via social media to relationships with romantic and sexual dimensions.

Unlike offline intimacy, online intimacy does not require physical copresence or tactile contact. Its development may be accelerated by anonymity or an increased sense of safety, which facilitates self-disclosure and the exchange of perceived social support. These experiences may form diverse configurations of relational proximal outcomes, some strengthening the individual (e.g., feelings of closeness and security), others potentially burdensome (e.g., pressure for immediate responsiveness or jealousy).

A review by Ian Kwok and Annie B. Wescott (2020) indicates that digital technologies can support all stages of the romantic relationship life cycle—initiation, maintenance, and, where applicable, dissolution. During initiation, technologies expand access to potential partners and facilitate self-disclosure, potentially accelerating the development of closeness. In the maintenance phase, messaging platforms and social media help sustain connection, particularly in long-distance relationships, yet may simultaneously intensify expectations of constant availability and foster misinterpretations arising from communicative ambiguity. During relationship dissolution, persistent "digital traces" (e.g., messages, photos, and shared content) may complicate emotional closure and prolong grieving processes.

A specific form of digital intimacy in which emotional closeness intertwines with symbolically represented corporeality is sexting—the digital expression of flirtation or sexuality. A systematic review by Yunhao Hu et al. (2023) suggests that in voluntary, consensual contexts grounded in mutual trust, sexting may constitute an adaptive form of sexual exploration, fostering intimacy and partner communication. In long-distance relationships or contexts of limited physical proximity, it may strengthen emotional bonds and relational continuity. Predictors of healthy, consensual sexting include positive peer norms and beliefs regarding its acceptability within close relationships.

With respect to cyberintimacy, increasing scholarly attention has focused on romantic relationships between humans and AI-driven agents. Among so-called "AI romantic companions" are conversational applications (e.g., Replika), virtual partners (e.g., VR Kanojo), embodied social robots (e.g., Harmony), and generative AI-based systems (e.g., Forever Companion AI) that adapt to users' communicative styles and construct relational narratives based on interactional data.

A review of 23 empirical studies (Ho et al., 2025) indicates that users form complex relational bonds with these technologies, encompassing emotional, companionate, and sexual components. The character of these relationships varies depending on the type of agent: interactions with chatbots are more frequently described as empathy-based and "safe" forms of intimacy, whereas relationships with social robots are characterized by greater sensory realism but reduced emotional flexibility. The authors argue that future research should focus on four key areas: (1) empirical validation of the positive effects of relationships with AI; (2) identification of factors protecting against excessive emotional dependency and affective manipulation; (3) cross-cultural and demographic analyses; and (4) comparative studies examining the role of embodiment, sensory modality, and affective responsiveness in shaping attachment dynamics. The development of this field should be accompanied by the construction of a dedicated theoretical model clarifying the functions of AI-mediated relationships in relation to human bonds, whether compensatory, substitutive, or destabilizing, as well as by the standardization of measurement tools capable of reliably assessing the quality and dynamics of human–AI relationships, including the subjective sense of reciprocity.

3.3.4.5 Meaning: Value-Driven Digital Experiences

Adaptive technology use associated with strengthening the Meaning domain in the PERMA model (Seligman, 2011) is linked to the generation of value-driven digital experiences. These constitute proximal outcomes of digital practices oriented toward the realization of moral, communal, or spiritual values. One example is self-transcendent media experiences, which may enable users to move beyond an egocentric perspective and evoke moral emotions that reinforce a sense of community, interdependence, and spiritual significance within digital participation (Oliver, 2022). Such experiences represent the eudaimonic dimension of digital life, in which meaning is expressed through engagement with the good and participation in something larger than the individual self.

Within digital ecosystems, individuals engage in reflective dialogues concerning life purpose, authenticity, and shared values, thereby forming communities of meaning (Baym, 2015). These communities are sustained through digital rituals and symbolic communication, in which repetitive acts of sharing, commenting, and co-creating content become practices of belonging and collective sense-making. As demonstrated by Tommaso Trillò et al. (2022), at least sixteen types of such rituals can be distinguished in online environments—from relational practices (e.g., public apologies and birthday wishes), through disclosure-oriented formats (e.g., "day-in-the-life" vlogs and Q&A sessions), to commemorative practices (e.g., collective mourning following the death of public figures). Each of these forms warrants empirical exploration within the framework of DWB analyses.

A theoretical foundation for studying digital rituals is provided by the concept of technology-mediated interaction rituals (TMIR) proposed by Lars E. F. Johannessen (2023). He argues that rituals traditionally associated with offline contexts may also occur in digital environments, provided they enable emotional synchronization, symbolic boundary formation, and a shared sense of meaning. In such practices, technology functions as a ritual mediator—it not only transmits content but also organizes communal experience through rhythmic communication patterns, repeated gestures (e.g., likes and shares), and collective participation in symbolically charged online events.

Religious and spiritual practices offer a salient example of value-driven digital experiences. A systematic review by Constantin Grigore and Alexandra Cobzeanu (2025) demonstrates that such practices are increasingly enacted through online communal rituals. Livestreamed prayers, virtual pilgrimages, prayer applications, and symbolic acts such as "holy selfies" do not merely substitute for offline practices but constitute novel sense-making forms in their own right. The COVID-19 pandemic acted as a catalyst in this transformation, fostering the emergence of transnational spiritual communities in which experiences of the sacred are co-constructed and negotiated within mediated spaces. These developments also reconfigure religious authority, shifting it from institutional structures toward community-based interactions, in which technology becomes a medium of transcendence rather than its negation.

Digital practices that foster the aforementioned eudaimonic proximal outcomes require active and intentional participation in online environments (Meier & Reinecke, 2023). Meaningfulness, understood as the experience of purpose, significance, and life coherence, does not arise from mere exposure to content but from the quality of interaction, dialogue, and collaborative narrative construction.

The cultivation of communicative rituals and authentic social bonds is therefore crucial for transcending purely hedonic gratifications. By contrast, passive content consumption may yield ambivalent effects, ranging from inspiration and elevation to feelings of emptiness and exclusion.

The factors shaping the quality and intensity of experiences that strengthen meaning and deepen spirituality require further systematic investigation. This includes research on the spontaneous formation of online communities of meaning as well as on the mechanisms facilitating solidarity, copresence, and shared significance. Moreover, analyses of ritualized social coordination in digital environments may provide valuable insights into phenomena such as group flow or collective emotional immersion, in which synchronized expressions, gestures, and affective states give rise to emergent communal experiences of meaning and transcendence.

3.3.4.6 Accomplishment: Learning, Work, Sport, and Creativity

Digital environments increasingly create opportunities for personal development through engagement in activities that strengthen the Accomplishment domain of the PERMA model (Seligman, 2011). Adaptive technology use in this respect is expressed in the generation of experiences that foster the development of competencies, enhance individuals' sense of efficacy, and provide satisfaction derived from achievement. This section examines analytical pathways related to the elicitation of such outcomes in the domains of digital learning, professional career development, electronic sports, and digital creativity.

3.3.4.6.1 Digital Learning

The term *digital learning*, often referred to as *online learning*, encompasses a broad spectrum of learning modalities implemented through digital technologies—ranging from blended and fully online instruction to mobile and adaptive learning, as well as immersive and collaborative educational environments. Collectively, these modalities form complex ecosystems that enable flexible, personalized, and socially embedded support for the development of cognitive, self-regulatory, and social competencies. Their impact on flourishing depends on how learning practices are regulated, as this regulation shapes the balance between beneficial and burdensome proximal outcomes generated through engagement with digital environments.

As emphasized by Yumei Zou et al. (2025) in "Digital Learning in the 21st Century: Trends, Challenges, and Innovations in Technology Integration," the integration of digital tools in education facilitates the construction of individualized learning pathways in which learners can monitor their progress, experiment with strategies, and cultivate metacognitive capacities. However, the optimal realization of these developmental opportunities depends on multiple interrelated factors that influence both the quality of learning experiences and objective educational outcomes (Hu & Xiao, 2025; Meng et al., 2024). At the individual level, key determinants include self-discipline, autonomous motivation, digital competence, and emotional engagement—resources that enable learners to plan their studies, monitor progress, and sustain effort under conditions of reduced external supervision and flexible scheduling. Equally important are socio-emotional factors such as the quality and intensity of interaction, collaboration, and a sense of belonging to a learning community, all of which counteract isolation and strengthen engagement. The effectiveness of online education further depends on the quality of instructional design, including a clear course structure, explicit instructions, diversified forms of activity, and access to timely feedback. These elements are reinforced by strategies of personalization, scaffolding, and gamification. At a more fundamental level, technological boundary conditions, such as infrastructure quality, Internet stability, access to hardware and digital resources, as well as platform ergonomics, usability, and multimedia integration, remain prerequisites for realizing these pedagogical intentions.

A significant research challenge concerns identifying how these determinants influence learning effectiveness, for instance, through the optimization of cognitive load. Excessive sensory stimulation, complex navigation, or overextended interactivity may generate extraneous load, thereby overtaxing working memory resources and limiting deep information processing. A promising line of inquiry involves empirical examination of the concept of cognitive alignment load, which postulates the alignment of digital environment complexity with the learner's competence level, the nature of the cognitive task, and intended learning outcomes (Skulmowski & Xu, 2022). This perspective motivates the design of educational ecosystems capable of dynamically monitoring cognitive and emotional indicators and adapting difficulty level, pacing, and content presentation accordingly.

An area of particularly intensive investigation within digital learning concerns the effectiveness of educational chatbots. This category includes AI-driven tutoring systems providing real-time guidance and feedback, socio-emotional chatbots that enhance motivation and reduce stress, task-oriented tools supporting collaboration and habit formation, as well as systems based on LLMs that enable semantically rich interaction, conceptual explanation, and the stimulation of cognitive creativity.

A review conducted by Lasha Labadze et al. (2023) indicates that the effectiveness of educational chatbots depends on their functional role, level of adaptive intelligence, and depth of user interaction. These systems can substantially support learning processes when designed as learning companions—tools that strengthen reflection, motivation, and self-regulation—rather than merely as information-delivery mechanisms. Particularly effective are solutions that engage learners in Socratic dialogue, provide personalized feedback, and support educational planning. Conversely, excessive automation and a lack of transparency regarding knowledge sources may undermine trust and diminish cognitive engagement.

3.3.4.6.2 Professional Growth in Digital Environments

The progressive digitalization and automation of work processes have increasingly positioned the question of well-being–supportive technology use in occupational contexts as a relatively autonomous research domain (POP 2.0; van Zyl et al., 2024). This development underscores the importance of designing human–AI collaborative workspaces that enhance both individual satisfaction and organizational effectiveness (Gladden et al., 2022; Ladhari et al., 2026; Modliński et al., 2022; Pollak et al., 2025; Rożnowski et al., 2026). Given the growing maturity of this field, the following section highlights a still emerging yet professionally consequential phenomenon: *digital entrepreneurship.*

Digital entrepreneurship represents an adaptive mode of digital tool use in which technologies are not merely instruments for executing predefined goals but become active environments for testing hypotheses about one's competencies, aspirations, and developmental trajectories. At the same time, they function as spaces for exploring the monetization potential embedded in digital ecosystem affordances. Analyses of this phenomenon should therefore concentrate on identifying the conditions under which an individual's creative response to the developmental opportunities perceived within digital environments translates into personal and professional success.

The significance of research on digital entrepreneurship is reinforced by the increasing number of professions in which digital technologies constitute the environment of occupational activity (e.g., influencers), its primary tool (e.g., designers), and in some cases even its product (e.g., programmers). Importantly, research on *digital entrepreneurship intention* (DEInt) indicates that the mechanisms underlying entrepreneurial engagement in digital contexts differ substantially from classical models of entrepreneurial intention (Alkhalaileh, 2021). Whereas traditional frameworks emphasize market experience, access to financial and social capital, and managerial competence, DEInt appears to depend more strongly on digital competencies, DL, and the capacity to learn under conditions of uncertainty and rapid feedback. Complementary findings reported by João M. Lopes et al. (2025), based on research conducted among Portuguese students, demonstrate that DEInt more frequently emerges from openness to experimentation and the desire to participate in innovation culture than from strictly economic motivations. Within this perspective, the question "Am I an entrepreneurial person?" gives way to a different inquiry: "Am I capable of creatively shaping the digital environment, and do I perceive it as my own sphere of action?"

A promising direction for future research involves comparing the dynamics of DWB among digital entrepreneurs with those observed in other technology user groups. Entrepreneurship is associated with elevated levels of risk and requires continuous monitoring of digital environments, identification of opportunities, reinterpretation of constraints as resources, and flexible configuration of relationships between goals, technologies, and contextual conditions (Ahmetoglu et al., 2017). Although demanding, this mode of functioning may also be developmentally enriching. It can be hypothesized that digital entrepreneurs interpret the proximal outcomes of digital practices differently, classifying them as benefits or harms not on the basis of immediate hedonic value but according to their instrumental and developmental significance—for example, interpreting costs as investments. Experiences that might constitute frustration or burden for other users may instead function as feedback signals, strengthen agency, and support long-term adaptation. Consequently, one may hypothesize the existence of a distinctive DWB profile among digital entrepreneurs, characterized by short-term well-being fluctuations coexisting with higher tolerance for uncertainty and a stronger orientation toward growth and achievement. These propositions require empirical verification through comparative studies that account for different phases of the entrepreneurial lifecycle.

3.3.4.6.3 Electronic Sports

The term *electronic sports* (*eSports*, *e-sports*, and *cybersports*) refers to "a form of sports where the primary aspects of the sport are facilitated by electronic systems," in which "the input of players and teams as well as the output of the eSports system are mediated by human–computer interfaces" (Hamari & Sjöblom, 2017, p. 211). This category encompasses both professional and recreational forms of participation. When players' activity is combined with the performative dimension of public exposure, it takes the form of live-streaming eSports. Importantly, the term *digital sports* carries a distinct meaning, referring to the digitization of traditional sport, including the use of technology in training (e.g., sensors and wearable devices), broadcasting, and performance analytics (Tang et al., 2023).

From a psychological perspective, eSport may be conceptualized as a domain of self-actualization in which individuals pursue achievement and mastery through technologically mediated competition. Empirical findings suggest that systematic engagement in eSport can support multidimensional human development (Hayburn et al., 2025). At the cognitive level, players demonstrate improvements in executive functioning, selective attention, motor control, and decision-making. At the emotional level, eSport participation may foster the acquisition of emotion regulation strategies, including preperformance routines, visualization techniques, and breath control. In the social domain, it may promote the development of collaboration, communication, and team coordination skills while strengthening a sense of belonging. Additionally, eSport competitions may generate material rewards and prestige. For example, the League of Legends World Championship offers a prize pool exceeding $2 million, and the Esports World Cup provides a total prize pool surpassing $70 million (Kachwala, 2025).

From the perspective of adaptive technology-use patterns, eSport offers a paradigmatic example of digital practice in which achievement and well-being are shaped through a dynamic balance between the exploitation of developmental opportunities (benefits) and the effective mitigation of associated costs (harms). A key mechanism underpinning both high performance and the maintenance of well-being in this domain is self-regulation (Riedl & Verschuuren, 2025). Self-regulatory capacities are essential for counteracting potential costs of eSport participation, including musculoskeletal strain, physical inactivity, circadian rhythm disruption, stress overload, and the risk of burnout. They also fulfill a normative and ethical function, enabling resistance to unethical behaviors such as prejudice and sexism, the use of e-doping practices, or the manipulation of competitive outcomes. In this respect, eSport constitutes an important field of inquiry not only in terms of performance enhancement but also in relation to the cultivation of digital responsibility among technology users.

3.3.4.6.4 Digital Creativity

One of the most dynamically developing domains of digital technology use is digital creativity (Lee, 2015). In this context, the adaptive use of innovation is expressed through the generation of experiences that signal an expansion of human creative capacities, for example, through collaboration in networked online environments and the exploration of new forms of partnership with generative AI systems. Understood in this way, digital creativity opens a space for innovative digital practices that generate diverse proximal outcomes, ranging from enhanced agency and competence, through experiences of authenticity, flow, and STEs, to engagement with beauty, satisfaction, and a heightened sense of meaning in life (see Giraldez-Hayes et al., 2025).

From a broader perspective, digital creativity constitutes a process that not only supports achievement but also fosters communal experiences through the democratization of access to creative tools. Its specificity is reflected in a paradigmatic shift in the understanding of creativity: from the model of the "individual genius" operating in isolation toward a conception of the human being as a networked agent, co-constructing meanings and artifacts within dynamic digital ecosystems (Samper-Márquez & Oropesa-Ruiz, 2025; Wulan et al., 2025). In this framework, the value of creative activity derives not only from the originality of individual ideas but also from the ability to share, develop, and reinterpret the ideas of others. In this sense, digital creativity may be conceptualized as a form of shared self-realization (co-agency), and its investigation aligns closely with the assumptions of the third wave of positive psychology.

A particularly promising line of inquiry concerns the synergistic collaboration between humans and AI systems, described as human–AI co-creativity (Haase & Pokutta, 2024). Within this approach, AI ceases to function merely as a supportive tool and becomes an active participant in the creative process. Four levels of AI integration in creative activity may be distinguished: from basic digital tools (Digital Pen), through specialized task-oriented systems (AI Task Specialist), interactive assistants (AI Assistant), to fully co-creative systems (AI Co-Creator), in which human and AI share intention, goals, and responsibility for the creative outcome. At the highest level of integration, a qualitatively new form of creativity may emerge—one in which satisfaction derives from relational interaction rather than competition with technology.

Within a DWB framework, one of the central questions concerns the nature of proximal outcomes generated within human–AI co-creativity processes. The evaluation of creative products depends not only on the subjectively assessed quality of creative experiences but also on the social appraisal of outputs—particularly in contexts marked by ambiguous authorship and contested authenticity. Generative models operate on opaque datasets and complex processing mechanisms, thereby blurring the boundaries between inspiration, transformation, and reproduction of content (Fortuna & Modliński, 2026). Consequently, aesthetic experiences of co-creation with AI may constitute both a source of developmental benefits, such as increased creative satisfaction and meaning, and potential harms associated with normative, ethical, and identity-related tensions. Empirical verification of how these experiential configurations contribute to or destabilize flourishing represents a significant and forward-looking research challenge.

3.3.5 Summary

The Enrichment perspective, by adopting DWB as an analytical framework, focuses on explaining the dynamic quality of everyday digital technology use and its potential to enrich human functioning. What is central in this approach is not the intensity or frequency of technology engagement, but the qualitative balance of proximal outcomes generated by digital practices embedded within the broader ecology of an individual's life.

Research conducted within this perspective is organized around four complementary dimensions of digital technology use quality. Balanced use refers to the harmonious integration of digital practices with daily rhythms, social roles, and personal goals. Healthy use concerns the conditions under which engagement with digital tools sustains, rather than undermines, psychophysiological functioning. Autonomous use emphasizes agentic and reflective regulation of technology engagement. In this form of use, the satisfaction of basic psychological needs coexists with systemic safeguards that prevent its transformation into compulsive or dependency-driven patterns. Adaptive use, in turn, denotes purpose-oriented and functionally appropriate deployment of digital tools. This deployment occurs across domains corresponding to a broad spectrum of flourishing components, including positive affect, engagement, relationships, meaning, and accomplishment.

The Enrichment perspective clearly differentiates three levels of analysis: digital practices, the proximal outcomes they generate (both benefits and costs), and distal outcomes related to components of flourishing. This distinction prevents the conflation of the quality of digital experiences with broad well-being indicators and enables precise modeling of mediating mechanisms and moderating conditions. Importantly, analyses conducted within the Enrichment perspective do not offer a normative prescription for "good" technology use. Rather, they provide the foundation for a coherent research program focused on conceptual clarification, operationalization, and empirical validation of high-quality patterns of digital engagement. In this way, the systematic accumulation of empirical findings expands the explanatory landscape of technology research beyond PTU-focused approaches.

3.4 Enhancement Perspective: PTIs

Within the epistemic model of PCyb, the Enhancement perspective organizes research on intentionally designed digital interventions aimed at strengthening flourishing. Its central research question can be formulated as follows: What conditions determine the effectiveness of PTIs?

The Enhancement perspective specifies the status of PTIs as a distinct category of PPIs in which technology is not merely a vehicle for content delivery but a constitutive element of the intervention protocol. Like classical PPIs, they are practices aimed at improving the well-being of individuals and groups (Schueller et al., 2014); however, their specificity lies in the deliberate use of digital affordances to intensify developmental effects. This anticipated beneficial impact of PTIs is captured by the term *enhancement* employed in the name of the perspective. In this sense, enhancement does not denote an escalation of experiential intensity. Rather, it refers to a qualitative transformation of functioning. Such transformation may be grounded in processes of regulation, stabilization, compensation, or the activation of resources.

The development and empirical testing of PTIs operationalize postulates articulated, among others, within the frameworks of Positive Technology (Riva et al., 2012) and Positive Computing (Calvo & Peters, 2014). A strong impetus for their expansion was the increased reliance on technological support and automation of PPIs observed during the COVID-19 pandemic. Their scope has gradually broadened to include interventions employing diverse types of digital tools, addressed to users representing different age groups, environments, and cultural contexts. Although knowledge about PTIs is integrated within the Enhancement perspective, the primary aim of analysis remains the elucidation of the psychological mechanisms underlying the user's positive transformation as the subject of intervention. This entails a focus not only on which PTIs, for whom, and under what conditions lead to desirable developmental changes, but above all on why and through which processes these changes occur.

A useful theoretical framework for this approach is provided by the work of Reuben Rusk and Lea Waters (2015). Based on an analysis of over 18,000 publications in positive psychology, they identified five domains of psychosocial functioning that mediate the impact of interventions on well-being. These domains are attention and awareness, comprehension and coping, emotions, goals and habits, and virtues and relationships. These domains may be treated not only as discrete end targets of PTIs but also as mediating variables linking intervention design to its outcomes.

Modeling the human–technology relationship at the level of mechanisms of change additionally requires consideration of factors that facilitate participant engagement in PTIs. In this regard, valuable insights are offered by concepts developed within HCI (e.g., Rogers et al., 2023), which enable the identification of interface affordances and design logics conducive to initiating and sustaining the change process.

A rigorous evaluation of PTI effectiveness requires the application of stringent experimental procedures analogous to those used in PPI research (van Zyl et al., 2019), as well as the selection of appropriate methods and indicators operationalizing intervention effects (see Table 3.5). In cases where the PTI under examination constitutes a technologically supported version of a classical PPI, it is advisable to design studies including a control group implementing an "analog" intervention protocol with established effectiveness. Although this approach expands the research model applied to PTIs, it is justified if the objective is not merely to multiply technologically supported interventions but to identify solutions that are most beneficial for individuals and supportive of their well-being.

The specific methodological features of designing and testing PTIs are discussed in greater detail in the following section.

3.4.1 Conceptual and Methodological Framework

This section outlines the conceptual and methodological foundations for research on PTIs. It presents a proposed typology of these interventions, identifies conditions that maximize both efficacy and effectiveness, and formulates guiding principles for their ethical design and implementation.

Table 3.5 Measurement categories, methods, and instruments/indicators used in the Enhancement perspective.

Measurement category	Method	Psychological target	Instruments/indicators
Behavioral observation	Behavioral metrics	Intervention fidelity	Adherence to the intervention protocol
Behavioral observation	Behavioral metrics	Engagement indicators	Retention; churn; and return visits
Behavioral observation	Behavioral metrics	Task effectiveness	Performance scores; completion accuracy
Behavioral observation	Digital trace and log data	Intervention engagement	Task completion frequency; time spent in the application; and number of completed modules
Behavioral observation	Digital trace and log data	User behavior patterns	Number of clicks; navigation paths; and interaction sequences
Behavioral observation	Online interaction data	Social engagement	Messages; comments; and interaction frequency
Behavioral observation	Real-time analytics	Adaptive intervention processes	Intervention tailoring in JITAI (just-in-time adaptive intervention)
Self-report	Questionnaire	Flourishing and well-being components	Standardized positive psychology instruments
Self-report	Questionnaire	Intervention adherence	Frequency and subjective compliance ratings (e.g., “How often did you complete the task?,” “To what extent did you follow the instructions?”)
Self-report	ESM (intensive longitudinal self-report)	Momentary experiences (e.g., emotions, flow, awe, and connectedness)	Repeated in situ self-reports
Self-report/behavioral observation	N-of-1 and intensive longitudinal designs	Within-person variability and individual change dynamics	Repeated time-series data; person-specific trajectories

Psychophysiological measures	Wearable and smartphone sensing	Physiological activation and regulation	Heart rate; HRV; and GSR
Qualitative approaches	Case studies	Intervention effectiveness and individual trajectories	Idiographic analysis
Qualitative approaches	Diary methods	Subjective experience and change processes	BPS exercises; savoring diaries
Qualitative approaches	In-depth interviews	Meanings and perceived impact	Semi-structured interviews; focus groups
Qualitative approaches	Narrative analysis	Transformation processes	Narrative accounts of change

Note: Behavioral observation refers to objective indicators derived from digital trace and log data, real-time analytics, and other digitally mediated data sources used to monitor engagement and intervention processes. Self-report methods include both global questionnaires and intensive longitudinal approaches such as experience sampling. Some approaches combine self-report and behavioral observation, including N-of-1 designs, to examine dynamic within-person processes over time. Psychophysiological measures capture physiological processes associated with engagement and regulation during intervention use, including data collected via wearable and mobile sensing technologies. Qualitative approaches are included as complementary research designs used to explore meanings, processes, and individual trajectories of change.

3.4.1.1 Conceptual Criteria

The term *positive technology intervention* is not new in the literature (Gradito Dubord et al., 2026). Semantically, it overlaps with expressions such as *online positive psychology interventions* (Parks, 2014) and *digital positive psychology interventions* (Biber & Davis, 2024), while more explicitly emphasizing its connection to the Positive Technology tradition (Riva et al., 2012).

To date, no coherent definition or typology of such interventions has been established. A central challenge lies in determining the criteria by which an intervention may be classified as "digital." It appears justified to assume that a defining feature of PTIs should be the use of digital technologies in a manner that makes a substantive contribution to positive individual change, rather than merely serving as a neutral medium for content delivery.

A useful analytical tool is provided by James Pawelski's Elements Model (2020), according to which any intervention may be examined through five constitutive elements responsible for its effectiveness. Technology may be incorporated at each of these levels:

- desired outcome—enabling the shaping of outcomes specific to digital environments (e.g., digital strengths);
- target system—constituting the environment within which and upon which the intervention acts (e.g., online interactions);
- target change—modifying the trajectory of change within the target system (e.g., immersive VR environments);
- active ingredient—generating the causal mechanism that produces change (e.g., VR-induced awe);
- activity—determining the mode of intervention delivery (e.g., notification systems).

On this basis, it is possible to distinguish between broad and narrow understandings of PTIs, while acknowledging that the legitimacy of such a distinction and the criteria defining the status of technology in the process should remain open to debate.

In the broad sense, PTIs encompass programs intentionally designed to strengthen components of flourishing in which technology performs a significant structural function (as a target system or activity), enabling automation, scalability, and integration within platform infrastructures. In this view, technology is constitutive when it shapes the intervention's structure and delivery, even if it does not directly generate the mechanism of change. This is particularly evident in AI-driven systems that enable continuous monitoring and adaptive personalization of interventions, dynamically shaping their structure and delivery over time (Thakkar et al., 2024). This allows the Enhancement perspective to include interventions employing behavior change technologies aimed at promoting or discouraging specific behaviors, for example, through warnings, prebunking strategies, or informational labels (e.g., Alberts et al., 2024).

In the narrow sense, technology constitutes a necessary condition for the mechanism of change (target change and active ingredient), such that the core transformative experience could not occur without it (e.g., immersive VR exposure). Here, technology plays a causal rather than merely supportive role.

Interventions occupying a borderline status include classical PPIs delivered through technological means (e.g., specialist-led group training conducted online). An example is Positive Emotions Training (PoET; Niemann et al., 2023), a multimodal online intervention targeting eleven constructs (e.g., hope, optimism, and spirituality). In such cases, technology functions as the target system, yet its contribution to intervention effectiveness requires empirical verification. In line with the principle that "the medium is the message," the digital environment may operate as a moderator of intervention effects and should therefore be treated as a theoretically and empirically relevant variable.

3.4.1.2 Typologies

The proposed typologies of PTIs are open and heuristic in nature. They are based on five criteria: intervention aims, theoretical basis, research status, type of technology used, and level of automation. Although the remainder of this chapter discusses PTIs primarily according to the criterion of intervention aims, each of these dimensions may serve as a valid basis for systematizing research within the Enhancement perspective.

3.4.1.2.1 Intervention Aims

The range of well-being outcomes attainable through PTIs is extensive and can be expected to expand systematically. PTIs may be either single-component or multicomponent in structure, exerting simultaneous effects across multiple domains of functioning.

Within the Positive Technology framework (Riva et al., 2012), beneficial effects were associated with the hedonic, eudaimonic, and social dimensions of well-being. More fine-grained classifications have been developed within positive psychology. For example, Acacia C. Parks and Stephen Schueller (2014) identified 12 areas of intervention (e.g., gratitude interventions and empathy-related interventions). Similarly, Jolanta Burke (2025) distinguished fifteen PPIs, labeling them according to their aim (e.g., kindness), the technique employed (e.g., counting blessings), or the term established in the literature (e.g., the Best Possible Self [BPS]).

An intermediate position may be derived from the concept of the flexible map of flourishing proposed by Tim Lomas et al. (2024b), which distinguishes physical, psychological, social, and spiritual dimensions of well-being, complemented by personal growth as a category permeating the remaining domains.

This framework enables consideration of a broad range of interventions that contribute to shaping specific components of flourishing—both through direct effects on lived experiences (e.g., positive affect and sense of meaning) and through the development of individual dispositions (e.g., psychological capital [PsyCap]) or the enhancement of cognitive functioning.

3.4.1.2.2 Theoretical Basis

The theoretical foundations of PTIs may be drawn from concepts developed within positive psychology (e.g., PsyCap) or adopted by it (e.g., SDT, flow, self-efficacy, and mindfulness). The PPI literature also includes interventions developed within an integrative approach, combining elements of positive psychology with other streams of contemporary psychology (see Groot et al., 2023). Examples include acceptance and commitment therapy (ACT) and cognitive-behavioral therapy (CBT) models, elements of which (e.g., acceptance exercises, cognitive restructuring, and progress tracking) are frequently implemented in digital applications.

Concepts from lifestyle medicine and Positive Health are also gaining importance in intervention design. These approaches conceptualize health as the outcome of dynamic interactions among psychological well-being, health-related behaviors, and psychosocial resources. Programs developed on this basis aim to support the cultivation of habits related to physical activity, healthy nutrition, sleep, and related domains. They have been provisionally termed *lifestyle-medicine-and-positive-psychology interventions* (Burke, 2025) and, within the context of PCyb, may be conceptualized as *healthy lifestyle PTIs.*

3.4.1.2.3 Research Status

Following the proposal of Stephen M. Schueller and Acacia C. Parks (2012), two categories of PTIs may be distinguished based on their research status:

- Evidence-based PTIs—interventions with empirically confirmed effectiveness and replicability;
- Intuitive practices—solutions grounded in design intuition or observed effects, yet lacking rigorous validation (e.g., the use of social media in home settings for relaxation purposes).

The market offers numerous applications providing programs for behavior change, personal development, or "self-improvement," whose theoretical foundations remain unclear and whose effectiveness has not been empirically established. Similarly, the literature contains many descriptions of practices that currently hold the status of preliminary proposals and require further experimental verification. For this reason, one of the key tasks of PCyb is to promote a standard of evidence-based PTIs supported by rigorous protocols and clearly specified conditions and limitations of application.

3.4.1.2.4 Type of Technology Used

PTIs may be classified according to their delivery environment, as well as the architecture of the interface and the modality of interaction. As technologies continue to evolve, these typologies will expand accordingly.

With respect to the delivery environment, the following categories may be distinguished:

- Online PTIs (web-based or Internet-based interventions)—psychoeducational programs and modular self-help interventions delivered via websites and online platforms (Collins et al., 2024a; Parks, 2014).
- App-based PTIs (mobile-based interventions)—automated, application-based interventions with options for personalization (e.g., AlSlaity et al., 2022).
- VR-based PTIs—interventions conducted in immersive VR environments (e.g., Meshkat et al., 2024).
- Game-based PTIs—programs implemented within mobile or video game environments, including so-called serious games developed for purposes other than entertainment (e.g., Saleme et al., 2020).
- AI-delivered PTIs (e.g., chatbot-delivered interventions)—interventions utilizing AI-driven systems, such as chatbots, that engage users in dialogic interaction (e.g., Li et al., 2023).

In terms of interface architecture and interaction modality, interventions may also be grouped according to whether they employ: screen-based interfaces (textual, visual, and touch-based), immersive interfaces (VR/AR), wearable and sensor-based interfaces (e.g., biofeedback and physiological monitoring), multisensory interfaces (haptic, auditory, and kinesthetic), or BCIs. Future developments may also involve advanced computational paradigms (e.g., quantum computing), which are already being applied in clinical care (Fairburn et al., 2025).

3.4.1.2.5 Level of Automation

Drawing on classifications developed in the field of mental health (Pineda et al., 2023), the following categories may be distinguished:

- Provider-administered PTIs—characterized by a high level of personalization but requiring the direct involvement of a supporting professional.
- Provider-administered PTIs with blended digital adjuncts—incorporating digital components such as applications, reminder SMS messages, or VR-based exercises.
- Self-help human-supported (guided) PTIs—minimal support from a specialist (e.g., consultant, coach, and online moderator) aimed at increasing engagement and program adherence.
- Self-help fully automated PTIs (digital interventions)—such as mobile applications, chatbots, e-learning platforms, or therapeutic games; these offer the

greatest scalability and low per-user cost, while ensuring anonymity and 24/7 accessibility.
- Artificial-provider PTIs—interventions in which an AI-driven support provider performs functions traditionally carried out by human professionals.

The proposed typology invites research aimed at comparing their effectiveness and identifying optimal intervention configurations within specific contexts.

3.4.1.3 Conditions of Efficacy

The development of effective PTIs requires the integration of methodological standards established within positive psychology with a critical reflection on the distinctive characteristics of digital environments. A key reference point is the framework articulated in *Best-practice guidelines for positive psychological intervention research design* (van Zyl et al., 2019), which identifies five core domains: design, recruitment and retention, adoption, fidelity, and evaluation.

In addition to guideline-based approaches, recent methodological proposals point toward more process-oriented frameworks for designing and evaluating PTIs. For example, Llewellyn E. van Zyl and Bryan J. Dik (2025) propose a six-stage methodological pipeline that integrates multimodal data capture, computational analysis, idiographic modeling, collaborative interpretation, and precision interventions within a continuous, iterative cycle. This framework complements domain-based models by providing a dynamic architecture that links data, analysis, and intervention design, thereby enabling the systematic development, testing, and optimization of PTIs in digitally mediated environments while addressing key limitations of top-down, population-level models of well-being. It further reflects a shift toward idiographic, person-centered research, in which intervention effects are examined at the level of the individual (e.g., N-of-1 designs) and continuously refined through iterative feedback loops based on real-time data. Importantly, this process-oriented perspective does not replace the domain-based framework; rather, it reconceptualizes domains such as design, recruitment, adoption, fidelity, and evaluation as dynamically interconnected phases within an ongoing intervention process.

In the case of PTIs, however, each of these approaches requires reconceptualization, as the intervention is not delivered through a neutral medium but within a dynamic socio-technical ecosystem that may itself generate psychological effects. A long-term objective of research in this area should therefore be to develop a document analogous to the one mentioned earlier—*Guidelines for PTI research design*—that explicitly addresses both the opportunities and the risks associated with embedding interventions within digital tools (see Table 3.6). Importantly, such guidelines should reflect the dynamic interdependencies between the core domains of PTI research design, rather than treating them as discrete categories.

Table 3.6 The potential opportunities and risks related to incorporating digital technologies into PTI protocols across research domains.

Research domains	Opportunities	Risks
Design	• Top-down design grounded in validated theoretical models. • Bottom-up design informed by observed affordances and emergent user practices. • Data-informed, idiographic design enabling dynamically adaptive interventions based on individual-level data. • Iterative linking of data collection, analysis, and intervention adjustment. • Application of EMA/ESM and EMIs to capture real-time processes and deliver context-sensitive support. • Use of AI-driven personalization and immersive technologies to enhance engagement.	• Limited access to technological infrastructure (economic and political barriers). • Algorithmic errors and bias in recommendation systems. • Overemphasis on technological sophistication at the expense of psychological content. • Overfitting interventions to idiosyncratic data and limited generalizability. • Misinterpretation of within-person data (non-ergodicity problem). • Increased system complexity reducing transparency and controllability.
Recruitment and retention	• Use of personalization, gamification, and digital nudging to increase engagement. • Implementation of supportive chatbots and real-time feedback systems. • Support for basic psychological need satisfaction (autonomy, competence, and relatedness). • Facilitation of flow states as a mechanism sustaining engagement through goal clarity, perceived control, and immediate feedback. • Process-based mapping enabling identification of engagement dynamics across intervention components.	• Overrepresentation of WEIRD populations and variability in DL. • Digital exclusion and unequal access. • Technofatigue and loss of trust in automated systems. • Misalignment between engagement strategies and users' psychological needs. • Fragmentation of engagement across intervention components.

(Continued)

Table 3.6 (Continued)

Research domains	Opportunities	Risks
Adoption	• Integration of PTIs into daily routines (e.g., micro-interventions embedded in apps or wearable devices). • Alignment with person–activity fit (values, preferences, and styles of functioning). • Adaptive adjustment of interventions to evolving user needs and contexts.	• Excessive integration leading to cognitive overload, technostress, and resource depletion. • Mismatch between intervention characteristics and individual profiles. • Failure to adapt to changing user needs over time. • Destabilization of digital-life balance.
Fidelity	• Automated fidelity tracking (logs, telemetry data, and user activity monitoring). • Use of AI to analyze engagement patterns and implementation quality in real time. • Reduction of human error and increased standardization of intervention delivery.	• Limited control over system stability (failures, updates, and unintended interactions). • Unauthorized protocol modifications and loss of intervention coherence. • Privacy concerns related to continuous monitoring. • Erosion of user autonomy in opaque monitoring systems. • Shift from supportive to controlling or disciplinary system functions.
Evaluation	• Application of real-time analytics and multimodal outcome measures (psychometric, behavioral, and physiological). • Use of Bayesian approaches, mixed-effects models, and trajectory analyses. • Modeling within-person dynamics and heterogeneity of change. • Integration of measurement within intervention processes (embedded assessment).	• Difficulty distinguishing intervention effects from technology effects. • Challenges in assessing long-term outcomes under continuous digital exposure. • Inflation of Type I error due to high-frequency data collection.

3.4.1.3.1 Design

The design of PTIs may follow different approaches, most commonly conceptualized as top-down and bottom-up. The former was proposed within the Positive Technology framework (e.g., Riva et al., 2016) as a structured procedure for designing e-experiences, involving the identification of experiential determinants, the specification of their key components, and the selection of appropriate technological strategies. This pathway is grounded in established and empirically validated theoretical models developed and debated within positive psychology.

In the bottom-up approach, design inspiration emerges from observations of the positive effects of digital tools used in everyday or experimental contexts. Beneficial outcomes may result from embedded design logics and affordances, as well as from algorithmic systems that learn from user behavior (i.e., personalization). Explaining such effects requires their integration into coherent theoretical frameworks that enable the identification of underlying mechanisms of change.

Extending these perspectives, PTI design may also incorporate a data-informed, idiographic design, in which intervention components are iteratively constructed and refined based on individual-level data (van Zyl & Dik, 2025). Within this approach, design is not treated as a one-time specification of intervention elements but as an ongoing process linking data collection, analysis, and intervention adjustment. Such an approach enables the identification of person-specific mechanisms of change and supports the development of dynamically adaptive interventions tailored to users' evolving states and contexts. From this perspective, personalization should be understood not merely as a technological feature (e.g., algorithmic tailoring) but as a process grounded in idiographic modeling through which interventions are continuously aligned with individuals' lived experiences, contexts, and evolving needs. This may, in turn, support the development of precision-oriented PTIs, in which intervention components are continuously calibrated in response to within-person dynamics over time.

Regardless of the design approach, it is advantageous to incorporate ecological momentary assessment (EMA) or the ESM into the intervention protocol. These approaches enable real-time monitoring of psychological processes, behaviors, and their contextual conditions. When combined with ecological momentary interventions (EMIs), they also allow for the delivery of micro-interventions in response to users' current states and needs (e.g., sending reminders that support goal pursuit).

3.4.1.3.2 Recruitment and Retention

At this stage a central issue concerns how technologies sustain user engagement in PTIs. Personalization, gamification, and chatbot-based support may enhance responsiveness and motivation while lowering barriers to entry. Although these solutions enable the delivery of content precisely tailored to users' current states and contexts, their implementation involves significant tensions. Algorithmic selection may exacerbate digital exclusion and the overrepresentation of WEIRD populations; intensive gamification may promote selective retention of only certain user segments; and overly proactive chatbots may generate technofatigue and diminish well-being.

Research on engagement in behavior change technologies and digital interventions highlights the crucial role of satisfying participants' basic psychological needs (Alberts et al., 2024). Sustained engagement may also be facilitated by experiences of flow, supported by clarity of goals, a sense of control, and immediate feedback (Stocchi et al., 2025). However, because engagement in PTIs fluctuates alongside users' energy levels and resource availability, approaches that explicitly account for this variability have been proposed. For example, Inbal Nahum-Shani and Carolyn Yoon (2024) introduce the concept of process-based mapping, which conceptualizes an intervention as a sequence of interrelated stimuli and tasks. According to their view, such mapping enables researchers to track user responses to each intervention component, identify moments of declining engagement, analyze interdependencies among components, and ultimately contribute to the design of dynamically optimized intervention models. These assumptions, however, require empirical validation.

3.4.1.3.3 Adoption

As noted by Llewellyn van Zyl et al. (2019), the adoption of an intervention depends on its alignment with the values, needs, and routines of target groups, as well as on its compatibility with existing patterns of action. Excessive integration of PTIs into daily life (e.g., through constant alerts, overly intensive micro-tasks, or extensive monitoring modules) may lead to cognitive overload, increase technostress, and activate spirals of resource depletion. Consequently, interventions intended to strengthen well-being may paradoxically destabilize individual functioning.

This observation is consistent with the positive activity model (PAM; Lyubomirsky & Layous, 2013), developed in the context of PPIs. According to PAM, intervention effectiveness depends on the interaction between the properties of the activity (e.g., frequency, variety, and level of social engagement), characteristics of the person (e.g., motivation, effort, self-regulation resources, and emotional state), and person–activity fit—that is, the alignment between an individual's values, preferences, and style of functioning and the nature of the intervention itself.

Importantly, such person–activity fit should not be inferred solely from generalized patterns of user behavior but rather understood as emerging from individual trajectories of experience that may vary across persons and over time (van Zyl & Dik, 2025). This implies that successful adoption depends not only on initial alignment but also on the capacity of PTIs to remain responsive to evolving user needs, resources, and contexts.

3.4.1.3.4 Fidelity

The possibilities afforded by continuous, automated monitoring of adherence to PTI protocols are accompanied by both the potential for optimization and significant methodological and ethical risks. High protocol fidelity constitutes a necessary condition for drawing valid inferences about the effectiveness of positive interventions (Toomey et al., 2020). In digital environments, however, ensuring such fidelity often requires advanced mechanisms for tracking user activity, automated checklists, log-data analyses, and adaptive algorithms regulating session flow. These solutions may reduce variability in implementation, minimize human error, and enable the rapid identification of deviations from the protocol. At the same time, they introduce new vulnerabilities. Intensive automation may paradoxically weaken oversight of PTI stability, rendering intervention delivery sensitive to system failures, flawed update procedures, or unforeseen interactions among technological components.

Moreover, detailed monitoring of participant activity raises substantial privacy concerns, particularly when users lack full transparency regarding the scope of data collection, methods of analysis, or meaningful opportunities to negotiate the level of monitoring. In digital environments where monitoring is not only continuous but also opaque, participants may lose their sense of autonomy, and the system may shift from a supportive to a disciplinary function. As a result, the automation of fidelity procedures may paradoxically undermine the very quality of fidelity it is intended to secure.

3.4.1.3.5 Evaluation

Assessment of the effectiveness of PTIs requires the application of experimental methodologies and, where justified, research designs including a control group implementing a non-digital counterpart of the PTI. As in the case of PPIs, it is equally important to replicate findings across diverse age groups, occupational settings, and cultural contexts.

In line with the recommendations of Llewellyn van Zyl et al. (2019), intervention evaluation should involve the parallel use of quantitative and qualitative measures while accounting for both immediate effects and longer-term impacts on well-being. In digital environments, however, the challenge of selecting appropriate measures becomes intensified, as measurement ceases to function solely as an evaluative tool and instead becomes embedded within the intervention itself. Advanced analytical tools enable the examination of change dynamics in real time, yet they also introduce methodological complexities related to disentangling intervention effects from technology effects. The abundance of quantitative data further increases the risk of Type I errors—that is, falsely detecting effects where none exist.

To distinguish short-term fluctuations in individual reactivity from enduring intervention effects, advanced process-oriented analytic models may be employed, including mixed-effects models, trajectory analyses, and Bayesian approaches. At the same time, caution is warranted when interpreting aggregated patterns of change as representative of individual-level processes, as temporal dynamics of well-being may differ substantially across persons (van Zyl & Dik, 2025). This underscores the importance of analytic approaches capable of capturing within-person variability and heterogeneity in response to PTIs over time.

3.4.1.4 Enhancing Effectiveness

The development of guidelines for the effective implementation of PTIs constitutes a significant research challenge, one that may be grounded in concepts developed within positive psychology. In the context of PPIs, it has been shown that the effectiveness and durability of outcomes may be strengthened by such conditions as adequate social support, autonomy of engagement (i.e., the sense that participation stems from personal choice), variety and flexibility of practices counteracting hedonic adaptation, and optimal dosage—neither too infrequent nor too intensive engagement in the intervention (Lyubomirsky & Layous, 2013).

Acacia C. Parks (2014), in her analysis of online positive psychological interventions (OPPIs), identified several principles influencing user engagement:

- Relative advantage—the perception that the intervention offers something unique compared to available alternatives;
- Compatibility—alignment of the intervention with the user's values, goals, and lifestyle;
- Complexity (ease of use)—the intervention should be simple, intuitive, and easy to understand;
- Observability—the possibility of monitoring progress and outcomes;
- Dosage—an appropriate level of intensity (neither too little nor too much);
- User choice—opportunities for selection and personalization of activities.

Empirical research has confirmed the relevance of several of these principles. A systematic review of digital mental health interventions (Borghouts et al., 2021) indicates that factors corresponding to relative advantage, compatibility, complexity, and user choice are particularly important for sustaining long-term engagement. Users were more likely to continue participation when they perceived the intervention as uniquely valuable, aligned with their lifestyle and values, intuitive and easy to use, and adaptable to personal preferences. Findings regarding observability and dosage, however, were less conclusive. In some studies, the ability to monitor progress enhanced motivation and perceived effectiveness, whereas in others, excessive amounts of data led to feelings of overload and reduced engagement. Similarly, in the case of dosage, overly long modules tended to diminish motivation, highlighting the lack of precise guidelines defining optimal duration and intensity.

3.4.1.5 Ethical Considerations

The application of rigorous methodological standards should lead to the development of PTIs whose design, implementation, and evaluation adhere to the highest scientific and practical standards. Their deployment as a form of evidence-based practice in psychology is inseparably linked to ethical responsibility (Brzeziński & Oleś, 2021; Fried & Jansen, 2023). In the domain of positive psychology practice, ethical standards have been articulated in the document "Ethical Guidelines for Positive Psychology Practice" (Jarden et al., 2021). Drawing on its principles, the following guidelines may be formulated with respect to PTIs:

- Beneficence and non-maleficence—the necessity of systematically assessing potential benefits and risks associated with the use of digital technologies, particularly in the context of autonomous algorithmic functioning and data-driven personalization;
- Responsible caring—designing PTIs that not only promote well-being but also ensure users' psychological, informational, and technological safety;
- Respect for autonomy—encompassing informed consent, procedural transparency, the possibility of withdrawal, and access to information regarding the functioning of digital systems;
- Justice and integrity—preventing digital exclusion, avoiding algorithmic bias, offering interventions appropriate to users' levels of competence, and communicating their capabilities and limitations honestly;
- Sensitivity to cultural and social context—ensuring that PTIs are aligned with the values, norms, and lived realities of their participants;
- Clear delineation of competence boundaries—applying both to professionals responsible for designing interventions and to the systems that implement their automated components;
- Monitoring of potential adverse effects—including both psychological and technological side effects (e.g., app dependency, technostress, and privacy violations).

Responsible practices in the development and implementation of PTIs should reflect the ethical orientation of PCyb as a whole, grounded in the professional code of ethics of psychologists and encompassing obligations toward research participants, intervention users, and society at large.

3.4.2 Healthy Lifestyle PTIs

Interest in the development and evaluation of PTIs aimed at strengthening physical well-being stems from the inclusion of physical health among the core components of flourishing (Kern, 2022; Lomas et al., 2024b; VanderWeele, 2017). Digital health-promoting interventions are being developed at the intersection of positive psychology and the fields of eHealth, mHealth, and uHealth (Murray et al., 2016). The technologies employed in this domain are most often examples of behavior change technologies, designed both for clinical contexts (e.g., disease-management apps and medication adherence apps) and for the promotion of healthy lifestyles (wellness apps).

The classical framing of PPIs as "happiness-boosting strategies" (Layous & Lyubomirsky, 2014) tended to marginalize psychologists' interest in solutions developed within clinical practice. However, the emergence of the positive health paradigm and the second and third waves of positive psychology have fostered greater integration of interventions targeting psychological and physical well-being, particularly within multicomponent health programs. In this context, wellness technologies have attracted increasing attention, forming the basis of a broader category of healthy lifestyle PTIs (see Table 3.7). These interventions may be analyzed within two principal domains: healthy behaviors and collective health engagement.

3.4.2.1 Healthy Behaviors

Existing research on the role of digital technologies in shaping health-promoting behaviors, conducted within the mHealth domain, points to the need for a stronger integration of psychological variables into models explaining intervention effectiveness. Previous analyses have primarily examined technological and contextual determinants of intervention efficacy, only rarely linking these factors to indicators of well-being and flourishing. The findings presented below should therefore be treated as a promising point of departure for further analyses aimed at identifying the psychological mechanisms underlying the operation of health-oriented PTIs.

In the domain of physical activity promotion, intervention effectiveness has been shown to increase through the use of adaptive training plans, workload monitoring, movement reminders, and progress visualizations (Wang et al., 2024). Among children and adolescents, gamification-based solutions and family support appear particularly effective, whereas during adolescence, the social component, enabling joint activity and peer comparison, plays a crucial role. Among adults and older individuals, multicomponent interventions integrating goal setting, self-monitoring, personalized feedback, and social support demonstrate the highest effectiveness.

Similar mechanisms have been observed in the domain of dietary habit formation. The most favorable outcomes are achieved by solutions combining

Table 3.7 Categories of healthy lifestyle applications with their intended aims, example applications, and core functions.

Category	Intended aims	Example applications	Core functions
Fitness and physical activity	• Promoting physical activity and improving fitness • Reducing sedentary behavior and supporting active lifestyle change • Strengthening perceived competence and exercise motivation • Preventing lifestyle-related diseases	Freeletics, Fitbod, TrainingPeaks, 8fit, Noom (partially), and Vida Health	• Adaptive training plans and workout timers • Progressive overload tracking • Daily step goals and movement reminders • Progress dashboards and goal visualizations • Cardio zone analysis and metabolic load estimation • Personalized coaching features
Healthy eating	• Promoting healthy dietary habits and informed food choices • Supporting calorie and macronutrient monitoring • Facilitating meal planning and consistent eating routines	MyFitnessPal, Lose It!, Lifesum, Noom, and Yazio	• Nutritional education and diet-quality scoring systems • Food logging with automated nutrient summaries • Personalized meal plans and shopping list generation • Healthier alternative recommendations • Meal reminders and routine tracking
Sleep improvement	• Improving sleep quality and circadian rhythm regulation • Early detection of irregular sleep patterns • Reducing fatigue and enhancing recovery	Sleep Cycle, Calm, Pillow, and Headspace (Sleep)	• Sleep stage detection and smart alarms • Chronotype insights and irregularity alerts • Trend anomaly detection • Sleep debt calculators and recovery scores • Guided bedtime routines and relaxation protocols
Social health and community-based	• Strengthening social support • Enhancing motivation through social interaction • Fostering belonging in health-promoting activities • Supporting sustained participation in healthy behaviors	Fitbit Communities, Strava Clubs, Garmin Connect Groups, and MyFitnessPal Communities	• Peer groups and health forums • Leaderboards and team challenges • Shared progress logs and community feeds • Social accountability tools and cooperative goal systems

clear action structures (e.g., challenges, daily tasks, and reward systems) with personalized recommendations and progress monitoring (Curtin et al., 2025; Gkintoni et al., 2024). These findings underscore the importance of feedback loops linking behavioral regulation with perceived competence and agency.

A broad set of factors contributing to the effectiveness of sleep-improvement interventions has also been identified (Al Mahmud et al., 2022). These include application usability and accessibility, engagement-sustaining mechanisms (goals, reminders, and feedback), integration with wearable devices, trust in technology grounded in transparency and measurement reliability, and personalization aligned with users' lifestyles and circadian rhythms. The factors listed above may be treated as a more general research heuristic, the validity of which requires further empirical verification across different categories of health-promoting PTIs.

3.4.2.2 Community-Based Health Engagement

A strong potential for developing effective PTIs lies in the use of community-based health applications. Their function is to reinforce the social foundations of a healthy lifestyle by leveraging interpersonal interaction as a key mechanism for sustaining motivation and consistency in health-promoting behaviors. The aim of such tools is therefore to build supportive environments in which users can exchange experiences, track shared progress, and engage in cooperative challenges.

Cross-sectional studies examining the use of commercial physical activity applications indicate that engagement with such tools generally promotes collective health practices (Petersen et al., 2020). Functions such as sharing results on social platforms, receiving encouragement from other users, and participating in community-based competitions were associated with higher levels of activity. Importantly, however, some users' activity decreased as a result of competitive pressure or unfavorable social comparison, suggesting that the social component is not unequivocally beneficial.

Realizing the full potential of these applications requires further systematic research. Nevertheless, there are clear grounds for designing multicomponent PTIs that simultaneously support physical and social well-being. Such interventions may facilitate the integration of individual health goals with processes of cooperation, mutual support, and resource sharing within social networks. Their effectiveness can be interpreted in light of the dual perspective model of social perception (Abele & Wojciszke, 2014), which posits that psychological functioning rests on a dynamic balance between agency and communion.

3.4.3 Mental Well-Being PTIs

Mental well-being refers to the extent to which individuals subjectively experience the quality of their psychological functioning, encompassing affect regulation, clarity of cognitive processes, and the capacity to cope with the demands of everyday life (Lomas et al., 2024b). This section discusses a broad range of PTIs whose positive effects on this component of flourishing have been empirically supported or are grounded in robust theoretical justification. These interventions include those targeting regulatory aspects of mental well-being, such as the cultivation of positive emotions, the development of mindfulness and stress reduction practices, savoring, the BPS exercise, self-compassion, and gratitude. Interventions aimed at enhancing cognitive performance are addressed separately in the section devoted to personal growth PTIs (section 3.4.6).

3.4.3.1 Positive Emotions

Technological innovations that facilitate the generation of positive emotions constitute a paradigmatic example of the so-called hedonic technologies identified within the Positive Technology framework (Riva et al., 2012). Their value lies in the fact that the induction of positive affect may extend beyond momentary pleasure, broaden individuals' cognitive–behavioral repertoires, and initiate subsequent well-being–enhancing activities (Fredrickson, 2001).

Within this context, the effectiveness of positive mood induction procedures (MIPs) has been successfully tested using immersive technologies (Baños et al., 2012). The general conclusion emerging from research on MIPs in such environments is that their application can effectively increase levels of positive emotions, thereby promoting well-being and mental health (Di Pompeo et al., 2023). Beneficial effects have been observed among adolescents, university students, older adults, clinical patients, and even isolated astronauts (Baños et al., 2017).

However, intervention effectiveness depends to a considerable extent on the sense of presence, enhanced by multisensory stimulation (e.g., visualizations of natural environments and audiovisual elements), as well as the opportunity for active interaction within the virtual environment. Studies comparing different forms of exposure to virtual nature (2D film, 360° video, and VR) indicate that immersive VR enabling free exploration produces the strongest improvements in mood and reductions in negative affect (Yeo et al., 2020). Similar findings have been reported in research on VR games, where motor and cognitive engagement were associated with increases in positive emotions and decreases in anxiety and tension (Pallavicini & Pepe, 2020). At the same time, recent reviews suggest that such positive effects are typically short-lived and strongly dependent on technological quality, underscoring the need for further investigation (Linares-Vargas & Cieza-Mostacero, 2025).

3.4.3.2 Mindfulness and Stress Reduction

The category of interventions targeting mindfulness and stress reduction encompasses a wide range of approaches to using digital technologies. Their number and diversity suggest that this trend is not merely a response to market demand but also reflects the stimulating influence of a well-established theoretical foundation on intervention design. Many of these programs are grounded in the extensively validated mindfulness-based stress reduction (MBSR; Kabat-Zinn, 1982) model, which promotes specific techniques such as breath-focused meditation, body scanning, relaxation exercises, and attentional focus on transient experiences. Given the rapid development of digital technologies, further solutions can be expected to emerge, effectively functioning as commercial experimental environments. In evaluating their effectiveness, levels of mindfulness may be assessed using the Mindful Attention Awareness Scale–State (MAAS-State; Brown & Ryan, 2003), while perceived stress can be measured with the Perceived Stress Scale (PSS-10; Cohen et al., 1983).

3.4.3.2.1 Online Interventions

Research on the effectiveness of online interventions aimed at enhancing mindfulness and reducing stress is conducted primarily within workplace contexts, as organizations increasingly provide employees with access to digital psychological support programs (e.g., BetterHelp for Organizations and Mindgram). Although these initiatives often take the form of intuitive practices that may only serve as a preliminary foundation for PTIs, their implementation can contribute to reductions in stress, anxiety, and burnout while simultaneously strengthening psychological well-being (Cameron et al., 2025). More favorable outcomes are associated with interventions grounded in established theoretical frameworks (e.g., CBT), thoughtfully designed and well-structured programs, opportunities for content personalization, and the availability of support (e.g., a coach or guidance). By contrast, fully self-guided solutions typically yield weaker or more heterogeneous effects, which may be linked to lower motivation, declining engagement, and limited personalization.

3.4.3.2.2 App-Based Interventions

In app-based interventions, applications such as Headspace, Calm, and Insight Timer are used to deliver brief, structured regulatory programs, including guided breathing, micro-meditations, grounding exercises, and features that facilitate reflection on affective states. Some solutions, often integrated with wearable devices, also incorporate the monitoring of physiological stress indicators (e.g., HRV). However, their effectiveness is strongly contingent upon users' level of engagement. Emma L. Osborne et al. (2023) identified three key factors in this regard: (1) individuals' subjective reactions to their own practice, which may undermine motivation through feelings of guilt, frustration, or the perception of meditation as an obligation; (2) the process of habit formation, which requires personalization of the intervention due to the need to reorganize daily routines; and (3) access to social support—both in the form of human contact (e.g., an instructor) and community components, the absence of which may foster isolation and practice discontinuation. These principles appear to be broadly applicable to other app-based PTIs as well; however, this assumption requires empirical verification.

3.4.3.2.3 VR-Based Interventions

Research indicates that immersive VR interventions can effectively reduce psychophysiological tension following exposure to stressors (Meshkat et al., 2024). This effect is facilitated by simulations of natural environments enriched with relaxation-oriented narration, ambient sounds, and low-arousal music (Wiederhold & Riva, 2020). Classic experiments employing the immersive environment The Secret Garden demonstrated that VR-based relaxation leads to significant reductions in state anxiety and normalization of physiological parameters (e.g., HRV) compared to traditional rest conditions (Gaggioli et al., 2020). These effects have been replicated in samples of healthcare professionals (Pallavicini et al., 2025). Intervention efficacy is further enhanced by the possibility of active interaction with digital objects, as evidenced in a study using an immersive environment based on a botanical garden project that enabled exploration and simple gardening activities (Kalantari et al., 2022). Improvements in mood, as well as increased feelings of calmness and relaxation, were observed particularly among older adults and individuals with limited mobility—importantly, without incurring costs in the form of fatigue or cybersickness.

3.4.3.2.4 Game-Based Interventions

Research on game-based interventions indicates that, among young adults, digital games may function as effective tools for stress reduction and as an engaging complement or alternative to classical mindfulness interventions (Veeral Desai et al., 2021). Positive effects have been observed particularly in immersive games, where strong cognitive engagement supports post-work recovery and positions gaming as a stress-management strategy complementary to mindfulness-based approaches (Mella et al., 2023). A novel line of inquiry is emerging from the recently identified potential to influence well-being through internal dialogues with game characters (Fortuna et al., 2026). Interviews conducted with players suggest that synthetic characters may become a form of "internal interlocutor." Participants reported that such interactions help them reduce tension, organize their thoughts, or distance themselves from daily burdens, thereby indicating a possible role in emotion regulation. However, the effectiveness of gaming activities in promoting mental well-being through mechanisms grounded in internal dialogue requires further empirical verification.

3.4.3.2.5 AI-Chatbot Interventions

A promising line of research concerns interventions employing conversational bots as mindfulness and stress-reduction coaches. However, existing evidence does not yet provide unequivocal conclusions regarding their effectiveness. For example, significant reductions in stress levels, depressive symptoms, and psychosomatic complaints were reported by participants in studies implementing a program based on the MISHA agent (Ulrich et al., 2024). Within several weeks of guided sessions, this chatbot delivered psychoeducational content on stress, relaxation, and mindfulness, proposed practical exercises (e.g., breathing and relaxation techniques), and encouraged regular practice. In contrast, a study testing the effectiveness of a three-week intervention based on the ELME chatbot (Schillings et al., 2024) did not observe a significant decrease in perceived stress. Nevertheless, increases in mindfulness and improvements in adaptive emotion regulation (reappraisal) were identified. These findings underscore the need for further research to examine the hypothesis that chatbots may support the development of key regulatory resources, even if their impact on direct stress reduction is indirect or delayed.

3.4.3.3 Savoring

Savoring is the process of consciously generating, maintaining, and amplifying positive experiences through the appreciation of life events (Bryant & Veroff, 2007). Unlike mindfulness, it focuses exclusively on positive moments—whether past (reminiscing), present (savoring the moment), or future (anticipating). Savoring interventions include exercises such as sharing positive events, intensifying sensory aspects of experience, constructing mental "photographs," counting blessings, and engaging in spontaneous expressions of joy.

Daniela Villani et al. (2023) tested the effectiveness of a self-guided, Internet-based e-savoring intervention among young adults during the COVID-19 pandemic. Participants in the experimental group completed six online exercises (two per week over three weeks). The tasks included recalling three positive moments from the past, elaborating and strengthening these memories, and reflecting on their broader capacity to enjoy present and future positive events. Compared to the control group, which did not receive any activity during the same period, the experimental group demonstrated significant increases both in savoring beliefs (particularly regarding the present and future) and in levels of positive emotions. Additionally, participants evaluated the platform as clear, engaging, and useful, which may facilitate sustained engagement.

3.4.3.4 The Best Possible Self

The BPS is one of the most widely recognized PPIs. Participants are invited to describe a scenario in which their lives have unfolded optimally: they have achieved important goals, developed their strengths, acted in accordance with their values, and experienced satisfying relationships (Sheldon & Lyubomirsky, 2006). The classical protocol involves a brief writing exercise lasting several minutes, often preceded by a short visualization designed to intensify positive emotions, enhance meaning, and increase overall well-being.

An example of a digital tool supporting structured self-reflection in line with the BPS framework is the Book of Life application. It constitutes a module of a self-administered system called EARTH, which has been shown to be effective in inducing positive moods. Within Book of Life, users create chapters devoted to different domains of their lives (e.g., personal, professional, social, and health-related) and subsequently elaborate on their vision of the future. The application further enables the enrichment of narratives with multimedia elements, such as photographs, audio recordings, and videos, which intensify the imaginal quality of the exercise and facilitate deeper memory consolidation. The saved content can be repeatedly accessed and visualized, allowing BPS to evolve into a sustained practice rather than a one-time writing task.

In studies involving patients with eating disorders, the use of this application was associated with increased positive expectations about the future and a reduction in negative expectations (Enrique et al., 2018).

3.4.3.5 Self-Compassion

Self-compassion practices are developed on the basis of Kristin Neff's (2003) conceptual framework. Their core aim is to alleviate suffering by offering oneself the kind of support that is typically reserved for close others. Rather than avoiding personal pain or responding with self-criticism, individuals are encouraged to approach their own distress with kindness. This stance enables a shift from harsh self-evaluation toward the recognition that mistakes, failures, and difficult emotions constitute a natural part of the human experience. The construct comprises three key components: self-kindness, referring to warmth and care toward oneself in moments of suffering; common humanity, defined as the acknowledgment that pain is a shared human condition; and mindfulness, expressed in the balanced acceptance of difficult thoughts and emotions as they are.

The range of digital tools supporting the practice of self-compassion includes mobile applications (e.g., compassion modules within Headspace or Calm), online platforms (e.g., Self-Compassion Online), conversational chatbots, VR technologies, and digital journaling tools. These solutions most commonly provide personalized and easily accessible programs based on brief writing exercises, psychoeducational modules, audio meditations, and relaxation tasks. However, determining their effectiveness—and the conditions under which they may be equivalent to or surpass traditional therapist-led interventions—requires further empirical investigation. Promising evidence concerns online interventions. According to a systematic review (Randhawa & Vella-Brodrick, 2025), approximately 75% of the analyzed programs resulted in significant increases in self-compassion compared to control conditions, with some studies demonstrating maintenance of these effects at follow-up assessments ranging from 1 to 12 months. Importantly, from the perspective of PTI design, the absence of direct therapeutic support did not attenuate the observed effects.

3.4.3.6 Gratitude

In positive psychology, *gratitude* is conceptualized both as an emotional experience arising from receiving a benefit from an external source and as a character strength expressed in noticing and appreciating the positive aspects of everyday life (Peterson & Seligman, 2004). This dual nature carries important implications for the design of PTIs. Interventions aimed at cultivating gratitude may elicit short-term positive emotions or, when practiced with sufficient intensity and over an extended period, modify dispositional tendencies.

Traditionally, research has focused on three primary forms of intervention: (1) gratitude lists based on the Three Good Things exercise, in which participants regularly record positive events or aspects of their day; (2) gratitude journals, involving more elaborate narratives that encourage deeper reflection on the context, meaning, and consequences of experienced benefits; and (3) interpersonal expressions of gratitude, encompassing the communication of appreciation to another person. The adaptation of these practices to technological environments has not only increased their accessibility but also enabled the automation of reminders, progress tracking, and the creation of supportive networks. Empirical evidence (Huston et al., 2025) suggests that functionalities supporting regularity and deeper engagement may facilitate more sustained participation in gratitude practice. However, the effectiveness of gratitude interventions remains mixed and appears to depend on contextual factors, individual characteristics, and life experiences. Accordingly, gratitude practice should be understood as a context-sensitive process in which consistent repetition, meaningful engagement, and interpersonal expression constitute key conditions for its effectiveness.

3.4.4 Social Well-Being PTIs

Supportive social relationships constitute one of the central pillars of flourishing, consistently present across its major conceptualizations. Their strengthening is facilitated by experiences that satisfy the need for relatedness, sustain a sense of belonging to a community, reinforce the perception of one's meaningful contribution to its functioning, cultivate a positive orientation toward others, and enhance the subjective sense of comprehensibility within the social world (Keyes, 1998; Ryan & Deci, 2000). Technological development opens new avenues for influencing these dimensions. Promising research directions concern three complementary pathways: the enhancement of digital social support, the cultivation of connectedness and social belonging within digital environments, and the stimulation of prosocial orientation.

3.4.4.1 Digital Social Support

Interventions aimed at providing or strengthening social support may employ a broad spectrum of embodied and virtual companion systems designed to regulate emotions, reduce loneliness, and stimulate social activity. These include, among others, companion systems that offer dialogue, cognitive activation, and nonjudgmental emotional support (e.g., ElliQ and AI chatbots); therapeutic systems that utilize multisensory interaction to reduce tension and enhance positive affective states (e.g., Paro); and socially facilitative systems that initiate and sustain interpersonal interactions while increasing social engagement in educational, caregiving, and therapeutic contexts (e.g., Pepper and NAO).

Positive interactions with such systems are shaped by their design and functional features. Particularly important are the capacities to adapt tone of voice, recognize emotions, and sustain the impression of engagement. These features foster a sense of being heard and understood, which in turn may support emotion regulation, reduce tension, and enhance subjective well-being. Additionally, in the case of chatbots, anonymity and the absence of social-evaluative threat may render them especially beneficial for individuals experiencing social anxiety or isolation.

For the development of effective PTIs, an important general conclusion emerging from meta-analyses (Merrill et al., 2025; Mitchell & Jeon, 2025) is that interactions with artificial agents, both embodied and virtual, can alleviate subjective feelings of loneliness; however, these effects appear to be primarily short-term. Such interactions rarely lead to durable strengthening of real-life social bonds or a sustained sense of belonging. Accordingly, the supportive function of artificial agents should be conceptualized as complementary to, rather than substitutive of, human relationships. Importantly, these systems may operate as a "bridge" that facilitates reengagement with social life. Research (Shen et al., 2025) suggests that AI-based systems can function as social proxies: they do not replace contact with others but instead provide mediated access to others' experiences and narratives, thereby stimulating empathy and perspective-taking, which indirectly reinforce feelings of connectedness.

In light of these findings, the utility of PTIs employing artificial agents may be particularly pronounced during critical periods of social isolation or diminished mood. Empirical support for this proposition is provided by an intervention described by Yahui Wang et al. (2025a), in which Chinese university students with elevated depressive symptoms and loneliness engaged in daily conversations with a CBT-informed chatbot over seven consecutive days. Compared to a control group, the intervention group demonstrated significant reductions in both depressive symptoms and loneliness. Nevertheless, the potential of such chatbot-based sessions requires further validation across age-diverse populations and varied cultural contexts.

3.4.4.2 Connectedness and Social Belonging

The development of PTIs grounded in shared activities within digital environments remains at an early stage. Nevertheless, immersive technologies and the expanding metaverse ecosystem open new possibilities for designing communal experiences across culturally and socially diverse populations. Particularly strong potential is demonstrated by interventions based on collaboration between individuals who, under offline conditions, would have no opportunity for contact.

A useful foundation for PTIs aimed at strengthening connectedness and social belonging lies in social VR environments, where spatial architecture and the design of social affordances modulate the quality of mutual orientation and interaction dynamics. Research conducted on the AltspaceVR platform (Kenyon et al., 2023) indicates that the formation of stable relational networks is especially facilitated by the possibility of creating personalized avatars, sharing virtual spaces, and participating in recurring events within immersive environments. Many users functioned within regularly meeting groups, which endowed their relationships with a community-like character extending beyond episodic online interactions. Active participation in such communities was associated with lower levels of loneliness and social anxiety, particularly when interactions were repeated and embedded in a sense of belonging. Importantly, participants described the experience of presence in VR as more immersive and "real" than communication via videoconferencing or traditional social media.

A second line of inquiry concerns cooperation-based interventions, in which joint action serves as a mechanism for generating connectedness and social belonging. An example is the project "KIMA: Color" (Gingrich et al., 2024), implemented with individuals with visual impairments. The intervention involved collectively transforming works of art into audiovisual experiences using a mobile application that translated colors into acoustic events within a 360° space. Participants explored the same images in real time, co-creating compositions and engaging in a shared process of discovery. This environment fostered experiences of participatory presence, generated a sense of communal synchrony, and strengthened social connectedness.

Similar mechanisms are observed in cooperative gaming environments. One example is a four-week home-based VR program for adolescents with physical disabilities (Lai et al., 2023). The intervention consisted of regular, moderated virtual meetings during which participants engaged in cooperation-based games. Findings indicated that the program facilitated peer relationship building in a safe and accessible manner. The majority of participants reported forming new friendships and experiencing satisfaction from social engagement in VR.

Collectively, these studies reveal the potential for developing PTIs that may offer unique opportunities for experiencing copresence and collaboration. With the implementation of robust protocols, individuals functioning under conditions of social isolation, such as those studying or working remotely, living alone or in care institutions, individuals with limited mobility, or incarcerated persons, may experience a sense of meaningful contribution to social interactions and access to social support, while also having opportunities to challenge stereotypes and prejudices. In this sense, the application of such PTIs may foster not only human flourishing but also humanity flourishing.

3.4.4.3 Prosocial Orientation

Existing research suggests that designing PTIs aimed at strengthening prosocial orientation is feasible; however, eliciting durable prosocial behaviors that extend beyond the digital context remains challenging. For example, Sharon T. Steinemann et al. (2020) tested a three-week intervention based on the Simple Acts platform, designed to support daily helping behaviors and enhance self-efficacy beliefs. Despite the system's advanced design features—such as task personalization, progress monitoring, and virtual badges—the intervention did not increase the frequency of prosocial behaviors.

More promising, albeit mixed, results emerge from a systematic review of prosocial digital games among children and adolescents (Saleme et al., 2020). The authors organized the observed effects into five domains: socio-emotional competencies, attitudes toward self and others, prosocial behaviors, behavioral problems, and stress. Overall, the most substantial changes were found in the domains of competencies and attitudes, whereas the translation of these changes into sustained behavioral outcomes and well-being indicators was generally weaker.

Compelling implications for PTI design arise from research by Zhiying Zhang et al. (2026), who demonstrated that prosocial attitudes and behaviors may be effectively shaped indirectly. A particularly promising strategy involves the peripheral integration of natural elements into game environments (techno-biophilia design). Notably, the games used in their study were not explicitly designed as prosocial tools, nor were participants instructed to attend to nature. Nevertheless, exposure to natural landscapes was associated with higher levels of prosocial behavior, with the perceived beauty of nature functioning as a key mediating mechanism. These effects extended to decisions made after gameplay (e.g., helping intentions and donation decisions), indicating a transfer effect beyond the immediate digital context. This finding aligns with analyses of beauty perception (natural, artistic, and moral), which suggest that the experience of beauty activates neural systems that, particularly in immersive environments such as VR, may be stimulated with heightened intensity, thereby strengthening feelings of connectedness and motivation to act for the benefit of others (Diessner, in press).

3.4.5 Spiritual Well-Being PTIs

Spiritual well-being refers to the subjective quality of life in its spiritual dimension and encompasses a sense of meaning, purpose, and inner harmony. As emphasized by Raymond F. Paloutzian and Craig W. Ellison (1982), this construct is not reducible to religious practices or denominational affiliation, as it pertains both to one's relationship with transcendence and to a secular sense of life meaning—an element central to the eudaimonic dimension of flourishing. It can be assessed using the Spiritual Well-Being Scale (SWBS) developed by these authors.

The design of PTIs aimed at strengthening spiritual well-being remains a relatively underdeveloped yet theoretically promising area. Research on such programs may be systematized by reference to three dimensions: affective, cognitive-existential (meaning-oriented), and behavioral (spiritual practices), corresponding to components identified in analyses of religiosity (e.g., Huber & Huber, 2012). Importantly, beyond testing intervention effectiveness, it is essential to identify factors that may limit the risk of instrumentalizing spiritual well-being—a risk potentially amplified in environments designed according to performance metrics or gamification logics.

3.4.5.1 Self-Transcendent Emotions

The category of STEs (*moral emotions* and *other-praising emotions*) includes awe, elevation, compassion, admiration, gratitude, and love (Yaden et al., 2017). According to Dacher Keltner (2024), their defining feature is that they "transport us out of our self-focused, threat-oriented, and status quo mindset to a realm where we connect to something larger than the self" (p. 28).

Among the affective states intensively studied in the context of interactions with digital technologies, awe occupies a central position. This emotion arises when an individual encounters perceived vastness combined with a need for accommodation—that is, the necessity to revise existing cognitive schemas in response to something that transcends one's current understanding of the world (Keltner & Haidt, 2003). Empirical findings indicate that experiencing awe fosters spiritual growth, personal transformation, and an increased sense of the self as part of a greater whole (Schaffer et al., 2024).

In laboratory settings, awe is most frequently induced through immersive technologies. These allow users to become immersed in virtual spaces presenting realistic panoramas of mountains, outer space, or the Earth viewed from orbit. For example, in a study by Denise Quesnel and Bernhard E. Riecke (2018), participants explored two immersive VR environments: Google Earth VR, enabling free movement from street-level perspectives to views of Earth from space, and a simulation of Mount Everest, in which they contemplated majestic, expansive mountain landscapes. Both stimuli effectively elicited awe; however, the former promoted dynamic wonder and cognitive reflection, whereas the latter evoked feelings of humility and smallness in the face of nature's grandeur. A substantial proportion of participants also reported physiological markers of awe (e.g., goose bumps).

A related state is the sublime, which can likewise be effectively induced in immersive environments. In one experiment, Alice Chirico et al. (2021) employed two contrasting virtual stimuli presented in immersive 360° video format to evoke experiences of the sublime: a photorealistic scene of Provençal nature and an immersive reconstruction inspired by Vincent van Gogh's The Starry Night. Both stimuli successfully elicited the sublime, though through distinct cognitive-affective mechanisms. The natural scene generated a stronger sense of vastness and a "small self," leading to feelings of humility before the magnitude of the world, whereas the immersive artwork evoked aesthetic sublimity grounded in admiration for color, rhythm, and movement. Regardless of stimulus source, both experiences facilitated cognitive accommodation and a sense of transcending prior interpretative frameworks.

From the perspective of spiritual well-being, STEs may be understood not merely as transient affective states but as potential mechanisms initiating processes of personal transformation. Together with experiences such as appreciation of beauty (Diessner et al., 2022) and aesthetic experience (Pizzolante et al., 2024), they function as affective "gateways" to existential reflection, attenuating egocentric and anthropocentric orientations and opening individuals to experiences of transcendence. In this sense, STEs may serve as catalysts of noetic processes, providing an emotional point of departure for subsequent, more structured engagement with questions of meaning and purpose. Promising avenues for future research include identifying the properties of digital stimuli (e.g., degree of immersion, interactivity, and aesthetic complexity) that effectively elicit different types of STEs; distinguishing between positive and negative awe, which appear to engage distinct neurophysiological and cognitive pathways and may differentially affect well-being (Schaffer et al., 2024); examining the durability of technology-induced STE effects; and exploring their relevance for the development of spiritual well-being across diverse cultural contexts.

3.4.5.2 Noetic Support

The term *noetic support* is introduced to distinguish interventions focused on affect regulation, discussed above, from those primarily aimed at the existential reorganization of meaning (these may be referred to as *noetic PTIs*). This terminology draws on Viktor E. Frankl's (1988) concept of logotherapy (nootherapy).

Frankl emphasized the fundamental role of the noetic (spiritual and existential) dimension in the structure of the human person. He further argued that the primary human motivation is the will to meaning, and that the capacity to discover and actualize meaning constitutes a central condition of mental health and existential resilience.

In recent years, an increasing number of applications have emerged that are explicitly designed to facilitate reflection on meaning and life purpose. Examples include Elixir: Find Balance & Purpose, Meaning of Life Experiment, and Ikigai Life Compass. These tools typically offer brief exercises, reflective prompts, and elements of EMA to enhance awareness of personal values, sources of meaning, and life direction. Their aim is not to provide ready-made answers but to support users in constructing their own existential narratives, defining long-term goals, and deepening their sense of life coherence. Systematic evaluation of the effectiveness of such applications—and of PTIs developed on their basis—constitutes a valuable analytical objective.

Against this backdrop, a well-documented, though still requiring further replication, intervention is the seven-day program proposed by Joep van Agteren et al. (2021). This short, low-intensity process targeted adults from the general population. Each day, participants completed a single 10–15-minute task, including identifying personal sources of meaning, reflecting on core values, formulating long-term goals, working on internal coherence, and composing an individual purpose statement. The intervention was complemented by brief repeated assessments of ongoing experience: three times daily, the application prompted participants to report their current sense of meaning and life satisfaction, thereby fostering attentiveness to everyday experiences. The results were unequivocally positive. Compared to a control group, participants demonstrated statistically significant increases in the presence of meaning in life, life satisfaction, and positive affect, with effects of moderate magnitude. Importantly, data analyses revealed a gradual increase in perceived meaning and satisfaction over the course of the intervention, suggesting that even very brief digital programs grounded in existential reflection may strengthen core components of well-being.

3.4.5.3 Spiritual Self-Care

The final category of interventions aimed at strengthening spiritual well-being involves systems that actively encourage the practice of spirituality. An example is the Skylight application, which offers activities such as nondenominational prayer, mindfulness exercises, meditations, intentional goal setting, reflection on meaning, and daily prompts designed to foster self-reflection. A distinctive feature of this solution is its worldview openness: use of the application does not require identification with any specific religious tradition or belief system, rendering it potentially accessible to a broad range of users, including those who identify as "spiritual but not religious."

Preliminary empirical evidence suggests that such programs show promise, although their benefits appear to be selective. A review conducted by Susanna Park et al. (2024), encompassing pioneering studies among members of Generation Z, indicates that the use of the Skylight application was associated with improvements in selected dimensions of spiritual well-being, particularly within the personal domain. These changes primarily concerned users' subjective perceptions of their spiritual lives, increased reflectiveness, enhanced sense of meaning, and more mindful engagement with everyday experiences. At the same time, the authors emphasize that the observed effects were moderate and did not extend across all analyzed dimensions of spirituality. This underscores the need for further research into underlying mechanisms, the durability of effects, and the conditions under which such applications may meaningfully strengthen spiritual well-being.

3.4.6 Personal Growth PTIs

This section integrates research on the effectiveness of PTIs designed to strengthen individual resources essential for flourishing. These include procedures targeting dispositions examined within conceptual frameworks developed in positive psychology (e.g., PsyCap and character strengths), as well as constructs adopted and further elaborated within the field (e.g., growth mindset). The scope may also encompass programs aimed at enhancing cognitive functioning and developing digital strengths (see Section 3.2.2).

3.4.6.1 Cognitive Optimization

Cognitive optimization refers to the strengthening of mental functions that enable individuals to sustain engagement, pursue goals, and function adaptively across diverse life domains. From a flourishing perspective, such interventions may be conceptualized as enabling mechanisms: they do not directly increase well-being but rather enhance the cognitive conditions that support self-regulation, perseverance, and the effective pursuit of valued goals.

Two primary lines of inquiry can be distinguished. The first concerns the impact of cognitive training interventions on psychological functioning and is rooted in models of adaptation and cognitive plasticity. The second focuses on neuro-enhancement practices, including biohacking activities inspired by the idea of augmenting cognitive capacities beyond compensatory aims. In the former case, change results from systematic training of cognitive systems; in the latter, it derives from direct modulation of their biological substrates.

Cognitive training interventions consist of structured exercise programs designed to improve working memory, attention, cognitive control, and executive functions (e.g., Birtwistle et al., 2025; Nęcka, 2018). In digital environments, they most commonly take the form of adaptive computer-based programs, including n-back tasks that dynamically adjust difficulty levels to users' current performance. Although screen-based solutions predominate, the development of this category increasingly includes multimodal and neurophysiologically monitored approaches, currently tested primarily under experimental conditions (e.g., Kwaśniak et al., 2025).

Research on the effectiveness of cognitive training has focused largely on older adult populations. Findings are promising yet inconclusive. For instance, a meta-analysis involving individuals over the age of 60 (Bonnechère et al., 2020) demonstrated that commercial computerized cognitive training games were associated with significant improvements in processing speed, working memory, executive functions, and verbal memory, but no significant effects were observed for attention or visuospatial abilities. At the same time, intervention effectiveness may be moderated by motivational factors, levels of technological competence, and subjective appraisal of the training context. Performance pressure or technology-related anxiety may reduce engagement and attenuate potential benefits, particularly among older adults.

The second analytical pathway within cognitive optimization concerns interventions aimed not solely at training specific cognitive processes but at regulating neurophysiological parameters in order to enhance cognitive and affective performance. This area is rapidly evolving within the field of neurotechnology and includes the use of neurofeedback, advanced wearable systems, and BCIs.

An important research challenge in this context involves intensifying analyses of transhumanist enhancement—that is, practices oriented toward exceeding normative developmental trajectories (see Section 1.4.1). Given the still limited, though growing, number of individuals experimenting with biotechnological augmentation, research strategies based on case studies, interviews, and qualitative analyses of biohackers' narratives appear particularly appropriate (e.g., Łukaszewicz-Alcaraz, 2020). From a PCyb perspective, it is also essential to link indicators of increased cognitive performance resulting from intentional biological intervention with sustained enhancement of flourishing. Equally important is the identification of conditions that minimize the risk of instrumentalizing mental performance at the expense of personal integration, and the embedding of these considerations within a broader ethical reflection.

3.4.6.2 Psychological Capital

PsyCap (Luthans et al., 2007) is defined as a positive developmental state comprising four core resources: hope, optimism, resilience, and self-efficacy. Together, these resources synergistically support individuals' motivation to act, perseverance in goal pursuit, and adaptive functioning in the face of adversity.

Pioneering research conducted by the team led by the originator of the concept demonstrated that PsyCap can be developed through a highly focused, two-hour web-based training intervention (Luthans et al., 2008). Subsequently, Justin W. Carter and Carolyn Youssef-Morgan (2022) compared interventions delivered in three formats: traditional face-to-face sessions, online e-learning platforms, and a micro-learning model administered via a mobile application. Despite differences in content delivery, all three variants resulted in significant increases in PsyCap immediately after program completion, and resource levels remained elevated six weeks later compared to baseline. Notably, the micro-learning format produced the strongest immediate gains, suggesting the potential advantage of brief, distributed modules over a single intensive session. The findings also indicated that improvements in goal attainment emerged with a temporal delay, implying that increases in PsyCap precede changes in behavior and performance outcomes.

Within this context, analyses should also address the individual components constituting PsyCap. For example, interventions targeting resilience—understood as the capacity to maintain psychological balance and adaptive functioning despite stress and adversity—have been extensively studied. A meta-analysis (Schäfer et al., 2024) encompassing over one hundred randomized studies indicates that the most commonly implemented formats include mobile applications, web-based courses, and blended programs (web plus application), often incorporating elements of CBT and mindfulness techniques. The effects of such interventions are small to moderate but statistically significant, involving the strengthening of resilience-related factors, with effectiveness comparable to traditional forms of psychological support. As with many of the interventions discussed earlier, further research is needed to examine the long-term durability of effects, identify the mechanisms underlying functional improvement, and explore the role of personalization in enhancing intervention efficacy across diverse user groups.

3.4.6.3 Character Strengths

Within the VIA framework, character strengths such as creativity, curiosity, kindness, gratitude, humor, and spirituality are defined as positive personality traits that reflect the core of an individual's identity, lead to beneficial outcomes for oneself and others, and contribute to the "greater good" (Niemiec, 2017). Among them, so-called *signature strengths* are distinguished—typically three to seven strengths that a person owns, celebrates, and frequently exercises. For one individual, these may include curiosity, love of learning, and humor; for another, kindness, gratitude, and spirituality.

In the context of PPIs, character strengths are most commonly applied in two complementary ways: (a) through relatively universal exercises targeting specific strengths (e.g., gratitude letters and "counting blessings" for gratitude; counting acts of kindness for kindness; "three funny things" for humor), and (b) through individualized strengths-based interventions, in which participants first identify their most pronounced strengths (e.g., top five VIA strengths) and subsequently integrate them intentionally into daily functioning. In the latter case, particularly well-documented effectiveness has been demonstrated for PPIs involving the "use of signature strengths in a new way" and the gradual formation of a habit of regular strengths application. Research indicates that such interventions increase positive affect, meaning in life, subjective well-being, and life satisfaction, while also reducing depressive symptoms and general distress in both general populations and individuals with health-related burdens (Casali & Feraco, 2025). Importantly, the greatest psychological benefits arise not from a one-time exercise, but from systematic and habitual use of one's strengths in everyday contexts.

Although character strengths are typically conceptualized in the literature as relatively stable traits, findings by Fabian Gander et al. (2024) suggest that they are amenable to change. In one-week and four-week programs, participants first learned the language of strengths and observed their manifestations, and then systematically applied their signature strengths in new contexts over subsequent days, aiming to transform this practice into a habit. These activities led not only to increases in subjective and social well-being and reductions in stress but also to increases in strengths-related states (more frequent enactment of strengths-based behaviors during the week) and, albeit to a lesser extent, changes at the trait level, including reductions in neuroticism. This mechanism may be described as a bottom-up process: repeated, intentional, episodic use of strengths (states), applied in novel and action-embedded ways (habit formation), strengthens self-identification with the given strength and consolidates associated behavioral patterns, gradually shifting the individual's trait profile.

In this context, an important challenge lies in transforming the established strengths builder program (Niemiec & McGrath, 2019) into scalable digital protocols delivered through applications, online platforms, or chatbots. An example is the chatbot-based version of the strengths assessment intervention, tested in a series of three studies conducted by Ivan Liu et al. (2024). The chatbot guided users through the identification of character strengths, contextualization within personal experiences, and deeper self-reflection on situations in which these strengths were, or could have been, applied. This process enhanced participants' awareness of their resources and served as a foundation for subsequent exercises involving active strengths use. Notably, mere identification of strengths proved insufficient to generate significant well-being effects. The strongest improvements were observed when the chatbot was capable of personalizing recommended activities, conducting multistage dialogue, and providing immediate, empathic feedback. These three elements emerged as key mechanisms of digital "strengths building," positioning the chatbot as a promising tool for designing engaging and effective interventions.

3.4.6.4 Growth Mindset

One of the key contributions of psychology has been the identification of the regulatory role of individuals' lay intuitions about their own traits and abilities. According to Carol S. Dweck's (2006) framework, two types of such beliefs can be distinguished: a growth mindset and a fixed mindset. A growth mindset assumes that intelligence, abilities, and competencies are not fixed attributes but can be developed through practice, perseverance, and constructive feedback. In contrast, a fixed mindset assumes that abilities are innate and immutable, and that failure reflects a lack of talent, which typically leads to the avoidance of challenging tasks and more rapid disengagement in the face of obstacles.

An example of a PTI designed to cultivate a growth mindset is the web-based self-help procedure We-SMILE (Web-based Single-session Intervention of Mindset on Intelligence, Failure, and Emotion) described by Yongyi Wang et al. (2025b). The protocol consists of a 45-minute intervention comprising five complementary components, including psychoeducational content on the role of failure and feedback in development, personal narratives, video materials, a panel addressing common misconceptions about growth mindset, and self-persuasive writing exercises. The procedure includes assessments of growth mindset, anxiety, and psychological well-being conducted before the intervention, as well as two and eight weeks afterward. The effectiveness of this intervention requires further empirical validation.

Growth mindset represents a particularly promising intervention target given its relevance to functioning in the face of challenges and its potential to moderate the effectiveness of other developmental interventions. Research indicates that it promotes the selection of more demanding tasks under conditions requiring immediate effort and may influence decisions to pursue more challenging educational pathways (Yeager et al., 2019). Future research should examine whether such beliefs moderate engagement in PTI protocols, persistence in their implementation despite temporary lack of observable effects, and the interpretation of feedback generated by digital systems.

3.4.7 Summary

The Enhancement perspective systematizes research on intentionally designed digital practices aimed at strengthening specific components of flourishing, here referred to as PTIs. It advances a conceptual and methodological framework for investigating such interventions. This framework specifies definitional criteria and proposes typologies based on intervention aims, theoretical foundations, stage of empirical validation, technological architecture, and level of automation. It further delineates conditions of efficacy, including design quality, recruitment and retention strategies, adoption processes, implementation fidelity, evaluation standards, and adherence to ethical principles.

Research on PTIs has been organized with reference to domains of physical, mental, social, and spiritual well-being, as well as personal growth. Within these broader domains, more specific intervention aims have been identified, resulting in the delineation of 18 distinct groups of interventions. The reviewed evidence suggests that digital interventions may strengthen diverse components of flourishing; however, many of the solutions discussed currently hold the status of promising yet insufficiently validated intuitive practices. Their effectiveness requires confirmation through rigorous experimental research that accounts not only for the durability of effects but also for their mechanisms and contextual determinants. Existing findings are heterogeneous, and the positive impact of interventions is substantially moderated by the quality and intensity of user engagement, levels of technological competence, contextual conditions, and person–activity fit.

Importantly, research conducted within the Enhancement perspective does not aim to multiply technologically supported interventions or to uncritically promote technological enhancement of human functioning. Rather, it constitutes an analytical laboratory in which practices derived from positive psychology are reorganized under the influence of digital affordances. Central challenges include identifying the psychological mechanisms underlying PTIs' effectiveness and examining the configurations of design features, motivational processes, and contextual conditions that, under specific circumstances, support the sustainable strengthening of flourishing through digital practices.

3.5 Integration Perspective: Upward Dynamics of Flourishing

The Integration perspective focuses on the systemic dynamics through which digitally mediated experiences become embedded in broader developmental processes. The central research question is: How do dynamic interrelations among individual, technological, and environmental conditions initiate and sustain upward trajectories of flourishing?

The use of the term *integration* in the name of this perspective underscores that the object of analysis is not isolated effects of technology use, but rather the dynamic relations and feedback loops among a broad constellation of factors that co-constitute the system of flourishing components. This does not imply replacing the previously distinguished analytical perspectives; instead, it involves their reorganization within a systemic explanatory architecture. This architecture is structured around complementary analytical pathways referring to three interrelated aspects: type of technology, well-being domains, and the flourishing system.

1. Type of technology. Attention is focused here on individuals' use of specific types of digital tools in order to identify the conditions under which their use exerts the most beneficial impact on life. Accordingly, the analysis should integrate those factors that ensure the associated digital practices are harmoniously embedded in the user's overall functioning, undertaken autonomously, and supportive of health and adaptive capacity. Conducting such analyses requires methodological strategies adequate to the heterogeneity and fragmentation of the available empirical evidence. Particularly valuable are systematic reviews complemented by systematic narrative synthesis, which enable the integration of findings derived from diverse research paradigms, levels of analysis, and types of operationalization. A desirable outcome of this line of inquiry is the development of conceptual models integrating conditions and outcomes, together with a specification of the logic linking these factors. The subsequent step involves their empirical testing across diverse user groups, types of technology, and cultural contexts, thereby allowing for the assessment of their validity and generalizability.
2. Well-being domains. Within this analytical pathway, attention shifts toward explaining how digitally generated experiences strengthen specific components of flourishing, as understood within established theoretical frameworks of psychological mechanisms. The central concern is therefore not when and under what conditions technology is used advantageously, but why and through which processes its use contributes to fostering specific domains of well-being. Accordingly, research methodology should remain aligned with the adopted theoretical assumptions while enabling the empirical testing of the functional equivalence of digital and non-digital experiences, as well as the modeling of the dynamic configurations through which they reinforce particular components of flourishing.
3. Flourishing system. The third pathway adopts a systems perspective on flourishing (Höltge et al., 2023), examining how digital technology use may strengthen specific well-being domains and thereby reconfigure their interrelations. This perspective shifts the emphasis from analyzing isolated components of flourishing toward examining their systemic interdependencies, thereby deepening the understanding of the phenomenon and opening space for the development and empirical testing of alternative modes of conceptualization. If flourishing is shaped by interactions among domains, contexts, and practices, its structure may not be adequately captured by a static aggregate model but may instead need to be analyzed as a dynamically configured system. At this stage, however, the primary aim is not to assert ontological emergence but to examine whether flourishing can be more adequately modeled as an emergent configuration at the epistemic level. Such modeling may constitute a preliminary step toward more robust ontological claims while remaining methodologically cautious and empirically grounded.

Using a vertical metaphor, analyses conducted within the technology-specific perspective may be described as a "bottom-up" approach to the formation of well-being domains. That is, they examine flourishing through the lens of how specific technologies are used while identifying the components of flourishing that are thereby strengthened. Research conducted within the well-being domains perspective, in contrast, enables a "top-down" view, proceeding from theoretical frameworks that explain the strengthening of well-being domains and identifying the configurations of online and offline experiences that support them. Analyses situated within the flourishing system perspective operate at a meta-systemic level, as they focus on the dynamic interrelations among the components of well-being themselves. Together, these three analytical lenses form a multilevel explanatory architecture of flourishing in digital contexts.

In the subsequent part of the chapter, a preliminary systematization of theoretical approaches and empirical studies associated with the distinguished analytical pathways is proposed. Importantly, many of the research directions presented here remain programmatic in nature and should be understood primarily as indications for further exploration.

3.5.1 Technology-Specific Developmental Configurations

Analyses conducted within this pathway are oriented toward identifying and modeling the conditions under which interactions with specific classes of digital systems may initiate flourishing trajectories. Owing to its focus on particular types of digital tools, this approach is complementary to UX analyses, while substantially extending their scope by incorporating psychological variables, including precisely operationalized components of flourishing. The integration of knowledge in this area is initiated by the examples presented below, which concern the use of social media, VR technologies, and video and mobile games. As the field continues to mature, the range of digital system classes subjected to analysis should be systematically expanded.

3.5.1.1 Social Media

Maya Gudka et al. (2021) conducted a systematic review of 118 studies from 26 countries, encompassing more than 50,000 participants and addressing seven major social media platforms. Their analysis demonstrated that the potentially beneficial effects of social media use are conditioned by six main categories of interrelated factors. The outcomes identified in the reviewed studies were organized with reference to the domains described within the Comprehensive Inventory of Thriving (Su et al., 2014), including relationships, subjective well-being, mastery/achievement, autonomy, engagement/meaning, and optimism. The distinguished conditions include:

1. Platform design. The architecture of digital platforms shapes patterns of interaction, intensity of engagement, and the psychological processes activated through features such as content visuality, speed of information flow, and the visibility of social reactions. Research indicates that solutions strongly emphasizing popularity metrics and algorithmic content selection may heighten orientation toward social evaluation and comparison, thereby modifying the impact of use on well-being.
2. Psychological needs and individual motivations. Social media use fosters flourishing when it supports the satisfaction of the basic needs for autonomy, competence, and relatedness described within SDT (Ryan & Deci, 2000), as well as the pursuit of personal goals and authentic identity expression. Externally oriented motivations, focused on self-presentation and social approval, are more frequently associated with intensified social comparisons and less favorable well-being indicators. At the same time, self-determination provides an important, though not exhaustive, interpretative framework for these relationships.
3. Usage/experience. The psychological consequences of platform use depend largely on patterns of engagement and the user's subjective experience. Active forms of engagement tend to promote connectedness, agency, and positive affect, whereas passive browsing is more often associated with social comparison and declines in mood.
4. Baseline well-being. Well-being functions both as an antecedent and a potential outcome of social media use, influencing the risk of problematic engagement and the adaptiveness of online practices. Although individuals with lower well-being may experience compensatory benefits through social support, they are simultaneously more vulnerable to the negative consequences of passive or compulsive use.
5. Individual differences. User characteristics such as personality, age, gender, cultural context, and life situation significantly moderate both patterns of social media use and their psychological consequences. For example, higher neuroticism is associated with greater susceptibility to negative affect, whereas for introverted individuals or those with lower social competencies, asynchronous communication may constitute a relatively safe environment for relationship building.
6. Social comparison. Social media intensifies social comparison processes, which are among the strongest predictors of lowered mood, reduced self-esteem, and stress. However, the nature of these effects depends on the type of comparison involved: opinion comparisons may have an inspiring function, whereas comparisons of abilities, achievements, or appearance more frequently lead to negative outcomes, creating feedback loops with diminished well-being.

The analyses indicate that the relationship between social media use and flourishing is contextual and bidirectional: social media can influence users' well-being, yet baseline well-being and individual characteristics simultaneously shape patterns of platform use. In the authors' conceptual framework, configurations of the identified factors may initiate a positive, reinforcing virtuous spiral between self-determination, individual traits, usage patterns, and flourishing, ultimately fostering increasingly intentional, reflective, and autonomous engagement with social media. The same feedback logic also allows for the anticipation of negative spirals, triggered under conditions of psychological resource deficits (e.g., loneliness, reduced autonomy, and low self-esteem). In such circumstances, media use may exacerbate existing difficulties and consolidate maladaptive well-being trajectories.

The proposed model does not constitute an explanatory theory in the strict sense but rather a general framework integrating existing empirical findings and offering a heuristic invitation for further research. Future work should expand the set of considered factors to include environmental conditions and clarify their interrelations with other determinants of social media use (see Section 3.5.2.3).

3.5.1.2 Video and Mobile Games

Christian M. Jones et al. (2014) presented a narrative review of research on the associations between video games and flourishing, situating their analysis within two complementary frameworks: flourishing as "more than the absence of disorder" (Huppert & So, 2013) and the PERMA model (Seligman, 2011). Although the authors did not propose a formal dynamic model, they synthesized the evidence in a manner that highlighted the most plausible moderators and mechanisms shaping the consequences of gaming, including its potential to support flourishing. These include:

1. Time spent gaming. Some studies suggest a curvilinear relationship, indicating that moderate gaming may be associated with more favorable well-being outcomes than either excessive gaming or complete nonengagement.
2. Style of engagement and self-regulation. A crucial distinction concerns harmonious versus obsessive engagement, which determines whether gaming serves a restorative function (e.g., relaxation and stress reduction) or becomes compulsive and conflict-generating.
3. Immersion and flow experience. Supported by optimal challenge–skill calibration and immediate feedback, gaming may facilitate relaxation and engagement; however, in certain vulnerability profiles, high immersion may hinder self-control and increase the risk of problematic gaming patterns.
4. Social context and online–offline transfer. Multiplayer games can foster relationships and social capital (e.g., through cooperation and belonging), while

playing with offline friends may strengthen cognitive–social "bridges" that support self-regulation.

5. Design logic and game characteristics. Clear goals, progressive difficulty scaling, rewards, and frequent micro-achievements may enhance experiences of competence and accomplishment.
6. Baseline well-being. Lower well-being (e.g., loneliness) may precede the risk of problematic gaming, with gaming then functioning as a short-term compensatory strategy.
7. Content (including violence). Within this framework, content is treated as part of a broader configuration of motives and context. Violent elements do not necessarily constitute the primary source of enjoyment; players often choose such games for the challenge, autonomy, and perceived "freedom of action" within virtual worlds.

Findings from a more recent meta-analysis conducted by Łukasz D. Kaczmarek et al. (2025) significantly refine these insights, particularly those concerning the role of gaming "dose." Integrating global data collected during the lockdown period (March 2020–December 2021), the authors identified only a slight increase in gaming time relative to the pre-pandemic period and, importantly, no significant association between time spent gaming and indicators of mental health—both positive (e.g., happiness, positive affect, and relaxation) and negative (e.g., depression, anxiety, stress, and loneliness). From a modeling perspective, this suggests that "amount of time" functions primarily as a contextual indicator or a potential "risk gateway" (e.g., for problematic gaming), rather than as a universal predictor of flourishing.

Parallel to research on video games, studies should also investigate how mobile game use may initiate and reinforce growth-oriented trajectories. Owing to their distinct usage context—shorter sessions, high accessibility, strong embedding in everyday micro-breaks, and widespread free-to-play models—mobile games are increasingly treated as a specific subcategory of gaming activity (e.g., Zendle et al., 2023). Regardless of the type of game analyzed, however, conceptual models should incorporate the broader context of engagement. For instance, a player who controls an attractive and self-confident character in a game may begin to display greater confidence in social interactions beyond the gaming environment (Szolin et al., 2023b). Similarly, it is necessary to account for indirect gaming involvement (Strojny et al., 2023), including the quality of experiences generated through associated cognitive and interpersonal activities.

3.5.1.3 Virtual Reality

Based on a scoping review encompassing 18,008 publications from the VR and well-being literature, of which 187 articles were coded for final analysis,

Jih-Hsuan T. Lin et al. (2025b) systematically organized the dispersed body of knowledge concerning the impact of VR technologies on user well-being. The outcome of this synthesis was the development of the conceptual VIEW model (Virtual Reality InducE Well-being), which explicitly models the beneficial mechanism of VR influence as a four-stage sequence: VR design features → experiential illusions → psychological mechanisms → outcomes in well-being domains. The VIEW model thus assumes that VR technologies do not affect well-being directly, but rather through user experience structured by specific design solutions.

The authors identified three key classes of design elements: the virtual environment, the interactions and events occurring within that environment, and the representation and properties of the virtual body. Their configuration gives rise to specific experiential illusions that function as mediators between technology and psychological processes relevant to well-being. These include: place illusion—the subjective sense of actually being in another location, strongly associated with affect regulation; plausibility illusion—engaging cognitive processes and enhancing perceived meaningfulness and agency; and virtual body ownership—enabling embodied perspective-taking, reorganization of the self-concept, and increases in self-efficacy, empathy, and prosocial behavior.

Modeling flourishing trajectories initiated through VR use requires moving beyond the analysis of immersive experiences per se and embedding them within the offline environment. Such a perspective is offered by the ERA (Enable–Reconnect–Augment) approach developed by Sigbjørn Litleskare et al. (2020) on the basis of a review of research on immersive virtual nature (IVN). The authors conceptualize the impact of virtual nature not as a one-time regulatory episode but as a set of potential levels of application that may support more enduring changes in the human–nature relationship and health. Within this framework, IVN may: (1) enable access to beneficial experiences, particularly when contact with real nature is limited (e.g., supporting stress reduction and increased positive affect); (2) reconnect users by strengthening connectedness to nature and motivating engagement with real natural environments; and (3) augment or "boost" the benefits of human–nature interaction through additional elements (e.g., attentional guidance, savoring, and mindfulness instructions) that may subsequently be transferred into offline practices.

VR may represent a privileged laboratory for studying flourishing as a dynamically induced process. Integrating factors identified in frameworks such as VIEW and ERA allows for a more comprehensive understanding of how experiences generated by immersive technologies can be incorporated into long-term, contextually embedded flourishing trajectories. The development of more complex models would benefit from incorporating variables identified in gaming research, particularly given the growing number of games employing immersive technologies, as well as VR-specific conditions related to the type and quality of technology (e.g., strength of immersion) and the phenomenon of cybersickness.

3.5.2 Fostering Well-Being Domains

Within this analytical pathway, attention is directed toward developmental trajectories structured by psychological mechanisms through which reciprocally configured experiences across virtual and material environments reinforce specific components of flourishing. To organize these considerations heuristically, three complementary pillars of flourishing are proposed, corresponding to the typology of positive technologies identified in the literature: hedonic, eudaimonic, and social (Riva et al., 2012). This distinction serves a purely analytical purpose and should not be interpreted as implying ontological separateness among these dimensions.

3.5.2.1 Hedonic Pillar of Flourishing

Explaining what makes individuals' use of digital technologies contribute to the pleasantness of their lives is embedded in a rich tradition of psychological research on the mechanisms underlying life satisfaction judgments. These studies indicate that people typically do not experience difficulty in forming such evaluations, and that a salient contextual cue informing this process may be momentary affect ("How do I feel about it?"; Schwarz & Clore, 1988). An analogous mechanism may be activated by experiences occurring in digital environments. For example, exposure to emotionally charged online content (e.g., memes) has been shown to effectively induce specific affective states, which subsequently color global evaluations of well-being (Myrick et al., 2022).

According to Prospect Theory (Kahneman & Tversky, 1979), more enduring changes in life satisfaction may arise from experiences that derive their significance not from their absolute hedonic intensity but from relational comparisons with a reference point, most often the current status quo. From this perspective, the strengthening of the hedonic component of flourishing depends on the subjective interpretation of technology-related outcomes in terms of perceived gains and losses (e.g., "it is better than before," "it is worse than I expected"). Such effects, however, require the experience to exceed an individual's subjective positivity threshold, which is not fixed but dynamically shifts in accordance with prior experiences and evolving expectations. Important constraints may stem from anhedonia—manifested as a reduced capacity to experience pleasure (Cangelosi et al., 2025)—as well as from the phenomenon of the hedonic treadmill, that is, rapid adaptation to favorable changes (Brickman & Campbell, 1971). Consequently, even seemingly intense and enjoyable experiences enabled by appropriate design solutions may gradually lose their capacity to reinforce the hedonic component of flourishing.

A broader theoretical framework for explaining the regulatory function of positive digital experiences within the wider context of human life is provided by Barbara Fredrickson's (2001) Broaden-and-Build Theory. According to this account, positive emotions broaden individuals' momentary thought–action repertoires, influencing information processing, cognitive flexibility, and readiness to engage in behaviors that foster exploration, learning, and relationship formation—both offline and online. Over time, this broadening effect contributes to the building of enduring psychological resources, which in turn facilitate further engagement in activities conducive to positive emotional experiences. The proposed sequence—emotions → cognitive processes → behavior → resources → subsequent emotions—describes a self-reinforcing upward spiral that promotes well-being. Digitally mediated positive experiences may serve as initiators or amplifiers of such spirals.

An ambitious, though ultimately unsuccessful, attempt to formalize this logic was the mathematical modeling of flourishing proposed by Fredrickson and Losada (2005). Drawing on concepts from dynamical systems theory, the authors sought to model the nonlinear interplay between positive and negative affect, assuming that affective dynamics evolve over time through reciprocal feedback loops. They suggested that different ratios of positive to negative affect could be associated with distinct patterns of system dynamics—ranging from complex, flexible, and relatively stable trajectories (interpreted as flourishing) to more rigid and simplified patterns characteristic of languishing. Although the model was later formally retracted (Fredrickson & Losada, 2013), it retains theoretical significance as an attempt to conceptualize the relationship between affect and well-being within a dynamic systems framework.

An empirical illustration of modeling a segment of the theoretically postulated upward spiral in a digital context is provided by Ye Chen et al. (2021) in their study of mobile social media use during travel. The authors demonstrated that mobile social media engagement was associated with increased positive affect among tourists, which subsequently broadened their cognitive and emotional involvement in the travel experience (e.g., heightened curiosity, environmental interest, and intensity of experience), ultimately contributing to higher levels of subjective well-being. In the proposed model, positive emotions functioned as a mediator, explaining how specific technology-use practices—particularly active and reflective engagement with mobile social media—activated processes of experiential broadening that supported well-being.

However, the analyses did not allow for inferences regarding the existence of a full upward spiral, as temporal change was not tracked and nonlinear dynamics were not tested. The findings documented only a single "turn" of the growth spiral (positive affect → broadened experience → higher well-being), without examining subsequent iterations of the process (e.g., whether enhanced well-being fosters later intensification of positive affect), potential bifurcation thresholds, or distinct patterns of affective dynamics. Nevertheless, these results provide a substantive rationale for further research on strengthening the hedonic component of flourishing within the framework of Broaden-and-Build Theory.

3.5.2.2 Eudaimonic Pillar of Flourishing

The eudaimonic pillar of flourishing can be strengthened through digital practices that support the enactment of personal values, stimulate personal growth, enhance a sense of meaning and personal agency, and foster satisfaction derived from achievement.

A particularly important analytical pathway within this domain involves explaining how digital practices contribute to human development through transformative experiences. According to the framework proposed by Alice Chirico et al. (2022), such experiences constitute a distinct class of psychological phenomena that function as turning points in an individual's life, substantially reconfiguring patterns of functioning. At the level of identity, this may manifest as a sense of "rebirth" or a redefinition of one's life role; at the existential level, as a revaluation of life meaning and long-term goals; and at the relational level, as heightened prosocial orientation or a deeper sense of embeddedness within communities.

The developmental trajectory through which a given experience acquires transformative status unfolds across several interrelated phases. A crucial element is the encounter with a stimulus that exceeds existing interpretative frameworks—a disorienting dilemma—arising either from extraordinary events or from cumulative processes of increasing novelty or complexity. This is accompanied by a state of heightened psychological (and, in some cases, neurobiological) plasticity, involving intensified emotional arousal, focused attention, and alterations in the perception of body, time, and space. The core of transformation lies in the dynamic interplay between epistemic expansion and complex, often ambivalent emotions, leading to the reorganization of belief systems, identity structures, and motivational orientations.

This complexity has important methodological implications. The specificity of transformative experiences often requires idiographic approaches. Such investigations are typically characterized by in-depth qualitative analyses of individual cases and, in the context of human–technology interaction, by the examination of the unique confrontation between particular technological design logics and the individual's sensitivity, biography, and existential concerns.

A coherent conceptual framework for this line of inquiry is provided by Transformative Experience Design (TED; Gaggioli, 2016), which conceptualizes transformative experience as discontinuous, emergent, and embedded in the dynamics of complex systems. Within this perspective, digital environments are understood as mediating tools capable of enabling epistemic expansion and the reconfiguration of self–world relations. TED emphasizes that immersive design logics are particularly effective in generating high-intensity experiences: through manipulations of perception, embodiment, and narrative, immersive environments can readily initiate disorienting dilemmas and temporarily increase psychological plasticity. Importantly, research on awe (Chirico et al., 2024) demonstrates that exposure to immersive environments generates experiences whose phenomenological core closely resembles that elicited in offline settings.

A complementary and design-relevant extension of this pathway is offered by Liminal Design (Liedgren et al., 2023), which specifies how digital systems may be intentionally structured to enable transformative experiences without presuming linear causality. The framework proposes that transformative potential emerges when technology creates a distinct, narratively organized liminal space—an "in-between" zone that is sufficiently stable to preserve psychological safety while remaining open enough to disrupt habitual sensemaking. Transformation is thus conceptualized as a consequence of narrative accommodation under conditions of semiotic ambiguity, supported by two key design mechanisms: optimized abstraction, which reduces competing stimuli and concentrates attention on a carefully staged experiential arc, and suspension of disbelief, which invites users to temporarily bracket ordinary assumptions and engage alternative narratives of self and world. In practical terms, this entails (a) articulating a compelling narrative desire that frames the experience as existentially meaningful rather than merely transactional; (b) designing a clearly demarcated, independent space—physical or virtual—that signals threshold crossing; (c) employing sensory reduction, focalization, and symbolic abstraction to sustain immersion; (d) incorporating friction, ritual, or ceremonial markers that structure the experiential arc; and (e) preserving "narrative room" to allow for personal projection and interpretative flexibility. Illustrative applications discussed by the authors include immersive VR scenarios that modulate perspective and embodiment to elicit awe or empathy, architecturally staged remote-presence environments designed to deepen interpersonal connection, and metaverse-based interventions that intentionally blur performative and real identities in order to provoke reflective destabilization.

Beyond immersive and episodic designs, transformative dynamics may also unfold in more durable and structurally embedded forms of human–technology integration. Processes of cyborgization are particularly amenable to analysis through the theoretical framework of transformative experience. The progressive integration of technological systems with the human body—whether in the form of wearable, implantable, or permanently embedded devices—should not be conceptualized solely as functional augmentation; it may also constitute a site of existential reconfiguration. From this perspective, cyborgization does not merely extend human capacities but may destabilize or gradually transform established self-concepts, reshape embodied experience, and reconfigure perceived boundaries between self and world (Łukaszewicz-Alcaraz, 2020). The transformative experience framework provides a robust analytical lens for examining these dynamics by clarifying how technologically mediated alterations in perception, embodiment, and agency may generate disorienting dilemmas and initiate adaptive restructuring at the levels of identity, value hierarchies, and long-term life orientation. In this sense, cyborgization can be conceptualized as a developmental process unfolding within the dynamics of psychological plasticity rather than solely as a technological or biomedical intervention.

3.5.2.3 Social Pillar of Flourishing

Relative to the hedonic and eudaimonic pillars of flourishing, the development of social dimensions of well-being has been more extensively conceptualized within frameworks emphasizing the interdependence of offline and online experiences. Their dynamic configurations can be interpreted within several complementary theoretical frameworks. According to social network theory (Holt-Lunstad, 2015), individual functioning is embedded within a relational structure understood as a configuration of nodes (actors) and ties (relationships). From this perspective, what is crucial for well-being is not isolated interactions but the diversity, reach, and distribution of social ties.

This approach is complemented by the concept of social capital (Arampatzi et al., 2018; Duradoni et al., 2024), which indicates that online interactions foster well-being primarily when they sustain and develop already existing relational networks. Digital environments may thus strengthen both bonding capital (close, strong ties) and bridging capital (connections across more heterogeneous social circles), provided they remain embedded within a broader relational ecosystem that also includes offline contexts.

Empirical analyses support these assumptions. In a study involving nearly 11,000 Chinese adults aged 18–69, Meijie Chu et al. (2023) demonstrated that the highest levels of life satisfaction were reported by individuals maintaining relationships both offline and online across diverse personal and professional groups. These findings are consistent with evidence from Western cultures, which likewise underscores the beneficial impact of diverse and multi-contextual group memberships on individual well-being.

At the same time, available data suggest that a substantial shift of relational investment from offline contexts toward digital environments may be associated with a weakening of key resources underpinning social well-being. As Giuseppe Riva (2025) argues, the qualitative depth of embodied social presence cannot be fully replaced by the comfortable yet potentially passivizing concept of a *digital we*. For example, Łukasz D. Kaczmarek and Dariusz Drążkowski (2014) showed in the context of MMORPGs that individuals motivated by escapism exhibited a systematic weakening of offline social support, particularly under conditions of prolonged engagement and strong beliefs in the realism of the game world. Importantly, digital relationships, even when subjectively experienced as meaningful, did not fully compensate for the functions fulfilled by ties rooted in offline environments and did not constitute an independent foundation for sustained social well-being.

Similar limitations have been observed in longitudinal research on social media use. In a nine-year study of Dutch adults, James A. Roberts et al. (2024) found that both passive and active social media engagement were associated with increases in perceived loneliness. The analyses identified a reinforcing feedback loop: heightened loneliness predicted greater online engagement, which in turn maintained or intensified experiences of social isolation.

Accumulated empirical evidence suggests that relational experiences generated in offline and online environments may not be functionally equivalent, even when they are subjectively perceived as comparable in terms of closeness or support (e.g., digital friendship). The difference concerns primarily their structural role within social networks. Offline relationships demonstrate a greater capacity to stabilize and integrate relational resources across multiple life contexts, whereas online relationships more often serve a complementary function—reinforcing or extending existing network configurations, but less frequently constituting their foundational core.

A parallel distinction can be drawn with respect to experiences generated in human–artificial agent interactions. Available evidence indicates a lack of full functional equivalence between support provided by other humans and that offered by advanced technologies, even at high levels of responsiveness (see Section 3.3.4.4). This issue, however, requires further empirical verification, particularly in relation to mechanisms central to upward social trajectories.

In this context, two processes well documented in the relational literature are of particular importance. The first is capitalizing on positive events (Gable & Reis, 2010), understood as sharing positive experiences and receiving an active and constructive response from an interaction partner. This mechanism amplifies psychological benefits, including increases in positive affect, closeness, trust, and intimacy. The second is self-expansion (Aron et al., 1992), which involves the gradual inclusion of the partner's representation into the structure of the self. This process broadens one's repertoire of roles, cognitive perspectives, and action possibilities, thereby strengthening agency, vitality, and relational well-being.

In both cases, the mere simulation of relational activity by artificial systems may prove insufficient to activate the full scope of these mechanisms. A potential moderator of the observed effects is the degree of anthropomorphization of technology. Its strength is closely linked to the process of mind perception (Gray et al., 2007), which positions an entity within a two-dimensional space defined by experience (the capacity to feel affective states) and agency (the capacity for intentional action). Research indicates that humanoid characteristics, such as mimicking facial expressions and gestures, generating empathic responses, and employing narratives that imply intentionality and affective experience (e.g., Cucciniello et al., 2023), shift robots and digital agents within this matrix. This shift may result in the attribution of moral status to artificial agents and their inclusion within the moral community, thereby subjecting them to norms governing acceptable behavior toward them (Wróblewski & Fortuna, 2023). However, the extent to which these processes influence the shaping of social flourishing trajectories in digital contexts remains an empirically open question.

3.5.3 Emergence of Flourishing

The diversity of ontological and epistemological assumptions underlying the concept of flourishing, together with the multiplicity of its operationalizations, necessitates a systematic reconsideration of its structural and dynamic properties. The inclusion of digital technology use as a constitutive context further amplifies this need by exposing additional layers of interdependence among well-being domains. A particularly promising direction of inquiry, therefore, involves examining the systemic organization of flourishing and empirically testing the hypothesis of its emergent character.

3.5.3.1 Systems Perspective on Flourishing

From a systemic perspective, flourishing does not constitute a simple aggregate of relatively independent domains of well-being; rather, it represents their dynamic and relationally interconnected configuration. A key reference point for such a conceptualization is the approach developed within psychopathology, particularly the network model of mental disorders proposed by Denny Borsboom (2017). This framework departs from viewing mental disorders as the effect of a single underlying causal variable (a latent construct) and instead understands them as states emerging from dynamic interactions among observable symptoms. Borsboom's approach is rooted in the paradigm of network psychometrics and is not equivalent to the reflective or formative models employed in structural equation modeling (SEM).

A theoretical impetus for adopting a systemic understanding of flourishing is provided by Centeredness Theory, proposed by Zephyr T. Bloch-Jørgensen et al. (2018). Although this concept has not yet developed into a clearly articulated and coherent research program, it contains several noteworthy assumptions. According to this perspective, no domain of well-being operates in isolation; disturbances or enhancements in one area may initiate cascading effects throughout the entire system. Moreover, the authors assume that the relatively endogenous center of the system is the domain of the Self, which performs an integrative function by organizing the individual's experiences, whereas the remaining domains constitute fields of influence of a more exogenous character.

In the context of flourishing research, it is also significant that this framework explicitly incorporates specific environments of individual functioning—such as educational and occupational contexts—into the definition of well-being.

This approach underscores the need for critical reflection on the legitimacy of conceptualizing flourishing separately within particular life spheres (e.g., McQuaid & Kern, 2017; Rautenbach & Rothmann, 2017). Correlations identified in workplace-based studies (Fortuna et al., 2025a) between occupational flourishing, measured with the Workplace PERMA-Profiler, and the domains of the PERMA-Profiler ($r = .53$–$.65$), as well as overall happiness ($r = .69$), indicate substantial and robust associations, while simultaneously preserving grounds for treating these constructs as non-reducible. Consequently, the current state of research does not allow for a definitive conclusion as to whether the domain of work should be regarded as a component of general flourishing or rather as a relatively autonomous field within the well-being system, whose significance and weight may vary depending on developmental stage, lifestyle, or cultural context.

Empirical support for the hypothesis of the systemic character of flourishing has been provided by Jan Höltge et al. (2023). Using network analysis based on the Secure Flourishing Measure (VanderWeele, 2017), they examined the structure of interrelations among key domains of well-being in a large sample of young adults (aged 18–29) from 10 countries. Their findings indicate that, at a general level, flourishing networks display high structural coherence—manifested, among other features, in strong connections between meaning and purpose in life, life satisfaction, and health. At the same time, however, significant differences emerged in local configurations of relationships among domains depending on cultural and socio-economic contexts. Particularly pronounced heterogeneity was observed in the associations between financial stability and the remaining components of flourishing, which supports its interpretation as a sustaining rather than a constitutive factor within the structure of well-being.

A theoretically significant result of the study was the observation that well-being networks exhibit stronger global connectivity among individuals with lower levels of flourishing, whereas at higher levels of well-being they become more loosely connected. The authors interpret this effect, among other perspectives, in terms of system reactivity: a more densely interconnected configuration of domains may be more susceptible both to negative cascades (e.g., the spread of deficits) and to positive feedback loops in response to interventions. In this sense, flourishing appears not only as a dynamic configuration of interdependent components and processes but as a system whose degree of internal connectivity also determines its level of reactivity.

Particularly relevant for analyses that should be integrated and conducted within the Integration perspective are studies revealing the impact of digital practices on changes in the system of well-being domains. Noteworthy analyses were conducted by Huaiyuan Qi et al. (2025). They compared configurations of well-being components between groups at high risk of PIU and groups at high risk of Internet gaming disorder (IGD), combining latent profile analysis with network analysis of well-being dimensions (hedonic, eudaimonic, and psychological richness indicators).

The authors demonstrated that risk profiles differ not only in mean levels of well-being but also in the pattern of interconnections among its components. Compared with the high-risk PIU group, the high-risk IGD group was characterized not only by higher levels of hedonic and eudaimonic well-being and psychological richness but also by stronger global connectivity within the well-being network. In addition, through the application of the NodeIdentifyR algorithm (NIRA), components were identified whose simulated modification generated the strongest changes across the entire well-being system. In the IGD group, life satisfaction emerged as the key component, whereas in the PIU group it was novel experiences, constituting a central element of the psychological richness dimension.

These findings reinforce the interpretation of flourishing as a system of interdependent components whose structure and dynamics may be reconfigured under the influence of specific digital practices. The differences observed between groups did not concern solely the levels of individual well-being domains; they also encompassed the pattern of interrelations among them—network density, global connectivity, and the centrality of key nodes. In this sense, the study shifts the analytical focus from the question of "how much" well-being characterizes a given group to the question of "how" it is structurally organized.

Such findings raise a fundamental methodological and theoretical question: Do the observed differences reflect variations in the level of a single underlying latent variable, or do they indicate distinct configurations of a system of mutually interacting components? When flourishing is conceptualized as a latent construct, changes in particular domains are theoretically relevant primarily insofar as they influence the level of the common underlying factor. From this perspective, it is of secondary importance which specific component is strengthened, provided that the global latent trait increases. By contrast, in formative or configurational models, the identity of the strengthened domain becomes substantively significant, as each component contributes uniquely to the overall composite. In such models, differences may concern not only the overall level of flourishing but also the architecture of interrelations among domains—their centrality, the strength of their connections, and the mechanisms through which changes propagate across the system (as illustrated by life satisfaction in the IGD group and novelty in the PIU group). The modeling framework is therefore not neutral: it determines whether analytical attention is directed primarily toward the magnitude of a common factor or toward the structure and differential contribution of its constituent domains.

In this context, the status of flourishing as a construct becomes a matter of particular importance. Should it be understood as a unidimensional latent variable, a second-order factor, a composite of domains, or as a configurational property emerging from the structural interdependencies among its components? This issue is not merely technical. It shapes how findings concerning the impact of digital practices on the well-being system are interpreted and defines the scope of conclusions that can legitimately be drawn.

From the perspective of future research, it is therefore essential not only to simulate potential changes within well-being networks but, more importantly, to empirically capture the actual processes through which the flourishing system reorganizes under the influence of digitally strengthened well-being domains. Clarifying these mechanisms—including the role of technology as a factor modulating systemic dynamics—opens a particularly promising field of inquiry, especially within the Integration perspective.

3.5.3.2 Flourishing as an Emergent Phenomenon Hypothesis

Beyond the classical conceptualizations of flourishing discussed in the first chapter of this book, methodological literature increasingly emphasizes the legitimacy of considering emergent approaches (Schamberger et al., 2023). Within this perspective, a construct may be conceptualized as a configurational property of a set of components, reconstructed from their patterned co-occurrence and structural interrelations. Importantly, this refers to *epistemic emergence*—that is, a particular way of modeling and representing a construct—rather than to ontological emergence, in which the emergent property would possess autonomous ontic status and causal agency with respect to its components.

Testing the epistemic emergence of flourishing constitutes a further step in developing its systemic conceptualization. Approaches such as confirmatory composite analysis (CCA) and the Henseler–Ogasawara procedure enable researchers to distinguish between two modes of representation: one in which flourishing is specified as a latent common cause of its indicators, and another in which it is modeled as a composite arising from the configuration of interrelated domains. Unlike reflective SEM models, composite approaches do not assume that flourishing underlies and explains its indicators; rather, they treat the global construct as emerging from a structured pattern of co-occurring components. Such modeling allows researchers to assess whether a global representation of flourishing maintains empirical coherence and predictive utility when specified as a configuration of domains, rather than as a single hidden trait accounting for their covariance.

An empirical attempt to examine the hypothesis of the emergent character of flourishing was undertaken by Paweł Fortuna and Marcin Wojtasiński (2026). In this study, flourishing was treated not as an abstract ontological problem but as a modeling question: whether the global PERMA construct is more appropriately represented as a higher-order reflective factor or as a composite derived from the configuration of five interrelated well-being domains. In other words, the aim was to determine whether the choice of modeling framework alters the interpretation of how individual domains contribute to overall flourishing.

The analyses were conducted on data (N = 1067) collected in the course of validating the Polish version of the Workplace PERMA-Profiler (Fortuna et al., 2025a). Two representations were compared: a reflective second-order latent model and a composite specification in which the global level of well-being results from the structural configuration of domains.

The findings demonstrated a remarkably high degree of convergence between the two approaches. Global flourishing scores derived from the latent and composite models were nearly identical, and their associations with external criteria—such as job satisfaction, self-rated health, stress, and negative emotions—were highly similar. These results indicate that PERMA contains a strong common core of well-being that remains stable across alternative model specifications.

At the same time, the composite model revealed nuances that reflective models do not explicitly foreground. It showed that individual domains need not contribute uniformly to the global representation. In certain configurations, the weights of specific components varied depending on the criterion, reflecting statistical interdependencies among domains rather than normative judgments about their intrinsic value. This does not imply that any domain is inherently less important; rather, it suggests that the contribution of a given domain depends on the overall structure of the flourishing system and the context in which flourishing is evaluated.

These findings do not definitively resolve whether flourishing should be understood as a latent or emergent construct. What they demonstrate, however, is that the composite specification makes the internal structure of flourishing analytically transparent. By rendering the relative contribution of individual domains explicit, it shifts attention from the mere level of a global score to the configuration through which flourishing is constituted. Although the present analyses do not directly test the dynamic reorganization of the well-being system, they clarify an important implication for PCyb: if digital practices are assumed to strengthen specific domains of well-being, then understanding their differentiated contribution becomes theoretically and methodologically essential. In this respect, composite modeling provides a framework for examining not only whether flourishing increases but which domains are reinforced and how their relative contribution shapes the global representation of flourishing. Its value, therefore, lies not in resolving the latent–composite debate but in expanding the analytical repertoire available for modeling flourishing as a structurally organized system whose global properties depend on the configuration of its domains.

3.5.4 Summary

The Integration perspective focuses on the analysis of upward trajectories of flourishing within a comprehensive and multilevel framework, integrating insights derived from research conducted at the other levels of analysis within the epistemic model of PCyb. Three complementary analytical pathways are distinguished in this chapter.

The first pathway centers on identifying configurations of factors that condition the beneficial use of specific classes of digital technologies. Illustrative analyses concerning social media, video games, and VR technologies demonstrate that the impact of technology on flourishing depends on complex interactions among design logics, user motivations, styles of engagement, and the broader social context.

The second pathway directs attention to the psychological mechanisms through which experiences generated in digital contexts, dynamically coupled with those emerging in offline environments, strengthen specific domains of well-being. These analyses are organized around three pillars of flourishing: hedonic, eudaimonic, and social, drawing on selected theoretical frameworks and the empirical findings associated with them.

The third pathway advances a systemic understanding of flourishing, conceptualizing it as a dynamic configuration of interdependent components whose structure may be reconfigured under the influence of digital practices. Preliminary findings from network-based studies indicate that relationships among well-being components are not fixed but vary depending on patterns of technology use and the contexts in which individuals function. Further progress in this area may be facilitated by analyses testing the hypothesis of epistemic emergence in flourishing, thereby clarifying how domain-specific technological reinforcement relates to the systemic configuration of flourishing and deepening reflection on the construct's ontological status.

Taken together, these analytical pathways position the Integration perspective as a research framework for examining dynamic and systemic trajectories of flourishing. This framework is grounded in established psychological theories while remaining open to the development of new strategies for modeling and interpreting complex well-being processes in the digital era.

The Future: Research and Practice

Positive cyberpsychology (PCyb) remains a provisionally defined, problem-oriented research domain, and its future will depend on critical evaluation by the scientific community. It is the community that will ultimately determine whether the proposed analytical pathways, modes of knowledge organization, and outlined research directions are regarded as conceptually sound, heuristically useful, and worthy of further development. Equally important will be researchers' willingness to strengthen collaboration, integration, and dialogue under the shared umbrella of PCyb. Such engagement may serve as a consolidating force for initiatives that have thus far remained dispersed, facilitating their institutionalization in the form of thematic conferences and, in the longer term, dedicated academic journals and professional associations.

A positive developmental scenario can be drawn from the history of positive psychology, which, despite initial controversies, managed to move beyond a normative manifesto phase and evolve into a recognizable research tradition. This transformation was made possible through the systematic operationalization of key concepts. It was further supported by the development of measurement instruments and the accumulation of empirical data. It also depended on a sustained readiness to subject its own assumptions to critical revision. By contrast, the proposal of a cognitive anthropology of the person (Cohen & Barrett, 2011) did not undergo a comparable process of scientific consolidation and largely remained at the level of interdisciplinary theoretical reflection, without crystallizing into a stable empirical research program.

At the same time, it is important to clarify that the emphasis placed in PCyb on human flourishing should not be interpreted as reflecting a reductionist or exclusively individualistic stance. Rather, it reflects the individual-level orientation that has historically dominated research within positive psychology. This point is especially important because the future development of PCyb depends not only on the expansion of its analytical ambitions but also on preserving a coherent developmental logic. At the present stage, the field requires not a premature escalation toward increasingly abstract levels of explanation, but a disciplined strengthening of the empirical and conceptual foundations on which such expansion could later rest.

Grounding: Zone of Proximal Development

Given the potential variability of the conditions that will shape the future status of PCyb, it is reasonable at this stage to conceptualize its development in terms of a "zone of proximal development." Such a framing captures both the openness of the field and the constraints that should guide its subsequent development. The developmental horizon of PCyb should not be interpreted as a departure from the individual-level foundation of the proposed epistemic model, but rather as a process that presupposes its further consolidation and systematic empirical grounding.

From the perspective of knowledge development, even the discussion concerning the status of PCyb may possess intrinsic value insofar as it contributes to intensifying scholarly inquiry and theoretical debate on the condition of the human being functioning in digital contexts. In particular, it is desirable to more clearly position flourishing as a central object of psychological inquiry and to systematically investigate the role of digital practices in processes that strengthen it. At the same time, the developmental trajectory of positive psychology—within which a relative balance has emerged among research traditions associated with its three waves—allows one to anticipate a progressive broadening of the analytical scope beyond individual flourishing. This expansion may extend toward social, environmental, and even global forms of the "peak of well-being." Such a direction remains consistent with a shift observable in cyberpsychology from studies focused on single technologies, media, or isolated effects toward relational, processual, and systemic approaches that capture the dynamic interplay among users, technological environments, and cultural–developmental contexts.

Research: Promising Lines of Inquiry

The proposed epistemic model of PCyb represents an attempt to organize a dynamically expanding field of inquiry, motivated by the ambition to comprehensively capture the spectrum of analyses concerning the "bright side" of technology use. The analytical perspectives distinguished within the model were identified through the recognition of thematic clusters and their associated theoretical frameworks and empirical findings. The model is heuristic in nature and functions as an organizing framework; as such, it should not be interpreted as exhaustive or definitive. At the same time, it serves as an invitation to further discussion regarding key research questions, criteria for integrating concepts developed within diverse theoretical traditions, their rigorous operationalization, and the selection of adequate analytical strategies.

At the present stage, the most important task is to transform this heuristic framework into a more stable architecture of research programs. This requires not only identifying broad thematic priorities but also formulating clearly specified lines of inquiry capable of generating cumulative findings, methodological innovation, and practice-relevant knowledge. In this respect, the future consolidation of PCyb depends on whether it can organize a sufficiently coherent agenda in at least four interrelated perspectives.

The first perspective concerns the study of individual resources that enable agentic, reflective, and developmentally beneficial management of digital contexts. Research in this area should move beyond narrow competencies related solely to technical proficiency and consider broader constellations of strengths that combine technological and humanistic capacities. Joseph Aoun's (2018) concept of humanics is instructive here, insofar as it emphasizes the need for the parallel development of technological and humanistic competencies. It may therefore be anticipated that the repertoire of digital strengths will also include dispositions that integrate "hard" and "soft" components. One such example is a disposition provisionally termed well-tech literacy, which combines elements of digital literacy and well-being literacy. The concept of digital literacy refers to competencies related to the informed and skillful use of digital tools and was discussed earlier. In turn, well-being literacy denotes an individual's capacity to understand, articulate, and purposefully apply knowledge concerning well-being, particularly through the use of appropriate conceptual and linguistic resources (Oades & Johnston, 2017). Accordingly, an expression of well-tech literacy would be an individual's ability to formulate informed and context-sensitive expectations regarding the well-being potential of digital technologies, as well as to recognize those features and functionalities that are conducive to flourishing.

The second perspective concerns the identification of conditions supporting the formation of harmonious, healthy, autonomous, and adaptive patterns of digital technology use. The significance of research on digital well-being is likely to increase as the interpenetration of offline and online worlds intensifies, particularly with the development of mixed reality and the metaverse. Efforts to integrate these realities are actively driven by marketing forces, and their ontological fusion is captured by the term "phygital" (Reilly & Dawson, 2021). At the same time, it cannot be ruled out that growing institutional, peer, and infrastructural pressures to engage with digital technologies may generate a boomerang effect (Brehm, 1966), as suggested by findings from a UK survey indicating that nearly half (47%) of respondents aged 16–21 would prefer to be young in a world without the internet (British Standards Institution, 2025). In this context, future research should examine not only processes of technological integration but also the subjective differentiation and strategic separation of offline and digitally mediated spheres of experience. As hybrid environments become increasingly normalized at the infrastructural level, it becomes analytically crucial to investigate how individuals negotiate boundaries between what they perceive as "offline" and "online," and how such boundary work relates to their well-being. Particular attention should therefore be devoted to examining the growing readiness among some individuals to regulate their digital practices, for example, by cultivating the state referred to as the Joy of Missing Out (JOMO; Barry et al., 2023), understood as a willingness to consciously refrain from selected online activities and to derive satisfaction from being temporarily and selectively unavailable. Equally important is examining potential shifts in how individuals subjectively evaluate the quality of proximal outcomes generated through digital practices. This includes evolving criteria for selecting digital tools and the increasing role of value-based and autonomy-oriented considerations in such choices. It also involves the cultivation of digital hygiene practices and a stronger valuation of autonomy in digital contexts. Researchers should also consider the possibility that desirable configurations of proximal outcomes may increasingly be informed by models of the good life originating in the offline world, such as hygge or slow living, which may be reinterpreted and selectively translated into hybrid environments.

The third perspective concerns the effectiveness of positive technology interventions (PTIs) and the mechanisms underlying their impact. One of the key challenges associated with testing the effectiveness of PTIs and implementing intervention protocols lies in sustaining participant engagement. A promising analytical pathway involves incorporating individual-level variables in the form of beliefs about the ontological foundations of one's own nature. The impulse for developing this line of inquiry stems from findings obtained outside the domain of digital technology use, which indicate meaningful associations between such beliefs and well-being–supportive behaviors. Research has shown that manipulating beliefs along the dimension of physicalism versus mind–body dualism leads to systematic differences in health-related decision-making (Burgmer & Forstmann, 2018; Forstmann et al., 2012). Individuals in whom a physicalist perspective was activated were more likely to make choices conducive to a healthy lifestyle. By analogy, it may be hypothesized that beliefs concerning human nature—whether construed as unified or dualistic, and as purely biological or hybrid—could function as moderators of PTI effectiveness. By shaping perceptions of self–intervention congruence, such beliefs may influence both the level of engagement and the interpretation of experienced outcomes.

The fourth perspective concerns the dynamic relationships and feedback loops among individual, technological, and environmental factors that co-constitute upward trajectories of flourishing. Here, the Integration perspective acquires special importance, because it is precisely at this point that PCyb may begin to move beyond a catalog of positive outcomes toward a more systemic model of developmental processes. A systemic and emergent understanding of flourishing shifts the focus from merely registering levels of well-being to examining the direction of growth and its internal organization. In this light, the "peak of well-being" appears not as a statistical maximum but as an ideal of development (e.g., Pawelski, 2016). Such a perspective more firmly situates PCyb within the tradition of humanistic psychology and encourages deeper reflection on the factors that orient developmental trajectories. These factors include aspirational attractors, understood here as value-laden developmental ideals that give trajectories direction and make some pathways more likely than others. An important dimension of analysis concerns how contemporary individuals navigate the tension between axiological transcendentals—truth, goodness, and beauty—and classical developmental tendencies such as the will to meaning (Viktor Frankl), the process of individuation (Carl G. Jung), or self-actualization (Abraham Maslow). It also involves examining tensions with cultural narratives of "super-well-being" and marketing projections of the "happy life," in which satisfaction is often reduced to the intensification of pleasurable experience. At the same time, analyses of the systemic organization of the components of flourishing invite an interpretation of this phenomenon in terms of internally coherent order rather than mere aggregation. Drawing on the concept of engagement in beauty (Diessner, 2019), this structure may be understood as a form of unity-in-diversity—an existential beauty in which the differentiation of experience does not lead to fragmentation but culminates in healthy transcendence (Kaufman, 2020). Within this perspective, aspirational attractors define the teleological vector of development, while unity-in-diversity expresses its structural form, such that flourishing can be understood both as movement toward value and as the lived experience of its realization.

At the same time, the integration of analyses across the distinguished perspectives has revealed numerous conceptual and empirical gaps. Several promising directions for further research were outlined in Chapter 3, together with their theoretical justification and methodological suggestions. What matters now is the extent to which these directions can be translated into sustained research programs capable of stabilizing the field, enhancing theoretical integration, and generating methodologically robust tools adequate for future system-level elaboration.

Applied Implications: Education and the Design of Technological Ecosystems

The scientific consolidation of PCyb depends on robust conceptual and empirical foundations and on its capacity to generate knowledge that meaningfully informs educational practice and the design of digital environments. Application should therefore not be treated as a secondary consequence of theory but as one of the crucial arenas in which the validity and usefulness of the framework are tested.

Max Tegmark (2017), reflecting on the possibility of the emergence of AI systems with superhuman capabilities, called for a global dialogue concerning the directions of artificial system development. He described this as "the most important conversation of our time," emphasizing that careful reflection on the values and goals to which technologies should be subordinated reduces the risk of outcomes misaligned with human well-being. PCyb contributes meaningfully to this debate by underscoring the importance of striving for well-being and flourishing, while simultaneously shifting the focus from what technology is capable of to the human capacities and resources that enable individuals to navigate and manage digital environments in optimal ways. The symbolic enactment of participation in this proposed dialogue may take the form of implementing the knowledge integrated within PCyb in the domains of education and the design of positive digital ecosystems.

In the sphere of education for flourishing in the digital age, the PCyb perspective calls for broadening the dominant prevention-oriented agenda. A substantial body of cyberpsychological literature documents a wide spectrum of risks and dysfunctions associated with online functioning. Consequently, digital education has developed a strong focus on so-called sensitive issues (e.g., cyberbullying, trolling, hate speech, reputational aggression, behavioral addictions, cyberchondria, sexting, online pornography, digital fraud, or misogynistic online communication), the discussion of which aims to foster prevention and harm minimization (Taylor et al., 2017). The PCyb perspective does not negate the importance of these concerns. Rather, it proposes broadening this agenda to include strengthening-oriented phenomena such as cyber-altruism, digital balance, sense of presence, digital flourishing, connectedness, and online social capital. Their introduction into educational contexts is most beneficial when framed within more fundamental categories developed in positive psychology. These include flourishing, well-being, character strengths, and the distinction between hedonic and eudaimonic orientations. Such knowledge can enrich textbooks, educational publications, podcasts, and other materials aimed at cultivating reflective and responsible engagement in digital environments.

The dissemination of knowledge about digital strengths may also benefit from the ongoing public debate concerning "future skills," which is often dominated by anxiety-driven narratives about the need to adapt to accelerating digitalization. Emphasizing the importance of developing digital literacy, digital self-control, and digital empathy enables a departure from a victimological image of the technology user. Instead, it supports tendencies toward agency and prosocial functioning in digital contexts. Importantly, research integrated within PCyb provides not only guidance on training digital strengths. It also offers tools for their reliable assessment. Equipped with these resources, educators can design developmental programs grounded in exercises, case analyses, and reflective tasks.

Research on digital well-being likewise offers a rich body of practically relevant insights. Of primary importance is the empirical verification of common assumptions regarding the central role of screen time and the intensity of digital artifact use. This verification should also examine assumptions about the significance of personal priorities and the quality of functioning in offline environments, including the level of basic psychological need satisfaction. It is therefore crucial to emphasize that design logics and affordance structures may become "traps" primarily when individuals experience deficits in offline rootedness, acceptance, recognition, or security.

Finally, research integrated within PCyb provides knowledge about procedures aimed at strengthening components of flourishing in the form of PTIs and programs aspiring to this status. In this context, cultivating a critical stance toward solutions promoted through marketing becomes especially important, as their long-term psychosocial consequences remain insufficiently examined. Disseminating knowledge about the conceptual, methodological, and ethical standards underlying PTI design should foster more informed expectations regarding the quality of available solutions and the standards governing their implementation.

The applied relevance of PCyb is equally visible in the project of designing flourishing-oriented technological ecosystems. Three primary environments can be identified in which the implementation of knowledge developed within PCyb may prove particularly valuable: the personal and domestic sphere, educational settings, and the workplace. In popular discourse, the term "digital wellness" is often used to describe the cultivation of a "healthy relationship" with technology across these domains. The PCyb perspective, however, endows this notion with a more systemic and axiological dimension.

In the context of private life, the key challenge lies in designing digital order in a way that integrates technology into everyday functioning so that it strengthens interpersonal relationships and processes of restoration rather than eroding them. This becomes especially significant under conditions of hybrid work, where the boundaries between professional and private spheres increasingly blur. The adoption of digital balance and digital hygiene practices may be supported through the development of reflective competencies in managing digital contexts and/or through the involvement of specialists in cyber-counseling. The emergence of such roles could be inspired by the development of PCyb, analogous to the role positive psychology played in the rise of positive coaching. The competencies of such experts would extend beyond individual-level interventions to include the optimization of broader hybrid life systems, encompassing conditions conducive to the satisfaction of basic psychological needs within one's immediate environment.

The application of PCyb-informed knowledge in education aligns with the tradition of educational positive psychology (Seligman et al., 2009). This perspective does not confine itself to enhancing cognitive achievement but emphasizes the role of digital practices in shaping well-being, engagement, and long-term developmental trajectories. It involves both cultivating competencies in the use of technologies that support flourishing and designing learning environments that minimize exposure to risk factors while strengthening students' psychological resources. An inspiring example is Sugata Mitra's (2010) "Hole in the Wall" experiment, conducted in India and Cambodia and later in African countries. Providing children, many of whom were illiterate, with unrestricted access to a computer transformed the artifact into a focal point of shared interest. The children spontaneously developed a collaborative system in which they first guided peers who had access to the keyboard and subsequently engaged in independent experimentation. This case illustrates how digital technologies may function as catalysts of autonomous learning and peer collaboration, provided that they are embedded in environmental contexts that frame them as spaces of exploration rather than instruments of control.

In the workplace, knowledge integrated within PCyb may serve as a foundation for evidence-based design of flourishing-oriented technological ecosystems. This perspective calls for moving beyond narrow criteria of efficiency and cost reduction toward consideration of the long-term impact of technology on employees' well-being, agency, relational quality, and professional development trajectories. Ideally, implementation should encompass the entire technology life cycle: (1) introducing tools in ways that foster their acceptance and establish them as supportive work resources; (2) dynamically adapting technologies to changing conditions and user needs, including monitoring technostress and potential resource-loss spirals; and (3) periodically evaluating solution quality, leading to modification, replacement, or withdrawal when necessary.

It should be emphasized that experiences gathered in workplace contexts, along with evaluations of technologies used in PTIs, constitute invaluable sources of information for designers. Such data enable the assessment of the relevance and quality of design solutions and significantly extend preliminary knowledge derived from traditional UX research. In alignment with the spirit of PCyb, user experiences encompassing both functional and psychological dimensions (e.g., autonomy, cognitive load, relational quality, or sense of meaning at work) should be treated as essential design data rather than merely subjective end-user feedback. Designers may already draw on substantial methodological support in this domain (e.g., Calvo & Peters, 2014; positivecomputing.org). Responsibility for improving technological ecosystems rests with all stakeholders: designers, managers, employees, and users. The core objective is not the maximization of isolated indicators of efficiency or well-being. Rather, it is the systemic strengthening of the quality of life under conditions of hybridization.

Upward Expansion: Toward Collective Flourishing

Building on the grounding process and the research directions outlined above, and assuming the acceptance of the current epistemic model—grounded in individual experience as an analytical entry point—the next stage of development involves extending this architecture "upward" toward collective and systemic flourishing. In line with emerging systemic and regenerative perspectives on well-being (e.g., Steger, 2025), such flourishing should be understood not as the simple sum of individual states but as an emergent property of interconnected social and technological systems. Accordingly, while preserving this analytical point of departure, the upward expansion requires modeling how interactions between individuals and sociotechnical structures are organized, amplified, or attenuated within systems in ways that may support or undermine flourishing at the collective level.

Importantly, although a growing number of theoretical approaches recognize the significance of collective and system-level well-being, fully standardized and widely accepted methods for assessing collective flourishing have not yet been established. Existing approaches—such as multilevel modeling, network-based analyses, and ecological frameworks—offer valuable tools for examining how well-being unfolds across interconnected systems; however, they often rely on aggregated individual-level data or remain limited in their ability to capture the dynamic and emergent nature of collective phenomena (e.g., Lomas et al., 2024a; VanderWeele et al., 2025). To date, collective flourishing is not typically measured directly as a predefined construct but is instead inferred from patterns of interaction, feedback loops, and system-level dynamics unfolding across individuals, technologies, and contexts.

Under these conditions, such an expansion of the epistemic model would require not simply the addition of a new level of analysis but a systematic re-specification of all major perspectives of the model at the collective and systemic level. This involves redefining the same analytical categories so that their core constructs, mechanisms, and units of analysis are appropriate for capturing qualitatively distinct system-level processes, rather than being confined to the individual level.

First, the Dispositional perspective would have to be reformulated in terms of *systemic/collective digital strengths.* These would refer not to aggregated personal traits but to system-level competencies and capacities that support collective engagement with digital technologies and enable the coordinated management of technological resources across groups, organizations, and societies. Such strengths would emerge from patterns of coordination, shared practices, institutional norms, and durable sociotechnical arrangements. They might include, for example, collective attentional governance, shared norms of digital self-limitation, organizational capacities for balancing innovation with psychosocial sustainability, and institutional abilities to coordinate digital participation in ways that protect agency and relational quality.

Second, the Enrichment perspective would require extension toward systemic digital enrichment, grounded in the more demanding construct of collective digital well-being. At this level, the object of analysis would no longer be solely the quality of an individual's digital practices, but rather the quality of technologically mediated functioning within broader systems. The central question would concern whether the sociotechnical arrangements through which people interact are themselves balanced, healthy, autonomous, and adaptive. This would direct research toward the quality of digital participation, coordination, dependence, communication, and technological embeddedness within institutions, communities, organizations, and broader populations.

Third, the Enhancement perspective should be broadened to encompass systemic digital enhancement through the analysis and design of *system-oriented PTIs*. Such interventions would aim to strengthen individual flourishing while supporting multiple domains of collective well-being by shaping digital environments, organizational practices, institutional routines, and policy frameworks governing their use. In this form, PTIs would serve not only as instruments of psychological intervention but also as tools of sociotechnical design. A comprehensive evaluation of their effectiveness would encompass both individual-level outcomes and system-level improvements in resilience, informational justice, relational quality, equitable access, sustainable rhythms of engagement, and robustness under stress.

Fourth, the Integration perspective would require development toward the analysis of the upward dynamics of collective flourishing. Here, the central object of inquiry would be the trajectories through which system-level well-being is strengthened, stabilized, or undermined over time. In this perspective, systemic flourishing would be approached as an emergent property arising from dynamic interactions among individuals who themselves experience flourishing, as well as from the structures and processes that organize these interactions. Research would therefore need to model how gains and losses propagate across systems, how supportive ecologies are formed or eroded, and under what conditions patterns of individual flourishing contribute to system-level flourishing without being sufficient, on their own, to constitute it.

A crucial implication of this upward expansion is that the relationship between individual and collective flourishing can no longer remain implicit. It must itself become a central research problem. This includes identifying the conditions under which individual-level well-being contributes to collective flourishing, the circumstances in which such translation fails, and the mechanisms through which flourishing scales across levels of organization. Such analyses are essential for understanding how collective flourishing emerges, why it sometimes does not emerge despite favorable individual-level conditions, and how sociotechnical systems may display stability or efficiency while simultaneously eroding the flourishing of persons within them.

For this reason, the systemic extension of PCyb should be approached as a carefully staged developmental project rather than as a completed theoretical move. Its feasibility depends on the continued strengthening of methodological approaches capable of capturing multilevel and temporally dynamic processes, including those proposed within Computational Positive Psychology (Hou et al., 2025). In this respect, the further evolution of PCyb may follow a developmental trajectory analogous to the successive "waves" observed in positive psychology, potentially leading toward more systemically oriented iterations of the field.

At the same time, this expansion must be situated within the broader context of rapidly evolving technologies that co-shape global economic, political, social, and cultural transformations in ways that are inherently difficult to anticipate (Benedikter et al., 2022). Research on the impact of digital practices on quality of life and flourishing is therefore particularly susceptible to "black swan" events, as described by Nassim N. Taleb (2007): rare occurrences with high systemic impact that escape dominant predictive models and whose significance is often reconstructed only retrospectively. A paradigmatic example is the COVID-19 pandemic, which within a short period led to a profound reconfiguration of digital practices across vast populations. At the time of writing, new classes of AI systems are emerging that may further intensify this dynamic. One such example is the emergence of "hyperagents"—AI systems designed not only to improve task performance but also to iteratively refine the processes through which those gains are achieved (Zhang et al., 2026). Such systems signal a shift toward forms of artificial agency that operate on both performance and meta-level adaptation, potentially redefining the dynamics of human–technology interaction.

In this context, the continued development of PCyb should depend not on the expectation of environmental stability but on the adequacy, flexibility, and revisability of the conceptual categories it offers for describing human–technology relations. Any future systemic elaboration of the field must therefore remain open to discontinuity, capable of learning from unexpected technological transformations, and sufficiently reflexive to revise its own assumptions when the ecology of digital life changes more rapidly than the theories built to interpret it.

Concluding Synthesis

Positioned between the relatively stable structures of human nature and the accelerating dynamics of technological transformation, individuals and groups in the digital era seek to maintain balance in their lives across hybrid online–offline environments of experience. In this context, PCyb should be understood not merely as a proposal for a new research domain but as an evolving framework for organizing knowledge, guiding empirical inquiry, and informing practice in a world increasingly shaped by digital systems. Its central ambition lies in identifying the conditions under which human–technology relations contribute to flourishing across levels of analysis—from individual experience to collective and systemic dynamics.

In this sense, the development of PCyb reflects a broader transformation in the human sciences: a shift from the analysis of isolated variables toward the understanding of complex, relational, and emergent processes. Such a shift advances methodological pluralism and interdisciplinary openness while redirecting the field's aims from prediction and control toward understanding the dynamic processes through which well-being is sustained, disrupted, and transformed within sociotechnical environments.

Whether PCyb will ultimately provide reliable guidance in this domain remains subject to empirical validation and institutional consolidation. What appears more certain, however, is that growing scholarly sensitivity to the impact of digital technological development on the human condition—combined with theoretical generativity, cumulative research efforts, and sustained empirical rigor—positions the systematic study of the "bright side" of technology use as an increasingly central endeavor within contemporary psychological science. The maturation of PCyb will therefore depend on the coherence of its conceptual architecture and its capacity to integrate diverse lines of inquiry into a cumulative and operationalizable body of knowledge.

At the same time, the significance of PCyb does not rest solely on its potential to establish a new disciplinary domain. The problems it addresses are unlikely to disappear. On the contrary, they will intensify as digital technologies become more deeply embedded in the structures of everyday life, social organization, and global systems. For this reason, the most enduring contribution of PCyb may lie not only in the answers it provides but also in the questions it renders unavoidable—questions concerning how human beings, technologies, and societies can coevolve in ways that sustain and deepen the conditions for flourishing.

From this perspective, PCyb delineates not a closed theoretical system but an open and evolving field of inquiry—one that remains responsive to empirical findings, sensitive to technological change, and oriented toward the long-term task of understanding and shaping the conditions under which flourishing becomes possible in a digitally mediated world.

References

Abele, A. E., & Wojciszke, B. (2014). Communal and agentic content in social cognition: A dual perspective model. *Advances in Experimental Social Psychology, 50*, 195–255. https://doi.org/10.1016/B978-0-12-800284-1.00004-7

Adadi, A., & Berrada, M. (2018). Peeking inside the black-box: A survey on explainable artificial intelligence (XAI). *IEEE Access, 6*, 52138–52160. https://doi.org/10.1109/ACCESS.2018.2870052

Adamowicz, K., & Jurczyk, M. (2023). Digital hygiene – selected methods and tools for managing time in the virtual space by students and working professionals. *Wychowanie w Rodzinie, 30*(1), 107–127. https://doi.org/10.61905/wwr/175095

Ahmetoglu, G., Chamorro-Premuzic, T., Klinger, B., & Karcisky, T. (Eds.). (2017). *The Wiley handbook of entrepreneurship*. John Wiley & Sons, Ltd. https://doi.org/10.1002/9781118970812

Ajzen, I. (1991). The theory of planned behavior. *Organizational Behavior and Human Decision Processes, 50*(2), 179–211. https://doi.org/10.1016/0749-5978(91)90020-T

Alberts, L., Lyngs, U., & Lukoff, K. (2024). Designing for sustained motivation: A review of self-determination theory in behaviour change technologies. *Interacting with Computers, 38*(3), 447–468. https://doi.org/10.1093/iwc/iwae040

Aldbyani, A., Chuanxia, Z., & Alhimaidi, A. (2025). The effect of mindfulness on smartphone addiction: The mediating role of self-regulation learning and the moderating role of digital detox. *Research Square*. https://doi.org/10.21203/rs.3.rs-6405697/v1

Alkhalaileh, M. Y. (2021). Systematic review: Digital entrepreneurship intention. *Network Intelligence Studies, 17*(1), 25–34.

Al Mahmud, A., Wu, J., & Mubin, O. (2022). A scoping review of mobile apps for sleep management: User needs and design considerations. *Frontiers in Psychiatry, 13*, 1037927. https://doi.org/10.3389/fpsyt.2022.1037927

Almourad, M. B., Alrobai, A., Skinner, T., Hussain, M., & Ali, R. (2021). Digital wellbeing tools through users' lens. *Technology in Society, 67*, 101778. https://doi.org/10.1016/j.techsoc.2021.101778

AlSlaity, A., Suruliraj, B., Oyebode, O., Fowles, J., Steeves, D., & Orji, R. (2022). Mobile applications for health and wellness: A systematic review. *Proceedings of the ACM on Human-Computer Interaction*, *6*, 1–29. https://doi.org/10.1145/3534525

Ancis, J. R. (2020). The age of cyberpsychology: An overview. *Technology, Mind, and Behavior*, *1*(1), 9–23. https://doi.org/10.1037/tmb0000009

Aoun, J. E. (2018). *Robot-proof: Higher education in the age of artificial intelligence.* MIT Press.

Arampatzi, E., Burger, M. J., & Novik, N. (2018). Social network sites, individual social capital and happiness. *Journal of Happiness Studies*, *19*, 99–122. https://doi.org/10.1007/s10902-016-9808-z

Arets, T. T. J. E., Perugia, G., Houben, M., & IJsselsteijn, W. A. (2025). The role of generative AI in facilitating social interactions: A scoping review. *arXiv*. https://doi.org/10.48550/arXiv.2506.10927

Armoogum, S., Armoogum, V., Chandra, A., Dewi, D. A., Kurniawan, T. B., Bappoo, S., Mohd Salikon, M. Z., & Alanda, A. (2025). A comprehensive review of cyber hygiene practices in the workplace for enhanced digital security. *JOIV: International Journal on Informatics Visualization*, *9*(1), 137–145. https://doi.org/10.62527/joiv.9.1.3787

Arnold, J. E. (1959). *Creative engineering*. Stanford University Press.

Aron, A., Aron, E. N., & Smollan, D. (1992). Inclusion of Other in the Self Scale and the structure of interpersonal closeness. *Journal of Personality and Social Psychology*, *63*(4), 596–612. https://doi.org/10.1037/0022-3514.63.4.596

Arslankara, V. B., Demir, A., Öztaş, Ö., & Usta, E. (2022). Digital well-being scale validity and reliability study. *Journal of Teacher Education and Lifelong Learning*, *4*(2), 263–274. https://doi.org/10.51535/tell.1206193

Attrill, A. (2015). *Cyberpsychology*. Oxford University Press.

Attrill-Smith, A., Fullwood, C., Keep, M., & Kuss, D. J. (Eds.). (2018). *The Oxford handbook of cyberpsychology*. Oxford University Press. https://doi.org/10.1093/oxfordhb/9780198812746.001.0001

Audrin, C., & Audrin, B. (2023). More than just emotional intelligence online: Introducing "digital emotional intelligence." *Frontiers in Psychology*, *14*, 1154355. https://doi.org/10.3389/fpsyg.2023.1154355

Ayyagari, R., Grover, V., & Purvis, R. (2011). Technostress: Technological antecedents and implications. *MIS Quarterly*, *35*(4), 831–858. https://doi.org/10.2307/41409963

Bailenson, J. (2018). *Experience on demand: What virtual reality is, how it works, and what it can do*. W. W. Norton & Company.

Bakker, A. B., & Demerouti, E. (2007). The job demands-resources model: State of the art. *Journal of Managerial Psychology*, *22*(3), 309–328. https://doi.org/10.1108/02683940710733115

Ballou, N., & Deterding, S. (2024). The basic needs in games model of video game play and mental health. *Interacting with Computers*, *38*(3), 469–486. https://doi.org/10.1093/iwc/iwae042

Bandura, A. (2001). Social cognitive theory: An agentic perspective. *Annual Review of Psychology, 52*, 1–26. https://doi.org/10.1146/annurev.psych.52.1.1

Baños, R. M., Carrillo, A., Etchemendy, E., & Botella, C. (2017a). Positive technologies for understanding and promoting positive emotions. *The Spanish Journal of Psychology, 20*, E50. https://doi.org/10.1017/sjp.2017.42

Baños, R. M., Etchemendy, E., Castilla, D., García-Palacios, A., Quero, S., & Botella, C. (2012). Positive mood induction procedures for virtual environments designed for elderly people. *Interacting with Computers, 24*(3), 131–138. https://doi.org/10.1016/j.intcom.2012.04.002

Baños, R. M., Etchemendy, E., Mira, A., Riva, G., Gaggioli, A., & Botella, C. (2017b). Online positive interventions to promote well-being and resilience in the adolescent population: A narrative review. *Frontiers in Psychiatry, 8*, 10. https://doi.org/10.3389/fpsyt.2017.00010

Barbed-Castrejón, N., Navaridas-Nalda, F., Mason, O., & Ortuño-Sierra, J. (2024). Prevalence of phubbing behaviour in school and university students in Spain. *Frontiers in Psychology, 15*, 1396863. https://doi.org/10.3389/fpsyg.2024.1396863

Bargh, J. A., McKenna, K. Y. A., & Fitzsimons, G. M. (2002). Can you see the real me? Activation and expression of the "true self" on the internet. *Journal of Social Issues, 58*(1), 33–48. https://doi.org/10.1111/1540-4560.00247

Barnes, S., & Prescott, J. (2025). *How digital technologies can support positive psychology*. Emerald Publishing Ltd.

Barry, C. T., Smith, E. E., Murphy, M. B., Halter, B. M., & Briggs, J. (2023). JOMO: Joy of missing out and its association with social media use, self-perception, and mental health. *Telematics and Informatics Reports, 10*, 100054. https://doi.org/10.1016/j.teler.2023.100054

Basch, J. M., Albus, P., & Seufert, T. (2025). Fighting Zoom fatigue: Evidence-based approaches in university online education. *Scientific Reports, 15*, 7091. https://doi.org/10.1038/s41598-025-90973-6

Bauman, Z. (2000). *Liquid modernity*. Polity Press.

Bauman, Z. (2007). *Consuming life*. Polity Press.

Baumeister, R. F., Vohs, K. D., & Tice, D. M. (2007). The strength model of self-control. *Current Directions in Psychological Science, 16*(6), 351–355. https://doi.org/10.1111/j.1467-8721.2007.00534.x

Baym, N. K. (2015). *Personal connections in the digital age* (2nd ed.). Polity Press/Wiley.

Benedikter, M., Gruber, M., & Kofler, I. (Eds.). (2022). *Re-globalization: New frontiers of political, economic and social globalization*. Routledge.

Bennett, D., Feng, F., & Mekler, E. D. (2025). Autonomous regulation of social media use: Implications for self-control, well-being, and UX. In *CHI '25: Proceedings of the 2025 CHI Conference on Human Factors in Computing Systems* (Article 960, pp. 1–22). Association for Computing Machinery. https://doi.org/10.1145/3706598.3713094

Bergmann, R., Rintel, S., Baym, N., Sarkar, A., Borowiec, D., Wong, P., & Sellen, A. (2023). Meeting (the) pandemic: Videoconferencing fatigue and evolving tensions of sociality in enterprise video meetings during COVID-19. *Computer Supported Cooperative Work, 32*, 347–383. https://doi.org/10.1007/s10606-022-09451-6

Betley, J., Warncke, N., Sztyber-Betley, A., Tan, D., Bao, X., Soto, M., Srivastava, M., Labenz, N., & Evans, O. (2026). Training large language models on narrow tasks can lead to broad misalignment. *Nature, 649*, 584–589. https://doi.org/10.1038/s41586-025-09937-5

Biber, D., & Davis, A. (2024). A digital positive psychology intervention for college student mental health and health behaviors. *Mental Health and Digital Technologies, 1*(2), 228–239. https://doi.org/10.1108/mhdt-02-2024-0007

Bieleke, M., Keller, L., & Gollwitzer, P. M. (2021). If-then planning. *European Review of Social Psychology, 32*(1), 88–122. https://doi.org/10.1080/10463283.2020.1808936

Bigaj, M., & Woynarowska, M. (Eds.). (2023). *Higiena cyfrowa dorosłych użytkowniczek i użytkowników internetu w Polsce* [Digital hygiene of adult internet users in Poland]. Wydawnictwo Newsline.

Bigaj, M., Woynarowska, M., Panczyk, M., & Wójcik, S. (2025). *Higiena cyfrowa dorosłych* [Digital hygiene of adults]. Wydawnictwo Newsline.

Birtwistle, E., Chernikova, O., Wünsch, M., & Niklas, F. (2025). Training of executive functions in children: A meta-analysis of cognitive training interventions. *SAGE Open, 15*(1), 1–18. https://doi.org/10.1177/21582440241311060

Bjureberg, J., Ljótsson, B., Tull, M. T., Hedman, E., Sahlin, H., Lundh, L.-G., Bjärehed, J., DiLillo, D., Messman-Moore, T., Hellner Gumpert, C., & Gratz, K. L. (2016). Development and validation of a brief version of the Difficulties in Emotion Regulation Scale: The DERS-16. *Journal of Psychopathology and Behavioral Assessment, 38*(2), 284–296. https://doi.org/10.1007/s10862-015-9514-x

Błachnio, A., & Przepiorka, A. (2016). Dysfunction of self-regulation and self-control in Facebook addiction. *Psychiatric Quarterly, 87*(3), 493–500. https://doi.org/10.1007/s11126-015-9403-1

Błachnio, A., Przepiórka, A., Ben-Ezra, M., Ciobanu, A. M., Senol-Durak, E., Durak, M., Rudnicka, P., & Fortuna, P. (2026). *Real me location, self-esteem, and satisfaction with life in Internet and Facebook addictions: Results from six countries* [Manuscript submitted for publication]. Department of Emotion and Motivation Psychology, The John Paul II Catholic University of Lublin.

Bloch-Jørgensen, Z. T., Cilione, P. J., Yeung, W. W. H., & Gatt, J. M. (2018). Centeredness theory: Understanding and measuring well-being across core life domains. *Frontiers in Psychology, 9*, 610. https://doi.org/10.3389/fpsyg.2018.00610

Bonnechère, B., Langley, C., & Sahakian, B. J. (2020). The use of commercial computerised cognitive games in older adults: A meta-analysis. *Scientific Reports, 10*(1), 15276. https://doi.org/10.1038/s41598-020-72281-3

Borghouts, J., Eikey, E., Mark, G., De Leon, C., Schueller, S. M., Schneider, M., Stadnick, N., Zheng, K., Mukamel, D., & Sorkin, D. H. (2021). Barriers to and facilitators of user engagement with digital mental health interventions: Systematic review. *Journal of Medical Internet Research, 23*(3), e24387. https://doi.org/10.2196/24387

Borsboom, D. (2017). A network theory of mental disorders. *World Psychiatry, 16*(1), 5–13. https://doi.org/10.1002/wps.20375

Bostrom, N. (2005). In defense of posthuman dignity. *Bioethics, 19*(3), 202–214. https://doi.org/10.1111/j.1467-8519.2005.00437.x

Bostrom, N. (2014). *Superintelligence: Paths, dangers, strategies.* Oxford University Press.

Botella, C., Riva, G., Gaggioli, A., Wiederhold, B. K., Alcañiz, M., & Baños, R. M. (2012). The present and future of positive technologies. *Cyberpsychology, Behavior, and Social Networking, 15*(2), 78–84. https://doi.org/10.1089/cyber.2011.0140

Boulianne, S. (2020). Twenty years of digital media effects on civic and political participation. *Communication Research, 47*(7), 947–966. https://doi.org/10.1177/0093650218808186

Braidotti, R. (2013). *The posthuman.* Polity Press.

Brand, M., Young, K. S., Laier, C., Wölfling, K., & Potenza, M. N. (2016). Integrating psychological and neurobiological considerations regarding the development and maintenance of specific internet-use disorders: An Interaction of Person–Affect–Cognition–Execution (I-PACE) model. *Neuroscience & Biobehavioral Reviews, 71*, 252–266. https://doi.org/10.1016/j.neubiorev.2016.08.033

Brehm, J. W. (1966). *A theory of psychological reactance.* Academic Press.

Brickman, P., & Campbell, D. T. (1971). Hedonic relativism and planning the good society. In M. H. Appley (Ed.), *Adaptation-level theory* (pp. 287–305). Academic Press.

British Standards Institution. (2025). Supporting a safe and secure world for adolescents: Building consumer trust in tomorrow's technology. https://www.bsigroup.com/en-GB/insights-and-media/media-centre/press-releases/2025/may/half-of-young-people-want-to-grow-up-in-a-world-without-internet

Brougham, D., & Haar, J. (2018). Smart technology, artificial intelligence, robotics, and algorithms (STARA): Employees' perceptions of our future workplace. *Journal of Management & Organization, 24*(2), 239–257. https://doi.org/10.1017/jmo.2016.55

Brown, K. W., & Ryan, R. M. (2003). The benefits of being present: Mindfulness and its role in psychological well-being. *Journal of Personality and Social Psychology, 84*(4), 822–848. https://doi.org/10.1037/0022-3514.84.4.822

Bryant, F. B., & Veroff, J. (2007). *Savoring: A new model of positive experience.* Lawrence Erlbaum Associates Publishers.

Brzeziński, J. M., & Oleś, P. K. (2021). *O psychologii i psychologach. Między uniwersytetem a praktyką społeczną* [*On psychology and psychologists: Between the university and social practice*]. Wydawnictwo Naukowe PWN.

Büchi, M. (2024). Digital well-being theory and research. *New Media & Society, 26*(1), 172–189. https://doi.org/10.1177/14614448211056851

Buck, R., Khan, M. M. H., Fagan, M., & Coman, E. (2018). The User Affective Experience Scale: A measure of emotions anticipated in response to pop-up computer warnings. *International Journal of Human–Computer Interaction, 34*(1), 25–34. https://doi.org/10.1080/10447318.2017.1314612

Burgmer, P., & Forstmann, M. (2018). Mind-body dualism and health revisited: How belief in dualism shapes health behavior. *Social Psychology, 49*(4), 219–230. https://doi.org/10.1027/1864-9335/a000344

Burke, J. (2021). Positive cyberpsychology: A conceptual framework of an emerging field. In A. Kostić & D. Chadee (Eds.), *Positive psychology: An international perspective* (pp. 85–101). Wiley-Blackwell.

Burke, J. (2025). *The foundation of positive psychology: A compilation of key studies, theory, and practice*. Routledge.

Burke, J., Boniwell, I., Frates, B., Lianov, L. S., & O'Boyle, C. A. (Eds.). (2023). *Routledge international handbook of positive health sciences: Positive psychology and lifestyle medicine research, theory, and practice*. Routledge.

Burleigh, T. L., Footitt, T., Colder Carras, M., Conkey-Morrison, C., Poulus, D. R., & Stavropoulos, V. (2025). Flowing in the net of disordered gaming: A network analysis approach. *Addictive Behaviors Reports, 21*, 100606. https://doi.org/10.1016/j.abrep.2025.100606

Burnell, R., Peters, D., Ryan, R. M., & Calvo, R. A. (2023). Technology evaluations are associated with psychological need satisfaction across different spheres of experience: An application of the METUX scales. *Frontiers in Psychology, 14*, 1092288. https://doi.org/10.3389/fpsyg.2023.1092288

Burr, C., Taddeo, M., & Floridi, L. (2020). The ethics of digital well-being: A thematic review. *Science and Engineering Ethics, 26*(4), 2313–2343. https://doi.org/10.1007/s11948-020-00175-8

Butler, J., & Kern, M. L. (2016). The PERMA-Profiler: A brief multidimensional measure of flourishing. *International Journal of Wellbeing, 6*(3), 1–48. https://doi.org/10.5502/ijw.v6i3.526

Button, M., Shepherd, D., Hawkins, C., & Tapley, J. (2024). Disseminating fraud awareness and prevention advice to older adults: Perspectives on the most effective means of delivery. *Crime Prevention & Community Safety, 26*, 385–400. https://doi.org/10.1057/s41300-024-00218-3

Bynum, T. W. (2006). Flourishing ethics. *Ethics and Information Technology, 8*(4), 157–173. https://doi.org/10.1007/s10676-006-9107-1

Calvo, R. A., & Peters, D. (2014). *Positive computing: Technology for wellbeing and human potential*. MIT Press.

Cameron, G., Mulvenna, M., Ennis, E., O'Neill, S., Bond, R., Cameron, D., & Bunting, A. (2025). Effectiveness of digital mental health interventions in the workplace: Umbrella review of systematic reviews. *JMIR Mental Health, 12*, e67785. https://doi.org/10.2196/67785

Campagna, G., & Rehm, M. (2025). A systematic review of trust assessments in human–robot interaction. *ACM Transactions on Human–Robot Interaction*, *14*(2), 1–35. https://doi.org/10.1145/3706123

Cangelosi, G., Biondini, F., Sguanci, M., Nguyen, C. T. T., Ferrara, G., Diamanti, O., Morales Palomares, S., Mancin, S., & Petrelli, F. (2025). Anhedonia in youth and the role of internet-related behavior: A systematic review. *Psychiatry International*, *6*(1), 1. https://doi.org/10.3390/psychiatryint6010001

Carrier, L. M., Spradlin, A., Bunce, J. P., & Rosen, L. D. (2015). Virtual empathy: Positive and negative impacts of going online upon empathy in young adults. *Computers in Human Behavior*, *52*, 39–48. https://doi.org/10.1016/j.chb.2015.05.026

Carter, J. W., & Youssef-Morgan, C. M. (2022). Psychological capital development effectiveness of face-to-face, online, and micro-learning interventions. *Education and Information Technologies*, *27*(5), 6553–6575. https://doi.org/10.1007/s10639-021-10824-5

Carvalko, J. (2012). *The techno-human shell: A jump in the evolutionary gap*. Sunbury Press.

Casali, N., & Feraco, T. (2025). Bridges over troubled water: A meta-analysis of the associations of character strengths with well-being and common mental health disorders. *European Journal of Personality*, *39*(6), 878–896. https://doi.org/10.1177/08902070251366765

Cassel, J. (1976). The contribution of the social environment to host resistance. *American Journal of Epidemiology*, *104*(2), 107–123. https://doi.org/10.1093/oxfordjournals.aje.a112281

Cattell, R. B. (1950). *Personality: A systematic theoretical and factual study*. McGraw-Hill.

Chalmers, D. J. (2022). *Reality+: Virtual worlds and the problems of philosophy*. W. W. Norton & Company.

Chang, E., Billinghurst, M., & Yoo, B. (2023). Brain activity during cybersickness: A scoping review. *Virtual Reality*, *27*, 2073–2097. https://doi.org/10.1007/s10055-023-00795-y

Charmaraman, L., Nesi, J., Schueller, S. M., Choukas-Bradley, S., Hernandez, J. M., & Davis, K. (2025). Youth digital wellbeing and social connectedness. In D. A. Christakis & L. Hale (Eds.), *Handbook of children and screens* (pp. 223–229). Springer. https://doi.org/10.1007/978-3-031-69362-5_31

Chen, S., Ebrahimi, O. V., & Cheng, C. (2025a). New perspective on digital well-being by distinguishing digital competency from dependency: Network approach. *Journal of Medical Internet Research*, *27*, e70483. https://doi.org/10.2196/70483

Chen, X., Jin, Y., Sun, S., Zhang, W., & Yu, C. (2025b). Research on propagation dynamics of emotional contagion using S3EIR model based on multiple social media platforms. *Frontiers in Communication*, *10*, 1582974. https://doi.org/10.3389/fcomm.2025.1582974

Chen, Y., Lin, Z., Filieri, R., & Liu, R. (2021). Subjective well-being, mobile social media and the enjoyment of tourism experience: A broaden-and-build perspective. *Asia Pacific Journal of Tourism Research, 26*(10), 1070–1080. https://doi.org/10.1080/10941665.2021.1952285

Chirico, A., Borghesi, F., Yaden, D. B., Pizzolante, M., Sarcinella, E. D., Cipresso, P., & Gaggioli, A. (2024). Unveiling the underlying structure of awe in virtual reality and in autobiographical recall: An exploratory study. *Scientific Reports, 14*, 12474. https://doi.org/10.1038/s41598-024-62654-3

Chirico, A., Clewis, R. R., Yaden, D. B., & Gaggioli, A. (2021). Nature versus art as elicitors of the sublime: A virtual reality study. *PLOS ONE, 16*(3), e0233628. https://doi.org/10.1371/journal.pone.0233628

Chirico, A., Pizzolante, M., Kitson, A., Gianotti, E., Riecke, B. E., & Gaggioli, A. (2022). Defining transformative experiences: A conceptual analysis. *Frontiers in Psychology, 13*, 790300. https://doi.org/10.3389/fpsyg.2022.790300

Chiu, K.-L., Collins, A., & Alexander, R. (2022a). Detecting hate speech with GPT-3. *arXiv*. https://doi.org/10.48550/arXiv.2103.12407

Chiu, T. K. F., Sun, J. C.-Y., & Ismailov, M. (2022b). Investigating the relationship of technology learning support to digital literacy from the perspective of self-determination theory. *Educational Psychology, 42*(10), 1263–1282. https://doi.org/10.1080/01443410.2022.2074966

Cho, M. E., & Kim, M. J. (2022). Smart homes supporting the wellness of one- or two-person households. *Sensors, 22*(20), 7816. https://doi.org/10.3390/s22207816

Christopher, J. C., & Hickinbottom, S. (2008). Positive psychology, ethnocentrism, and the disguised ideology of individualism. *Theory & Psychology, 18*(5), 563–589. https://doi.org/10.1177/0959354308093396

Chu, M., Ma, H., Lee, C.-Y., Zhao, Z., Chen, T., Zhang, S., & Chiang, Y.-C. (2023). Effect of online and offline social network group clusters on life satisfaction across age groups. *Heliyon, 9*(5), e16176. https://doi.org/10.1016/j.heliyon.2023.e16176

Cocking, D., & Matthews, S. (2000). Unreal friends. *Ethics and Information Technology, 2*(4), 223–231. https://doi.org/10.1023/A:1011414704851

Cohen, E., & Barrett, J. L. (2011). In search of "Folk anthropology": The cognitive anthropology of the person. In J. W. Van Huyssteen & E. Wiebe (Eds.), *In search of self: Interdisciplinary perspectives on personhood* (pp. 104–124). Eerdmans Publishing Company.

Cohen, S., Kamarck, T., & Mermelstein, R. (1983). A global measure of perceived stress. *Journal of Health and Social Behavior, 24*(4), 385–396. https://doi.org/10.2307/2136404

Collins, A. C., Price, G. D., Woodworth, R. J., & Jacobson, N. C. (2024a). Predicting individual response to a web-based positive psychology intervention: A machine learning approach. *Journal of Positive Psychology, 19*(4), 675–685. https://doi.org/10.1080/17439760.2023.2254743

Collins, A. M., Warburton, W. A., Bussey, K., & Sweller, N. (2024b). Factor structure and psychometric properties of the Digital Communication Empathy Scale

(DCES). *International Journal of Human-Computer Studies, 183*, 103183. https://doi.org/10.1016/j.ijhcs.2023.103183

Collins, A. M., Warburton, W. A., Sweller, N., & Bussey, K. (2025). Further validation of the Digital Communication Empathy Scale (DCES). *Computers in Human Behavior Reports, 19*, 100721. https://doi.org/10.1016/j.chbr.2025.100721

Collu, R., Ferrazzano, E., Murgia, V., Salis, C., & Barbaro, M. (2025). The technological and psychological aspects of upper limb prostheses abandonment: A narrative review. *Prosthesis, 7*(6), 167. https://doi.org/10.3390/prosthesis7060167

Cooper, H., Coutanche, M. N., McMullen, L. M., Panter, A. T., Rindskopf, D., & Sher, K. J. (Eds.). (2023). *APA handbook of research methods in psychology* (2nd ed.). American Psychological Association.

Csikszentmihalyi, M. (1975). *Beyond boredom and anxiety: Experiencing flow in work and play*. Jossey-Bass.

Csikszentmihalyi, M., & Csikszentmihalyi, I. S. (Eds.). (1988). *Optimal experience: Psychological studies of flow in consciousness*. Cambridge University Press.

Csikszentmihalyi, M., & Csikszentmihalyi, I. S. (Eds.). (2006). *A life worth living: Contributions to positive psychology*. Oxford University Press.

Cucciniello, I., Sangiovanni, S., Maggi, G., & Rossi, S. (2023). Mind perception in HRI: Exploring users' attribution of mental and emotional states to robots with different behavioural styles. *International Journal of Social Robotics, 15*, 867–877. https://doi.org/10.1007/s12369-023-00989-z

Cudo, A., Kopiś, N., Jarząbek-Cudo, A., Szewczyk, R., & Demczuk, M. (2019). The relationship between problematic internet use and the need for cognitive closure. *Advances in Psychiatry and Neurology, 28*(3), 199–207. https://doi.org/10.5114/ppn.2019.89136

Cudo, A., Lelonek-Kuleta, B., & Bartczuk, R. P. (2024). Psychometric assessment and gender/age invariance of the Polish adaptation of the Risky Loot Box Index. *Advances in Cognitive Psychology, 20*(2), 105–120. https://doi.org/10.5709/acp-0421-y

Culkin, J. M. (1967, March 18). A schoolman's guide to Marshall McLuhan. *The Saturday Review*, 51–53, 70–72.

Curtin, E., Green, R., Brown, K. A., Nájera Espinosa, S., Chandrasekar, A., Hopkins, L., Turner, G., Alae-Carew, C., Ullian, K., & Scheelbeek, P. (2025). The effectiveness of mobile app-based interventions in facilitating behavior change towards healthier and more sustainable diets: A systematic review and meta-analysis. *International Journal of Behavioral Nutrition and Physical Activity, 22*, 122. https://doi.org/10.1186/s12966-025-01823-7

Dadischeck, M. (2021). Conceptualizing digital well-being and technology addiction in I-O psychology. *Industrial and Organizational Psychology, 14*(3), 401–403. https://doi.org/10.1017/iop.2021.87

Davis, F. D. (1989). Perceived usefulness, perceived ease of use, and user acceptance of information technology. *MIS Quarterly, 13*(3), 319–340. https://doi.org/10.2307/249008

Deci, E. L., & Ryan, R. M. (1985). *Intrinsic motivation and self-determination in human behavior*. Plenum Press.

Deleuze, G. (1992). Postscript on the societies of control. *October*, *59*, 3–7. http://www.jstor.org/stable/778828

Dellermann, D., Ebel, P., Söllner, M., & Leimeister, J. M. (2019). Hybrid intelligence. *Business & Information Systems Engineering*, *61*(5), 637–643. https://doi.org/10.1007/s12599-019-00595-2

Derks, D., Bakker, A. B., Peters, P., & van Wingerden, P. (2016). Work-related smartphone use, work–family conflict and family role performance: The role of segmentation preference. *Human Relations*, *69*(5), 1045–1068. https://doi.org/10.1177/0018726715601890

Dernbecher, S., & Beck, R. (2017). The concept of mindfulness in information systems research: A multi-dimensional analysis. *European Journal of Information Systems*, *26*(2), 121–142. https://doi.org/10.1057/s41303-016-0032-z

Desai, V., Gupta, A., Andersen, L., Ronnestrand, B., & Wong, M. (2021). Stress-reducing effects of playing a casual video game among undergraduate students. *Trends in Psychology*, *29*(3), 563–579. https://doi.org/10.1007/s43076-021-00062-6

Desmet, P. M. A., & Pohlmeyer, A. E. (2013). Positive design: An introduction to design for subjective well-being. *International Journal of Design*, *7*, 5–19. https://repository.tudelft.nl/islandora/object/uuid%3A06ec60ac-0363-43ea-9ccd-8426ef0d6b64

Diener, E. (1984). Subjective well-being. *Psychological Bulletin*, *95*(3), 542–575. https://doi.org/10.1037/0033-2909.95.3.542

Diener, E., Lucas, R. E., & Oishi, S. (2002). Subjective well-being: The science of happiness and life satisfaction. In C. R. Snyder & S. J. Lopez (Eds.), *Handbook of positive psychology* (pp. 63–73). Oxford University Press.

Diener, E., Wirtz, D., Tov, W., Kim-Prieto, C., Choi, D. W., Oishi, S., & Biswas-Diener, R. (2010). New well-being measures: Short scales to assess flourishing and positive and negative feelings. *Social Indicators Research*, *97*(2), 143–156. https://doi.org/10.1007/s11205-009-9493-y

Diessner, R. (2019). *Understanding the beauty appreciation trait: Empirical research on seeking beauty in all things*. Palgrave Macmillan.

Diessner, R. (in press). The role of sense and perception education in moral flourishing: Natural, artistic, and moral beauty. In V. Domingo & K. Kristjánsson (Eds.), *Educating character for human flourishing: The integrative dynamics of human moral growth*. Springer.

Diessner, R., Klebl, C., Mowry, G., & Pohling, R. (2022). Natural and moral beauty have indirect effects on proenvironmental behavior. *Ecopsychology*, *14*(2), 71–82. https://doi.org/10.1089/eco.2021.0038

Dietvorst, B. J., Simmons, J. P., & Massey, C. (2015). Algorithm aversion: People erroneously avoid algorithms after seeing them err. *Journal of Experimental Psychology: General*, *144*(1), 114–126. https://doi.org/10.1037/xge0000033

Digital and Population Data Services Agency. (2022). *Digital skills report 2022: Digitally brave is confident about the future.* https://dvv.fi/documents/16079645/141915645/Digitaitoraportti_2022_ENG

Di Pompeo, I., D'Aurizio, G., Burattini, C., Bisegna, F., & Curcio, G. (2023). Positive mood induction to promote well-being and health: A systematic review from real settings to virtual reality. *Journal of Environmental Psychology*, *91*, 102095. https://doi.org/10.1016/j.jenvp.2023.102095

Du, J., van Koningsbruggen, G. M., & Kerkhof, P. (2018). A brief measure of social media self-control failure. *Computers in Human Behavior*, *84*(July), 68–75. https://doi.org/10.1016/j.chb.2018.02.002

Duckworth, A. L., Steen, T. A., & Seligman, M. E. P. (2005). Positive psychology in clinical practice. *Annual Review of Clinical Psychology*, *1*, 629–651. https://doi.org/10.1146/annurev.clinpsy.1.102803.144154

Dunin-Kozicka, M., Fortuna, P., Szubielska, M., Kopiś-Posiej, N., Kaczmarczyk, Ł., & Iwińska, J. (2025). Presence in virtual art environments affects the perception of novel affordances in real-world objects. *Ecological Psychology*, *37*(3), 226–250. https://doi.org/10.1080/10407413.2025.2491339

Dunn, D. S., & Dougherty, S. B. (2008). Flourishing: Mental health as living life well. *Journal of Social and Clinical Psychology*, *27*(3), 314–316. https://doi.org/10.1521/jscp.2008.27.3.314

Duradoni, M., Colombini, G., Battistoni, V., Zagaglia, V., & Guazzini, A. (2025). Exploring the role of online social capital in differentiating technology addiction effect on well-being. *Human Behavior and Emerging Technologies*, *2025*, 6211572. https://doi.org/10.1155/hbe2/6211572

Duradoni, M., Meacci, S., Panerai, G., Salvatori, G., & Guazzini, A. (2022a). Development and validation of the Social Media Capital Scale (SMC): A brand new measure for online social capital. *Human Behavior and Emerging Technologies*, *2022*, 9903615. https://doi.org/10.1155/2022/9903615

Duradoni, M., Serritella, E., Avolio, C., Arnetoli, C., & Guazzini, A. (2022b). Development and validation of the digital life balance (DLB) scale: A brand-new measure for both harmonic and disharmonic use of ICTs. *Behavioral Sciences*, *12*(12), 489. https://doi.org/10.3390/bs12120489

Duradoni, M., Serritella, E., Severino, F. P., & Guazzini, A. (2024). Exploring the relationships between digital life balance and internet social capital, loneliness, fear of missing out, and anxiety. *Human Behavior and Emerging Technologies*, *2024*, 5079719. https://doi.org/10.1155/2024/5079719

Dweck, C. S. (2006). *Mindset: The new psychology of success.* Random House.

Dziak, M. (2022). Digital intelligence. *EBSCO Knowledge Advantage.* https://www.ebsco.com/research-starters/education/digital-intelligence

Ekefjärd, S., Piussi, R., & Hamrin Senorski, E. (2024). Physical symptoms among professional gamers within eSports: A survey study. *BMC Sports Science, Medicine and Rehabilitation*, *16*(1), 18. https://doi.org/10.1186/s13102-024-00810-y

Elliott, M. A., Paterson, A., Orr, S., Marshall, C., Wood, C., Toye, M., & Wilson, C. (2021). Evidence that implementation intentions reduce drivers' use of mobile phones while driving. *Transportation Research Part F: Traffic Psychology and Behaviour, 78*, 381–397. https://doi.org/10.1016/j.trf.2021.03.002

Enrique, Á., Bretón-López, J., Molinari, G., Roca, P., Llorca, G., Guillén, V., Fernández-Aranda, F., Baños, R. M., & Botella, C. (2018). Implementation of a positive technology application in patients with eating disorders: A pilot randomized control trial. *Frontiers in Psychology, 9*, 934. https://doi.org/10.3389/fpsyg.2018.00934

European Commission. (2021). *Industry 5.0: Towards a sustainable, human-centric and resilient European industry*. Publications Office of the European Union. https://research-and-innovation.ec.europa.eu/knowledge-publications-tools-and-data/publications/all-publications/industry-50-towards-sustainable-human-centric-and-resilient-european-industry_en

European Union. (2019). *Key competences for lifelong learning*. Publications Office of the European Union. https://doi.org/10.2766/569540

Fairburn, S. C., Jehi, L., Bicknell, B. T., Wilkes, B. G., & Panuganti, B. (2025). Applications of quantum computing in clinical care. *Frontiers in Medicine, 12*, 1573016. https://doi.org/10.3389/fmed.2025.1573016

Faria, D. R., Godkin, A. L., & da Silva Ayrosa, P. P. (2025). Advancing emotionally aware child–robot interaction with biophysical data and insight-driven affective computing. *Sensors, 25*(4), 1161. https://doi.org/10.3390/s25041161

Fendel, J. C., Vogt, A., Brandtner, A., & Schmidt, S. (2024). Mindfulness programs for problematic usage of the internet: A systematic review and meta-analysis. *Journal of Behavioral Addictions, 13*(2), 327–353. https://doi.org/10.1556/2006.2024.00024

Feng, S., Mäntymäki, M., Dhir, A., & Salmela, H. (2021). How self-tracking and the quantified self promote health and well-being: Systematic review. *Journal of Medical Internet Research, 23*(9), e25171. https://doi.org/10.2196/25171

Ferdman, A. (2024). Human flourishing and technology affordances. *Philosophy & Technology, 37*(1), 1. https://doi.org/10.1007/s13347-023-00686-9

Flecha Ortiz, J. A., Santos Corrada, M. A., López, E., & Dones, V. (2021). Analysis of the use of memes as an exponent of collective coping during COVID-19 in Puerto Rico. *Media International Australia, 178*(1), 168–181. https://doi.org/10.1177/1329878X20966379

Floridi, L. (2014). *The fourth revolution: How the infosphere is reshaping human reality*. Oxford University Press.

Floridi, L. (2023). *The ethics of artificial intelligence: Principles, challenges, and opportunities*. Oxford University Press.

Fogg, B. J. (2003). *Persuasive technology: Using computers to change what we think and do*. Morgan Kaufmann.

Forstmann, M., Burgmer, P., & Mussweiler, T. (2012). The mind is willing, but the flesh is weak: The effects of mind-body dualism on health behavior. *Psychological Science, 23*(10), 1239–1245. https://doi.org/10.1177/0956797612442392

Fortuna, P. (2012). *Pozytywna psychologia porażki: Jak z cytryn zrobić lemoniadę* [The positive psychology of failure: How to turn lemons into lemonade]. Gdańskie Wydawnictwo Psychologiczne.

Fortuna, P. (2021). *Optimum. Idea cyberpsychologii pozytywnej* [Optimum: The idea of positive cyberpsychology]. Wydawnictwo Naukowe PWN.

Fortuna, P. (2023). Positive cyberpsychology as a field of study of the well-being of people interacting with and via technology. *Frontiers in Psychology*, *14*, 1053482. https://doi.org/10.3389/fpsyg.2023.1053482

Fortuna, P. (2024). *Optimum 2.0. Idea cyberpsychologii pozytywnej* [Optimum 2.0: The idea of positive cyberpsychology]. Wydawnictwo Naukowe PWN.

Fortuna, P. (2026). Dobrostan pracowników w technosferze – perspektywa cyberpsychologii pozytywnej [Employee well-being in the technosphere – a positive cyberpsychology perspective]. In P. Fortuna & A. Czerw (Eds.), *Psychologia pozytywna pracy i organizacji* [Positive organizational and work psychology] (pp. 313–345). Wydawnictwo Naukowe PWN.

Fortuna, P., Czerw, A., Ostafińska-Molik, B., & Chudzicka-Czupała, A. (2025a). Flourishing at work: Psychometric properties of the Polish version of the Workplace PERMA-Profiler. *PLOS ONE*, *20*(5), e0319088. https://doi.org/10.1371/journal.pone.0319088

Fortuna, P., & Gorbaniuk, O. (2022). What is behind the buzzword for experts and laymen: Representation of "artificial intelligence" in the IT-professionals' and non-professionals' minds. *Europe's Journal of Psychology*, *18*(2), 207–218. https://doi.org/10.5964/ejop.5473

Fortuna, P., & Modliński, A. (2026). Contextual cues influencing the evaluation of AI-generated artworks by laypeople. In R. Ladhari (Ed.), *Encyclopedia of artificial intelligence in marketing* (pp. 1–12). Springer. https://doi.org/10.1007/978-3-031-75316-9_88-1

Fortuna, P., Puchalska-Wasyl, M., Kaczmarczyk, Ł., & Cudo, A. (2026). A new look at the relationship between the gamer and the game character: An exploratory study of internal dialogical activity. *Cyberpsychology: Journal of Psychosocial Research on Cyberspace*, *20*(3), Article 12. https://doi.org/10.5817/CP2026-3-12

Fortuna, P., Puchalska-Wasyl, M., Kaczmarczyk, Ł., Cudo, A., & McNeill, M. (2025b). Who are you really, the creator of the future? Forming identity in the age of 'soft cyborgization'. In P. Fortuna & A. Dutkowska (Eds.), *The creators of tomorrow: An interdisciplinary perspective on shaping the future* (pp. 13–34). Brill. https://doi.org/10.1163/9789004748194_003

Fortuna, P., & Wojtasiński, M. (2026). *Latent factor or composite index? Modeling flourishing as an emergent configuration of well-being domains* [Manuscript submitted for publication]. Department of Experimental Psychology, The John Paul II Catholic University of Lublin.

Fortuna, P., Wróblewski, Z., & Gorbaniuk, O. (2021). The structure and correlates of anthropocentrism as a psychological construct. *Current Psychology*, *42*, 3630–3642. https://doi.org/10.1007/s12144-021-01835-z

Fortuna, P., Wróblewski, Z., Gut, A., & Dutkowska, A. (2024). The relationship between anthropocentric beliefs and the moral status of a chimpanzee, humanoid robot, and cyborg person: The mediating role of the assignment of mind and soul. *Current Psychology, 43*, 12664–12679. https://doi.org/10.1007/s12144-023-05313-6

Fourcade, A., Malandrone, F., Roellecke, L., Ciston, A., Mooij, J. D., Villringer, A., Carletto, S., & Gaebler, M. (2025). AffectTracker: Real-time continuous rating of affective experience in immersive virtual reality. *Frontiers in Virtual Reality, 6*, 1567854. https://doi.org/10.3389/frvir.2025.1567854

Fowers, B. J., Novak, L. F., Calder, A. J., & Kiknadze, N. C. (2024). Can a theory of human flourishing be formulated? Toward a science of flourishing. *Review of General Psychology, 28*(2), 123–142. https://doi.org/10.1177/10892680231225223

Francuz, P. (Ed.). (1999). *Psychologiczne aspekty odbioru telewizji* [Psychological aspects of television reception]. TN KUL.

Frankl, V. E. (1988). *The will to meaning: Foundations and applications of logotherapy*. Meridian.

Fredrickson, B. L. (2001). The role of positive emotions in positive psychology: The broaden-and-build theory of positive emotions. *American Psychologist, 56*(3), 218–226. https://doi.org/10.1037/0003-066X.56.3.218

Fredrickson, B. L., & Losada, M. F. (2005). Positive affect and the complex dynamics of human flourishing. *American Psychologist, 60*(7), 678–686. https://doi.org/10.1037/0003-066X.60.7.678

Fredrickson, B. L., & Losada, M. F. (2013). "Positive affect and the complex dynamics of human flourishing": Correction to Fredrickson and Losada (2005). *American Psychologist, 68*(9), 822. https://doi.org/10.1037/a0034435

Fried, A. L., & Jansen, K. L. (2023). Ethics in psychological research: Guidelines and regulations. In H. Cooper, M. N. Coutanche, L. M. McMullen, A. T. Panter, D. Rindskopf, & K. J. Sher (Eds.), *APA handbook of research methods in psychology: Foundations, planning, measures, and psychometrics* (2nd ed., pp. 59–81). American Psychological Association. https://doi.org/10.1037/0000318-003

Friedman, B., & Hendry, D. G. (2019). *Value sensitive design: Shaping technology with moral and technical imagination*. MIT Press.

Friesem, Y. (2016). Developing digital empathy: A holistic approach to media literacy research methods. In M. N. Yildiz & J. Keengwe (Eds.), *Handbook of research on media literacy in the digital age* (pp. 145–160). IGI Global. https://doi.org/10.4018/978-1-4666-9667-9.ch007

Gable, S. L., & Haidt, J. (2005). What (and why) is positive psychology? *Review of General Psychology, 9*(2), 103–110. https://doi.org/10.1037/1089-2680.9.2.103

Gable, S. L., & Reis, H. T. (2010). Good news! Capitalizing on positive events in an interpersonal context. In M. P. Zanna (Ed.), *Advances in experimental social psychology* (Vol. 42, pp. 195–257). Academic Press. https://doi.org/10.1016/S0065-2601(10)42004-3

Gaggioli, A. (2016). Transformative experience design. In A. Gaggioli, A. Ferscha, G. Riva, S. Dunne, & I. Viaud-Delmon (Eds.), *Human computer confluence:*

Transforming human experience through symbiotic technologies (pp. 97–122). De Gruyter. https://doi.org/10.1515/9783110471137-006

Gaggioli, A., Gianotti, E., & Chirico, A. (2020). Psycho-physiological effects of a virtual reality relaxation experience after acute stressor exposure. *Annual Review of CyberTherapy and Telemedicine, 18*, 123–126.

Gaggioli, A., Villani, D., Serino, S., Baños, R. M., & Botella, C. (2019a). Editorial: Positive technology: Designing e-experiences for positive change. *Frontiers in Psychology, 10*, 1571. https://doi.org/10.3389/fpsyg.2019.01571

Gaggioli, A., Villani, D., Serino, S., Baños, R. M., & Botella, C. (Eds.). (2019b). *Positive technology: Designing e-experiences for positive change*. Frontiers Media. https://doi.org/10.3389/978-2-88963-023-3

Gander, F., Wagner, L., & Niemiec, R. M. (2024). Do character strengths-based interventions change character strengths? Two randomized controlled intervention studies. *Collabra: Psychology, 10*(1), 108604. https://doi.org/10.1525/collabra.108604

Gehlen, A. (1940). *Der Mensch: Seine Natur und seine Stellung in der Welt*. Alfred Kröner Verlag.

Giardina, A., Schimmenti, A., Starcevic, V., King, D. L., Di Blasi, M., & Billieux, J. (2024). Problematic gaming, social withdrawal, and escapism: The compensatory-dissociative online gaming (C-DOG) model. *Computers in Human Behavior, 155*, 108187. https://doi.org/10.1016/j.chb.2024.108187

Gibson, J. J. (1979). *The ecological approach to visual perception*. Houghton Mifflin.

Gilster, P. (1997). *Digital literacy*. John Wiley & Sons, Inc.

Gingrich, O., Havsteen-Franklin, D., Grant, C., Renaud, A., & Hignell-Tully, D. (2024). Participatory presence – social connectedness through collaborative art practices. *International Journal of Performance Arts and Digital Media, 20*(2), 296–320. https://doi.org/10.1080/14794713.2024.2340418

Giraldez-Hayes, C., Seligman, M., & Burke, J. (Eds.). (2025). *Routledge international handbook of wellbeing arts*. Routledge.

Gkintoni, E., Vantaraki, F., Skoulidi, C., Anastassopoulos, P., & Vantarakis, A. (2024). Promoting physical and mental health among children and adolescents via gamification: A conceptual systematic review. *Behavioral Sciences, 14*(2), 102. https://doi.org/10.3390/bs14020102

Gladden, M., Fortuna, P., & Modliński, A. (2022). The empowerment of artificial intelligence in post-digital organizations: Exploring human interactions with supervisory AI. *Human Technology, 18*(2), 98–121. https://doi.org/10.14254/1795-6889.2022.18-2.2

Godden, D. R., & Baddeley, A. D. (1975). Context-dependent memory in two natural environments: On land and under water. *British Journal of Psychology, 66*(3), 325–331. https://doi.org/10.1111/j.2044-8295.1975.tb01468.x

Gollwitzer, P. M. (1999). Implementation intentions: Strong effects of simple plans. *American Psychologist, 54*(7), 493–503. https://doi.org/10.1037/0003-066X.54.7.493

Gomes, R., Mathew, J., Nair, S., Mulasi, A., & Yadav, P. (2023). Design and validation of the digital well-being scale. *Journal of Theories and Research in Education, 18*(1), 239–251. https://doi.org/10.6092/issn.1970-2221/16365

Gómez-Vallarta, A. C., Rivera Magos, S., García-Rojas, A. D., & Hernando-Gómez, Á. (2025). Digital emotional intelligence: Construction of a model and validation of a measurement instrument. *Alteridad, 20*(2), 226–237. https://doi.org/10.17163/alt.v20n2.2025.06

Goodyear, V., & Pallan, M. (2025, February 12). School bans alone not enough to tackle negative impacts of phone and social media use. *University of Birmingham.* https://www.birmingham.ac.uk/news/2025/school-bans-alone-not-enough-to-tackle-negative-impacts-of-phone-and-social-media-use

Gradito Dubord, M. A., Gagné, M., Dubreuil, P., & Forest, J. (2025). Finding your totem: Unveiling the effects of a positive technology intervention on employees' well-being and perceived team effectiveness with self-determination theory. *European Journal of Work and Organizational Psychology*, 1–21. https://doi.org/10.1080/1359432X.2025.2566811

Graffigna, G., Barello, S., Wiederhold, B. K., Bosio, A. C., & Riva, G. (2013). Positive technology as a driver for health engagement. *Studies in Health Technology and Informatics, 191*, 9–17. https://doi.org/10.3233/978-1-61499-282-0-9

Gray, H. M., Gray, K., & Wegner, D. M. (2007). Dimensions of mind perception. *Science, 315*(5812), 619. https://doi.org/10.1126/science.1134475

Grigore, C., & Cobzeanu, A. (2025). The impact of digitalization on religious practices and community dynamics following the COVID-19 pandemic: A systematic review. *Revista Românească Pentru Educaţie Multidimensională, 17*(2), 302–343. https://doi.org/10.18662/rrem/17.2/984

Groot, J., MacLellan, A., Butler, M., Todor, E., Zulfiqar, M., Thackrah, T., Clarke, C., Brosnan, M., & Ainsworth, B. (2023). The effectiveness of fully automated digital interventions in promoting mental well-being in the general population: Systematic review and meta-analysis. *JMIR Mental Health, 10*, e44658. https://doi.org/10.2196/44658

Grüning, D. J., Kamin, J., Panizza, F., Katsaros, M., & Lorenz-Spreen, P. (2024). A framework for promoting online prosocial behavior via digital interventions. *Communications Psychology, 2* Article 6. https://doi.org/10.1038/s44271-023-00052-7

Gudka, M., Gardiner, K. L. K., & Lomas, T. (2021). Towards a framework for flourishing through social media: A systematic review of 118 research studies. *The Journal of Positive Psychology, 18*(1), 86–105. https://doi.org/10.1080/17439760.2021.1991447

Gunning, D. (2019). DARPA's explainable artificial intelligence (XAI) program. *Proceedings of the 24th International Conference on Intelligent User Interfaces (IUI'19)*, ii. ACM. https://doi.org/10.1145/3301275.3308446

Haase, J., & Pokutta, S. (2024). Human-AI co-creativity: Exploring synergies across levels of creative collaboration. *arXiv:2411.12527*. https://arxiv.org/abs/2411.12527

Haff, P. K. (2014). Technology as a geological phenomenon: Implications for human well-being. *The Geological Society, London, Special Publications, 395*(1), 301–309. https://doi.org/10.1144/SP395.4

Haidt, J. (2024). *The anxious generation: How the great rewiring of childhood is causing an epidemic of mental illness*. Penguin Press.

Hamari, J., & Sjöblom, M. (2017). What is eSports and why do people watch it? *Internet Research, 27*(2), 211–232. https://doi.org/10.1108/IntR-04-2016-0085

Hansen, T., Johansen, R., Kirkøen, B., Stene-Larsen, K., Straiton, M., Tornes, R. A., & Reneflot, A. (2025). Digital bridges to social connection: A systematic review and meta-analysis of digital interventions for loneliness and social isolation. *Internet Interventions, 41*, 100856. https://doi.org/10.1016/j.invent.2025.100856

Hao, Z., Jin, L., & Huang, J. (2023). Offline and online basic need satisfaction and smartphone use behaviors: A mediation model. *Journal of Psychiatric Research, 161*, 99–105. https://doi.org/10.1016/j.jpsychires.2023.03.016

Hargittai, E. (2005). Survey measures of web-oriented digital literacy. *Social Science Computer Review, 23*(3), 371–379. https://doi.org/10.1177/0894439305275911

Hassenzahl, M. (2010). *Experience design: Technology for all the right reasons*. Morgan & Claypool Publishers.

Hatfield, E., Cacioppo, J. T., & Rapson, R. L. (1993). Emotional contagion. *Current Directions in Psychological Science, 2*(3), 96–100. https://doi.org/10.1111/1467-8721.ep10770953

Hayburn, J., Jowett, G. E., & Gledhill, A. (2025). Cognition, lifestyle, and gender: An umbrella review of esport performance, participation, and well-being. *Journal of Electronic Gaming and Esports, 3*(1), 1–16. https://doi.org/10.1123/jege.2024-0005

Hayles, N. K. (1999). *How we became posthuman: Virtual bodies in cybernetics, literature, and informatics*. University of Chicago Press.

Heckhausen, H., & Gollwitzer, P. M. (1987). Thought contents and cognitive functioning in motivational versus volitional states of mind. *Motivation and Emotion, 11*(2), 101–120. https://doi.org/10.1007/BF00992338

Heidegger, M. (1927/2008). *Being and time* (J. Macquarrie & E. Robinson, Trans.). Harper Perennial Modern Thought.

Hekler, E. B., Michie, S., Pavel, M., Rivera, D. E., Collins, L. M., Jimison, H. B., Garnett, C., Parral, S., & Spruijt-Metz, D. (2016). Advancing models and theories for digital behavior change interventions. *American Journal of Preventive Medicine, 51*(5), 825–832. https://doi.org/10.1016/j.amepre.2016.06.013

Held, B. S. (2002). The tyranny of the positive attitude in America: Observation and speculation. *Journal of Clinical Psychology, 58*(9), 965–991. https://doi.org/10.1002/jclp.10093

Helne, T., & Hirvilammi, T. (2015). Wellbeing and sustainability: A relational approach. *Sustainable Development, 23*(3), 167–175. https://doi.org/10.1002/sd.1581

Henrich, J., Heine, S. J., & Norenzayan, A. (2010). The weirdest people in the world? *Behavioral and Brain Sciences, 33*(2–3), 61–83. https://doi.org/10.1017/S0140525X0999152X

Hiernaux, Q. (2021). The ethics of plant flourishing and agricultural ethics: Theoretical distinctions and concrete recommendations in light of the environmental crisis. *Philosophies, 6*(4), 91. https://doi.org/10.3390/philosophies6040091

Ho, J. Q. H., Hu, M., Chen, T. X., & Hartanto, A. (2025). Potential and pitfalls of romantic Artificial Intelligence (AI) companions: A systematic review. *Computers in Human Behavior Reports, 19*, 100715. https://doi.org/10.1016/j.chbr.2025.100715

Hobfoll, S. E. (1989). Conservation of resources: A new attempt at conceptualizing stress. *American Psychologist, 44*(3), 513–524. https://doi.org/10.1037/0003-066X.44.3.513

Hofmans, L., van der Stappen, A., & van den Bos, W. (2024). Developmental structure of digital maturity. *Computers in Human Behavior, 157*, 108239. https://doi.org/10.1016/j.chb.2024.108239

Höltge, J., Cowden, R. G., Lee, M. T., Bechara, A. O., Joynt, S., Kamble, S., Khalanskyi, V. V., Shtanko, L., Kurniati, N. M. T., Tymchenko, S., Voytenko, V. L., McNeely, E., & VanderWeele, T. J. (2023). A systems perspective on human flourishing: Exploring cross-country similarities and differences of a multisystemic flourishing network. *The Journal of Positive Psychology, 18*(5), 695–710. https://doi.org/10.1080/17439760.2022.2093784

Holt-Lunstad, J. (2015). Social integration, social networks, and health. In J. D. Wright (Ed.), *International encyclopedia of the social & behavioral sciences* (2nd ed., pp. 365–370). Elsevier.

Hone, L. C., Jarden, A., Schofield, G., & Duncan, S. (2014). Measuring flourishing: The impact of operational definitions on the prevalence of high levels of well-being. *International Journal of Wellbeing, 4*(1), 62–90. https://doi.org/10.5502/ijw.v4i1.4

Horton, D., & Wohl, R. R. (1956). Mass communication and para-social interaction: Observations on intimacy at a distance. *Psychiatry, 19*(3), 215–229. https://doi.org/10.1080/00332747.1956.11023049

Hou, H., Liu, I., Kong, F., & Ni, S. (2025). Computational positive psychology: Advancing the science of wellbeing in the digital era. *The Journal of Positive Psychology, 20*(1), 1–14. https://doi.org/10.1080/17439760.2024.2362443

Hu, J., & Xiao, W. (2025). What are the influencing factors of online learning engagement? A systematic literature review. *Frontiers in Psychology, 16*, 1542652. https://doi.org/10.3389/fpsyg.2025.1542652

Hu, Y., Clancy, E. M., & Klettke, B. (2023). Longitudinal sexting research: A systematic review. *Psych*, *5*(2), 526–544. https://doi.org/10.3390/psych5020035

Huber, S., & Huber, O. W. (2012). The Centrality of Religiosity Scale (CRS). *Religions*, *3*(3), 710–724. https://doi.org/10.3390/rel3030710

Hubig, C. (2008). Mensch-Maschine-Interaktion in hybriden Systemen. In C. Hubig & P. Koslowski (Eds.), *Maschinen, die unsere Brüder werden: Mensch-Maschine-Interaktion in hybriden Systemen* (pp. 9–17). Wilhelm Fink.

Hui, B. P. H. (2022). Prosocial behavior and well-being: Shifting from the 'chicken and egg' to positive feedback loop. *Current Opinion in Psychology*, *44*, 231–236. https://doi.org/10.1016/j.copsyc.2021.09.017

Humanity+. (n.d.). Our mission. https://www.humanityplus.org/about

Huppert, F. A., & So, T. T. C. (2013). Flourishing across Europe: Application of a new conceptual framework for defining well-being. *Social Indicators Research*, *110*(3), 837–861. https://doi.org/10.1007/s11205-011-9966-7

Huston, G. E., Law, K. H., Teague, S., Pardon, M., Muller, J. L., Jackson, B., & Dimmock, J. A. (2025). Understanding and optimising gratitude interventions: The right methods for the right people at the right time. *Psychology & Health*, *40*(9), 1515–1531. https://doi.org/10.1080/08870446.2024.2336042

IEEE. (2019). *Ethically aligned design: A vision for prioritizing human well-being with autonomous and intelligent systems* (1st ed.). IEEE. https://ethicsinaction.ieee.org

Influencer Marketing Hub. (2024). Influencer marketing benchmark report 2024. https://influencermarketinghub.com/influencer-marketing-benchmark-report-2024/

International Organization for Standardization. (2019). *Ergonomics of human–system interaction – Part 210: Human-centred design for interactive systems (ISO 9241-210: 2019)*. ISO. https://www.iso.org/standard/77520.html

Ioannou, A., Lycett, M., & Marshan, A. (2024). The role of mindfulness in mitigating the negative consequences of technostress. *Information Systems Frontiers*, *26*(2), 523–549. https://doi.org/10.1007/s10796-021-10239-0

Jackson, S. A., & Eklund, R. C. (2002). Assessing flow in physical activity: The Flow State Scale–2 and Dispositional Flow Scale–2. *Journal of Sport and Exercise Psychology*, *24*(2), 133–150. https://doi.org/10.1123/jsep.24.2.133

Jackson, S. A., & Marsh, H. W. (1996). Development and validation of a scale to measure optimal experience: The Flow State Scale. *Journal of Sport and Exercise Psychology*, *18*(1), 17–35. https://doi.org/10.1123/jsep.18.1.17

Janicke-Bowles, S. H., Buckley, T. M., Rey, R., Wozniak, T., Meier, A., & Lomanowska, A. (2023). Digital flourishing: Conceptualizing and assessing positive perceptions of mediated social interactions. *Journal of Happiness Studies*, *24*(3), 1013–1035. https://doi.org/10.1007/s10902-023-00619-5

Jarden, A., Rashid, T., Roache, A., & Lomas, T. (2021). Ethical guidelines for positive psychology practice (Version 2.0: English). *International Journal of Wellbeing*, *11*(3), 1–38. https://doi.org/10.5502/ijw.v11i3.1819

Jarzyna, C. L. (2021). Parasocial interaction, the COVID-19 quarantine, and digital age media. *Human Arenas*, *4*(3), 413–429. https://doi.org/10.1007/s42087-020-00156-0

Johannessen, L. E. F. (2023). Interaction rituals and technology: A review essay. *Poetics*, *98*, 101765. https://doi.org/10.1016/j.poetic.2023.101765

Jonas, H. (1984). *The imperative of responsibility: In search of an ethics for the technological age*. University of Chicago Press.

Jones, C. M., Scholes, L., Johnson, D., Katsikitis, M., & Carras, M. C. (2014). Gaming well: Links between videogames and flourishing mental health. *Frontiers in Psychology*, *5*, 260. https://doi.org/10.3389/fpsyg.2014.00260

Joseph, S., & Linley, P. A. (2006). Positive psychology versus the medical model? Comment. *American Psychologist*, *61*(4), 332–333. https://doi.org/10.1037/0003-066X.60.4.332

Joshanloo, M. (2016). Revisiting the empirical distinction between hedonic and eudaimonic aspects of well-being using exploratory structural equation modeling. *Journal of Happiness Studies: An Interdisciplinary Forum on Subjective Well-Being*, *17*(5), 2023–2036. https://doi.org/10.1007/s10902-015-9683-z

Joshanloo, M., Weijers, D., Jiang, D.-Y., Han, G., Bae, J., Pang, J. S., Ho, L. S., Ferreira, M. C., Demir, M., Rizwan, M., Khilji, I. A., Achoui, M., Asano, R., Igarashi, T., Tsukamoto, S., Lamers, S. M. A., Turan, Y., Sundaram, S., Yeung, V. W. L., ... Natalia, A. (2015). Fragility of happiness beliefs across 15 national groups. *Journal of Happiness Studies*, *16*(5), 1185–1210. https://doi.org/10.1007/s10902-014-9553-0

Jupiter, A. (2016). The human-cyborg continuum: Why AI is pointless and why we should all become cyborgs instead. https://medium.com/@AlexJupiter/the-human-cyborg-continuum-why-ai-is-pointless-and-why-we-should-all-become-cyborgs-instead-4de0c4bb476f

Kabat-Zinn, J. (1982). An outpatient program in behavioral medicine for chronic pain patients based on the practice of mindfulness meditation: Theoretical considerations and preliminary results. *General Hospital Psychiatry*, *4*(1), 33–47. https://doi.org/10.1016/0163-8343(82)90026-3

Kachwala, Z. (2025, April 10). Esports World Cup returns to Riyadh with a record $70 million prize pool amid Saudi gaming push. *Reuters*. https://www.reuters.com/world/middle-east/esports-world-cup-returns-riyadh-with-record-70-million-prize-pool-amid-saudi-2025-04-10/

Kaczmarek, Ł. D. (2020). Happiness. In V. Zeigler-Hill & T. K. Shackelford (Eds.), *Encyclopedia of personality and individual differences* (pp. 1875–1879). Springer International Publishing. https://doi.org/10.1007/978-3-319-28099-8_522-1

Kaczmarek, Ł. D., Chwiłkowska, P., Behnke, M., & Drążkowski, D. (2025). Video game play and well-being during the COVID-19 pandemic: A meta-analysis of global findings. *Humanities and Social Sciences Communications*, *12*, 1388. https://doi.org/10.1057/s41599-025-05581-6

Kaczmarek, L. D., & Drążkowski, D. (2014). MMORPG escapism predicts decreased well-being: Examination of gaming time, game realism beliefs, and online social support for offline problems. *Cyberpsychology, Behavior, and Social Networking, 17*(5), 298–302. https://doi.org/10.1089/cyber.2013.0595

Kaczmarek, L. D., & Drążkowski, D. (2025). Interpersonal capitalization in esports enhances players' psychological resources and well-being. *Scientific Reports, 15*, 32826. https://doi.org/10.1038/s41598-025-17968-1

Kahneman, D., & Tversky, A. (1979). Prospect theory: An analysis of decision under risk. *Econometrica, 47*(2), 263–291. https://doi.org/10.2307/1914185

Kalantari, S., Xu, T. B., Mostafavi, A., Lee, A., Barankevich, R., Boot, W. R., & Czaja, S. J. (2022). Using a nature-based virtual reality environment for improving mood states and cognitive engagement in older adults: A mixed-method feasibility study. *Innovation in Aging, 6*(3), igac015. https://doi.org/10.1093/geroni/igac015

Kamieński, Ł. (2022). *Mimowolne cyborgi: Mózg i wojna przyszłości* [Unintentional cyborgs: The brain and the war of the future]. Wydawnictwo Czarne.

Kaufman, S. B. (2020). *Transcend: The new science of self-actualization.* TarcherPerigree.

Keller, J., Roitzheim, C., Radtke, T., Schenkel, K., & Schwarzer, R. (2021). A mobile intervention for self-efficacious and goal-directed smartphone use in the general population: Randomized controlled trial. *JMIR mHealth and uHealth, 9*(11), e26397. https://doi.org/10.2196/26397

Keltner, D. (2024). *Awe: The transformative power of everyday wonder*. Penguin Books.

Keltner, D., & Haidt, J. (2003). Approaching awe, a moral, spiritual, and aesthetic emotion. *Cognition and Emotion, 17*(2), 297–314. https://doi.org/10.1080/02699930302297

Kemp, S. (2025). *Digital 2025: Global overview report*. https://datareportal.com/reports/digital-2025-global-overview-report

Kenyon, K., Kinakh, V., & Harrison, J. (2023). Social virtual reality helps to reduce feelings of loneliness and social anxiety during the COVID-19 pandemic. *Scientific Reports, 13*, 19282. https://doi.org/10.1038/s41598-023-46494-1

Kern, M. L. (2022). PERMAH: A useful model for focusing on well-being in schools. In K.-A. Allen, M. J. Furlong, D. Vella-Brodrick, & S. M. Suldo (Eds.), *Handbook of positive psychology in schools: Supporting process and practice* (3rd ed., pp. 12–24). Routledge. https://doi.org/10.4324/9781003013778-3

Kern, M. L., Williams, P., Spong, C., Colla, R., Sharma, K., Downie, A., Taylor, J. A., Sharp, S., Siokou, C., & Oades, L. G. (2019). Systems informed positive psychology. *The Journal of Positive Psychology, 15*(6), 705–715. https://doi.org/10.1080/17439760.2019.1639799

Keyes, C. L. M. (1998). Social Well-Being Scale. *APA PsycTests*. https://doi.org/10.1037/t13598-000

Keyes, C. L. M. (2002). The mental health continuum: From languishing to flourishing in life. *Journal of Health and Social Behavior, 43*(2), 207–222. https://doi.org/10.2307/3090197

Keyes, C. L. M., & Haidt, J. (Eds.). (2003). *Flourishing: Positive psychology and the life well-lived*. American Psychological Association. https://doi.org/10.1037/10594-000

Keyes, C. L. M., Wissing, M., Potgieter, J. P., Temane, M., Kruger, A., & van Rooy, S. (2008). Evaluation of the Mental Health Continuum–Short Form (MHC–SF) in Setswana-speaking South Africans. *Clinical Psychology & Psychotherapy, 15*(3), 181–192. https://doi.org/10.1002/cpp.572

Kim, J., Popowski, L., Fang, A., Pyle, C., Freeman, G., Kelly, R. M., Lee, A. Y., Liu, F., Smith, A. D. R., To, A., & Zhang, A. X. (2024). Envisioning new futures of positive social technology: Beyond paradigms of fixing, protecting, and preventing. *arXiv*. https://doi.org/10.48550/arXiv.2407.17579

King, D. L., Billieux, J., & Delfabbro, P. H. (2024). Red box, green box: A self-report behavioral frequency measurement approach for behavioral addictions research. *Journal of Behavioral Addictions, 13*(1), 21–24. https://doi.org/10.1556/2006.2023.00079

Kirwan, G., Connolly, I., Barton, H., & Palmer, M. (Eds.). (2024). *An introduction to cyberpsychology* (2nd ed.). Routledge.

Klichowski, M. (2014). *Narodziny cyborgizacji. Nowa eugenika, transhumanizm i zmierzch edukacji* [The birth of cyborgization: New eugenics, transhumanism, and the decline of education]. Wydawnictwo Naukowe UAM.

Klisanin, D. (2011). Is the internet giving rise to new forms of altruism? *Media Psychology Review, 3*(1), 1–11.

Knobel, M., & Lankshear, C. (2007). Online memes, affinities, and cultural production. In M. Knobel & C. Lankshear (Eds.), *A new literacies sampler* (pp. 199–227). Peter Lang.

Kramer, A. D. I., Guillory, J. E., & Hancock, J. T. (2014). Experimental evidence of massive-scale emotional contagion through social networks. *Proceedings of the National Academy of Sciences of the United States of America, 111*(24), 8788–8790. https://doi.org/10.1073/pnas.1320040111

Kruglanski, A. W. (2023). New developments in goal systems theory. In A. W. Kruglanski, A. Fishbach, & C. Kopetz (Eds.), *Goal systems theory: Psychological processes and applications* (pp. 9–24). Oxford University Press. https://doi.org/10.1093/oso/9780197687468.003.0002

Kruglanski, A. W., & Webster, D. M. (1996). Motivated closing of the mind: "Seizing" and "freezing." *Psychological Review, 103*(2), 263–283. https://doi.org/10.1037/0033-295X.103.2.263

Krys, K., Haas, B. W., Igou, E. R., Kosiarczyk, A., Kocimska-Bortnowska, A., Kwiatkowska, A., Lun, V. M.-C., Maricchiolo, F., Park, J., Poláčková Šolcová, I., Sirlopú, D., Uchida, Y., Vauclair, C.-M., Vignoles, V. L., Zelenski, J. M., Adamovic, M., Akotia, C. S., Albert, I., Appoh, L., ... Bond, M. H. (2023). Introduction to a culturally sensitive measure of well-being: Combining life satisfaction and interdependent happiness across 49 different cultures. *Journal of Happiness Studies, 24*(2), 607–627. https://doi.org/10.1007/s10902-022-00588-1

Krys, K., Kostoula, O., van Tilburg, W. A. P., Mosca, O., Lee, J. H., Maricchiolo, F., Kosiarczyk, A., Kocimska-Bortnowska, A., Torres, C., Hitokoto, H., Liew, K.,

Bond, M. H., Lun, V. M.-C., Vignoles, V. L., Zelenski, J. M., Haas, B. W., Park, J., Vauclair, C.-M., Kwiatkowska, A., ... Uchida, Y. (2025). Happiness maximization is a WEIRD way of living. *Perspectives on Psychological Science, 20*(5), 874–902. https://doi.org/10.1177/17456916231208367

Kuhn, T. S. (1962). *The structure of scientific revolutions.* University of Chicago Press.

Kumano, M. (2018). On the concept of well-being in Japan: Feeling shiawase as hedonic well-being and feeling ikigai as eudaimonic well-being. *Applied Research in Quality of Life, 13*(2), 419–433. https://doi.org/10.1007/s11482-017-9526-5

Kumar, N. (2025). *Smartphone Addiction Statistics of 2025.* DemandSage. https://www.demandsage.com/smartphone-addiction-statistics/

Kumar, P. S. (2024). Technostress: A comprehensive literature review on dimensions, impacts, and management strategies. *Computers in Human Behavior Reports, 16*, 100475. https://doi.org/10.1016/j.chbr.2024.100475

Kurzweil, R. (2005). *The singularity is near: When humans transcend biology.* Viking Press.

Kwaśniak, R., Zapała, D., Augustynowicz, P., & Szubielska, M. (2025). Motor imagery in individuals with congenital aphantasia. *Scientific Reports, 15*, 36337. https://doi.org/10.1038/s41598-025-20168-6

Kwok, I., & Wescott, A. B. (2020). Cyberintimacy: A scoping review of technology-mediated romance in the digital age. *Cyberpsychology, Behavior, and Social Networking, 23*(10), 657–666. https://doi.org/10.1089/cyber.2019.0764

Laaber, F., Florack, A., Koch, T., & Hubert, M. (2023). Digital maturity: Development and validation of the Digital Maturity Inventory (DIMI). *Computers in Human Behavior, 143*, 107709. https://doi.org/10.1016/j.chb.2023.107709

Laaber, F., Koch, T., Hubert, M., & Florack, A. (2024). Young people's digital maturity relates to different forms of well-being through basic psychological need satisfaction and frustration. *Computers in Human Behavior, 152*, 108077. https://doi.org/10.1016/j.chb.2023.108077

Labadze, L., Grigolia, M., & Machaidze, L. (2023). Role of AI chatbots in education: Systematic literature review. *International Journal of Educational Technology in Higher Education, 20*, 56. https://doi.org/10.1186/s41239-023-00426-1

Ladhari, R., Knani, M., & Merkouche, W. (2026). Employee well-being and the integration of artificial intelligence in the workplace. In R. Ladhari (Ed.), *Encyclopedia of artificial intelligence in marketing.* Springer. https://doi.org/10.1007/978-3-031-75316-9_10-1

La Guardia, J. G., Ryan, R. M., Couchman, C. E., & Deci, E. L. (2000). Within-person variation in security of attachment: A self-determination theory perspective on attachment, need fulfillment, and well-being. *Journal of Personality and Social Psychology, 79*(3), 367–384. https://doi.org/10.1037/0022-3514.79.3.367

Lai, B., Young, R., Craig, M., Chaviano, K., Swanson-Kimani, E., Wozow, C., Davis, D., & Rimmer, J. H. (2023). Improving social isolation and loneliness among adolescents with physical disabilities through group-based virtual reality gaming: Feasibility pre-post trial study. *JMIR Formative Research*, *7*, e47630. https://doi.org/10.2196/47630

Lakatos, I. (1978). *The methodology of scientific research programmes: Philosophical papers volume 1* (J. Worrall & G. Currie, Eds.). Cambridge University Press.

Langer, E. J. (1992). Matters of mind: Mindfulness/mindlessness in perspective. *Consciousness and Cognition*, *1*(3), 289–305. https://doi.org/10.1016/1053-8100(92)90066-J

Lau, G. R., Low, W. Y., Koh, S. M., & Hartanto, A. (2025). Evaluating AI alignment in eleven LLMs through output-based analysis and human benchmarking. *arXiv*. https://doi.org/10.48550/arXiv.2506.12617

Layous, K., & Lyubomirsky, S. (2014). The how, why, what, when, and who of happiness: Mechanisms underlying the success of positive activity interventions. In J. Gruber & J. T. Moskowitz (Eds.), *Positive emotion: Integrating the light sides and dark sides* (pp. 473–495). Oxford University Press.

Lazarus, R. S., & Folkman, S. (1984). *Stress, appraisal, and coping*. Springer.

Lee, K. C. (2015). Digital creativity: New frontier for research and practice. *Computers in Human Behavior*, *42*, 1–4. https://doi.org/10.1016/j.chb.2014.06.001

Lem, S. (1964/2013). *Summa technologiae* (J. Zylinska, Trans.). University of Minnesota Press.

Lemahieu, L., Vander Zwalmen, Y., Mennes, M., Koster, E. H. W., Vanden Abeele, M. M. P., & Poels, K. (2025). The effects of social media abstinence on affective well-being and life satisfaction: A systematic review and meta-analysis. *Scientific Reports*, *15*, 7581. https://doi.org/10.1038/s41598-025-90984-3

Lewis, C. (1879). *A Latin dictionary*. Clarendon Press.

Li, H., Li, Q., Xu, Z., & Ye, X. (2024a). Digital technologies. *Journal of Digital Economy*, *3*, 240–248. https://doi.org/10.1016/j.jdec.2025.02.001

Li, H., Zhang, R., Lee, Y.-C., Kraut, R. E., & Mohr, D. C. (2023). Systematic review and meta-analysis of AI-based conversational agents for promoting mental health and well-being. *npj Digital Medicine*, *6*, 236. https://doi.org/10.1038/s41746-023-00979-5

Li, J., Ju, S.-Y., Zhu, C., Yuan, Y., Fu, M., Kong, L.-K., & Li, M. (2024b). The development of a digital intelligence quotient scale: A new measuring instrument for primary school students in China. *Heliyon*, *10*(16), e36437. https://doi.org/10.1016/j.heliyon.2024.e36437

Li, W., Qin, X., Yam, K. C., Deng, H., Chen, C., Dong, X., Jiang, L., & Tang, W. (2024c). Embracing artificial intelligence (AI) with job crafting: Exploring trickle-down effect and employees' outcomes. *Tourism Management*, *104*, 104935. https://doi.org/10.1016/j.tourman.2024.104935

Liedgren, J., Desmet, P. M. A., & Gaggioli, A. (2023). Liminal design: A conceptual framework and three-step approach for developing technology that delivers transcendence and deeper experiences. *Frontiers in Psychology*, *14*, 1043170. https://doi.org/10.3389/fpsyg.2023.1043170

Lin, C.-H., Shih, H.-Y., & Sher, P. J. (2007). Integrating technology readiness into technology acceptance: The TRAM model. *Psychology & Marketing*, *24*(7), 641–657. https://doi.org/10.1002/mar.20177

Lin, H., Fan, H., Fu, Q., Li, S., & Liu, Q. (2025a). The mediating role of self-control between physical activity and mobile phone addiction in adolescents: A meta-analytic structural equation modeling approach. *Frontiers in Psychiatry*, *16*, 1446872. https://doi.org/10.3389/fpsyt.2025.1446872

Lin, J.-H. T., Hsieh, J.-H. E., Wang, P.-C. P., & Lin, C.-W. D. (2025b). Virtual Reality (VR) Induce Well-Being (VIEW): A scoping review of VR design, mechanisms, and well-being outcomes. *Humanities and Social Sciences Communications*, *12*, 1766. https://doi.org/10.1057/s41599-025-06043-9

Lin, X., Su, W., & Potenza, M. N. (2018). Development of an online and offline integration hypothesis for healthy internet use: Theory and preliminary evidence. *Frontiers in Psychology*, *9*, 492. https://doi.org/10.3389/fpsyg.2018.00492

Linares-Vargas, B. G. P., & Cieza-Mostacero, S. E. (2025). Interactive virtual reality environments and emotions: A systematic review. *Virtual Reality*, *29*, 3. https://doi.org/10.1007/s10055-024-01049-1

Lindes, P. (2020). Intelligence and agency. *Journal of Artificial General Intelligence*, *11*(2), 47–49.

Linton, M. J., Dieppe, P., & Medina-Lara, A. (2016). Review of 99 self-report measures for assessing well-being in adults: Exploring dimensions of well-being and developments over time. *BMJ Open*, *6*(7), e010641. https://doi.org/10.1136/bmjopen-2015-010641

Litleskare, S., MacIntyre, T. E., & Calogiuri, G. (2020). Enable, reconnect and augment: A new ERA of virtual nature research and application. *International Journal of Environmental Research and Public Health*, *17*(5), 1738. https://doi.org/10.3390/ijerph17051738

Liu, I., Liu, F., Xiao, Y., Huang, Y., Wu, S., & Ni, S. (2024). Investigating the key success factors of chatbot-based positive psychology intervention with retrieval- and generative pre-trained transformer (GPT)-based chatbots. *International Journal of Human–Computer Interaction*, *41*(1), 341–352. https://doi.org/10.1080/10447318.2023.2300015

Liu, Z., & Wang, Z. (2025). The impact of emotional design on multimedia learning outcomes: The moderating role of task difficulty. *Behavioral Sciences*, *15*(3), 397. https://doi.org/10.3390/bs15030397

Livingstone, S., & Haddon, L. (2012). Theoretical framework for children's internet use. In S. Livingstone, L. Haddon, & A. Görzig (Eds.), *Children, risk and safety on the internet: Research and policy challenges in comparative perspective* (pp. 1–14). Bristol University Press. https://doi.org/10.46692/9781847428844.001

Livingstone, S., Mascheroni, G., & Stoilova, M. (2021). The outcomes of gaining digital skills for young people's lives and wellbeing: A systematic evidence review. *New Media & Society*, *25*(5), 1176–1202. https://doi.org/10.1177/14614448211043189

Lomanowska, A. M., & Guitton, M. J. (2016). Online intimacy and well-being in the digital age. *Internet Interventions, 4*, 138–144. https://doi.org/10.1016/j.invent.2016.06.005

Lomas, T. (2018). *Translating happiness: A cross-cultural lexicon of well-being*. MIT Press.

Lomas, T., Bradshaw, M., Case, B., Cowden, R. G., Crabtree, S., English, C., Fogleman, A., Johnson, K. A., Ritter, Z., Johnson, B. R., & VanderWeele, T. J. (2025). The development of the Global Flourishing Study questionnaire: Charting the evolution of a new 109-item inventory of human flourishing. *BMC Global and Public Health, 3*, 30. https://doi.org/10.1186/s44263-025-00139-9

Lomas, T., & Ivtzan, I. (2016). Second wave positive psychology: Exploring the positive–negative dialectics of wellbeing. *Journal of Happiness Studies, 17*(4), 1753–1768. https://doi.org/10.1007/s10902-015-9668-y

Lomas, T., Padgett, R. N., Lai, A. Y., Pawelski, J. O., & VanderWeele, T. J. (2024a). A multidimensional assessment of global flourishing: Differential rankings of 145 countries on 38 wellbeing indicators in the Gallup World Poll, with an accompanying principal components analyses of the structure of flourishing. *The Journal of Positive Psychology, 20*(3), 397–421. https://doi.org/10.1080/17439760.2024.2370538

Lomas, T., Pawelski, J. O., & VanderWeele, T. J. (2024b). A flexible map of flourishing: The dynamics and drivers of flourishing, well-being, health, and happiness. *International Journal of Wellbeing, 13*(4), 3665, 1–38. https://doi.org/10.5502/ijw.v13i4.3665

Lomas, T., Waters, L., Williams, P., Oades, L. G., & Kern, M. L. (2021). Third wave positive psychology: Broadening towards complexity. *The Journal of Positive Psychology, 16*(5), 660–674. https://doi.org/10.1080/17439760.2020.1805501

Long, D., & Magerko, B. (2020). What is AI literacy? Competencies and design considerations. *Proceedings of the 2020 CHI Conference on Human Factors in Computing Systems*, 1–16. ACM. https://doi.org/10.1145/3313831.3376727

Lopatovska, I., & Williams, H. (2018). Personification of the Amazon Alexa: BFF or a mindless companion. *Proceedings of the 2018 Conference on Human Information Interaction & Retrieval (CHIIR '18)*, 265–268. https://doi.org/10.1145/3176349.3176868

Lopes, J. M., Gomes, S., & Nogueira, E. (2025). Educational insights into digital entrepreneurship: The influence of personality and innovation attitudes. *Journal of Innovation and Entrepreneurship, 14*(1), 16. https://doi.org/10.1186/s13731-025-00475-y

Lu, Y. (2024). Impact of digital technologies on organizational change strategies: A review. *Research Journal in Business and Economics, 2*(1), 1–11. https://doi.org/10.61424/rjbe.v2i1.128

Łukaszewicz-Alcaraz, A. (2020). *Are cyborgs persons? An account of futurists ethics*. Palgrave Macmillan.

Lupton, D. (2016). *The quantified self: A sociology of self-tracking*. Polity Press.
Luthans, F., Avey, J. B., & Patera, J. L. (2008). Experimental analysis of a web-based training intervention to develop positive psychological capital. *Academy of Management Learning & Education*, *7*(2), 209–221. https://doi.org/10.5465/amle.2008.32712618
Luthans, F., Youssef, C. M., & Avolio, B. J. (2007). *Psychological capital: Developing the human competitive edge*. Oxford University Press.
Lyubomirsky, S., & Layous, K. (2013). How do simple positive activities increase well-being? *Current Directions in Psychological Science*, *22*(1), 57–62. https://doi.org/10.1177/0963721412469809
Mahzunah, A. K., Sari, I. Y., Paradela, B. V., Murti, B., & Tursina, E. (2024). The impact of cyberbullying on self-harming behavior and suicidal thoughts among adolescents: A meta-analysis. *Journal of Health Promotion and Behavior*, *9*(4), 357–369. https://doi.org/10.26911/thejhpb.2024.09.04.07
Mameli, C., Albani, A., Mazzetti, G., Saccà, A., Cavallini, F., & Grazia, V. (2025). A preliminary evaluation of an online parent training based on self-determination theory aimed at digital parenting. *Child & Youth Care Forum*, *54*, 93–115. https://doi.org/10.1007/s10566-024-09809-5
Manathunga, C., & Brew, A. (2012). Beyond tribes and territories: New metaphors for new times. In P. Trowler, M. Saunders, & V. Bamber (Eds.), *Tribes and territories in the 21st-century: Rethinking the significance of disciplines in higher education* (pp. 44–56). Taylor & Francis. https://doi.org/10.4324/9780203136935
Manz, R., Bäcker, J., Cramer, S., Meyer, P., Müller, D., Muzalyova, A., Rentschler, L., Wengenmayr, C., Hinske, L. C., Huss, R., Raffler, J., & Soto-Rey, I. (2025). Do explainable AI (XAI) methods improve the acceptance of AI in clinical practice? An evaluation of XAI methods on Gleason grading. *Journal of Pathology: Clinical Research*, *11*(2), e70023. https://doi.org/10.1002/2056-4538.70023
Maran, T. K., Liegl, S., Davila, A., Moder, S., Kraus, S., & Mahto, R. V. (2022). Who fits into the digital workplace? Mapping digital self-efficacy and agility onto psychological traits. *Technological Forecasting and Social Change*, *175*, 121352. https://doi.org/10.1016/j.techfore.2021.121352
Marnewick, C., & Marnewick, A. (2021). Digital intelligence: A must-have for project managers. *Project Leadership and Society*, *2*, 100026. https://doi.org/10.1016/j.plas.2021.100026
Martin Coesel, A., Biancardi, B., & Buisine, S. (2024). A theoretical review of the Proteus effect: Understanding the underlying processes. *Frontiers in Psychology*, *15*, 1379599. https://doi.org/10.3389/fpsyg.2024.1379599
Maslow, A. H. (1954). *Motivation and personality*. Harper.
Mayiwar, L., Asutay, E., Tinghög, G., Västfjäll, D., & Barrafrem, K. (2025). Determinants of digital well-being. *AI & Society*, *40*(4), 3063–3073. https://doi.org/10.1007/s00146-024-02071-2

McCarthy, J., Minsky, M., Rochester, N., & Shannon, C. E. (1955). *A Proposal for the Dartmouth summer research project on artificial intelligence*. http://raysolomonoff.com/dartmouth/boxa/dart564props.pdf

McKenna, K. Y. A., Green, A. S., & Gleason, M. E. J. (2002). Relationship formation on the internet: What's the big attraction? *Journal of Social Issues*, *58*(1), 9–31. https://doi.org/10.1111/1540-4560.00246

McLuhan, M. (1964/1994). *Understanding media: The extensions of man*. MIT Press.

McQuaid, M., & Kern, P. (2017). *Your wellbeing blueprint: Feeling good and doing well at work*. McQuaid Ltd.

Medeiros, M., Ozturk, A., Hancer, M., Weinland, J., & Okumus, B. (2022). Understanding travel tracking mobile application usage: An integration of self-determination theory and UTAUT2. *Tourism Management Perspectives*, *42*, 100949. https://doi.org/10.1016/j.tmp.2022.100949

Meier, A., & Reinecke, L. (2023). Social media and mental health: Reviewing effects on eudaimonic well-being. In R. L. Nabi & J. Gall Myrick (Eds.), *Emotions in the digital world: Exploring affective experience and expression in online interactions* (pp. 215–234). Oxford University Press. https://doi.org/10.1093/oso/9780197520536.003.0012

Mella, J., Iacovides, I., & Cox, A. L. (2023). Gaming for post-work recovery: The role of immersion. *Proceedings of the 2023 CHI Conference on Human Factors in Computing Systems*, 288, 1–15. https://doi.org/10.1145/3544548.3581510

Meng, W., Yu, L., Liu, C., Pan, N., Pang, X., & Zhu, Y. (2024). A systematic review of the effectiveness of online learning in higher education during the COVID-19 pandemic period. *Frontiers in Education*, *8*, 1334153. https://doi.org/10.3389/feduc.2023.1334153

Merrill, K., Jr., Mikkilineni, S. D., & Dehnert, M. (2025). Artificial intelligence chatbots as a source of virtual social support: Implications for loneliness and anxiety management. *Annals of the New York Academy of Sciences*, *1549*(1), 148–159. https://doi.org/10.1111/nyas.15400

Meshkat, S., Edalatkhah, M., Di Luciano, C., Martin, J., Kaur, G., Hee Lee, G., Park, H., Torres, A., Mazalek, A., Kapralos, B., Dubrowski, A., & Bhat, V. (2024). Virtual reality and stress management: A systematic review. *Cureus*, *16*(7), e64573. https://doi.org/10.7759/cureus.64573

Messinger, P. R., Ge, X., Stroulia, E., Lyons, K. A., Smirnov, K., & Bone, M. (2008). On the relationship between my avatar and myself. *Journal of Virtual Worlds Research*, *1*(2), 1–17.

Michailidis, L., Balaguer-Ballester, E., & He, X. (2018). Flow and immersion in video games: The aftermath of a conceptual challenge. *Frontiers in Psychology*, *9*, 1682. https://doi.org/10.3389/fpsyg.2018.01682

Michalec, B., Keyes, C., & Nalkur, S. (2009). Flourishing. In S. J. Lopez (Ed.), *The encyclopedia of positive psychology* (pp. 391–394). Wiley-Blackwell.

Michelotto, F., & Joia, L. A. (2024). Organizational digital transformation readiness: An exploratory investigation. *Journal of Theoretical and Applied Electronic Commerce Research, 19*(4), 3283–3304. https://doi.org/10.3390/jtaer19040159

Michie, S., Richardson, M., Johnston, M., Abraham, C., Francis, J., Hardeman, W., Eccles, M. P., Cane, J., & Wood, C. E. (2013). The behavior change technique taxonomy (v1) of 93 hierarchically clustered techniques: Building an international consensus for the reporting of behavior change interventions. *Annals of Behavioral Medicine, 46*(1), 81–95. https://doi.org/10.1007/s12160-013-9486-6

Miller, L. M. S., Callegari, R. A., Abah, T., & Fann, H. (2024). Digital literacy training for low-income older adults through undergraduate community-engaged learning: Single-group pretest–posttest study. *JMIR Aging, 7*, e51675. https://doi.org/10.2196/51675

Mitchell, J. J., & Jeon, M. (2025). Exploring emotional connections: A systematic literature review of attachment in human-robot interaction. *International Journal of Human–Computer Interaction, 41*(18), 11753–11774. https://doi.org/10.1080/10447318.2024.2445100

Mitra, S. (2010). New experiments in self-teaching [Video]. YouTube. https://www.youtube.com/watch?v=dk60sYrU2RU

Modliński, A., Fortuna, P., & Rożnowski, B. (2022). Human–machine trans roles conflict in the organization: How sensitive are customers to intelligent robots replacing the human workforce? *International Journal of Consumer Studies, 47*(1), 100–117. https://doi.org/10.1111/ijcs.12811

Modliński, A., Fortuna, P., Wojtasiński, M., & Tużnik, P. (2025). Getting in sync: Measuring perceived technological sustainability in organisations through the lens of employee well-being. *Employee Relations: The International Journal, 47*(9), 289–319. https://doi.org/10.1108/ER-03-2025-0194

Moradbakhti, L., Leichtmann, B., & Mara, M. (2024). Development and validation of a basic psychological needs scale for technology use. *Psychological Test Adaptation and Development, 5*(1), 26–45. https://doi.org/10.1027/2698-1866/a000062

Moravec, H. (1998). When will computer hardware match the human brain? *Journal of Evolution and Technology, 1*(1), 10.

Mori, M. (1970). The uncanny valley. *Energy, 7*(4), 33–35.

Mumford, L. (1934). *Technics and civilization.* Harcourt, Brace and Company.

Murray, E., Hekler, E. B., Andersson, G., Collins, L. M., Doherty, A., Hollis, C., Rivera, D. E., West, R., & Wyatt, J. C. (2016). Evaluating digital health interventions: Key questions and approaches. *American Journal of Preventive Medicine, 51*(5), 843–851. https://doi.org/10.1016/j.amepre.2016.06.008

Muthuswamy, V. V., & Esakki, S. (2024). Impact of cybersecurity and AI's related factors on incident reporting suspicious behavior and employees' stress: Moderating role of cybersecurity training. *International Journal of Cyber Criminology, 18*(1), 83–107. https://doi.org/10.5281/zenodo.4766805

Myrick, J. G., Nabi, R. L., & Eng, N. J. (2022). Consuming memes during the COVID pandemic: Effects of memes and meme type on COVID-related stress and coping efficacy. *Psychology of Popular Media*, *11*(3), 316–323. https://doi.org/10.1037/ppm0000371

Nahum-Shani, I., & Yoon, C. (2024). Toward the science of engagement with digital interventions. *Current Directions in Psychological Science*, *33*(4), 239–246. https://doi.org/10.1177/09637214241254328

Naneva, S., Sarda Gou, M., Webb, T. L., & Prescott, T. J. (2020). A systematic review of attitudes, anxiety, acceptance, and trust towards social robots. *International Journal of Social Robotics*, *12*, 1179–1201. https://doi.org/10.1007/s12369-020-00659-4

Nascimento, L., Correia, M. F., & Califf, C. B. (2024). Towards a bright side of technostress in higher education teachers: Identifying several antecedents and outcomes of techno-eustress. *Technology in Society*, *76*, 102428. https://doi.org/10.1016/j.techsoc.2023.102428

Nass, C., & Moon, Y. (2000). Machines and mindlessness: Social responses to computers. *Journal of Social Issues*, *56*(1), 81–103. https://doi.org/10.1111/0022-4537.00153

Nęcka, E. (2015). Self-control scale AS-36: Construction and validation study. *Polish Psychological Bulletin*, *46*, 488–497. https://doi.org/10.1515/ppb-2015-0055

Nęcka, E. (2018). *Trening poznawczy: Czy umysł można trenować tak jak trenuje się mięśnie?* [Cognitive training: Can the mind be trained like muscles?]. Smak Słowa.

Neff, K. D. (2003). Self-compassion: An alternative conceptualization of a healthy attitude toward oneself. *Self and Identity*, *2*(2), 85–101. https://doi.org/10.1080/15298860309032

Newport, C. (2019). *Digital minimalism: Choosing a focused life in a noisy world*. Portfolio/Penguin.

Ng, W. (2012). Can we teach digital natives digital literacy? *Computers & Education*, *59*(3), 1065–1078. https://doi.org/10.1016/j.compedu.2012.04.016

Nguyen, C. T. (2020). Echo chambers and epistemic bubbles. *Episteme*, *17*(2), 141–161. https://doi.org/10.1017/epi.2018.32

Niemann, L., von Gruner, C., Zhang, X. C., Margraf, J., & Totzeck, C. (2023). Positive Emotions Training (PoET) as an online intervention to improve mental health: A feasibility study. *BMC Public Health*, *23*, 1543. https://doi.org/10.1186/s12889-023-16424-x

Niemiec, R. M. (2017). *Character strengths interventions: A field guide for practitioners*. Hogrefe.

Niemiec, R. M., & McGrath, R. E. (2019). *The power of character strengths: Appreciate and ignite your positive personality*. VIA Institute on Character.

Nomura, T., Suzuki, T., Kanda, T., & Kato, K. (2006). Measurement of negative attitudes toward robots. *Interaction Studies*, *7*, 437–454. https://doi.org/10.1075/is.7.3.14nom

Norman, K. L. (2017). *Cyberpsychology: An introduction to human-computer interaction* (2nd ed.). Cambridge University Press.

Novak, T. P., Hoffman, D. L., & Yung, Y.-F. (2000). Measuring the customer experience in online environments: A structural modeling approach. *Marketing Science, 19*(1), 22–42. https://doi.org/10.1287/mksc.19.1.22.15184

Nowotny, H., Scott, P., & Gibbons, M. (2001). *Re-thinking science: Knowledge and the public in an age of uncertainty*. Polity Press.

Nuttall, M., Machin, T., Peel, R., Abel, S., & Brown, S. (2025). Online prosocial behaviors: A scoping review of definitions, actions, and motivators. *Cyberpsychology, Behavior, and Social Networking, 28*(6), 387–398. https://doi.org/10.1089/cyber.2024.0481

Oades, L. G., & Johnston, A. L. (2017). Wellbeing literacy: The necessary ingredient in positive education. *Psychology and Behavioral Science International Journal, 3*(5), 555621. https://doi.org/10.19080/PBSIJ.2017.03.555621

O'Brien, H. L., & Cairns, P. (2016). *Why engagement matters: Cross-disciplinary perspectives and innovations on user engagement with digital media*. Springer.

OECD. (2005). The definition and selection of key competencies: Executive summary. https://www.oecd.org/pisa/35070367.pdf

OECD. (2015). *Frascati Manual 2015: Guidelines for collecting and reporting data on research and experimental development, the measurement of scientific, technological and innovation activities*. OECD Publishing. https://doi.org/10.1787/9789264239012-en

Oettingen, G. (2014). *Rethinking positive thinking: Inside the new science of motivation*. Penguin Random House.

Ogonowska, A. (Ed.). (2021). *Cyberpsychologia. Media – użytkownicy – zastosowania* [Cyberpsychology: Media – users – applications]. Oficyna Wydawnicza Impuls.

Oishi, S., & Diener, E. (2014). Residents of poor nations have a greater sense of meaning in life than residents of wealthy nations. *Psychological Science, 25*(2), 422–430. https://doi.org/10.1177/0956797613507286

Oishi, S., & Westgate, E. C. (2022). A psychologically rich life: Beyond happiness and meaning. *Psychological Review, 129*(4), 790–811. https://doi.org/10.1037/rev0000317

Olech, M., & Jurek, P. (2022). *Technostres: Skale do pomiaru sposobu postrzegania technologii* [Technostress: Measurement scales for technology perception]. Pracownia Testów Psychologicznych i Pedagogicznych.

Oliveira, W., & Hamari, J. (2025). Flow experience in gameful approaches: A systematic literature review, scientometric analysis, and research agenda. *International Journal of Human–Computer Interaction, 41*(20), 13113–13139. https://doi.org/10.1080/10447318.2025.2470279

Oliver, M. B. (2022). Social media use and eudaimonic well-being. *Current Opinion in Psychology, 45*, 101307. https://doi.org/10.1016/j.copsyc.2022.101307

Olson, J. A., Sandra, D. A., Chmoulevitch, D., Raz, A., & Veissière, S. P. L. (2023). A nudge-based intervention to reduce problematic smartphone use: Randomised controlled trial. *International Journal of Mental Health and Addiction, 21*(6), 3842–3864. https://doi.org/10.1007/s11469-022-00826-w

Oreg, S., Michel, A., & By, R. T. (Eds.). (2013). *The psychology of organizational change: Viewing change from the employee's perspective*. Cambridge University Press.

Osborne, E. L., Ainsworth, B., Hooper, N., & Atkinson, M. J. (2023). Experiences of using digital mindfulness-based interventions: Rapid scoping review and thematic synthesis. *Journal of Medical Internet Research, 25*, e44220. https://doi.org/10.2196/44220

Öztürk, F., Çalışkan, B., & Oğuz-Duran, N. (2025). Digital resilience: A systematic literature review on definitions, measurements, and interventions. *European Psychologist*. https://doi.org/10.1027/1016-9040/a000570

Padilla-Coreano, N., & Martínez-Rivera, F. J. (2025). How dopamine guides our social world. *Pharmacological Reviews, 77*(5), 100085. https://doi.org/10.1016/j.pharmr.2025.100085

Pallavicini, F., Orena, E., Arnoldi, L., Achille, F., Stefanini, S., Cassa, M., Pepe, A., Veronese, G., Bernardelli, L., Sforza, F., Fascendini, S., Defanti, C. A., Gemma, M., Clerici, M., Riva, G., & Mantovani, F. (2025). Effects and acceptability of a 1-week home-based virtual reality training for supporting the management of stress and anxiety: Randomized pilot trial. *JMIR Serious Games, 13*, e50326. https://doi.org/10.2196/50326

Pallavicini, F., & Pepe, A. (2020). Virtual reality games and the role of body involvement in enhancing positive emotions and decreasing anxiety: Within-subjects pilot study. *JMIR Serious Games, 8*(2), e15635. https://doi.org/10.2196/15635

Paloutzian, R. F., & Ellison, C. W. (1982). Loneliness, spiritual well-being and the quality of life. In L. A. Peplau & D. Perlman (Eds.), *Loneliness: A sourcebook of current theory, research and therapy* (pp. 224–236). Wiley.

Pandey, S. K., & Pravesh, R. (2025). Workplace surveillance and its psychological impacts on employee: A review. *OPUS HR Journal, 16*(1), 18–35.

Parasuraman, A. (2000). Technology readiness index (TRI): A multiple-item scale to measure readiness to embrace new technologies. *Journal of Service Research, 2*(4), 307–320. https://doi.org/10.1177/109467050024001

Pariser, E. (2011). *The filter bubble: What the internet is hiding from you*. Penguin Press.

Park, S. Y., Do, B., Yourell, J., Hermer, J., & Huberty, J. (2024). Digital methods for the spiritual and mental health of Generation Z: Scoping review. *Interactive Journal of Medical Research, 13*, e48929. https://doi.org/10.2196/48929

Parks, A. C. (2014). A case for the advancement of the design and study of online positive psychological interventions. *The Journal of Positive Psychology, 9*(6), 502–508. https://doi.org/10.1080/17439760.2014.936969

Parks, A. C., & Schueller, S. (Eds.). (2014). *The Wiley Blackwell handbook of positive psychological interventions*. John Wiley & Sons.

Parks, M. R., & Floyd, K. (1996). Making friends in cyberspace. *Journal of Communication, 46*(1), 80–97. https://doi.org/10.1111/j.1460-2466.1996.tb01462.x

Passey, D., Shonfeld, M., Appleby, L., Judge, M., Saito, T., & Smits, A. (2018). Digital agency: Empowering equity in and through education. *Technology, Knowledge and Learning, 23*(3), 425–439. https://doi.org/10.1007/s10758-018-9384-x

Pastwa, R., & Dutkowska, A. (Eds.). (2025). *Kompetencje przyszłości: Podręcznik* [*Competencies of the future: Handbook*]. Wydawnictwo KUL.

Pawelski, J. O. (2016). Defining the "positive" in positive psychology: Part II. A normative analysis. *The Journal of Positive Psychology, 11*(4), 357–365. https://doi.org/10.1080/17439760.2015.1137628

Pawelski, J. O. (2020). The elements model: Toward a new generation of positive psychology interventions. *The Journal of Positive Psychology, 15*(5), 675–679. https://doi.org/10.1080/17439760.2020.1789710

Pearce, D. (1995). *The hedonistic imperative*. David Pearce. https://www.hedweb.com

Pečiuliauskienė, P. (2025). The relationship between information literacy and digital self-efficacy in teaching information literacy for new teachers in Lithuania. *Social Sciences & Humanities Open, 11*(2), 101304. https://doi.org/10.1016/j.ssaho.2025.101304

Peters, D., Calvo, R. A., & Ryan, R. M. (2018). Designing for motivation, engagement and wellbeing in digital experience. *Frontiers in Psychology, 9*, 797. https://doi.org/10.3389/fpsyg.2018.00797

Petersen, J. M., Kemps, E., Lewis, L. K., & Prichard, I. (2020). Associations between commercial app use and physical activity: Cross-sectional study. *Journal of Medical Internet Research, 22*(6), e17152. https://doi.org/10.2196/17152

Peterson, C., & Seligman, M. E. P. (2004). *Character strengths and virtues: A handbook and classification*. Oxford University Press; American Psychological Association.

Picard, R. W. (1997). *Affective computing*. MIT Press.

Pineda, B. S., Mejia, R., Qin, Y., Martinez, J., Delgadillo, L. G., & Muñoz, R. F. (2023). Updated taxonomy of digital mental health interventions: A conceptual framework. *mHealth, 9*, 28. https://doi.org/10.21037/mhealth-23-6

Pizzolante, M., Pelowski, M., Demmer, T. R., Bartolotta, S., Sarcinella, E. D., Gaggioli, A., & Chirico, A. (2024). Aesthetic experiences and their transformative power: A systematic review. *Frontiers in Psychology, 15*, 1328449. https://doi.org/10.3389/fpsyg.2024.1328449

Ploke, V., Batinic, B., & Stieger, S. (2024). Evaluating flourishing: A comparative analysis of four measures using item pool visualization. *Frontiers in Psychology, 15*, 1458946. https://doi.org/10.3389/fpsyg.2024.1458946

Podolak, J., Łukasik, S., Balawender, P., Ossowski, J., Piotrowski, J., Bakowicz, K., & Sankowski, P. (2024). LLM generated responses to mitigate the impact of hate speech. *arXiv*. https://doi.org/10.48550/arXiv.2311.16905

Pollak, A., Biolik, E., & Chudzicka-Czupała, A. (2025). New Luddites? Counterproductive work behavior and its correlates, including work characteristics, stress at work, and job satisfaction among employees working with industrial and collaborative robots. *Human Factors and Ergonomics in Manufacturing & Service Industries, 35*(4), e70016. https://doi.org/10.1002/hfm.70016

Prochnow, T., Senthil, R., Poulos, A., Patterson, M. S., Blake, J., & Massey, P. (2025). Virtual bonds; real emotions: Systematic review exploring online social connections and adolescent mental health. *Cyberpsychology, Behavior, and Social Networking, 28*(10), 658–671. https://doi.org/10.1177/21522715251377377

Przybylski, A. K., Mishkin, A., Shotbolt, V., & Gladwell, V. (2014). *Building children's online resilience*. Oxford Internet Institute.

Qamaria, R. S., Kuswandi, D., Setiyowati, N., & Bahodirovna, A. M. (2025). Digital resilience in adolescence: A systematic review of models, methods and theoretical perspectives. *Multidisciplinary Reviews, 8*(9), e2025287. https://doi.org/10.31893/multirev.2025287

Qi, H., Dong, Z., Wei, Q., Chen, X., & Luo, Y. (2025). Are gamers happier? Multidimensional well-being differences in risk groups for problematic internet use and internet gaming disorder. *Personality and Individual Differences, 246*, 113334. https://doi.org/10.1016/j.paid.2025.113334

Quesnel, D., & Riecke, B. E. (2018). Are you awed yet? How virtual reality gives us awe and goose bumps. *Frontiers in Psychology, 9*, 2158. https://doi.org/10.3389/fpsyg.2018.02158

Radtke, T., Apel, T., Schenkel, K., Keller, J., & von Lindern, E. (2021). Digital detox: An effective solution in the smartphone era? A systematic literature review. *Mobile Media & Communication, 10*(2), 190–215. https://doi.org/10.1177/20501579211028647

Rahayu, F. S., Nastiti, P., & Arthajanvian, T. (2025). The role of hedonic motivation in influencing TikTok use and how it relates to Generation Z characteristics. *Advances in Human–Computer Interaction, 2025*, 5971465. https://doi.org/10.1155/ahci/5971465

Randhawa, A. K., & Vella-Brodrick, D. A. (2025). Online self-compassion interventions and wellbeing outcomes: A systematic review of RCTs. *Mindfulness, 16*, 1795–1820. https://doi.org/10.1007/s12671-025-02606-8

Rautenbach, C., & Rothmann, S. (2017). Psychometric validation of the Flourishing-at-Work Scale—Short Form (FWS-SF): Results and implications of a South African study. *Journal of Psychology in Africa, 27*(4), 303–309. https://doi.org/10.1080/14330237.2017.1347748

Reilly, P., & Dawson, I. (2021). Track and trace, and other collaborative art/archaeology bubbles in the phygital pandemic. *Open Archaeology, 7*(1), 291–313. https://doi.org/10.1515/opar-2020-0137

Reinecke, L., Vorderer, P., & Knop, K. (2014). Entertainment 2.0? The role of intrinsic and extrinsic need satisfaction for the enjoyment of Facebook use. *Journal of Communication, 64*(3), 417–438. https://doi.org/10.1111/jcom.12099

Riedl, E., & Verschuuren, P. (2025). A systematic literature review of esports integrity. *The International Sports Law Journal*, *25*, 99–118. https://doi.org/10.1007/s40318-025-00295-y

Riva, G. (2012). What is positive technology and its impact on cyberpsychology. *Studies in Health Technology and Informatics*, *181*, 37–41. https://doi.org/10.3233/978-1-61499-121-2-37

Riva, G. (2025). Digital "we": Human sociality and culture in the era of social media and artificial intelligence. *American Psychologist*, *80*(9), 1535–1549. https://doi.org/10.1037/amp0001577

Riva, G., Baños, R. M., Botella, C., Wiederhold, B. K., & Gaggioli, A. (2012). Positive technology: Using interactive technologies to promote positive functioning. *Cyberpsychology, Behavior, and Social Networking*, *15*(2), 69–77. https://doi.org/10.1089/cyber.2011.0139

Riva, G., Serino, S., Chirico, A., & Gaggioli, A. (2019). Positive technology: From communication to positive experience. In J. A. Muñiz Velázquez & C. M. Pulido (Eds.), *The Routledge handbook of positive communication: Contributions of an emerging community of research on communication for happiness and social change* (pp. 267–277). Routledge.

Riva, G., Villani, D., Cipresso, P., & Gaggioli, A. (2016). Positive technology: The use of technology for improving and sustaining personal change. In D. Villani, P. Cipresso, A. Gaggioli, & G. Riva (Eds.), *Integrating technology in positive psychology practice* (pp. 1–37). Information Science Reference. https://doi.org/10.4018/978-1-4666-9986-1.ch001

Roberts, J. A., Young, P. D., & David, M. E. (2024). The epidemic of loneliness: A 9-year longitudinal study of the impact of passive and active social media use on loneliness. *Personality and Social Psychology Bulletin*, *52*(5), 1111–1125. https://doi.org/10.1177/01461672241295870

Roffarello, A. M., & De Russis, L. (2023). Achieving digital wellbeing through digital self-control tools: A systematic review and meta-analysis. *ACM Transactions on Computer-Human Interaction*, *30*(4), 1–66. https://doi.org/10.1145/3571810

Rogers, E. M. (1962). *Diffusion of innovations*. Free Press of Glencoe.

Rogers, Y., Sharp, H., & Preece, J. (2023). *Interaction design: Beyond human-computer interaction* (6th ed.). Wiley.

Rosenfield, M. (2011). Computer vision syndrome: A review of ocular causes and potential treatments. *Ophthalmic and Physiological Optics*, *31*(5), 502–515. https://doi.org/10.1111/j.1475-1313.2011.00834.x

Rosič, J., Janicke-Bowles, S. H., Carbone, L., Lobe, B., & Vandenbosch, L. (2022). Positive digital communication among youth: The development and validation of the Digital Flourishing Scale for Adolescents. *Frontiers in Digital Health*, *4*, 975557. https://doi.org/10.3389/fdgth.2022.975557

Rowland, L., & Klisanin, D. (2018). Cyber-kindness: Spreading kindness in cyberspace. *Media Psychology Review*, *12*(1). https://mprcenter.org/review/cyber-kindness-spreading-kindness-in-cyberspace/

Rożnowski, B., Matłacz, K., & Mamcarz, P. (2026). Synergy of silicon and sentiment: The interplay of emotional intelligence, technology acceptance, and employee well-being in human–AI collaborative workspaces. *International Journal of Social Robotics, 18*, 14. https://doi.org/10.1007/s12369-025-01342-2

Rudnicka, P. (2021). *Gotowość wobec technologii. Konteksty, definicja i pomiar* [Readiness for technology: Contexts, definition, and measurement]. Wydawnictwo Uniwersytetu Śląskiego.

Rusk, R. D., & Waters, L. (2015). A psycho-social system approach to well-being: Empirically deriving the five domains of positive functioning. *The Journal of Positive Psychology, 10*(2), 141–152. https://doi.org/10.1080/17439760.2014.920409

Russell, S. (2019). *Human compatible: Artificial intelligence and the problem of control.* Viking.

Ryan, R. M., & Deci, E. L. (2000). Self-determination theory and the facilitation of intrinsic motivation, social development, and well-being. *American Psychologist, 55*(1), 68–78. https://doi.org/10.1037/0003-066X.55.1.68

Ryff, C. D. (1989). Happiness is everything, or is it? Explorations on the meaning of psychological well-being. *Journal of Personality and Social Psychology, 57*(6), 1069–1081. https://doi.org/10.1037/0022-3514.57.6.1069

Ryff, C. D. (2024). The privilege of well-being in an increasingly unequal society. *Current Directions in Psychological Science, 33*(5), 300–307. https://doi.org/10.1177/09637214241266818

Ryff, C. D., & Keyes, C. L. M. (1995). The structure of psychological well-being revisited. *Journal of Personality and Social Psychology, 69*(4), 719–727. https://doi.org/10.1037/0022-3514.69.4.719

Ryff, C. D., Dienberg Love, G., Urry, H. L., Muller, D., Rosenkranz, M. A., Friedman, E. M., Davidson, R. J., & Singer, B. (2006). Psychological well-being and ill-being: Do they have distinct or mirrored biological correlates? *Psychotherapy and Psychosomatics, 75*(2), 85–95. https://doi.org/10.1159/000090892

Ryff, C. D., & Singer, B. H. (2008). Know thyself and become what you are: A eudaimonic approach to psychological well-being. *Journal of Happiness Studies: An Interdisciplinary Forum on Subjective Well-Being, 9*(1), 13–39. https://doi.org/10.1007/s10902-006-9019-0

Saleme, P., Pang, B., Dietrich, T., & Parkinson, J. (2020). Prosocial digital games for youth: A systematic review of interventions. *Computers in Human Behavior Reports, 2*, 100039. https://doi.org/10.1016/j.chbr.2020.100039

Samper-Márquez, J. J., & Oropesa-Ruiz, N. F. (2025). Scoping review on digital creativity: Definition, approaches, and current trends. *Education Sciences, 15*(2), 202. https://doi.org/10.3390/educsci15020202

Sander, T. (2011). Positive computing. In R. Biswas-Diener (Ed.), *Positive psychology as social change* (pp. 309–326). Springer.

Sauro, J., & Lewis, J. R. (2016). Quantifying the user experience: Practical statistics for user research (2nd ed.). Morgan Kaufmann.

Schäfer, S. K., von Boros, L., Schaubruch, L. M., Kunzler, A. M., Lindner, S., Koehler, F., Werner, T., Zappalà, F., Helmreich, I., Wessa, M., Lieb, K., & Tüscher, O. (2024). Digital interventions to promote psychological resilience: A systematic review and meta-analysis. *npj Digital Medicine*, *7*, 30. https://doi.org/10.1038/s41746-024-01017-8

Schaffer, V., Huckstepp, T., & Kannis-Dymand, L. (2024). Awe: A systematic review within a cognitive behavioral framework and proposed cognitive behavioral model of awe. *International Journal of Applied Positive Psychology*, *9*(1), 101–136. https://doi.org/10.1007/s41042-023-00116-3

Schamberger, T., Schuberth, F., & Henseler, J. (2023). Confirmatory composite analysis in human development research. *International Journal of Behavioral Development*, *47*(1), 89–100. https://doi.org/10.1177/01650254221117506

Schillings, C., Meißner, E., Erb, B., Bendig, E., Schultchen, D., & Pollatos, O. (2024). Effects of a chatbot-based intervention on stress and health-related parameters in a stressed sample: Randomized controlled trial. *JMIR Mental Health*, *11*, e50454. https://doi.org/10.2196/50454

Schleidgen, S., Friedrich, O., Gerlek, S., Assadi, G., & Seifert, J. (2023). The concept of "interaction" in debates on human–machine interaction. *Humanities and Social Sciences Communications*, *10*(1), 551. https://doi.org/10.1057/s41599-023-02060-8

Schramm, H., Liebers, N., Biniak, L., & Dettmar, F. (2024). Research trends on parasocial interactions and relationships with media characters: A review of 281 English and German-language studies from 2016 to 2020. *Frontiers in Psychology*, *15*, 1418564. https://doi.org/10.3389/fpsyg.2024.1418564

Schubert, T., Friedmann, F., & Regenbrecht, H. (2001). The experience of presence: Factor analytic insights. *Presence: Teleoperators and Virtual Environments*, *10*(3), 266–281. https://doi.org/10.1162/105474601300343603

Schueller, S., Kashdan, T., & Parks, A. (2014). Synthesizing positive psychological interventions: Suggestions for conducting and interpreting meta-analyses. *International Journal of Wellbeing*, *4*(1), 91–98. https://doi.org/10.5502/ijw.v4i1.5

Schueller, S. M., & Parks, A. C. (2012). Disseminating self-help: Positive psychology exercises in an online trial. *Journal of Medical Internet Research*, *14*(3), e63. https://doi.org/10.2196/jmir.1850

Schultz, D. P., & Schultz, S. E. (2015). *A history of modern psychology* (11th ed.). Cengage Learning Custom Publishing.

Schultz, W. (2016). Dopamine reward prediction-error signalling: A two-component response. *Nature Reviews Neuroscience*, *17*(3), 183–195. https://doi.org/10.1038/nrn.2015.26

Schwarz, N., & Clore, G. L. (1988). How do I feel about it? The informative function of affective states. In K. Fiedler & J. Forgas (Eds.), *Affect, cognition, and social behavior* (pp. 44–62). C. J. Hogrefe.

Sciara, S., Villani, D., Di Natale, A. F., & Regalia, C. (2021). Gratitude and social media: A pilot experiment on the benefits of exposure to others' grateful interactions on Facebook. *Frontiers in Psychology*, *12*, 667052. https://doi.org/10.3389/fpsyg.2021.667052

Seligman, M. E. P. (2011). *Flourish: A visionary new understanding of happiness and well-being*. Free Press.

Seligman, M. E. P., & Csikszentmihalyi, M. (2000). Positive psychology: An introduction. *American Psychologist*, *55*(1), 5–14. https://doi.org/10.1037/0003-066X.55.1.5

Seligman, M. E. P., Ernst, R. M., Gillham, J. E., Reivich, K., & Linkins, M. (2009). Positive education: Positive psychology and classroom interventions. *Oxford Review of Education*, *35*(3), 293–311. https://doi.org/10.1080/03054980902934563

Seligman, M. E. P., Steen, T. A., Park, N., & Peterson, C. (2005). Positive psychology progress: Empirical validation of interventions. *American Psychologist*, *60*(5), 410–421. https://doi.org/10.1037/0003-066X.60.5.410

Selye, H. (1956). *The stress of life*. McGraw-Hill.

Setty, E. (2023). Risks and opportunities of digitally mediated interactions: Young people's meanings and experiences. *Journal of Youth Studies*, *27*(8), 1188–1206. https://doi.org/10.1080/13676261.2023.2211929

Sevilla-Fernández, D., Díaz-López, A., Caba-Machado, V., Machimbarrena, J. M., Ortega-Barón, J., & González-Cabrera, J. (2025). Parental mediation and the use of social networks: A systematic review. *PLOS ONE*, *20*(2), e0312011. https://doi.org/10.1371/journal.pone.0312011

Sewaybricker, L. E., & Massola, G. M. (2022). Against well-being: A critique of positive psychology. *History of the Human Sciences*, *36*(1), 131–148. https://doi.org/10.1177/09526951221114733

Shaholli, D., Manai, M. V., Iantorno, F., Di Giampaolo, L., Nieto, H. A., Greco, E., La Torre, G., & De Sio, S. (2024). Teleworking and mental well-being: A systematic review on health effects and preventive measures. *Sustainability*, *16*(18), 8278. https://doi.org/10.3390/su16188278

Sheldon, K. M. (2004). *Optimal human being: An integrated multi-level perspective*. Lawrence Erlbaum Associates.

Sheldon, K. M., & Lyubomirsky, S. (2006). How to increase and sustain positive emotion: The effects of expressing gratitude and visualizing best possible selves. *The Journal of Positive Psychology*, *1*(2), 73–82. https://doi.org/10.1080/17439760.2 00500510676

Shen, J., Lee, A., Alghowinem, S., Adkins, R., Breazeal, C., & Park, H. W. (2025). Social robots as social proxies for fostering connection and empathy towards humanity. *arXiv*. https://arxiv.org/abs/2502.00221

Siddiq, F., Røkenes, F. M., Lund, A., & Scherer, R. (2024). New kid on the block? A conceptual systematic review of digital agency. *Education and Information Technologies*, *29*, 5721–5752. https://doi.org/10.1007/s10639-023-12038-3

Simondon, G. (2017). *On the mode of existence of technical objects* (C. Malaspina & J. Rogove, Trans.). Univocal Publishing.

Skulmowski, A., & Xu, K. M. (2022). Understanding cognitive load in digital and online learning: A new perspective on extraneous cognitive load. *Educational Psychology Review*, *34*, 171–196. https://doi.org/10.1007/s10648-021-09624-7

Slater, M., & Wilbur, S. (1997). A framework for immersive virtual environments (FIVE): Speculations on the role of presence in virtual environments. *Presence: Teleoperators & Virtual Environments*, *6*, 603–616. https://doi.org/10.1162/pres.1997.6.6.603

Smahel, D., Machackova, H., Mascheroni, G., Dedkova, L., Staksrud, E., Ólafsson, K., Livingstone, S., & Hasebrink, U. (2020). EU Kids Online 2020: Survey results from 19 countries. https://doi.org/10.21953/lse.47fdeqj01ofo

Small, G. W., Lee, J., Kaufman, A., Jalil, J., Siddarth, P., Gaddipati, H., Moody, T. D., & Bookheimer, S. Y. (2020). Brain health consequences of digital technology use. *Dialogues in Clinical Neuroscience*, *22*(2), 179–187. https://doi.org/10.31887/DCNS.2020.22.2/gsmall

Springer, K. W., & Hauser, R. M. (2006). An assessment of the construct validity of Ryff's scales of psychological well-being: Method, mode, and measurement effects. *Social Science Research*, *35*(4), 1080–1102. https://doi.org/10.1016/j.ssresearch.2005.07.004

Statista. (n.d.). *Number of available applications in the Google Play Store from April 2018 to January 2026*. https://www.statista.com/statistics/266210/number-of-available-applications-in-the-google-play-store/

Steger, M. F. (2025). Regenerative positive psychology: A call to reorient wellbeing science to meet the realities of our world. *The Journal of Positive Psychology*, *20*(3), 373–396. https://doi.org/10.1080/17439760.2024.2365259

Stein, J.-P., Breves, P. L., & Anders, N. (2024). Parasocial interactions with real and virtual influencers: The role of perceived similarity and human-likeness. *New Media & Society*, *26*(6), 3433–3453. https://doi.org/10.1177/14614448221102900

Steinemann, S. T., Geelan, B. J., Zaehringer, S., Mutuura, K., Wolkow, E., Frasseck, L., & Opwis, K. (2020). Potentials and pitfalls of increasing prosocial behavior and self-efficacy over time using an online personalized platform. *PLOS ONE*, *15*(6), e0234422. https://doi.org/10.1371/journal.pone.0234422

Steinhaeusser, S. C., Oberdörfer, S., von Mammen, S., Latoschik, M. E., & Lugrin, B. (2022). Joyful adventures and frightening places – Designing emotion-inducing virtual environments. *Frontiers in Virtual Reality*, *3*, 919163. https://doi.org/10.3389/frvir.2022.919163

Stephanidis, C., & Salvendy, G. (Eds.). (2024). *Human-computer interaction: Foundations and advances*. Routledge.

Stevens, M. W. R., Radünz, M., Galanis, C., Quinney, B., Zajac, I., Billieux, J., Delfabbro, P. H., & King, D. L. (2025). Red box, green box: Psychometric evaluation of a self-report behavioral frequency measurement approach for behavioral addictions research. *Addiction*. Advance online publication. https://doi.org/10.1111/add.70192

Stiegler, B. (2019). *The age of disruption: Technology and madness in computational capitalism*. Polity Press.

Stocchi, L., Michaelidou, N., Pourazad, N., Alevizou, P.-J., & Appiah-Campbell, R. (2025). Psychological drivers of the intention to continue using health apps amongst young users. *European Journal of Marketing*, *59*(13), 452–487. https://doi.org/10.1108/EJM-07-2024-0580

Strojny, A., & Strojny, P. (2025). Post-gaming return to reality: A key factor in predicting the positive and negative outcomes of escapism (Version 1). *PsyArXiv*. https://doi.org/10.31234/osf.io/g9vhs_v1

Strojny, P., Kiszka, P., Starosta, J., Szyszka, P. D., Starzec, S., Winiarska, A., Strojny, A., & Zajas, A. (2023). It's not just about how long you play: Indirect gaming involvement and genre preferences in predicting gaming disorder risk – Evidence from preregistered studies. *Frontiers in Psychiatry*, *14*, 1230774. https://doi.org/10.3389/fpsyt.2023.1230774

Su, R., Tay, L., & Diener, E. (2014). The development and validation of the comprehensive inventory of thriving (CIT) and the brief inventory of thriving (BIT). *Applied Psychology: Health and Well-Being*, *6*(3), 251–279. https://doi.org/10.1111/aphw.12027

Suler, J. R. (2016). The dimensions of cyberpsychology architecture. In J. Gackenbach & J. Brown (Eds.), *Boundaries of self and reality online: Implications of digitally constructed realities* (pp. 1–26). Academic Press.

Sweetser, P., & Wyeth, P. (2005). GameFlow: A model for evaluating player enjoyment in games. *Computers in Entertainment*, *3*(3), 1–24. https://doi.org/10.1145/1077246.1077253

Szolin, K., Kuss, D. J., Nuyens, F. M., & Griffiths, M. D. (2023a). "I am the character, the character is me": A thematic analysis of the user-avatar relationship in videogames. *Computers in Human Behavior*, *143*, 107694. https://doi.org/10.1016/j.chb.2023.107694

Szolin, K., Kuss, D. J., Nuyens, F. M., & Griffiths, M. D. (2023b). Exploring the user-avatar relationship in videogames: A systematic review of the Proteus effect. *Human–Computer Interaction*, *38*(5–6), 374–399. https://doi.org/10.1080/07370024.2022.2103419

Taleb, N. N. (2007). *The black swan: The impact of the highly improbable*. Random House.

Tandoc, E. C., Jr., Goh, Z. H., Wong, D. K. J., & Zhang, L. (2023). The good, the bad, and the internet: Investigating the impact of online prosocial and anti-social behaviors on well-being. *Cogent Social Sciences*, *9*(1), 2225834. https://doi.org/10.1080/23311886.2023.2225834

Tang, D., Sum, R. K.-W., Li, M., Ma, R., Chung, P., & Ho, R. W.-K. (2023). What is esports? A systematic scoping review and concept analysis of esports. *Heliyon*, *9*(12), e23248. https://doi.org/10.1016/j.heliyon.2023.e23248

Tarafdar, M., Cooper, C. L., & Stich, J. F. (2019). The technostress trifecta – techno eustress, techno distress and design: Theoretical directions and an agenda for research. *Information Systems Journal, 29*(1), 6–42. https://doi.org/10.1111/isj.12169

Tarafdar, M., Stich, J. F., Maier, C., & Laumer, S. (2024). Techno-eustress creators: Conceptualization and empirical validation. *Information Systems Journal, 34*(6), 2097–2131. https://doi.org/10.1111/isj.12515

Tarafdar, M., Tu, Q., Ragu-Nathan, B. S., & Ragu-Nathan, T. S. (2007). The impact of technostress on role stress and productivity. *Journal of Management Information Systems, 24*(1), 301–328. https://doi.org/10.2753/MIS0742-1222240109

Tatarkiewicz, W. (1976). *Analysis of happiness*. Martinus Nijhoff.

Taylor, J., & Armes, G. (2024). Social comparison on Instagram, and its relationship with self-esteem and body-esteem. *Discover Psychology, 4*, 126. https://doi.org/10.1007/s44202-024-00241-3

Taylor, J., McAlaney, J., Muir, S., & Cole, T. (2017). Teaching sensitive issues in cyberpsychology. *Psychology Teaching Review, 23*(1), 56–62. https://doi.org/10.53841/bpsptr.2017.23.1.56

Tegmark, M. (2017). *Life 3.0: Being human in the age of artificial intelligence*. Alfred A. Knopf.

ten Brummelhuis, L. L., & Bakker, A. B. (2012). A resource perspective on the work–home interface: The work–home resources model. *American Psychologist, 67*(7), 545–556. https://doi.org/10.1037/a0027974

Terry, C., & Cain, J. (2016). The emerging issue of digital empathy. *American Journal of Pharmaceutical Education, 80*(4), 58. https://doi.org/10.5688/ajpe80458

Thakkar, A., Gupta, A., & De Sousa, A. (2024). Artificial intelligence in positive mental health: A narrative review. *Frontiers in Digital Health, 6*, 1280235. https://doi.org/10.3389/fdgth.2024.1280235

Thatcher, J. B., Wright, R. T., Sun, H., Zagenczyk, T. J., & Klein, R. (2018). Mindfulness in information technology use: Definitions, distinctions, and a new measure. *MIS Quarterly, 42*(3), 831–848, A1–A14. https://www.jstor.org/stable/26635055

Thomas, J., Al Juraib, N., & Izadi, S. (2025). Mindfulness-based approaches to problematic technology use. In M.-J. Martín-Vázquez & C. Hocaoglu (Eds.), *Mental health – innovations in therapy and treatment* (pp. 63–122). IntechOpen. https://doi.org/10.5772/intechopen.1010097

Thompson, R. A. (1994). Emotion regulation: A theme in search of definition. In N. A. Fox (Ed.), *The development of emotion regulation: Biological and behavioral considerations* (pp. 25–52). University of Chicago Press.

Toomey, E., Hardeman, W., Hankonen, N., Byrne, M., McSharry, J., Matvienko-Sikar, K., & Lorencatto, F. (2020). Focusing on fidelity: Narrative review and recommendations for improving intervention fidelity within trials of health behavior change interventions. *Health Psychology and Behavioral Medicine, 8*(1), 132–151. https://doi.org/10.1080/21642850.2020.1738935

Tov, W., & Diener, E. (2009). Culture and subjective well-being. In E. Diener (Ed.), *Culture and well-being* (Social Indicators Research Series, Vol. 38, pp. 9–41). Springer. https://doi.org/10.1007/978-90-481-2352-0_2

Trentowski, B. F. (1843). *Stosunek filozofii do cybernetyki czyli sztuki rządzenia narodem: Rzecz treści politycznej* [The relation of philosophy to cybernetics, or the art of governing a nation]. J. K. Żupański.

Triberti, S., Sapone, C., & Riva, G. (2025). Being there but where? Sense of presence theory for virtual reality applications. *Humanities and Social Sciences Communications, 12*, 79. https://doi.org/10.1057/s41599-025-04380-3

Trillò, T., Hallinan, B., & Shifman, L. (2022). A typology of social media rituals. *Journal of Computer-Mediated Communication, 27*(4), zmac011. https://doi.org/10.1093/jcmc/zmac011

Trzebińska, E. (2008). *Psychologia pozytywna* [Positive psychology]. Wydawnictwa Akademickie i Profesjonalne.

TVP Info. (2018). *Robot Sophia otrzymał indeks AGH i zamierza rozpocząć naukę w Polsce* [Robot Sophia received an AGH student ID and intends to begin studying in Poland]. https://www.tvp.info/37651483/robot-sophia-otrzymal-indeks-agh-i-zamierza-rozpoczac-nauke-w-polsce

Uchida, Y., & Ogihara, Y. (2012). Personal or interpersonal construal of happiness: A cultural psychological perspective. *International Journal of Wellbeing, 2*(4), 354–369. https://doi.org/10.5502/ijw.v2.i4.5

Ulfert-Blank, A.-S., & Schmidt, I. (2022). Assessing digital self-efficacy: Review and scale development. *Computers & Education, 191*, 104626. https://doi.org/10.1016/j.compedu.2022.104626

Ulrich, S., Lienhard, N., Künzli, H., & Kowatsch, T. (2024). A chatbot-delivered stress management coaching for students (MISHA App): Pilot randomized controlled trial. *JMIR mHealth and uHealth, 12*, e54945. https://doi.org/10.2196/54945

UNESCO. (1978). Recommendation concerning the international standardization of statistics on science and technology. https://www.unesco.org/en/legal-affairs/recommendation-concerning-international-standardization-statistics-science-and-technology

Vallor, S. (2016). *Technology and the virtues: A philosophical guide to a future worth wanting*. Oxford University Press.

van Agteren, J., Bartholomaeus, J., Steains, E., Lo, L., & Gerace, A. (2021). Using a technology-based meaning and purpose intervention to improve well-being: A randomised controlled study. *Journal of Happiness Studies, 22*, 3571–3591. https://doi.org/10.1007/s10902-021-00383-4

Vanden Abeele, M. M. P. (2020). Digital wellbeing as a dynamic construct. *Communication Theory, 31*(4), 932–955. https://doi.org/10.1093/ct/qtaa024

van der Maden, W., Lomas, D., & Hekkert, P. (2024). Developing and evaluating a design method for positive artificial intelligence. *Artificial Intelligence for Engineering Design, Analysis and Manufacturing*, *38*, e14, 1–22. https://doi.org/10.1017/S0890060424000155

VanderWeele, T. J. (2017). On the promotion of human flourishing. *Proceedings of the National Academy of Sciences of the United States of America*, *114*(31), 8148–8156. https://doi.org/10.1073/pnas.1702996114

VanderWeele, T. J., Johnson, B. R., Bialowolski, P. T., Bonhag, R., Bradshaw, M., Breedlove, T., Case, B., Chen, Y., Chen, Z. J., Counted, V., Cowden, R. G., de la Rosa, P. A., Felton, C., Fogleman, A., Gibson, C., Grigoropoulou, N., Gundersen, C., Jang, S. J., Johnson, K. A., ... Yancey, G. (2025). The global flourishing study: Study profile and initial results on flourishing. *Nature Mental Health*, *3*(6), 636–653. https://doi.org/10.1038/s44220-025-00423-5

van Zyl, L. E., & Dik, B. J. (2025). Beyond universal prescriptions: Toward a person-centered, bottom-up science of wellbeing. *International Journal of Applied Positive Psychology*, *10*, 42. https://doi.org/10.1007/s41042-025-00232-2

van Zyl, L. E., Dik, B. J., Donaldson, S. I., Klibert, J. J., di Blasi, Z., van Wingerden, J., & Salanova, M. (2024). Positive organisational psychology 2.0: Embracing the technological revolution. *The Journal of Positive Psychology*, *19*(4), 699–711. https://doi.org/10.1080/17439760.2023.2257640

van Zyl, L. E., Efendic, E., Rothmann, S., & Shankland, R. (2019). Best-practice guidelines for positive psychological intervention research design. In L. van Zyl & S. Rothmann Sr. (Eds.), *Positive psychological intervention design and protocols for multi-cultural contexts* (pp. 1–32). Springer. https://doi.org/10.1007/978-3-030-20020-6_1

Venkatesh, V., Morris, M. G., Davis, G. B., & Davis, F. D. (2003). User acceptance of information technology: Toward a unified view. *MIS Quarterly*, *27*(3), 425–478. https://doi.org/10.2307/30036540

Venkatesh, V., Thong, J. Y. L., & Xu, X. (2012). Consumer acceptance and use of information technology: Extending the unified theory of acceptance and use of technology. *MIS Quarterly*, *36*(1), 157–178. https://doi.org/10.2307/41410412

Verbeek, P.-P. (2011). *Moralizing technology: Understanding and designing the morality of things*. University of Chicago Press.

Verplanken, B., & Orbell, S. (2003). Reflections on past behavior: A self-report index of habit strength. *Journal of Applied Social Psychology*, *33*(6), 1313–1330. https://doi.org/10.1111/j.1559-1816.2003.tb01951.x

Villamil, A., & Heshmati, S. (2023). Engaging in the good with technology: A framework for examining positive technology use. *Frontiers in Psychology*, *14*, 1175740. https://doi.org/10.3389/fpsyg.2023.1175740

Villani, D., Pancini, E., Pesce, F., & Scuzzarella, L. (2023). Savoring life during pandemic: An online intervention to promote well-being in emerging adults. *BMC Psychology*, *11*(1), 196. https://doi.org/10.1186/s40359-023-01225-z

Villani, D., Sorgente, A., Iannello, P., & Antonietti, A. (2019). The role of spirituality and religiosity in subjective well-being of individuals with different religious status. *Frontiers in Psychology, 10*, 1525. https://doi.org/10.3389/fpsyg.2019.01525

Vishwanath, A., Neo, L. S., Goh, P., Lee, S., Khader, M., Ong, G., & Chin, J. (2020). Cyber hygiene: The concept, its measure, and its initial tests. *Decision Support Systems, 128*, 113160. https://doi.org/10.1016/j.dss.2019.113160

Vita-More, N. (2002). Radical body design: Primo posthuman. *KurzweilAI*.

Vohs, K. D., & Baumeister, R. F. (Eds.). (2016). *Handbook of self-regulation: Research, theory, and applications* (3rd ed.). The Guilford Press.

Wang, J.-W., Zhu, Z., Shuling, Z., Fan, J., Jin, Y., Gao, Z.-L., Chen, W.-D., & Li, X. (2024). Effectiveness of mHealth app–based interventions for increasing physical activity and improving physical fitness in children and adolescents: Systematic review and meta-analysis. *JMIR mHealth and uHealth, 12*, e51478. https://doi.org/10.2196/51478

Wang, Y., Li, X., Zhang, Q., Yeung, D., & Wu, Y. (2025a). Effect of a cognitive behavioral therapy–based AI chatbot on depression and loneliness in Chinese university students: Randomized controlled trial with financial stress moderation. *JMIR mHealth and uHealth, 13*, e63806. https://doi.org/10.2196/63806

Wang, Y., Xi, A., Wong, S. S. K., Yam, K., Leung, J. T. Y., & Zhu, S. (2025b). Efficacy of a web-based integrated growth mindset intervention on reducing anxiety among social work and counseling practicum trainees: Protocol for a 2-arm randomized controlled trial. *JMIR Research Protocols, 14*, e67234. https://doi.org/10.2196/67234

Wang, Y. Y., & Wang, Y. S. (2019). Development and validation of an artificial intelligence anxiety scale: An initial application in predicting motivated learning behavior. *Interactive Learning Environments, 30*(4), 619–634. https://doi.org/10.1080/10494820.2019.1674887

Washington, H., Piccolo, J., Gomez-Baggethun, E., Kopnina, H., & Alberro, H. (2021). The trouble with anthropocentric hubris, with examples from conservation. *Conservation, 1*(4), 285–298. https://doi.org/10.3390/conservation1040022

Watson, D., Clark, L. A., & Tellegen, A. (1988). Development and validation of brief measures of positive and negative affect: The PANAS scales. *Journal of Personality and Social Psychology, 54*(6), 1063–1070. https://doi.org/10.1037/0022-3514.54.6.1063

Wauters, R. (2009). Google: Actually, we count only 16,000 apps in Android Market. *TechCrunch*. https://techcrunch.com/2009/12/16/google-android-market/

Wells, J., Scheibein, F., Pais, L., Rebelo dos Santos, N., Dalluege, C.-A., Czakert, J. P., & Berger, R. (2023). A systematic review of the impact of remote working referenced to the concept of work–life flow on physical and psychological health. *Workplace Health & Safety, 71*(11), 507–521. https://doi.org/10.1177/21650799231176397

Werthner, H. (2024). *Digitaler humanismus: Über digitalisierung und künstliche intelligenz*. Picus.

West, M., Rice, S., & Vella-Brodrick, D. (2024). Adolescent social media use through a self-determination theory lens: A systematic scoping review. *International Journal of Environmental Research and Public Health, 21*(7), 862. https://doi.org/10.3390/ijerph21070862

WHOQOL Group. (1995). The World Health Organization Quality of Life Assessment (WHOQOL): Position paper from the World Health Organization. *Social Science & Medicine, 41*(10), 1403–1409. https://doi.org/10.1016/0277-9536(95)00112-K

Wiederhold, B. K., & Riva, G. (Eds.). (2020). *Annual review of cybertherapy and telemedicine* (Vol. 18). Interactive Media Institute.

Wiener, N. (1948/1961). *Cybernetics: Or control and communication in the animal and the machine* (2nd ed.). MIT Press.

Willemse, C., Marchesi, S., & Wykowska, A. (2018). Robot faces that follow gaze facilitate attentional engagement and increase their likeability. *Frontiers in Psychology*, 9, 70. https://doi.org/10.3389/fpsyg.2018.00070

Willen, S. S., Williamson, A. F., Walsh, C. C., Hyman, M., & Tootle, W. (2022). Rethinking flourishing: Critical insights and qualitative perspectives from the U.S. Midwest. *SSM Mental Health, 2*, 100057. https://doi.org/10.1016/j.ssmmh.2021.100057

Williams, D. (2006). On and off the 'net: Scales for social capital in an online era. *Journal of Computer-Mediated Communication, 11*(2), 593–628. https://doi.org/10.1111/j.1083-6101.2006.00029.x

Wissing, M. P. (2022). Beyond the "third wave of positive psychology": Challenges and opportunities for future research. *Frontiers in Psychology, 12*, 795067. https://doi.org/10.3389/fpsyg.2021.795067

Witowska, J., Ogden, R., Schoetensack, C., Goncikowska, K., Wittmann, M., Černohorská, V., Codina, N., Martin-Soelch, C., Fernández Boente, M., Giner, G., Pestana, J. V., & Papastamatelou, J. (2025). New measurements of digital technology use: The immersion in digital life and quality of digital experience scales. *Frontiers in Psychiatry, 16*, 1595536. https://doi.org/10.3389/fpsyt.2025.1595536

Wong, P. T. P. (2011). Positive psychology 2.0: Towards a balanced interactive model of the good life. *Canadian Psychology, 52*(2), 69–81. https://doi.org/10.1037/a0022511

Wood, A. M., Linley, P. A., Maltby, J., Baliousis, M., & Joseph, S. (2008). The authentic personality: A theoretical and empirical conceptualization and the development of the authenticity scale. *Journal of Counseling Psychology, 55*(3), 385–399. https://doi.org/10.1037/0022-0167.55.3.385

World Health Organization. (1948). *Preamble to the constitution of the World Health Organization*. World Health Organization.

World Health Organization. (2023). *Classification of digital interventions, services and applications in health: A shared language to describe the uses of digital technology for health* (2nd ed.). World Health Organization.

Wróblewski, Z., & Fortuna, P. (2023). Moral subjectivity and the moral status of artificial intelligence: A philosophical and psychological perspective. *Ethos, 36*(4), 29–48. https://doi.org/10.12887/36-2023-4-144-05

Wulan, D. K., Agustiani, H., Purba, F. D., & Lubis, F. Y. (2025). Mapping empirical factors of digital creativity: A systematic review. *Journal of Creativity*, *35*(2), 100103. https://doi.org/10.1016/j.yjoc.2025.100103

Yaden, D. B., Haidt, J., Hood, R. W., Jr., Vago, D. R., & Newberg, A. B. (2017). The varieties of self-transcendent experience. *Review of General Psychology*, *21*(2), 143–160. https://doi.org/10.1037/gpr0000102

Yang, F.-C., Acevedo, P., Guo, S., Choi, M., & Mousas, C. (2025). Embodied conversational agents in extended reality: A systematic review. *IEEE Access, 13*, 79805–79824. https://doi.org/10.1109/ACCESS.2025.3566698

Yeager, D. S., Hanselman, P., Walton, G. M., Murray, J. S., Crosnoe, R., Muller, C., Tipton, E., Schneider, B., Hulleman, C. S., Hinojosa, C. P., Paunesku, D., Romero, C., Flint, K., Roberts, A., Trott, J., Iachan, R., Buontempo, J., Yang, S. M., Carvalho, C. M., ... Dweck, C. S. (2019). A national experiment reveals where a growth mindset improves achievement. *Nature*, *573*, 364–369. https://doi.org/10.1038/s41586-019-1466-y

Yee, N., & Bailenson, J. (2007). The Proteus effect: The effect of transformed self-representation on behavior. *Human Communication Research*, *33*(3), 271–290. https://doi.org/10.1111/j.1468-2958.2007.00299.x

Yeo, N. L., White, M. P., Alcock, I., Garside, R., Dean, S. G., Smalley, A. J., & Gatersleben, B. (2020). What is the best way of delivering virtual nature for improving mood? An experimental comparison of high definition TV, 360° video, and computer generated virtual reality. *Journal of Environmental Psychology*, *72*, 101500. https://doi.org/10.1016/j.jenvp.2020.101500

Yeşilyurt, E., & Vezne, R. (2023). Digital literacy, technological literacy, and internet literacy as predictors of attitude toward applying computer-supported education. *Education and Information Technologies*, *28*(8), 9885–9911. https://doi.org/10.1007/s10639-022-11311-1

Yosep, I., Suryani, S., Mediani, H. S., Mardhiyah, A., & Ibrahim, K. (2024). Types of digital mindfulness: Improving mental health among college students – a scoping review. *Journal of Multidisciplinary Healthcare*, *17*, 43–53. https://doi.org/10.2147/JMDH.S443781

Young, K. S. (2009). Internet addiction: Diagnosis and treatment considerations. *Journal of Contemporary Psychotherapy*, *39*(4), 241–246. https://doi.org/10.1007/s10879-009-9120-x

Yousefi, M., Crowe, S. E., Hoermann, S., Sharifi, M., Romera, A., Shahi, A., & Piumsomboon, T. (2024). Advancing prosociality in extended reality: Systematic review of the use of embodied virtual agents to trigger prosocial behaviour in extended reality. *Frontiers in Virtual Reality*, *5*, 1386460. https://doi.org/10.3389/frvir.2024.1386460

Yudkowsky, E. (2001). *Creating friendly AI 1.0: The analysis and design of benevolent goal architectures.* Singularity Institute for Artificial Intelligence. https://intelligence.org/files/CFAI.pdf

Zendle, D., Flick, C., Halgarth, D., Ballou, N., Demediuk, S., & Drachen, A. (2023). Cross-cultural patterns in mobile playtime: An analysis of 118 billion hours of human data. *Scientific Reports, 13,* 386. https://doi.org/10.1038/s41598-022-26730-w

Zhang, Z., Chen, J., Geng, L., & Qi, Y. (2026). Techno-biophilia design in video games and its positive social outcomes. *International Journal of Psychology, 61*(2), e70169. https://doi.org/10.1002/ijop.70169

Zhao, Y., Li, Y., & Bandyopadhyay, K. (2024). The role of techno-eustress in technology-enhanced IT learning. *Journal of Computer Information Systems, 64,* 607–621. https://doi.org/10.1080/08874417.2023.2240723

Zielonka, J. T., & Rothlauf, F. (2021). Techno-eustress: The impact of perceived usefulness and perceived ease of use on the perception of work-related stressors. In *Proceedings of the 54th Hawaii International Conference on System Sciences* (pp. 6287–6296). https://doi.org/10.24251/HICSS.2021.780

Zou, Y., Kuek, F., Feng, W., & Cheng, X. (2025). Digital learning in the 21st century: Trends, challenges, and innovations in technology integration. *Frontiers in Education, 10,* 1562391. https://doi.org/10.3389/feduc.2025.1562391

Zuboff, S. (2019). *The age of surveillance capitalism: The fight for a human future at the new frontier of power.* Profile Books.

Index

Note: Page numbers in *italics* and **bold** refer to figures and tables respectively.